# WOMEN OF COLOR

## IN U.S. SOCIETY

*In the series* Women in the Political Economy,
*edited by Ronnie J. Steinberg*

# WOMEN OF COLOR

# IN U.S.

# SOCIETY

*Edited by*
*Maxine Baca Zinn*
*and Bonnie Thornton Dill*

**TEMPLE UNIVERSITY PRESS:** PHILADELPHIA

Portions of Chapter 3 were previously published under the title "Black Females'
'Place' in Desegregated Classrooms," *Sociology of Education* 57, no. 2 (1984): 57–76.

Portions of Chapter 4 appear in Karen Hossfeld, *Divisions of Labor, Divisions of Lives:
Immigrant Women Workers in Silicon Valley*, forthcoming from University of California
Press. Used by permission of the University of California Press.

Portions of Chapter 8 were previously published under the title "Our Mothers'
Grief: Racial-Ethnic Women and the Maintenance of Families," *Journal of Family
History* 13, no. 4 (1988): 415–431.

Portions of Chapter 15 were previously published under the author's copyright in
*Uncertain Terms: Negotiating Gender in American Culture*, ed. Faye Ginsburg and Anna
Lowenhaupt Tsing (Boston: Beacon Press, 1990).

The paper used in this publication meets the minimum requirements of American
National Standard for Information Sciences—Permanence of Paper for Printed
Library Materials, ANSI Z39.48-1984 ∞

**Library of Congress Cataloging-in-Publication Data**
Women of color in U.S. society / edited by Maxine Baca Zinn and Bonnie
Thornton Dill.
    p. cm.—(Women in the political economy)
    Includes bibliographical reference (p. ) and index.
    ISBN 1-56639-105-9 (cl: alk. paper).—ISBN 1-56639-106-7 (pb:
alk. paper)
    1. Minority women—United States. I. Baca Zinn, Maxine.
II. Dill, Bonnie Thornton. III. Title: Women of color in US
society. IV. Series.
HQ1421.W655 1994
305.48'9693—dc20                        93-9448

*To our mothers,*
*Luisa Duran Baca and Hilda Branch Thornton;*
*and to all of those women of color whose lives*
*have inspired our research and guided our scholarship*

# Contents

## III SOCIAL AGENCY: CONFRONTING THE "WALLS"

## IV RETHINKING GENDER

# Preface

This book grew out of our concern about the exclusion of women of color from feminist scholarship and the misinterpretation of our experiences. Our conversations began at a time when race and class differences were absent from dominant feminist thinking. We were part of a cohort of women of color scholars, dispersed throughout the United States, who were working to define women's lives in a way that reflected our own experiences. Through the work of the Center for Research on Women at Memphis State University, many of us came together, built a network, and began to influence the development of a national discussion of these issues. The Center provided a space for our determination to examine race and class in convergence with gender and to have our scholarship taken seriously.

Since we began this volume, feminist scholarship has taken on the challenge of studying the diversities of women's experiences. This new direction is transforming much of what we know about women and the social worlds we occupy. Our book now joins the movement to enlarge women's studies by examining the multiple interactions that differences in power and privilege create for women of color. The chapters in this book reveal that women's lives are shaped as much by relations of dominance based on race and class as those based on gender.

Producing this book has underscored the parallels between the lives of the authors and those of the women we write about. The contributors, ourselves women of color and progressive white women, have struggled to survive within our institutions of higher education, to reform them, and to produce inclusive scholarship. Those struggles have made this process longer and more arduous than any of us had anticipated. The result, to paraphrase Gloria Anzaldua, is a book which is not only *about* women of color and the redefinition of difference and domination, but embodies the very process of redefining difference and domination that is central to the lives of women of color in the United States.

## Acknowledgments

This book could not have been completed without the support, concern, and commitment of many people. We are indebted to the Inter-University Research Group Exploring the Intersection of Race and Gender, where early discussions about comparative research on women of color took place. We are grateful to the Ford Foundation for funding part of the preparation of this volume, and particularly to the program officers who agreed that this was an important venture: Mariam Chamberlain and Alison Bernstein. Michael Ames of Temple University Press and Ronnie Steinberg, series editor for the Press, have been enthusiastic about this volume from its inception and have provided consistent encouragement and invaluable editorial direction. We're also grateful to Diane Illig of the University of Maryland at College Park, Karen Lambourne of Michigan State University, and Jo Ann Ammons of the Center for Research on Women at Memphis State University for their work on the manuscript.

Our colleagues and friends Margaret Andersen, Patricia Hill Collins, Elizabeth Higginbotham, Sandra Morgen, and Lynn Weber have believed in and encouraged us at each step in this process and have engaged us in debates and discussions that are transforming gender studies.

Our families—Alan, Prentice, and Gabby; John, Kamau, Anika, and Nandi—have been both patient and enthusiastic supporters of our project. We thank them for the many ways they have helped us juggle our several roles.

Together, a Chicana and an African American woman edited this book. Within our commonalities and differences, we discovered the challenges and rewards of multiracial work. We treasure this experience. It has transformed our lives and is, we believe, an essential step in transforming feminist scholarship.

# Foreword

## Patricia Hill Collins

"People are interested in new ways of life, not just new ways of thinking," suggests philosopher Cornel West (hooks and West 1991:109). The illusion that political and intellectual unity exists in the United States represents one old way of life that requires new ways of thinking. American citizens have long been told that politically we are one people, "indivisible with liberty and justice for all." But how accurate or meaningful can this political unity be if it has been attained through the exploited labor of people of color, with land stolen from Native Americans, and if it is supported by the media-constructed objectification of women and invisibility of gays, lesbians, and bisexuals, and the deliberate silencing of anyone who complains too loudly? African-Americans, women, Latinos, Native Americans, gays and lesbians, older people, and persons with disabilities have all begun to challenge this putative political unity by claiming that such unity has long been gained at their/our expense and by demanding justice. Such charges threaten those who may sincerely believe that we should all speak one language, adhere to one set of values, accept only one version of history, and worship the same gods. From the perspective of those long in the political center, these challenges that democracy make good on its constitutional promises seem to endanger the very future of the United States.

Intellectually, an illusory unity has long been attained through the epistemological sleight of hand of using the ideas and experiences of one small yet powerful group of individuals, elite White men, as the normative experience for all humans, and constructing an intellectual unity based on this fundamental assumption. In one variation of this approach, intellectual unity is achieved by assessing the experiences of women, people of color, and others deemed different based on their proximity to the normative White male center. In another variation, while the search for human universals continues, the idea of a "human universal" that is expressed differently by diverse groups based on their distinctive backgrounds replaces the normative White male center. Upon closer inspection, however, the supposed human universal constructed through difference comes surprisingly close to the same normative White male center. This intellectual unity, which is based on silencing those who do not reflect the White, male, English-speaking, heterosexual, and economically privileged norm, is being challenged by demands for multicultural curricula, women's studies programs, more diverse teaching staffs, bilingual education, and other educational reforms.

How can a nation call itself "United" when it is based on this type of illusory political and intellectual unity? Can a unity based on subordinating diversity really be unity at all? Sometimes it is difficult to admit that old ways of thinking and old ways of life simply don't work anymore. But in the absence of alternatives, we often cling to the old and thereby obstruct changes that we so sorely need.

How can we come to terms with the past without becoming trapped in it? You and I are not responsible for the decisions and actions of those who came before us, but we are accountable to each other in the here and now. Moreover, we are responsible for those who hopefully will follow us and who will inherit the results of our responses to the difficult task of constructing a redefined unity from the political and intellectual diversity that characterizes our times.

Given the importance of finding new ways of creating unity on the foundation of diversity, we need all the ideas we can get. *Women of Color in U.S. Society* adds important voices to the dialogue that will be needed to address this concern. This volume does an admirable job of bringing together articles that promise to shift our thinking about how we might build unified intellectual and political coalitions across diversity.

The editors and authors of this volume attempt to grapple with the subject matter of women of color in a way that recognizes the formidable difficulties, both political and intellectual, in doing this type of work. For example, we still lack a language that facilitates this process. The editors and authors inherited the problematic language of the past and remain sensitive to, yet constrained by, its assumptions and approaches. Some readers may find the term "women of color" itself troublesome because it reflects less the actual experiences of Native American women, African-American women, Latinas, and Asian-

American women than it does the type of intellectual and political coalition that joins these groups. The term "women of color" aims to foster unity and unwillingly flattens diversity. Yet diversity pervades this volume. The editors include a wide range of articles that do not collapse the experiences of women from different backgrounds into a "woman of color" defined solely in response and opposition to White women as the new normative center.

From this overarching tension emerge opportunities to rethink some of the most cherished Eurocentric notions regarding the categories that frame so much of Western thinking. One such category is the very notion of gender itself. By demonstrating that women of color do not automatically have a shared sisterhood, this volume challenges the assumption that women can have a sisterhood based on universal centers. So much feminist scholarship assumes that when we cut through all of the diversity among women created by differences of racial classification, ethnicity, social class, and sexual orientation, a "universal truth" concerning women and gender lies buried underneath. But if we can face the scary possibility that no such certainty exists and that persisting in such a search will always distort or omit someone's experiences, with what do we replace this old way of thinking? Gender differences and gender politics begin to look very different if there is no essential woman at the core.

The articles in *Women of Color in U.S. Society* address the difficulty, if not impossibility, of maintaining an illusory unity within feminist communities when those communities subordinate the experiences of women of color to normative centers based on middle-class White women's experiences. The resulting volume disrupts old ways of thinking about a range of troubled relationships such as those between men and women within Vietnamese immigrant communities, those within families, and those facing women of color in educational and employment situations. But the volume's significance goes far beyond the ideas and experiences of women of color. We need volumes like *Women of Color in U.S. Society* if we are to construct new political and intellectual communities. Unless we know more about each other, how can we possibly hope to envision new models of unity and the types of communities that might emerge?

## Reference

hooks, bell, and Cornel West. 1991. *Breaking Bread: Insurgent Black Intellectual Life*. Boston: South End Press.

**WOMEN OF COLOR**
IN U.S. SOCIETY

# I
# INTRODUCTION

# 1

## Difference and Domination

### Maxine Baca Zinn
### Bonnie Thornton Dill

The experiences of women of color have challenged feminist scholarship to rethink the relationship between race and gender for everyone. Since the 1980s, women's studies scholars have increasingly acknowledged that differences among women arise from inequalities of power and privilege. For African American women, Latinas, Asian American women, and Native American women, gender is part of a larger pattern of unequal social relations; how gender is experienced depends on how it intersects with other inequalities.

While women's studies scholars are now seeking to emphasize the importance of diversity to understanding women's lives, acknowledging diversity is not enough. Today we face the new task of going beyond the mere recognition and inclusion of differences, to permitting them to reshape the basic concepts and theories of the discipline. We must avoid the current fashion in mass culture, where "ethnicity becomes spice, seasoning that can liven up the dull dish that is mainstream white culture" (hooks 1992:21).

The growing diversity movement in gender studies is occurring just as the United States is undergoing a demographic shift from a predominantly White/European or Anglo population rooted in Western culture to one characterized by increased racial and cultural diversity. The combination of population changes with efforts to rethink and revise social and cultural ideology has generated a backlash—fear that the United States may become a mostly non-White and non-Western society. Intellectual attacks labeling multiculturalism as divisive, political exploitation of people's fears of difference, and increases in racially directed violence are examples of this backlash. *Women of Color in U.S. Society* seeks to offer alternative interpretations of the social world. Not only are the subjects of the essays racial-ethnic[1] women but the authors are predominantly African American, Latina, Asian American, and Native American women whose analyses of this topic are shaped by their unique perspectives as outsiders within, marginal intellectuals whose social location provides them a special perspective on self and society (Collins 1986).

## The Constraining Walls of Social Location

People of color, both men and women, have encountered severe economic and social dislocations from the time of their arrival in the United States until the present. In colonial America, American Indians faced war, disease, and a deliberate program of extermination. Africans died in large numbers in the "middle passage," the journey that brought them from their native continent to enslavement in the United States. Mexicans were incorporated into the United States as the result of a war and, along with Asian workers who were forced to live and work in "bachelor" communities far from their homes and families, died in large numbers working to build the mines and railroads. Up through the present, these groups have experienced periods of severe animosity marked by lynchings, race riots, and other forms of public violence.

Today, women of color on average receive the lowest wages, hold the worst jobs, and are more likely to be unemployed. They have the highest rates of infant mortality and births out of wedlock. They are also more likely to live in poverty and to be single mothers than their White counterparts.

Women of color are subordinated in this way because patterns of hierarchy, domination, and oppression based on race, class, gender, and sexual orientation are built into the structure of our society. Inequality, in other words, is structural or socially patterned. Too often explanations of these inequalities suggest that biology or culture is key. We argue, however, that biological traits, such as race and gender, are relevant only because they are socially ranked and rewarded. It is the *social* response to these biological characteristics that results in inequality. Though we do not discount the importance of culture, the problem with cultural differences as the primary explanation of inequality is the tendency to marginalize each cultural group, to view it as unique, and to imply that each differs from some presumed standard. This often leads to blaming a people's cultural values and practices for their subordination.

An image that helps convey how social structure limits opportunity and represents the relationship between structure and culture is found in Gloria Naylor's novel *The Women of Brewster Place*. The characters in this story live on a dead-end street that has been closed off by a brick wall. The wall separates Brewster Place from the rest of the community. It shuts out light to apartments, it creates a dark and unprotected area where destructive activities occur, and its presence suggests that there is only one way out. The wall on Brewster Place is a powerful symbol of the ways racial oppression, sexual exploitation, and class domination constrain the life chances and choices of the women who live there. For women of color, the social structures that are identified and discussed in this book are similar to the wall; they create barriers, limit opportunities, and constrain choices.

We begin this book with the recognition that race, class, and gender stratification affects the experiences of all, not just those who are most victimized (Andersen and Collins 1992). At the same time that the structures of race, class, and gender create disadvantages for women of color, they provide unacknowledged benefits for those who are at the top of these hierarchies—Whites, members of the upper classes, and males. The privileges of those at the top of the hierarchy are dependent on the exploitation of those at the bottom.

For women of color, this has meant that their work often involves providing services to more privileged people; that their families and communities have access to fewer resources and are more likely to become dependent on the "social largess" of more privileged people; and that their sexuality is more likely to be used and abused by more privileged people.

Part II of this book explores distinct social conditions constraining women's lives. Although these authors examine different groups of women, they uncover consistent patterns of subordination, restricted participation in social institutions, and structured placement in roles with limited opportunities. This social location is constructed through particular historical struggles and denies African American, Latina, Asian, and American Indian women access to resources and power.

Labor arrangements are at the core of race and gender inequalities. Social location in the labor market means that opportunities are influenced by *who* people are—by their being male or female; White, Black, Latina, American Indian, or Asian; rich or poor—rather than what their skills and abilities are. Denise Segura uncovers structural conditions in the labor market that operate as barriers to decent jobs for Chicanas and Mexican immigrant women. She shows how these features combine with social relations in the workplace to limit occupational mobility. Karen Hossfeld's essay exposes the racial and cultural stereotypes in the microelectronics industry today and demonstrates how racially defined hiring expectations become discriminatory hiring practices.

Although labor arrangements are fundamental determinants of social inequality, all social institutions are "conduits for oppression" (Andersen and Collins 1992:172). Ruth Zambrana traces Puerto Rican women's problems to discrimination in education, employment, housing, and health care. Educational institutions, though a primary avenue of social mobility for women of color, have also contributed to the process of social placement. Despite the rhetoric of equal opportunity, schools are key institutional sites where race, class, and gender inequalities are reproduced. Linda Grant's study of Black female students in elementary school classrooms describes a sorting process based on race and gender. Elizabeth Higginbotham confronts the societal legend that upward social mobility is the "happy ending" for African American women who have achieved professional stature and the economic buying power of the middle class. She illustrates that African American and White professional women, though both concentrated in traditionally female occupations, face different barriers due to race. Her data show the high concentration of professional Black women in public sector employment (Whites are more likely to be employed in the private sector), where salaries are lower.

## Social Agency: Confronting the "Walls"

Women of color, however, are not merely acted upon by oppressive social relations but are also shapers of their own lives. Our analysis stresses the primacy of external forces in making women's lives unequal, yet it views the lives of women of color as an outgrowth of the interaction between structured inequalities and the agency of the women who are coping and resisting.

Race, class, and gender create a matrix of domination that women of color "experience (and resist) on three levels, namely the level of personal biography, the group level of the cultural context created by race, class and gender, and the systemic level of social institutions" (Collins 1986:364–65). Part III of the book provides an analysis of the ways women cope and survive in the face of these structures. Though we have separated structure from culture and biography for the purposes of organizing this volume, the relationship between them is an interactive one.

At the conclusion of *The Women of Brewster Place*, the wall at the end of the street becomes the focus of collective social action. In a final act of rage and defiance, the residents of the street tear the wall down. The wall and the responses and reaction of the residents to it provide a useful device for illustrating the relationship of social structure to human choice and action. Within the "walls" constructed by race, class, and gender oppression, women of color create lives for themselves, their families, and their communities. Their lives are an active outgrowth of the continuous interplay between their cultural backgrounds, their personal abilities, and their struggles with the constraints of social structure.

In addition to the formal limits of social structure, women of color have also been subjected to cultural assaults (Caulfield 1974). Cultural assaults are systematic attacks on the institutions and forms of social organization that are fundamental to the maintenance and flourishing of a group's culture. They are a way dominant groups control and manage subordinate groups of people. They range from legal prohibitions against the use of drums among African slaves, and against the immigration of the wives of Chinese men, to informal practices that denigrate the cultural patterns of these groups while elevating the values and practices of the dominant groups.

In spite of these obstacles, women of color have shaped their lives and those of their families through acts of quiet dignity and steadfast determination. Their actions have included revolt and rebellion, creative conflict and social change, adaptation and accommodation.

The involvement of women in slave rebellions, American Indian wars, labor revolts in the fields and mines of the West and Southwest, and contemporary urban uprisings is well documented. As the primary laborers in families, kinship networks, and communities, women have also been engaged in more subtle forms of resistance. In their families and communities, many worked to create new institutions and to help their children maintain an autonomous cultural identity—a vision of self in society based on their own distinctive culture, separate from the ideals and images that the dominant culture sought to impose upon them.

The essay by Bonnie Thornton Dill opening Part III of the book identifies this process historically and contrasts the support provided European Americans for family life and women's roles within families with the policies of deliberate destruction or benign neglect directed toward African slaves, Chinese sojourners, and colonized Mexicans. It argues that families of color sustained cultural assaults as a direct result of the organization of the labor systems in which this group participated. On the other hand, the chapters by Jennie Joe and Dorothy Lonewolf Miller and by Cheryl Townsend Gilkes show how community can be a tool in resisting cultural assaults. Joe and Miller point out that the assimilation of American Indians was brutally enforced by U.S. government policies and that American Indian cultural autonomy today is threatened by wide-scale urbanization of Native American populations. Their study of American Indian women from the Tohono O'odham and Yaqui tribes in Tucson, Arizona, provides examples of the ways mothers promote cultural heritage as a way to help them and their children cope with racism, poverty, and discrimination.

Gilkes's essay illustrates the ways contemporary Black women's community work was designed to "combat racism and empower communities for growth and survival." She suggests that women's community work is a characteristic strategy not only for survival but also for change and empowerment among all people of color. Women, she argues, are "particularly rebellious" because they are oppressed as women; experience the oppressions of the "menfolk" in very personalized ways as lovers, wives, daughters or sisters; and are the primary caretakers of children.

Resistance does not always lead to socially desirable results. Some women have been defeated by the triple burdens of race, class, and gender, and have victimized themselves and others as a result of their anger and/or alienation and lack of choices. "Passing" is one strategy that people of color have used to escape the burden of race. Crime, drugs, and dangerous alternative lifestyles are other responses to lack of opportunity. Regina Arnold's discussion of how young African American women become criminals suggests that the process begins with the rebellious acts of victims of destructive family patterns, an alienating educational system, and poverty. Seeing no alternatives other than running away, they become part of a street culture, which leads to a life of crime, drug abuse, prostitution, and ultimately incarceration.

Constructing their responses to social structural constraints, women of color draw upon resources from their culture, family, kin, and community. These realms, however, are contested sites. They provide the resources the women have used to resist oppression and exploitation. Yet, because of their potential as a source of resistance, the dominant society has actively sought to control them. In addition, as the essay by Esther Ngan-Ling Chow demonstrates, the contrast between their own cultural norms and those of the dominant society may create circumstances that are especially problematic for women of color. Chow points out that for Asian American women, the stereotypes of obedience, docility, and submissiveness seem to suggest a perfect "fit" with the needs of U.S. bureaucracies. In fact, they, like other minorities, may feel out of place in such work environments.

A further paradox is that within racial-ethnic communities women have often had to oppose traditional customs and values to obtain the freedom to develop their full potential. Nazli Kibria's article on Vietnamese American women argues that the ethnic community is a source both of solidarity and of oppression for women. It facilitates adaptation to a new society and provides support in facing discrimination from outside the group, but its traditional and patriarchal patterns oppress women within the group. Kibria's contention is that the ethnic community is also an arena of struggle between men and women.

## Rethinking Gender

Social location is a complex (and often contradictory) determinant of women's distinctive experiences. For example, Patricia Hill Collins, in *Black Feminist Thought* (1990:150), argues that "a self-defined, articulated Black feminist standpoint" exists and that it has been the source of Black women's ability to resist the controlling images of the dominant society, which depicted them as mammies, matriarchs, whores, welfare recipients, and unwed mothers. This standpoint provided alternative images that encouraged them to fight to change the world in which they and their children lived. Leith Mullings explores this issue in depth in her article in Part IV of this volume. She argues that images and ideologies about women of color are used not only to control them but also to rationalize their subordinate position in the society.

Grounding gender studies in women's differences can reveal relations that remain obscure from other vantage points. Starting with women of color can lead, for example, to what Collins (1990) calls the "matrix of domination," an analysis that raises questions about the primacy of gender as an analytic category. Carol Stack's essay examines moral reasoning in a context that combines gender, race, class, and culture. Although conventional wisdom within women's studies treats moral reasoning as a gendered process, Stack's findings challenge the dichotomous portrayal of moral reasoning. Problematizing gender allows Stack to develop a more complex understanding of gender relations. By looking at social context along the way, we discover that within a social order that is racially formed and class based, the categories "women" and "men" do not exist as broad universals, although there are women and men in particular historically located relations. "There are no gender relations per se, but only gender relations as constructed by and between classes, races, and cultures" (Harding 1991:179). Many women of color are oppressed not only by race, class, and gender but by systems that privilege heterosexuality. The discriminations that lesbians of color face occur within this matrix of domination.

The study of women of color makes women's studies less partial and less distorted. More important, it transcends the reductionism of explaining the complexity of women's experiences with only "the analytic category of gender" (Zavella 1989:28). Focusing on women's varied locations, we do more than simply understand women better. Through our examination of the multiple conditions shaping women's lives, we begin to identify those interlocking systems of power which render some women more privileged and some more oppressed. Beyond simply asserting that gender is socially constructed, we can begin to account for the multiple connections shaping all women's experiences.

Diversity, in other words, reveals how genders are constructed out of interlocking systems of inequality. The lives of women of color are not a variation of a more general model of American womanhood. Instead, their experiences are formed by many of the same forces that shape the lives of others. In given historical moments, those forces combine to create differences among women.

However, women's experiences are not merely different, they are *relational*. As Evelyn Nakano Glenn explains, each is made up of categories (e.g., male/female, Anglo/Latino) that are positioned and therefore gain meaning in relation to each other. To represent race and gender as relationally constructed is to assert that the experiences of White women and women of color are not just different, but connected in systematic ways (Glenn 1992:34).

The insight that genders are relational challenges us to rethink every conceptualization of gender based solely on the experiences of Anglo middle-class women. Hence, Maxine Baca Zinn's essay pushes for a feminist reconstruction of the family through incorporating race as a dimension of social structure rather than merely an expression of cultural differences. She argues that race places families in different social locations, giving some greater access to resources and rewards, and denying or limiting access to these same items for others. Privileged family forms rest on the exploited labor of women and men in subordinated race and class locations.

The chapters in this book refute some of the conventional wisdom about women of color and women in general. In this way they challenge some of our basic assumptions about how society coheres and why people behave in certain ways. Ultimately, they force us to look at our most studied population, White males, in new ways—not as the actors who set the standards by which all social action is measured, but as part of a social order in which their privilege as a group is dependent on the subordination of others. We must then look at all of these populations together and ask questions that focus on the interconnectedness rather than the separateness of social phenomena. The crucial question that emerges is, How do the existences and experiences of all people, women and men, different racial-ethnic groups, and different classes, shape each other?

Once we acknowledge that all women are affected by the racial order of society, we gain "new starting points for feminist thought and action" (Andersen 1993:349). Emergent in this collection of essays is the framework of a body of theory and practice we label "multiracial feminism." Growing primarily out of the experiences of racial-ethnic women, which are themselves varied, multiracial feminism does not offer a singular or unified feminism but a body of knowledge situating women and men in multiple systems of domination. Nevertheless, it treats racial inequality as a vital shaper of women's and men's lives and advances a coherent and powerful premise—that racial ancestry, ethnic heritage, and economic status are as important as gender for analyzing the social construction of women and men.

The insights of the authors in this book lead to a reformulation of the feminist agenda by asking a basic sociological question of each reform strategy: Who benefits? In the book *Backlash*, journalist Susan Faludi (1991:xx) provides an example:

> In the last decade, some women did make substantial advances before the backlash hit, but millions of others were left behind, stranded. Some women now enjoy the right to legal abortions— but not the 44 million women from the indigent to the military work force, who depend on the federal government for their medical care. Some women can now walk into high paying professional careers—but not the more than 19 million still in the typing pool or behind the department store sales counter.

Multiracial feminism is a potential antidote to this aspect of the backlash. It charges us to look beyond those women who supposedly "have it all" to those who "have none of it." It provides the motives that compel us to make our teaching as well as our programs and policies address the varied circumstances and needs of all women.

## Note

1. The term *racial-ethnic* refers to groups that are socially and legally subordinated and remain culturally distinct within U.S. society. It is meant to include (1) the systematic discrimination of socially constructed racial groups and (2) their distinctive cultural arrangements. Historically, the

categories of African American, Latino, Asian American, and Native American were constructed as both racially and culturally distinct. Each group has a distinctive culture, shares a common heritage, and has developed a common identity within a larger society that subordinates them. The racial characteristics of these groups have become meaningful within a society that continues to change.

Terms of reference are also changing. For example, Blacks increasingly use the term *African Americans* and Hispanics often refer to themselves as *Latinos*. All the groups included sometimes use the term *people of color*. In this book we use such terms interchangeably because they are currently used in both popular and scholarly discourse.

# References

Andersen, Margaret L. 1993. *Thinking About Women*, 3d ed. New York: Macmillan.

Andersen, Margaret, and Patricia Hill Collins. 1992. *Race, Class, and Gender: An Anthology*. Belmont, Calif.: Wadsworth.

Caulfield, Mina Davis. 1974. "Imperialism, the Family, and Cultures of Resistance." *Socialist Review* 4 (2) (October): 67–85.

Collins, Patricia Hill. 1986. "Learning from the Outsider Within: The Sociological Significance of Black Feminist Thought." *Social Problems* 33:6 (December):514–532.

———. 1990. *Black Feminist Thought: Knowledge, Consciousness, and the Politics of Empowerment*. Boston: Unwin Hyman.

Faludi, Susan. 1991. *Backlash*. New York: Crown Publishers.

Glenn, Evelyn Nakano. 1992. "From Servitude to Service Work: Historical Continuities in the Racial Division of Paid Reproductive Labor." *Signs: Journal of Women in Culture and Society* 18 (1): 1–43.

Harding, Sandra. 1991. *Whose Science? Whose Knowledge?* Ithaca, N.Y.: Cornell University Press.

hooks, bell. 1992. *Black Looks: Race and Representation*. Boston: South End Press.

Naylor, Gloria. 1983. *The Women of Brewster Place*. New York: Penguin.

Zavella, Patricia. 1989. "The Problematic Relationship of Feminism and Chicana Studies." *Women's Studies* 17: 25–36.

# 2

# *Women of Color: A Demographic Overview*

## Vilma Ortiz

**R**ecent scholarship in the social sciences has focused on the integration of race, ethnicity, gender, and class, building on earlier feminist research that focused primarily on gender. The earliest feminist literature documented the role of patriarchal systems in oppressing women, such that women had little power in the home and few opportunities for success in the labor market. Because this early literature was based primarily on the experiences of White, middle-class women, recent contributions to the feminist literature have pointed out that it is not possible to generalize from these experiences to all women, particularly women of color. Women of color carry the additional burden of race and class, which relegates them to the lowest socioeconomic positions in society. Although women of color have made tremendous economic gains since the 1950s, they still experience considerable discrimination and oppression.

The purpose of the present chapter is to demonstrate the importance of race, ethnicity, gender, and class when describing the experiences of women of color in American society. In particular, this chapter focuses on the demographic, family, and socioeconomic characteristics of Black, Latina, Asian, and American Indian women. Fortunately, data now exist that allow us to document the importance of race, class, and gender simultaneously.

Just as we cannot make generalizations about all women as a single group, so we cannot generalize about women of color, since this group includes women from numerous racial, ethnic, and national origin backgrounds. Blacks, Latinas, Asians, and American Indians are considered women of color because of their non-White or mixed racial backgrounds. And within these broad categories, there are important distinctions as well—the most important being that of country of origin among Latina and Asian women. Among Latinas, the primary groups are Mexican, Puerto Rican, and Cuban women; among Asians, there are more than twenty national origins, including Chinese, Japanese, Filipino, Korean, Asian Indian, and Vietnamese.

The data presented in this chapter are organized into three sections. In the first section, information on each group's historical background and demographic characteristics—including age, migration background, and place of residence—is presented. This information is organized by racial-ethnic group in order to give a comprehensive portrait of each group. The second section compares women of color of different origins along family characteristics, including marital status, fertility, and the extent to which households are headed by women. In the third section, comparisons are made on socioeconomic indicators, including education, employment, income, and poverty. Because of the dramatic changes that have occurred over time among women of color, the analysis includes a historical dimension.

This chapter documents the lower socioeconomic position of groups that have a long history of discrimination and oppression in the United States—Blacks, Mexicans, Puerto Ricans, and American Indians. Among these groups, we see lower levels of education, work status, and income. Cubans and most Asian women fare better since they are immigrants from countries that have been somewhat selective in their migration experience. Vietnamese women are quite disadvantaged relative to other Asians because they are primarily refugees, some with limited literacy. Among all racial-ethnic groups, as expected, women fare much worse than men.

## Background and Demographic Characteristics

### AFRICAN AMERICANS

African Americans have historically been one of the most oppressed groups in the United States. Slavery and pervasive and persistent discrimination have kept most Blacks from attaining any meaningful measure of success. The early 1960s were a turning point for the Black population with the passage of the Civil Rights Act of 1964 and the launching of the War on Poverty. Although empirical evidence shows that on some indicators, such as educational and occupational status, conditions for Blacks are improving, on many other indicators, such as poverty, conditions have remained dismal or have deteriorated (Allen and Farley 1987; Farley 1984; Wilson 1987).[1] Black women have long suffered from the dual disadvantage of race and gender, especially in the labor force. Initially, they were largely agricultural laborers in the post-slavery period; subsequently, Black women worked primarily in domestic service; and more recently, they are concentrated in low-level service and clerical jobs. Many Black women are single mothers who earn considerably less than men and experience difficulty in providing for their families.

As can be seen from Table 2.1, the African American population has grown modestly since the 1960s, in contrast to other groups (see the Appendix at the end of this chapter for a description of the methods and data sources). This is because Blacks are neither an immigrant population (see Table 2.2) nor a population with particularly high fertility (see Table 2.5), the main reasons for population growth among other groups. The Black population is fairly young (see Table 2.2), urban (Table 2.3),[2] and more likely to be concentrated in the southern region of the country (see Table 2.3).

## LATINAS

The Latino population has grown considerably, more than doubling in size between 1960 and 1985 (see Table 2.1). This is due to a combination of a large influx of immigrants (see Table 2.2) and high fertility (see Table 2.5). Among Latinos, 59 percent are of Mexican origin, 14 percent are Puerto Rican, 6 percent are Cuban, and the remaining 21 percent are from various Central and South American nations. Differences by national origin are so pervasive that each group will be discussed separately.

**Mexican-Origin Population.** The Mexican-origin population is the largest (see Table 2.1) and is concentrated geographically in the southwestern United States, particularly California and Texas (see Table 2.3). The majority of Mexican Americans are U.S.-born (see Table 2.2)[3] and commonly referred to as Chicanos and Chicanas. The high percentage of native-born is partly due to the population being indigenous to the Southwest prior to the territory being taken over by the United States in 1848, and to the continuous history of immigration from Mexico since the early 1900s. The level of immigration and the level of acceptance of Mexican Americans by Anglo society have varied depending on economic conditions: restrictive during economic downturns and welcoming during labor shortages (Bean and Tienda 1988). Since the revision of immigration laws in 1965, immigration has increased; consequently immigrant origin increased from 15 percent in

**Table 2.1.** Population Size by Race/Ethnicity, 1960–1988 (in Thousands)

|                 | 1960    | 1970    | 1980    | 1985    | 1988    |
| --------------- | ------- | ------- | ------- | ------- | ------- |
| White           | 158,838 | 177,749 | 189,035 | 199,117 | 203,869 |
| Black           | 18,849  | 22,550  | 26,482  | 28,151  | 29,333  |
| Latino          | —       | 9,073   | 14,604  | 16,940  | 19,431  |
| Mexican         | 3,465   | 4,532   | 8,679   | 10,262  | 12,110  |
| Puerto Rican    | 893     | 1,429   | 2,005   | 1,036   | 2,471   |
| Cuban           | 124     | 545     | 806     | 1,003   | 1,035   |
| Asian           | —       | —       | 3,726   | —       | —       |
| Chinese         | 236     | 432     | 812     | —       | —       |
| Japanese        | 473     | 588     | 716     | —       | —       |
| Filipino        | 182     | 337     | 782     | —       | —       |
| Korean          | 20      | 70      | 357     | —       | —       |
| Asian Indian    | 25      | 76      | 387     | —       | —       |
| Vietnamese      | —       | —       | 245     | —       | —       |
| American Indian | 546     | 764     | 1,479   | —       | —       |

1960 to 26 percent in 1980. Although Mexican immigrants have typically been poor peasants from rural areas who come to the United States to work in agriculture, the majority currently reside in urban areas (see Table 2.3). Although Mexican American women have long been characterized as adhering to traditional roles in the family (that is, placing their families ahead of themselves, deferring to husbands and fathers, and carrying all of the household responsibilities), empirical evidence demonstrates that Chicanas are active participants in both home and work environments (e.g., Zavella 1987).

**Puerto Ricans.** Although a small community of Puerto Ricans has resided in New York City since the 1920s, large-scale migration did not begin until the late 1940s, with the largest migration during the 1950s and early 1960s. Approximately half of the Puerto Rican population in 1980 was not born in the mainland United States (see Table 2.2).[4] Puerto Rican migrants tend to be young (see Table 2.2), with little education and few occupational skills; they migrate as a result of the limited employment opportunities in Puerto Rico and the lure of plentiful, low-skill, manufacturing jobs in New York City (Ortiz 1986). Puerto Rican women work largely as operatives and in other unskilled

**Table 2.2.** Median Age and Migration History by Race/Ethnicity, 1980

| | Median Age | Foreign Born (%) | Recent Immigrant[a] (%) |
|---|---|---|---|
| White | 32.9 | 4.9 | — |
| Black | 26.1 | 3.1 | — |
| Latino | 23.8 | 35.2 | 25.0 |
| Mexican | 22.1 | 26.0 | 28.5 |
| Puerto Rican | 23.3 | 51.0 | 20.0 |
| Cuban | 39.1 | 77.9 | 7.2 |
| Asian | 29.4 | 58.6 | 44.7 |
| Chinese | 29.8 | 63.3 | 35.1 |
| Japanese | 36.2 | 28.4 | 35.9 |
| Filipino | 29.1 | 64.7 | 34.8 |
| Korean | 27.1 | 81.9 | 50.1 |
| Asian Indian | 28.6 | 70.4 | 43.9 |
| Vietnamese | 22.3 | 90.5 | 77.5 |
| American Indian | 23.4 | 2.5 | — |

[a]Calculated among those foreign born.

occupations. In the mainland United States, Puerto Ricans are an urban population concentrated mostly in New York City and the Northeast (see Table 2.3).

**Cubans.** Cubans are a primarily immigrant population (see Table 2.2) who arrived in the United States during the late 1950s and early 1960s. Because of little migration in the following twenty years and low fertility (see Table 2.5), Cubans are older than other Latinos. Cuban immigrants were largely professionals and entrepreneurs who fled the communist government in Cuba. They were given special refugee status and provided settlement assistance by the U.S. government, which helped them to do well economically. In the early 1980s, another influx of Cubans entered the United States (commonly referred to as the "Marielitos" because they left from the Cuban port of Mariel); they have not fared as well economically because of their lower socioeconomic status. In contrast to other Latinos, Cubans have settled primarily in Florida and other southeastern states (see Table 2.3). By actively participating in the labor force, Cuban women contribute significantly to the socioeconomic status of their families.

**Table 2.3.**  Geographic Characteristics by Race/Ethnicity, 1980

| | | Geographic Distribution (%) | | | |
|---|---|---|---|---|---|
| | Urban (%) | North East | North Central | South | West |
| White | 71.4 | 22.8 | 27.7 | 31.2 | 18.3 |
| Black | 85.3 | 18.7 | 20.2 | 53.0 | 8.1 |
| Latino | 89.9 | 18.6 | 8.5 | 30.8 | 42.2 |
| Mexican | 87.7 | 1.0 | 9.1 | 36.1 | 53.8 |
| Puerto Rican | 97.0 | 75.6 | 9.8 | 8.2 | 6.3 |
| Cuban | 98.0 | 22.0 | 4.0 | 65.3 | 8.7 |
| Asian | 93.1 | 19.0 | 10.4 | 19.3 | 51.3 |
| Chinese | 97.0 | 26.6 | 8.8 | 11.2 | 53.5 |
| Japanese | 91.6 | 6.8 | 6.2 | 7.7 | 79.3 |
| Filipino | 92.4 | 10.4 | 11.2 | 11.3 | 67.2 |
| Korean | 92.9 | 18.4 | 18.2 | 21.4 | 42.2 |
| Asian Indian | 92.2 | 33.3 | 23.4 | 23.6 | 19.8 |
| Vietnamese | 95.3 | 9.3 | 13.4 | 31.3 | 45.8 |
| American Indian | 54.6 | 5.8 | 18.2 | 26.3 | 49.7 |

## ASIANS

Asians include persons of many nationalities, of which Chinese, Japanese, Filipinos, Koreans, Asian Indians, and Vietnamese are the largest groups now residing in the United States. As with Latinas, it is not possible to generalize about all Asian women since the history and experiences of the different groups vary tremendously.

**Chinese.** The Chinese, the oldest Asian community, dating back to the 1840s, settled mostly in California (Kitano 1981). The initial migration was mostly males, who came as sojourners expecting to return to their homeland. In 1882, Congress passed the Chinese Exclusion Act, which prohibited Chinese immigration and expelled many Chinese from this country; it was not repealed until 1943. Changes in the immigration law in 1965, lifting national origin quotas especially restrictive to Asians, have meant a dramatic increase in Chinese immigration, including more women (Cafferty et al. 1983). Consequently, the Chinese population has increased in size since 1960 (see Table 2.1) and is largely immigrant (see Table 2.2). The Chinese

VILMA ORTIZ

are an urban population that resides primarily in the West and Northeast (see Table 2.3).

**Japanese.** The second Asian group to migrate in significant numbers were the Japanese. They came after 1890, also as sojourners, although many brought their wives. The most important historical event in the U.S. experience of the Japanese is their relocation and internment during World War II, an experience that affected all Japanese regardless of their national loyalty or their place of birth (Kitano 1981). Recent immigration from Japan, even after the immigration law changes in 1965, has been low, so that the Japanese population in the United States is largely second generation or later (see Table 2.2). Japanese are older than other Asians (see Table 2.2) and reside almost entirely in the West (see Table 2.3).

**Filipinos.** Filipinos are one of the more recent immigrant groups in the United States. They were allowed to enter the United States freely prior to 1946 since they were nationals because of the colonial relationship of the Philippines with the United States after the Spanish-American War. After 1946, they also faced restrictions. Since the 1965 changes in the immigration law, a large number of Filipinos have immigrated (reflected in the high percentage who are foreign-born presented in Table 2.2), and the population has increased in size (see Table 2.1). While the early immigrants were mostly agricultural workers, more recent immigrants from the Philippines tend to be professionals, with many among the women being nurses (Kitano 1981). Like other Asian groups, Filipinos reside primarily in urban areas in the West (see Table 2.3).

**Koreans and Asian Indians.** Koreans and Asian Indians (from the country of India) have immigrated largely since the 1965 immigration law changes. Therefore, both groups increased dramatically in size between 1960 and 1980 (see Table 2.1) and are primarily immigrant (see Table 2.2). The immigrants among both groups are mainly highly educated professionals (Gardner et al. 1985). Both groups are urban, with Koreans tending to reside in the West and Asian Indians in the Northeast (see Table 2.3).

**Vietnamese.** The Vietnamese population is a refugee population that settled in the United States between 1975 and 1980, after the Vietnam War ended (see Table 2.2). This population tends to come from rural communities, with some subgroups, such as the Hmong, possessing few literacy or economic skills (Kitano 1981). They have settled primarily in the West (see Table 2.3).

## AMERICAN INDIANS

American Indians,[5] indigenous to the United States, have been one of the most oppressed groups. They have been affected by laws unique to them because they are part of separate nations rather than citizens of the United States. In the first half of this century, they lived on reservations and followed fairly traditional lifestyles. Subsequently, particularly in the 1960s, they have moved off the reservations in large numbers and are becoming considerably more politically active (Deloria 1981). The American Indian population grew between 1960 and 1980 (see Table 2.1).[6] It is a young population relative to other racial-ethnic groups and only a very small percentage is immigrant (see Table 2.2).[7] They are less urban than other groups and reside mostly in the West (see Table 2.3).

## Family Characteristics Summary

Overall, Black and Puerto Rican women have experienced the most dramatic changes in their marital and family status since 1960—they are less likely to be married and more likely to head families on their own. In addition, they are more likely to have children at younger ages prior to marriage. In contrast, the percentage of women not married or heading families has increased modestly among Mexican, Cuban, Asian, and American Indian women. Moreover, Mexican, Vietnamese, and American Indian women tend to have more children than other women.

## MARITAL STATUS

Table 2.4 shows changes in the marital status of women in each group over time. For almost all groups, the percentage of women who are married has declined while the percent single and the percent divorced, widowed, or separated (referred to as marital disruptions) has grown. However, the increase in marital disruptions occurred primarily between 1960 and 1970, and the increase in remaining single between 1970 and 1980. In comparison to other women, Black and Puerto Rican women have experienced the most dramatic changes in their distribution of marital status. By 1980, they had the lowest rates of marriage and the highest rates of being single, divorced, widowed, or separated of all groups. In comparison to Black and Puerto Rican

**Table 2.4.** Marital Status of Women by Race/Ethnicity, 1960–1980

| | Married (%) | | | Never Married (%) | | | Maritally Disrupted (%) | | |
|---|---|---|---|---|---|---|---|---|---|
| | 1960 | 1970 | 1980 | 1960 | 1970 | 1980 | 1960 | 1970 | 1980 |
| White | 64.0 | 60.1 | 57.5 | 19.0 | 18.4 | 21.2 | 17.0 | 21.4 | 21.4 |
| Black | 51.3 | 44.2 | 35.1 | 21.7 | 23.4 | 34.4 | 26.9 | 32.4 | 30.6 |
| Latina | — | 58.2 | 52.8 | — | 23.2 | 27.5 | — | 18.7 | 19.7 |
| Mexican | 61.2 | 58.8 | 55.6 | 24.6 | 23.4 | 27.3 | 14.2 | 17.9 | 17.1 |
| Puerto Rican | 61.4 | 55.0 | 43.0 | 21.9 | 19.5 | 31.1 | 16.6 | 25.5 | 25.9 |
| Cuban | — | 58.5 | 54.5 | — | 18.7 | 22.3 | — | 22.8 | 23.2 |
| Asian | — | — | 61.7 | — | — | 25.0 | — | — | 13.3 |
| Chinese | 68.9 | 58.9 | 59.3 | 22.0 | 27.7 | 28.4 | 9.1 | 13.4 | 12.2 |
| Japanese | 69.0 | 63.8 | 60.9 | 21.1 | 20.2 | 24.3 | 9.9 | 16.0 | 14.7 |
| Filipino | 66.2 | 58.3 | 62.4 | 27.7 | 27.8 | 26.0 | 6.1 | 14.1 | 11.7 |
| Korean | — | — | 68.2 | — | — | 18.6 | — | — | 13.2 |
| Asian Indian | — | — | 71.5 | — | — | 15.1 | — | — | 13.4 |
| Vietnamese | — | — | 56.7 | — | — | 31.7 | — | — | 11.6 |
| American Indian | 55.1 | 54.3 | 48.0 | 29.1 | 22.2 | 28.6 | 15.7 | 23.4 | 23.3 |

*Note:* In 1960, based on fourteen years old and over; in 1970, based on sixteen years old and over; in 1980, based on fifteen years old and over.

women, Mexicans have experienced a modest change in their marital status and Cubans do not appear to have changed much.

Asian women experienced less change in their marital status than other women. Chinese, Japanese, and Filipino had the lowest levels of marital disruption in both 1960 and 1980, even though the level among them increased in this period. All three groups have relatively high rates of remaining single. This, coupled with the lower rates of marital disruptions, makes the percent married (about 60 percent) among Filipino, Chinese, and Japanese similar to that of Whites (58 percent). In 1980, the rate of marital disruptions among Korean, Asian Indians, and Vietnamese was similar to other Asian groups. However, Koreans and Asian Indians have lower rates of remaining single and slightly higher rates of being married than other Asians. On the other hand, the Vietnamese have an unusually high percentage of being single (31 percent) and a low rate of marriage (57 percent), which may be due to being younger than other groups.

Among American Indian women, the percent married decreased and the percent experiencing a marital disruption increased, but to a lesser extent than other groups. The percent single declined and then increased, showing a slightly different pattern than among other groups.

### FERTILITY

Table 2.5 presents fertility rates by age in 1980.[8] Fertility among those fifteen to twenty-four reflects a different process than fertility among those twenty-five to thirty-four or thirty-five to forty-four years old. Higher fertility among younger women means that the women are having children at a young age, often before marriage. On the other hand, the fertility rate among the older women reveals the total number of children a woman has in her lifetime.

Younger Black and Puerto Rican women have a high rate of fertility, which has been shown to occur primarily before marriage (Darabi and Ortiz 1987). Young Mexican-origin women also have a high fertility rate, although they tend to have a child after marriage (Darabi and Ortiz 1987). Young Cuban women, on the other hand, have an especially low fertility rate, which is consistent with the fact that they tend to marry at an older age (Gurak 1978). Among older women, Mexican women have the highest fertility levels, followed by Puerto Rican and Black women, with Cubans having a low level of fertility.

Generally, fertility among Asian women is lower than among other women, especially among Chinese and Japanese women. Viet-

**Table 2.5.** Fertility Rate by Age and Race/Ethnicity, 1980 (per Thousand Women)

|  | *15–24* | *25–34* | *35–44* |
|---|---|---|---|
| White | 269 | 1,404 | 2,544 |
| Black | 537 | 1,816 | 3,077 |
| Latina | 475 | 1,922 | 3,202 |
|   Mexican | 528 | 2,105 | 3,646 |
|   Puerto Rican | 548 | 1,986 | 3,202 |
|   Cuban | 192 | 1,186 | 2,033 |
| Asian | 217 | 1,233 | 2,272 |
|   Chinese | 82 | 939 | 2,233 |
|   Japanese | 106 | 908 | 1,872 |
|   Filipino | 278 | 1,270 | 2,216 |
|   Korean | 229 | 1,244 | 2,045 |
|   Asian Indian | 236 | 1,336 | 2,197 |
|   Vietnamese | 305 | 1,775 | 3,391 |
| American Indian | 530 | 2,012 | 3,450 |

namese women have the highest fertility among Asian women and higher fertility than other women of color. The fertility of Filipino, Korean, and Asian Indian women falls between these two extremes. Although there is little research on the causes of fertility among these groups, we do know that the especially low fertility rate among Japanese is largely due to the older age at which they first marry (Gurak 1978, 1980).

Generally, American Indian women have high fertility at all ages. At younger ages, their fertility level is about that of Black and Puerto Rican women, while at older ages, it is similar to Mexican and Vietnamese women.

## FAMILIES HEADED BY WOMEN

Table 2.6 presents the percent of families headed by women for each group over time. Overall, there has been an increase in the percent of families headed by women in every group, although the growth varies by group. Black and Puerto Rican families have experienced a very high increase in female headship—by the mid-1980s, the rate among Blacks was almost double that in 1960, and among Puerto Ricans it had tripled. Among Mexicans and Cubans the percent of

**Table 2.6.** Percentage of Female-Headed Families by Race/Ethnicity, 1960–1988

|  | 1960 | 1970 | 1980 | 1985 | 1988 |
|---|---|---|---|---|---|
| White | 9.3 | 9.0 | 11.2 | 12.8 | 12.9 |
| Black | 21.7 | 27.4 | 37.8 | 43.7 | 42.8 |
| Latina | — | 15.3 | 19.9 | 23.0 | 23.4 |
|   Mexican | 11.9 | 13.4 | 16.4 | 18.6 | 18.5 |
|   Puerto Rican | 15.3 | 24.4 | 35.3 | 44.0 | 44.0 |
|   Cuban | — | 12.3 | 14.9 | 16.0 | 16.1 |
| Asian | — | — | 11.0 | — | — |
|   Chinese | 6.1 | 6.7 | 8.6 | — | — |
|   Japanese | 7.8 | 10.3 | 12.3 | — | — |
|   Filipino | 5.5 | 8.6 | 12.1 | — | — |
|   Korean | — | — | 11.5 | — | — |
|   Asian Indian | — | — | 4.8 | — | — |
|   Vietnamese | — | — | 15.4 | — | — |
| American Indian | 16.4 | 18.4 | 23.5 | — | — |

families headed by women had increased to slightly less than 20 percent by the late 1980s.

Asian women tend to have lower levels of heading families than other women. Chinese and Asian Indian women have the lowest level (between 5 and 9 percent), while other Asian groups—Japanese, Filipinos, Koreans, and Vietnamese—have moderate levels. Among the Filipinos, Japanese, and Chinese (for whom we have information over time), the rate of families headed by women increased over time, although less so than among other groups. American Indian women also experienced an increase in the percent heading families between 1960 and 1980, but not to an especially high level.

## Socioeconomic Characteristics

Overall, Black, Latina, and American Indian women are in a lower socioeconomic position than White and Asian women. In addition to higher educational levels, Asian women are more advantaged workers since they are more likely to be professionals (Filipino, Chinese, Japanese, and Asian Indian) or to work in their own businesses (Chinese, Japanese, and Korean), and to earn more (all groups except the Vietnamese). Consequently, Asian families have higher incomes, and lower poverty rates, than other families. The only Asian group that is significantly disadvantaged is the Vietnamese.

Women are in a worse economic position than men. For instance, families headed by women have lower income levels and are much poorer than families in general among all groups. Also, women of all racial-ethnic origins earn considerably less, work fewer hours, and are less likely to work in their own businesses than men. Although women of some racial-ethnic origins are more likely to be professionals than men, they are concentrated in female-dominated occupations with lower prestige and pay.

**EDUCATIONAL ATTAINMENT**

Although the percentage of high school and college graduates has increased among most groups, some groups have not achieved parity with Whites (see Table 2.7). For instance, graduation rates among Black women more than doubled between 1960 and 1980, yet their opportunities do not equal those of other groups. Black men and women had a similar educational level in 1980.

Latina women have especially low educational levels, although they have increased over time. Mexican and Puerto Rican women are similar in their educational levels. In 1960, less than 20 percent had completed high school; by 1980, less than 40 percent had completed high school. Cuban women have a higher educational level than other Latinas. Among Mexicans and Puerto Ricans, men and women are similar in their educational attainment, while among Cubans, men have slightly higher educational levels than women.

Asian women have higher educational levels. Japanese and Filipino women have the highest rates of high school completion and Vietnamese have the lowest rate; Chinese, Korean, and Asian Indian women fall in between. All Asian groups except the Vietnamese have higher rates of completing college than other women. Filipino and Asian Indian women have the highest level of completing college, followed by Chinese women (30 percent), Korean women (22 percent), and Japanese women (20 percent). The group with the lowest rate of completing college is Vietnamese women—only 8 percent have completed college. To a large extent, the high educational levels of Asian women reflect the fact that immigrants from these countries have tended to be of fairly high status.

Comparing the educational levels of Asian men and women, we see large differences, in particular among the recently arrived groups. For instance, among Korean and Asian Indian men, the percent who have completed high school is about 90 percent, while the percent

**Table 2.7.** Educational Attainment by Gender and Race/Ethnicity, 1960–1980

| | High School Graduates (%) | | | | College Graduates (%) | | | |
| | Women | | | Men | Women | | | Men |
| | 1960 | 1970 | 1980 | 1980 | 1960 | 1970 | 1980 | 1980 |
|---|---|---|---|---|---|---|---|---|
| White | 44.7 | 55.0 | 68.1 | 69.6 | 6.0 | 8.4 | 13.3 | 21.3 |
| Black | 22.6 | 32.5 | 51.5 | 50.8 | 2.8 | 4.6 | 8.3 | 8.4 |
| Latina/o | — | 31.0 | 42.7 | 45.4 | — | 3.2 | 6.0 | 9.4 |
| Mexican | 18.7 | 22.9 | 36.3 | 38.9 | 1.3 | 1.7 | 3.7 | 6.1 |
| Puerto Rican | 16.1 | 22.7 | 39.1 | 41.3 | 1.3 | 1.9 | 4.8 | 6.5 |
| Cuban | — | 40.9 | 53.3 | 57.7 | — | 8.3 | 13.2 | 19.7 |
| Asian | — | — | 71.4 | 78.8 | — | — | 27.0 | 39.8 |
| Chinese | 48.3 | 54.9 | 67.4 | 75.2 | 12.5 | 19.5 | 29.5 | 43.8 |
| Japanese | 55.3 | 67.1 | 79.5 | 84.2 | 6.0 | 11.1 | 19.7 | 35.1 |
| Filipino | 42.8 | 63.7 | 75.1 | 73.1 | 10.9 | 30.5 | 41.2 | 32.2 |
| Korean | — | — | 70.6 | 90.0 | — | — | 22.0 | 52.4 |
| Asian Indian | — | — | 71.5 | 88.8 | — | — | 35.5 | 68.5 |
| Vietnamese | — | — | 53.6 | 71.3 | — | — | 7.9 | 18.2 |
| American Indian | 18.0 | 32.9 | 54.3 | 57.3 | 1.3 | 3.1 | 6.4 | 9.2 |

*Note:* In 1960, based on fourteen years old and over; in 1970 and 1980, based on twenty-five years old and over.

completing high school is around 70 percent for Korean and Asian Indian women and 54 percent for Vietnamese women. Among the Japanese, Chinese, and Vietnamese, there are also fairly large sex differences in the percent having completed college. The only group in which women have higher educational levels than men is among Filipinos.

American Indian women have low educational levels, comparable to those of Black women. In 1980, 54 percent had completed high school and 6 percent had completed college. In 1980, the educational levels of American Indian men and women were similar to each other.

### LABOR FORCE PARTICIPATION

Table 2.8 presents labor force participation, meaning the percentage of women who are employed or looking for working. As has been well documented in the literature, labor force participation among women has increased dramatically since about 1965, as can be seen among White women. Black women increased their participation from 1960 to the mid-1980s, although not to the same extent as other groups, since they started out with higher labor force participation rate in 1960.

The labor force participation of Latina women has also increased, but not to the same extent for all groups (see Table 2.8). Among Mexican women, participation went from 29 percent in 1960 to 52 percent in 1988. Puerto Rican women have an unusual pattern of participation, in that their rate actually declined between 1960 and 1970. This may be due to the decline of manufacturing jobs in New York City, in which Puerto Rican women were concentrated. Cuban women had a higher rate of participation in 1970 and continued to do so in the 1980s.

Asian women tend to have fairly high rates of labor force participation (see Table 2.8). Chinese and Japanese had high rates in 1960 and continued to do so in 1980 (58 percent among both groups). Filipino women, who did not have an especially high participation rate in 1960 (36 percent), had the highest rate in 1980 (68 percent). On the other hand, Asian Indian women and Vietnamese women had lower rates of participation in 1980 (47 percent and 49 percent, respectively).

American Indian women had the lowest rate of labor force participation in 1960. Their participation increased over the next two decades, so that they still had a low level, but not the lowest level of all groups.

### LABOR FORCE PARTICIPATION BY MARITAL STATUS

Table 2.8 also presents the labor force participation rates by marital status for women with children. It is generally true that nonmarried

**Table 2.8.** Labor Force Participation of Women by Race/Ethnicity, 1960–1988

| | All Women (%) | | | | Women with Children, 1980 (%) | | |
|---|---|---|---|---|---|---|---|
| | 1960 | 1970 | 1980 | 1988 | Not Married | Married | Difference |
| White | 33.6 | 40.6 | 49.4 | 56.4 | 71.9 | 51.4 | + 20.5 |
| Black | 42.2 | 47.5 | 53.3 | 58.0 | 60.0 | 67.8 | − 7.8 |
| Latina | — | 39.3 | 49.3 | 52.1 | 50.6 | 48.2 | + 2.4 |
| Mexican | 28.8 | 36.4 | 49.0 | 52.4 | 58.6 | 46.7 | + 11.9 |
| Puerto Rican | 36.3 | 32.3 | 40.1 | 40.9 | 27.4 | 42.9 | − 15.5 |
| Cuban | — | 51.0 | 55.4 | 53.6 | 67.5 | 60.3 | + 7.2 |
| Asian | — | — | 57.7 | — | 69.3 | 58.8 | + 10.5 |
| Chinese | 44.2 | 49.5 | 58.3 | — | 74.2 | 60.4 | + 13.8 |
| Japanese | 44.1 | 49.4 | 58.5 | — | 77.2 | 53.2 | + 24.0 |
| Filipino | 36.2 | 55.2 | 68.1 | — | 75.4 | 73.5 | + 1.9 |
| Korean | — | — | 55.2 | — | 72.7 | 55.5 | + 17.2 |
| Asian Indian | — | — | 47.1 | — | 71.6 | 53.4 | + 18.2 |
| Vietnamese | — | — | 48.9 | — | 54.7 | 49.3 | + 5.4 |
| American Indian | 25.5 | 35.3 | 48.3 | — | 56.3 | 50.7 | + 5.6 |

*Note:* Based on population sixteen years old and over.

women with children are more likely to be in the labor force than married women with children.[9] This is not surprising, given that unmarried women with children have an economic necessity to work in order to support their families, while some married women have spouses who help support the family and have more flexibility about working (although many married women, even those with young children, work outside the home).

This relationship is clearly evident among all groups of women except Blacks and Puerto Ricans. Among Puerto Ricans, unmarried women are especially likely to work less because they have few opportunities to find employment that will adequately support their families. One reason for this is that they reside in the North, where lower-skilled jobs are declining and higher-skilled jobs are increasing (Karsada 1985), which may discourage them from working. On the other hand, married Black women have an especially high participation rate. They may find that their husbands cannot support the family, given the employment difficulties that minority men face in a declining economy (Farley and Allen 1988). Consequently, married Black and Puerto Rican women work to supplement their family's income.

## EMPLOYMENT EXPERIENCES

**Full-time, Year-round Employment.** Table 2.9 presents characteristics of employed women and men in 1980. The first column presents the percent of women who worked full-time and year-round (among employed persons) in 1979. Three groups have an especially high level (over 45 percent) working full-time and year-round: Cuban, Japanese, and Filipino. Among the other groups, between 35 and 40 percent work full-time and year-round. In all groups, men are more likely to work full-time and year round than are women.

**Professional Occupations.** The second column of Table 2.9 shows the percent of employed women in professional occupations. Asian women are more likely to be professional workers than other groups of women, with Asian Indian women having an especially high rate of working in professional jobs (33 percent). In addition, among all Asian groups except Filipinos, a higher percentage of the men are professionals than women. The higher percentage of Filipino women professional workers results from the men having a lower rate of professional employment than other groups, not from the women having a higher rate. Among

**Table 2.9.** Employment Characteristics Among Employed Persons by Race/Ethnicity and Gender, 1979

| | Women | | | | | Men | | | |
|---|---|---|---|---|---|---|---|---|---|
| | Emp. FT Yr-Rd (%) | Prof. Occ. (%) | Self Emp. (%) | Income FT Yr-Rd Workers | | Emp. FT Yr-Rd (%) | Prof. Occ. (%) | Self Emp. (%) | Income FT Yr-Rd Workers |
| White | 40.2 | 22.4 | 4.0 | 10,512 | | 63.1 | 25.0 | 9.9 | 17,986 |
| Black | 40.3 | 16.5 | 1.2 | 9,583 | | 51.3 | 11.7 | 3.5 | 12,657 |
| Latina/o | 37.4 | 12.5 | 2.1 | 8,923 | | 54.0 | 12.0 | 4.9 | 12,970 |
| Mexican | 35.0 | 10.8 | 2.0 | 8,616 | | 52.7 | 9.0 | 4.4 | 12,623 |
| Puerto Rican | 38.1 | 13.4 | 1.2 | 9,390 | | 55.1 | 11.4 | 2.9 | 12,108 |
| Cuban | 47.1 | 15.7 | 2.6 | 8,982 | | 61.4 | 22.3 | 8.3 | 14,168 |
| Asian | 42.4 | 23.8 | 4.0 | 11,502 | | 57.4 | 33.2 | 7.9 | 17,403 |
| Chinese | 40.5 | 24.9 | 5.0 | 11,891 | | 57.3 | 38.6 | 9.0 | 17,945 |
| Japanese | 47.1 | 23.1 | 4.5 | 11,916 | | 63.0 | 33.5 | 11.1 | 20,262 |
| Filipino | 45.8 | 27.4 | 1.9 | 12,007 | | 55.4 | 22.4 | 3.6 | 15,101 |
| Korean | 37.0 | 17.4 | 7.8 | 10,263 | | 52.4 | 33.1 | 16.5 | 17,363 |
| Asian Indian | 37.4 | 33.4 | 4.0 | 11,799 | | 64.1 | 56.6 | 4.5 | 21,125 |
| Vietnamese | 36.4 | 11.3 | 2.6 | 9,261 | | 44.0 | 14.8 | 2.0 | 13,179 |
| American Indian | 34.9 | 17.7 | 3.0 | 9,286 | | 48.8 | 14.7 | 6.2 | 13,876 |

*Note:* Based on population sixteen years old and over.

Blacks, Mexicans, Puerto Ricans, and American Indians, an extremely low percentage of the men are professionals and a slightly higher percentage of the women are professionals. However, the percentage of women professionals among Blacks, Mexicans, Puerto Ricans, and American Indians is still lower than other women of color. We should keep in mind that women professionals tend to be in female-dominated, lower-paying occupations, such as nursing and teaching.

**Self-Employment.** The third column in Table 2.9 shows the percent that is self-employed, that is, owns a business. Asian women are more likely to be self-employed than Black, Latina, and American Indian women. This is true of all Asian groups except Filipinos and Vietnamese. Among groups of Asian women with high rates of self-employment, the men are also apt to be self-employed. It is likely that many of these are family businesses where women work for little or no compensation.

**Income of Full-Time, Year-round Workers.** The last column of Table 2.9 shows the income of full-time, year-round workers, which serves as a proxy for personal earnings.[10] Asian women have higher earnings than Black, Latina, and American Indian women. The only Asian group not having high earnings is the Vietnamese. For all groups, men earn more than women—at least $3,000 more a year.

Interestingly, Puerto Rican women earn more than other Latinas and have slightly higher levels of working full-time, year-round and being professional workers than Mexican women (although not Cuban women). This is in sharp contrast to the lower rates of labor force participation noted in Table 2.8. One reason they do better once in the labor force than other groups is that they are concentrated in the Northeast, where relatively higher wages and better employment conditions are found. However, paired with these higher wages are requirements for greater skills; consequently, fewer Puerto Rican women and men work and, overall, conditions are worse for the group as a whole.

## FAMILY INCOME AND POVERTY

Table 2.10 presents family income over time and poverty levels for 1979. For most groups, income increased substantially between 1959 and 1969, increased only slightly between 1969 and 1979, then decreased slightly after 1979 as a result of the downturn in the economy. Overall, Black, Latino, and American Indian families have lower

**Table 2.10.** Median Family Income (in 1979 Dollars) and Poverty by Race/Ethnicity

| | Median Family Income | | | | | Poverty Level, 1979 (%) |
|---|---|---|---|---|---|---|
| | *1959* | *1969* | *1979* | *1984* | *1987* | |
| White | 14,675 | 19,722 | 20,835 | 19,961 | 20,622 | 7.0 |
| Black | 7,872 | 12,012 | 12,598 | 10,623 | 11,564 | 26.5 |
| Latino | — | 14,550 | 14,712 | 12,839 | 12,975 | 21.3 |
| Mexican | 9,530 | 13,786 | 14,765 | 13,090 | 12,759 | 20.6 |
| Puerto Rican | 8,629 | 12,208 | 10,734 | 8,680 | 9,703 | 34.9 |
| Cuban | — | 16,889 | 18,245 | 18,198 | 17,440 | 11.7 |
| Asian | — | — | 22,713 | — | — | 10.7 |
| Chinese | — | 21,010 | 22,559 | — | — | 10.5 |
| Japanese | — | 24,782 | 27,354 | — | — | 4.2 |
| Filipino | — | 18,451 | 23,687 | — | — | 6.2 |
| Korean | — | — | 20,459 | — | — | 13.4 |
| Asian Indian | — | — | 24,993 | — | — | 7.4 |
| Vietnamese | — | — | 12,840 | — | — | 35.1 |
| American Indian | 7,393 | 11,549 | 13,678 | — | — | 23.7 |

incomes (below $15,000) than do Asian families. Japanese have the highest family income ($27,400); other Asian groups have annual income levels between $20,000 and $25,000, except the Vietnamese ($12,800).

Most Latino families experienced an increase in income levels between 1959 and 1969, a slight increase between 1969 and 1979, and a slight decrease from 1979 to the mid-1980s. In contrast, family income among Puerto Ricans has declined continuously since 1969. Mexican and Puerto Rican families had similar income levels in 1960, but by 1980, Puerto Rican families had lower income levels. In contrast, Cuban families had a higher income level throughout.

Table 2.10 also presents poverty rates in 1979. Again we see a pattern of Black, Latino, and American Indian families having higher poverty levels than Asian families. Among Latinos, Puerto Rican families have the highest poverty level, which is consistent with other socioeconomic indicators. Among Asian families, Filipinos, Japanese, and Asian Indian families have low poverty levels and Vietnamese have an especially high poverty rate.

## POVERTY AMONG FEMALE-HEADED FAMILIES

Table 2.11 presents poverty rates between 1969 and 1987 and median family income in 1979 among female-headed families.[11] Among all groups, female-headed families have considerably lower income levels than other families—the average income for female-headed families was less than half the income of families in general. Consequently, women heading families have considerably fewer resources to support their families, especially Black, Latina, and American Indian women. Among Latinas, Puerto Ricans have the lowest income level of all groups, followed by Mexican families; Cubans have income levels comparable to White and Asian families. Among Asian families, Vietnamese have the lowest income levels, and Korean families the next lowest.

The poverty levels of female-headed families are considerably higher than among all families. Among Black, Latino, and American Indian families, roughly half of female-headed families were classified as poor in 1979; and among Puerto Rican female-headed families, approximately two-thirds were poor in 1979. Among Asian families, Vietnamese had a poverty rate of almost half, while other Asian female-headed families have poverty rates of less than 30 percent. Between 1969 and 1979, poverty declined or remained the same for most groups. One exception to this is Puerto Rican families, for whom poverty increased in this period, probably reflecting the negative impact of a declining manufacturing base in the New York City area, where Puerto Ricans are concentrated. In the early 1980s, poverty increased for most groups, an indication of the economic downturn. Poverty rates declined between 1984 and 1987.

# Conclusion

We have seen that on most indicators, women of color are extremely disadvantaged relative to men. This was demonstrated in the incomes and poverty levels of families headed by women and in the earnings of women. Even among groups that were doing better economically, such as Asians, women earned less than men, and families headed by women had considerably lower incomes and were poorer than families generally. Given that there has been an increase in the percentage of families headed by women, more women, and consequently more children, live under worse economic conditions.

Clearly, women in some racial-ethnic groups are in a much worse economic position than others. Black, Mexican, Puerto Rican, Ameri-

**Table 2.11.** Median Family Income and Poverty Among Female-Headed Families by Race/Ethnicity

| | Median Family Income 1979 | Poverty Level (%) | | | |
|---|---|---|---|---|---|
| | | 1969 | 1979 | 1984 | 1987 |
| White | 9,138 | 25.7 | 22.3 | 27.1 | 26.7 |
| Black | 6,448 | 53.0 | 46.3 | 51.7 | 51.8 |
| Latina | 5,948 | 47.9 | 48.2 | 53.4 | 51.8 |
| Mexican | 6,627 | 50.6 | 44.3 | 43.8 | 47.1 |
| Puerto Rican | 4,593 | 58.0 | 66.8 | 74.4 | 65.3 |
| Cuban | 8,017 | 30.7 | 27.2 | — | — |
| Asian | 9,370 | — | 25.7 | — | — |
| Chinese | 10,763 | 20.3 | 22.3 | — | — |
| Japanese | 11,199 | 24.7 | 14.5 | — | — |
| Filipino | 10,743 | 39.6 | 20.4 | — | — |
| Korean | 8,165 | — | 32.1 | — | — |
| Asian Indian | 10,326 | — | 21.0 | — | — |
| Vietnamese | 6,851 | — | 47.8 | — | — |
| American Indian | 6,596 | 55.7 | 46.5 | — | — |

can Indian, and Vietnamese women were much worse off than Cuban, Filipino, Chinese, Japanese, Korean, and Asian Indian women. What might explain this difference? The key feature that most distinguishes these racial-ethnic groups is that the more successful have a highly selective immigration history. Migration from these countries involves persons of higher socioeconomic status than other immigrant groups.[12] As a consequence, these immigrants bring with them personal characteristics, motivation, and economic resources that ease their integration into American society.[13] The less successful groups are not immigrants but long-oppressed minority groups in the United States. Obviously, this includes Blacks, with a history of slavery and pervasive discrimination; Mexicans and American Indians, both conquered populations in the United States; and Puerto Ricans, a colonized population. The history of these groups has been one of tremendous oppression and exploitation.

Although Mexicans and Puerto Ricans are also immigrants, for both groups migration is not as selective with respect to socioeconomic characteristics because they cross less restrictive barriers (Ortiz 1986).

This is true for Mexicans because of their proximity to the United States, the existing Mexican community here that extends a kinship network to newcomers, and their entrance into a community of long-term oppression. Puerto Ricans are U.S. citizens who can enter freely; moreover, there are strong factors that push them to leave Puerto Rico. Consequently, Mexicans and Puerto Ricans have not done as well as Asians or Cubans.

Among Puerto Rican women, however, there is much worse economic deterioration than among other women. Particularly with respect to family indicators and economic well-being, Puerto Ricans are very poor and becoming more so. One factor mentioned earlier appears to be that they are residentially concentrated in the Northeast, where low-skill jobs have declined drastically. Decline of low-skill jobs is only one aspect of the many structural economic changes that have taken place since the 1970s. Higher-level service jobs in sectors such as information processing, real estate, and professional services have increased more than lower-level ones at the same time that unskilled jobs have worse working conditions (such as lower pay and few benefits). While Puerto Rican women are the most affected by these structural changes, other groups, such as Blacks and Mexicans, have also been affected (Ortiz 1991; Wilson 1987).

For conditions to improve for all women, particularly as heads of families, they need increased access to better jobs with higher pay and more opportunities for advancement. One mechanism for creating opportunities would be to provide opportunities for women to increase their educational levels, especially given the structural shifts in our economy from less-skilled jobs toward more-skilled ones. Puerto Rican women would obviously benefit from meaningful educational opportunities, since they have been particularly affected by structural changes in the availability of unskilled, well-paying jobs. However, they are not alone in needing education, especially job-relevant training, since women of color generally have been negatively affected by downgrading of job conditions and upgrading of job requirements.

Strategies that focus only on the individual skills of women are clearly inadequate. In order for women to work productively, conditions of employment need to be improved. This means providing benefits such as affordable child care and adequate health insurance even for the lowest-paid jobs (Smith and Tienda 1978). Moreover, these benefits need to be attached to part-time as well as full-time jobs, since many mothers work, or would prefer to work, part-time (Ellwood 1988).

This chapter points to the complex interplay of race, ethnicity, class, and gender in understanding the position of women of color in U.S. society. The strategies mentioned above cannot completely eradicate the oppressed economic position of women of color since many of the causes of women's position are historical and structural. Nevertheless, strategies must be attempted that acknowledge the structural nature of women's inequality.

## Appendix: Data Sources and Methodological Issues

The data presented in this chapter come from published U.S. census sources (see References under U.S. Bureau of the Census for a list of the data sources). The groups selected are those for whom 1980 census data are available. Among Latinas, detailed information is available for Mexicans, Puerto Ricans, and Cubans. The "Other" category, about 20 percent of all Latinas, is composed of numerous recent immigrants, such as Dominicans, Colombians, and Salvadorans, and of Spanish-origin persons indigenous to the Southwest. This group is excluded here because it combines different populations.

Of the more than twenty groups of Asian origin, we focus on the Chinese, Japanese, Filipino, Korean, Asian Indian, and Vietnamese populations because detailed information is available for them in the 1980 census. Although the 1980 census identified other groups of Asian ancestry (e.g., Hawaiian, Samoan, Guamanian), they are quite small (no more than 180,000), comprise a very small percentage of all Asians (less than 5 percent), and have little information available; therefore they are not included in this chapter.

To examine historical changes, 1960 and 1970 census data are used to the extent that they were available. Among Latinas, we have information on the Mexican and Puerto Rican population in 1960 and 1970 and information on the Cuban population in 1970. For the Asian groups, data are readily available for Filipino, Chinese, and Japanese in 1960 and 1970 but not for the other groups before 1980. Because the Census Bureau has changed the manner in which it measures race/ethnicity over time, every effort was made to ensure that the definitions used are comparable across time.

Since 1980 figures are outdated, more recent figures are presented from the Current Population Surveys (CPS). Figures for Whites, Blacks, and Latinas are available from the 1985 and 1988 CPS. Because the CPS are smaller efforts than the census, figures are not available for Asians and American Indians. Also, CPS reports do not include all the characteristics provided in the census.

VILMA ORTIZ

# Notes

*Acknowledgments:* I would like to acknowledge comments by Maxine Baca Zinn, Bonnie Thornton Dill, Antonio Serrata, and Ruth Milkman. Please address correspondence to the author at Department of Sociology, UCLA, Los Angeles, CA 90024.

1. Interpretations of these changes differ. Some scholars stress the considerable gains toward equality made by Blacks, others argue that the progress has been superficial, and still others argue that the Black population has become polarized between a middle class and an increasing number who are becoming persistently poor and concentrated in ghettos.

2. The figures presented on urban concentration are based on the total population of males and females, rather than just females, since they are not available for the latter. However, these characteristics for the total population are similar to what they would be for females because there are few gender differences in geographic distribution.

3. The figures presented on immigration are based on the total population of males and females, rather than just females, since they are not available for the latter. However, these characteristics among females are expected to be similar to those for the total population.

4. Since Puerto Rico is a territory of the United States, Puerto Ricans on the island are U.S. citizens and thus technically are not immigrants. However, given the distinctively Hispanic culture of Puerto Rico and their adjustment experiences on the mainland, Puerto Ricans are more like immigrants and are considered foreign-born for the purposes of this discussion.

5. Although the term "Native Americans" is preferred by some, it includes other groups, such as Eskimos and Aleuts. In order to be more precise, I use the term "American Indian."

6. To some extent this reflects more persons identifying as American Indians who either had no American Indian ancestry or reclaimed their ancestry as a result of more positive perceptions since the activism of the 1970s (Deloria 1981).

7. This most likely represents individuals of Latin American descent who are either of mixed racial-ethnic background or are choosing to identify as an "indigenous" group.

8. Figures from the prior censuses are not presented here because they are available only for married women. Since the groups differ considerably in the extent to which fertility occurs outside of marriage, focusing on marital fertility confounds these comparisons.

9. Women without children tend to work less than women with

children. While this may seem counterintuitive, it is due to the fact that women without children tend to be younger and to be enrolled in school.

10. This is the closest indicator to earnings that is available in the census publications. Measures of income include earnings, farm and nonfarm self-employment income, interest and dividends, Social Security, public assistance, and other sources. Earnings includes earnings and farm and nonfarm self-employment income. For full-time year-round workers, earnings should be fairly similar to measures of income.

11. Poverty rates are presented in Table 2.11 because income levels are not available for female-headed families in the 1980s from the Current Population Survey information. The income level for 1979 is presented in this table to allow for comparisons with the figures for all families presented in Table 2.10.

12. Gardner et al. (1985) provide further support for this in their comparison of the educational levels of Filipinos and Koreans aged twenty-five to twenty-nine, who immigrated during 1975 to 1980, with the population in their country of origin. The overwhelming majority of the Filipino and Korean immigrants were high school graduates (85 and 94 percent, respectively), in contrast to a much smaller percentage in the Philippines (27 percent) and Korea (54 percent).

13. Cuban immigrants are of higher socioeconomic status than nonmigrants from Cuba and other Latinos. They were classified as refugees from a communist regime and were provided extensive assistance by the U.S. government. For both reasons Cubans have successfully integrated in the United States.

## References

Allen, Walter, and Reynolds Farley. 1987. *The Color Line and the Quality of Life in America.* New York: Russell Sage Foundation.

Alvarez, Rodolfo. 1973. "The Psycho-Historical and Socioeconomic Development of the Chicano Community in the United States." *Social Science Quarterly* 53 (March): 920–942.

Auletta, Ken. 1982. *The Underclass.* New York: Random House.

Bean, Frank, and Marta Tienda. 1988. *The Hispanic Population of the United States.* New York: Russell Sage Foundation.

Cafferty, Pastora, Barry Chiswick, Andrew Greeley, and Teresa Sullivan. 1983. *The Dilemma of American Immigration: Beyond the Golden Door.* New Brunswick, N.J.: Transaction Books.

Cooney, Rosemary. 1979. "Intercity Variations in Puerto Rican Female Participation." *Journal of Human Resources* 14: 222–235.

Darabi, Katherine, and Vilma Ortiz. 1987. "Childbearing Among Young

Latino Women in the United States." *American Journal of Public Health* 77 (1): 25–28.

Deloria, Vine. 1981. "Native Americans: The American Indian Today." In Milton Gordon, ed., *America as a Multicultural Society. The Annals of the American Academy of Political and Social Science* 454: 139–149.

Ellwood, David. 1988. *Poor Support: Poverty in the American Family.* New York: Basic Books.

Farley, Reynolds. 1984. *Blacks and Whites: Narrowing the Gap.* Cambridge, Mass.: Harvard University Press.

Farley, Reynolds, and Allen Walter. 1988. *The Color Line and the Quality of Life in America.* New York: Russell Sage Foundation.

Gardner, Robert, Bryant Robey, and Peter Smith. 1985. "Asian Americans: Growth, Change, and Diversity." *Population Bulletin* 40(4): 1–43.

Gurak, Douglas. 1978. "Sources of Ethnic Fertility Differences: An Examination of Five Minority Groups." *Social Science Quarterly* 59(2): 295–310.

———. 1980. "Assimilation and Fertility: A Comparison of Mexican American and Japanese American Women." *Hispanic Journal of Behavioral Sciences* 2 (3): 219–239.

Karsada, John. 1985. "Urban Change and Minority Opportunities." In Paul Peterson, ed., *The New Urban Reality.* Washington, D.C.: The Brookings Institution.

Kitano, Harry. 1981. "Asian-Americans: The Chinese, Japanese, Koreans, Filipinos, and Southeast Asians." In Milton Gordon, ed., *America as a Multicultural Society. The Annals of the American Academy of Political and Social Science,* 454: 125–138.

Ortiz, Vilma. 1986. "Changes in the Characteristics of Puerto Rican Migrants from 1955 to 1980." *International Migration Review* 20 (3): 612–628.

———. 1991. "Latinos and Industrial Change in New York and Los Angeles." In Edwin Melendez et al., eds., *Hispanics in the Labor Force.* New York: Plenum Press.

Pachon, Harry, and Joan Moore. 1981. "Mexican Americans." In Milton Gordon, ed., *America as a Multicultural Society. The Annals of the American Academy of Political and Social Science,* 454: 111–124.

Portes, Alejandro, and Robert Bach. 1985. *Latin Journey.* Berkeley: University of California Press.

Smith, Shelley, and Marta Tienda. 1978. "The Doubly Disadvantaged: Women of Color in the U.S. Labor Force." In Ann Stromberg and Shirley Harkess, eds., *Women Working.* Palo Alto, Calif.: Mayfield.

Teauber, Cynthia, and Victor Valdisera. 1986. *Women in the American Economy.* U.S. Bureau of the Census, Current Population Reports, P-23, no. 146.

U.S. Bureau of the Census. 1963a. *Census of Population, 1960. Characteristics of the Population,* vol. 1. "U.S. Summary," pt. 1.

------. 1963b. *Nonwhite Population by Race.* Census of Population, 1960. Subject Reports, PC(2)-1C.

------. 1963c. *Persons of Spanish Surname.* Census of Population, 1960. Subject Reports, PC(2)-1B.

------. 1963d. *Puerto Ricans in the United States.* Census of Population, 1960. Subject Reports, PC(2)-1D.

------. 1973a. *American Indians. Census of Population, 1970.* Subject Reports, PC(2)-1F.

------. 1973b. *Census of Population, 1970. Characteristics of the Population,* vol. 1. "General Population Characteristics," ch. B, "U.S. Summary," pt. 1.

------. 1973c. *Census of Population, 1970. Characteristics of the Population,* vol. 1. "General Social and Economic Characteristics," ch. C, "U.S. Summary," pt 1.

------. 1973d. *Japanese, Chinese, and Filipinos in the United States.* Census of the Population, 1970. Subject Reports, PC(2)-1G.

------. 1973e. *Negro Population.* Census of Population, 1970. Subject Reports, PC(2)-1B.

------. 1973f. *Persons of Spanish Origin.* Census of Population, 1970. Subject Reports, PC(2)-1C.

------. 1973g. *Puerto Ricans in the United States.* Census of the Population, 1970. Subject Reports, PC(2)-1E.

------. 1983a. Census of Population, 1980. *Characteristics of the Population,* vol. 1. "General Population Characteristics," ch. B," "U.S. Summary," Pt. 1. PC80-1-B1.

------. 1983b. Census of Population, 1980. *Characteristics of the Population,* vol. 1. "General Social and Economic Characteristics," ch. C, "U.S. Summary," pt. 1. PC80-1-C1.

------. 1986. *The Hispanic Population in the United States, March 1985.* Current Population Reports, P-20, no. 422.

------. 1987. *Estimates of the Population in the United States, by Age, Sex, and Race 1980 to 1985.* Current Population Reports, P-25, no. 965.

------. 1989a. *The Black Population in the United States, March 1988.* Current Population Reports, P-20, no. 442.

------. 1989b. *The Hispanic Population in the United States, March 1988.* Current Population Reports, P-20, no. 438.

Wilson, William. 1978. *The Declining Significance of Race.* Chicago: University of Chicago Press.

------. 1987. *The Truly Disadvantaged: The Inner City, the Underclass, and Public Policy.* Chicago: University of Chicago Press.

Zavella, Patricia. 1987. *Women's Work and Chicano Families: Cannery Workers of the Santa Clara Valley.* Ithaca, N.Y.: Cornell University Press.

# II

# THE CONSTRAINING WALLS OF SOCIAL LOCATION

# 3

## Helpers, Enforcers, and Go-Betweens: Black Females in Elementary School Classrooms

### Linda Grant

### Schools and Social Placement

Students attending public schools in the United States learn lessons that go far beyond the formal curriculum. Through the informal curriculum (sometimes termed the hidden curriculum) they learn about status relationships among persons of various race-gender groups in society (Chesler and Cave 1981; C. Grant and Sleeter 1986; L. Grant 1984, 1985; Sadker and Frazier 1973). The hidden curriculum consists of routine, everyday interchanges that provide students with information about the placement of persons of various race-gender groups. The informal social roles that students come to assume in schools closely parallel adult roles deemed appropriate for persons of their race-gender configurations.

Schools are important sites for learning about social rankings related to race, gender, and class, even though they operate under the rhetoric of "equal opportunity" (Bowles and Gintis 1976). For many students, attending a desegregated public elementary school provides their first sustained contact with children of other races (and other socioeconomic classes). Impressions thus formed may be long-lasting. The transmission of status arrangements through schooling occurs despite dedicated educators' efforts to provide race- and gender-equitable learning environments (C. Grant and Sleeter 1986; Guttentag and Bray 1976; Schofield 1982).

# Black Females in Schools

I concentrate here on effects of schooling on the social placement of Black females, whose experiences in schools, as in other domains of social life, have been underexplored (Allen 1979; Davis 1971; Hare 1980; Luttrell 1989; Murray 1975). Available research suggests that Black girls' experiences in school differ significantly from those of other race-gender students (see, e.g., Hare 1979, 1980; Irvine 1985; Scott-Jones and Clark 1986). Black girls achieve more highly than Black boys but more poorly than White students. They have higher self-esteem than White girls but lower self-esteem than Black males. Black females' schooling experiences cannot be wholly understood by extrapolating from research on girls or research on Blacks (Hare 1979).

I suggest that complex, subtle processes in schools encourage Black girls, more so than other students, to assume distinctive roles: helper, enforcer, and go-between. These roles develop their social skills more than their academic abilities. In doing so, they encourage Black females toward adult roles stressing service and nurturance. Skills developed via these roles are consistent with occupational roles in which Black women currently are overrepresented (for example, nurse and teacher's aide). These roles do not stress the intellectual skills and individual attainment associated with high-status professional positions, such as lawyer and political leader.

# Setting and Methods

This study is based primarily on observations in six desegregated first-grade classrooms in working-class communities near a large Midwestern city. Enrollment ranged from 21 to 96 percent Black. Three had White teachers (Maxwell, Avery, Delby) and three had Black teachers (Todd, Horton, and Douglas). (All teacher and student names are fictitious.) Table 3.1 shows specific characteristics of each room.

I observed each room from twenty to thirty hours over several months. I also interviewed all teachers but Avery at the conclusion of observations. (More information on settings and data collection is provided in L. Grant 1984, 1985).

These data are supplemented by in-progress observations in four first- and second-grade rooms in a desegregated rural Southern primary school. Table 3.2 provides information on these rooms. Black enrollment ranges from 30 to 92 percent in each room. The first-grade teachers (Carson and Hilton) are White; the second-grade teachers (Jordan and Parker) are Black.

**Table 3.1.** Percentage of Black Students and Teacher Race, Six First-Grade Midwestern Classrooms

| Teacher Name[a] | Teacher Race | Black Pupils in Classroom[b] (%) | School District[a] |
|---|---|---|---|
| Maxwell | White | 22 | Glendon |
| Avery | White | 21 | Glendon |
| Delby | White | 22 | Ridgeley |
| Todd | Black | 59 | Ridgeley |
| Horton | Black | 29 | Ridgeley |
| Douglas | Black | 96 | Ridgeley |

[a]All teacher and school district names are fictitious.
[b]Includes only those students enrolled in the classroom for 80 percent or more of the total observation period.

Numerical data cited below are from the Midwestern schools only. Examples of Black girls' classroom roles come from both settings. Despite geographical and time separations in these two settings, classroom roles played by Black females are remarkably consistent. Furthermore, in both settings Black girls took on similar roles in White-teacher and in Black-teacher rooms.

## Black Girls' Classroom Roles

### THE HELPER OR CARETAKER

Helpers or caretakers provided nonacademic aid in classrooms, mostly to peers but occasionally to teachers. I distinguish between academic helpers, those providing academic aid, and helpers or caretakers, who provided nonacademic assistance. Caretaking or helping included helping peers locate lost materials or providing comfort to an emotionally distressed child. As I have reported elsewhere (see Grant 1985), tutoring was provided primarily by White students. In all classrooms, black girls were overrepresented relative to their proportions of enrollment, as helpers. Furthermore, they provided nonacademic help to diverse race-gender peers, sometimes interrupting their own academic work or risking sanctions to do so.

Sandra (Black), in Jordan's class, exemplified the helper. She often returned early from recess to sweep the classroom floor. Jordan praised her efforts and occasionally asked her to carry out additional tasks, such as sweeping up sand in the hall. Jordan confirmed that Sandra's

**Table 3.2.** Grade Level, Academic Track, Percentage of Black Students, and Teacher Race of the Southern Primary School Classrooms

| Teacher Name[a] | Teacher Race | Grade Level | Track Level[b] | Black Pupils in Class-rooms (%) |
|---|---|---|---|---|
| Taylor | White | 1 | Middle | 74 |
| Hilton | White | 1 | Low | 92 |
| Jordan | Black | 2 | High | 30 |
| Parker | Black | 2 | Middle | 65 |

[a]All teacher names are fictitious.
[b]Classes at each grade level were tracked as high, middle, or low on the basis of standardized test scores and teacher recommendations. Each room was subdivided into two to four ability-graded reading groups.

sweeping of the room was voluntary and referred to her as "our little housekeeper."

Celeste (Black), in Todd's room, stationed herself near the door to help peers on and off with outerwear. When Celeste was absent, other children tried to play her role but were rejected by classmates and told by Todd to sit down. Gloria (Black), in Carson's room, was the informal monitor who ensured that students left each afternoon with the correct coats, lunch boxes, and schoolbags.

Helpers sometimes became so concerned with aiding others that they neglected their academic work. Juliette (Black), in Avery's room, often failed to complete assignments because she ran errands for tablemates (finding lost crayons, getting tissues from the teacher's desk, etc.). Todd described Meredith (Black) as "bright but an underachiever." She also characterized her as a "busybody," too often abandoning her work to help with or check on someone else's. In a sixty-five-minute observation period, Todd reprimanded Meredith eleven times for stopping work on math to carry out tasks such as helping a friend search for a barrette and settling a noisy verbal dispute between two boys at the next table.

Helpers occasionally gave up privileges, or risked sanctions, to aid peers. Marvin (Black), in Hilton's room, cried because a punishment forced him to sit on the pavement adjacent to the playground rather than participate in recess games. Sheila (Black) voluntarily relinquished participation in games to comfort Marvin for the entire thirty-minute period. Millie (Black), in Horton's room, defied Horton's angry "Get back to that seat NOW" and continued to approach Horton to tell her that tablemates Gregory (Black), Cynthia (White), and Adam (White) lacked marker pens for an assignment. The students got the needed materials, but Millie lost her free-time activity privilege for defying the teacher's command.

The willingness to risk reprimands to aid a peer was a distinctive characteristic of Black girls. White females often helped peers, though their efforts tended to concentrate on a narrow range of close friends rather than on the diverse students aided by Black girls. White girls rarely persisted in helping when teachers threatened sanctions.

The helping and caretaking activities of Black girls likely contributed to other students' social comfort in the classroom and aided in maintenance of order and peace. Nevertheless, these actions had costs that might diminish intellectual achievement and favorable evaluation. Academic work was interrupted, and teachers occasionally reprimanded the helpers.

## THE ENFORCER

A second role overplayed by Black girls, relative to their enrollment, was that of self-appointed enforcer. Without explicit requests from teachers, the girls urged peers to comply with class or school rules. Black girls enforced more than other students in all Midwestern and Southern rooms.

When teacher Parker left the room briefly to greet a parent, she told students to "stay seated and be quiet." Nevertheless, several students left their seats. When Gerald (White) walked past Pamela (Black), Pamela rose, placed her hands on his shoulders, gently kicked the back of his legs, told him to "move it," and pushed him several feet back to his desk. She then pointed a finger at Steven (Black) and threatened: "You're next." Steven quickly took his seat. She then shook her head sternly at Renee (White), who had started to rise but sat down in response to Pamela's action.

Enforcements appeared to have many motivations. Some appeared to be genuine attempts to aid the teacher. Cheryl (Black), in Delby's room, was near tears when classmates ignored her pleas to be quiet, as Delby had requested. Sometimes enforcements seemed to be bids to gain the teacher's favorable attention, as when Juliette (Black), invariably called Avery's attention to her enforcements. Some appeared to be attempts to protect peers, as when Camille (Black), in Maxwell's room, told classmates to "look busy" when she perceived that Maxwell was ready to move around the room to check work.

Enforcers typically restated teacher messages, often exaggerating the teachers' threats about consequences of noncompliance. When

Horton warned that students not completing work would be unable to see a movie, Angela (Black) told inattentive and nonworking classmates Clifton (Black) and Yvonne (Black) that the teacher had threatened to "cut their fingers off" if they did not complete their work on time.

The enforcer role could be risky. Some peers resisted enforcements, as when Joel (White), in Jordan's room, slapped Ramona (Black) when she reminded him to keep hands off science experiment materials, as the teacher had requested. Teachers often reprimanded self-appointed enforcers, as when Douglas told Carolyn (Black) to "get back to your seat where you belong" when the child attempted to have peers return books to a shelf.

Enforcers demonstrated considerable knowledge of, and loyalty to, classroom roles. Whatever their motivations, successful enforcements served social control functions in the classrooms and minimized overt resistance to teacher rules. Successful enforcements also revealed that Black girls had substantial influence with peers of diverse race-gender attributes. It is not clear, however, that teachers were cognizant of this effect. Most ignored or discouraged enforcements.

## THE GO-BETWEEN

The most complex, but also the most influential, role assumed by Black girls was that of the go-between. Camille (Black), in Maxwell's room, was a go-between. An excerpt from field notes illustrates the scope of the role:

> Camille responds to Felix's (Black) appeal that he needs a replacement for a broken shoelace, comes to his side, then contacts the teacher. When Maxwell becomes engaged in a conversation (with a White female from another grade who came with a message), Camille goes to see George (White) to see if he has a shoelace in a box of odds-and-ends he keeps on his desk. He does not. Camille relays a request from George to Babs (White) to borrow a marker pen, then hammers out the details of the trade between George and Babs when they disagree. Camille scowls at Bradford (White) as he tries to trip her in the aisle, tells him to mind his own business, then giggles with Penny (White) as she laughs in response to Camille's remark to Bradford. Camille repeats her request to Maxwell, coming to the teacher's desk, then suggests that Maxwell send Sylvia (White) to see if the special education teacher in the adjoining room has a shoelace. Maxwell agrees and Camille calls to Sylvia as she leaves: "And it doesn't matter what color." Enroute to her own desk, Camille tells Gary (White) to

pick up his coat from the floor so it does not get dirty and stepped on. She responds to a hand motion from Tobin (Black) for help in reading a word, which she gives. Camille whispers to Sarah (Black), who smuggles her a handful of jellybeans. Camille, at her desk, shares some jellybeans with Clarissa (White). Camille is called to Maxwell's desk to relay a message to Felix to see the special education teacher to get a shoelace. Camille thanks Sylvia for running the errand when the teacher says nothing to her, then goes to stand at the corner of Maxwell's desk, where Maxwell looks at her and says, "Camille, what are you doing up here? It's time for math."

Camille's actions in the ten minutes covered above involved one-third of the class, plus the teacher. She provided links and transmitted influence from teacher to student, student to teacher, and student to student. She, like the other go-betweens, had easy access to the teacher and high status in the class. Camille often was chosen by peers to give out treats or lead games.

Not all rooms had go-betweens. In the Midwest schools they did not appear in the Black teachers' classrooms. In the Southern school, however, go-betweens emerged in both White teachers' and Black teachers' rooms. Where the role existed, it inevitably was filled by a Black female.

Mona was the go-between in Jordan's room. Jordan usually made participation in recess contingent on completion of work. Mona engaged in complex negotiations with adults and students around this issue. At the beginning of the seven-minute excerpt below, Mona has finished work and reads an enrichment book. Christopher and David across the aisle have been working off and on a math assignment, frequently interrupting their work for mock sword fights with small plastic rulers used in their work.

Christopher (White) and David (Black) complain to Mona (Black) that Jordan warned them that they would have no recess if they do not complete math worksheets in the next six minutes. Mona tells Christopher: "Well, you two been screwing around." Christopher tells her: "I didn't have no recess yesterday either." Mona tells him, "Gimme that," and grabs his worksheet. David stands over her desk. Jordan tells David: "Sit down, please, I think you've got work to do." Mona goes to Jordan for a whispered conversation and apparently gets her approval to work at a back table with the boys. Mona tells them: "I ain't done this one yet. I don't know how." She then goes to Gail (White), who tells her:

"Go away." Mona tells Gail, "You're a bitch," then goes to Anita (White), who gives help. Mona returns to the table and writes an answer on Christopher's paper. David copies this. The recess bell rings, and Christopher groans: "We ain't finished. We ain't going to get to go out." David puts both hands over his eyes in an exaggerated gesture of frustration (but then giggles at Christopher and Mona). As the rest of the class leaves, Mona goes to Jordan, who talks with Ms. Kyle (White), a teacher's aide from another room. Mona asks: "If they get done before ten minutes, can they have part of their recess? They're getting it now." Jordan smiles, then says: "What do you think, Ms. Kyle?" Ms. Kyle nods in the affirmative, and Jordan says, "Well, okay, but have them bring [their papers] to me before they go off [a paved area near the playground]." Christopher overhears and clasps his hands together over his head in a "victory" gesture, and David laughs and slaps him gently across the back. As Jordan puts papers in a cabinet near the door, Mona asks Ms. Kyle the answer to the next problem. Ms. Kyle and Mona return to the table to work with the boys as Jordan [on playground duty] leaves. They complete the work in about two minutes. The boys grab papers and run off, with David calling out: "OKAY." Ms. Kyle tells Mona: "That was nice of you," and puts her arm around Mona as they leave the room.

Mona displayed the same pattern of multiple contacts with teachers and peers visible in Camille's actions. She interacted easily with students and teachers and persisted in the face of obstacles. Although other students negotiated with teachers, Black girls were virtually the only ones to negotiate about matters not directly related to themselves or their needs. Mona's actions produce a positive outcome for her classmates (recess time) and for the teacher (completion of work by students who do not always do so). To play the role, Mona has relinquished some of her own work and leisure time.

Erving Goffman (1959) believes that go-betweens operate in many social settings. He labels the actions of a go-between in social encounters as a "discrepant role." It makes sense, he argues, only when one considers the go-between's position as a constituent member of two or more "teams" that have few positive ties. The go-between maintains a delicate balance, sometimes involving subtle distortions of one group's orientation to the other, so that a closer relationship between the teams is possible. Playing the role successfully requires access to both groups and extensive knowledge of their operating norms. It also requires the willingness to take personal risks in the interests of social harmony.

## COMMONALITIES AMONG THE ROLES

The three roles characteristically assumed by Black girls put a premium on social, rather than academic, skills. Helpers, enforcers, and go-betweens frequently neglect academic work to meet the needs of others in the room. This brings them disproportionate amounts of praise from teachers for social actions, but also causes a relative neglect of their academic work. Teacher praise skewed toward social deeds rather than academic work likely strengthens Black girls' tendencies to stress social skills as the primary mode of attainment. In a cyclical fashion teachers' tendencies to see Black girls primarily in terms of social behaviors (see below) increases over time.

## *Emergence and Maintenance of Roles*

Understanding the complex dynamics by which Black girls' roles emerged and were maintained in classrooms requires consideration of teachers' perceptions of these students, teacher–student interactions, and peer interactions in the desegregated rooms. Some authors have argued that minority parents, more so than White parents, socialize their children, and especially their daughters, to take care of peers (Ladner 1971; Lewis 1975). Black girls may arrive at school primed for service roles. The school environment reinforces this predisposition. Helpers, for example, usually first performed their roles spontaneously. Over time, teachers and peers increasingly looked to them to perform certain tasks. When Sandra was absent one day, Jordan told students: "Things just won't be as tidy today."

### TEACHERS' PERCEPTIONS

Interviews with five of the six observed Midwestern teachers provided information on teacher perceptions. Teachers were asked: "Tell me about [child's name]'s academic skills and performance" and "Tell me about [child's name]'s relationships with other children in the class." The open-ended questions allowed discernment of the direction of assessments as well as criteria teachers believed relevant in evaluating students of each race-gender group. When interviewed, teachers had no standardized achievement test data, except for a few students referred for special testing.

### ACADEMIC SKILLS RATINGS

Black girls' academic skills were rated as average or slightly below average compared with the other three race-gender groups in these classes. Of the twenty-six Black girls assigned to the five interviewed teachers, 23 percent were rated as high, 42 percent as average, and 35 percent as low or below average. Black girls' skills were rated most similarly to White males and were lower than those of White females but higher than those of Black males. Avery, who was not formally interviewed, mentioned spontaneously that one of her three Black female students was average in academic skills, while the other two were below average.

Even though skills of White males and Black females were similarly rated, teachers' assessments of White boys differed in one important respect. For 20 percent of the White boys rated average and 11 percent rated below average, teachers commented that these students were immature. Teachers thought their performances might improve with time. They did not make such comments about any Black female student. Evaluations of Black females differed from those of other students in another important respect. Unlike children of all other race-gender configurations, no Black female was singled out as having outstanding skill in a specific area—athletics, music, art. The "ho-hum" quality of most teachers' assessments of most Black girls is reflected in Maxwell's comments about Carrie: "She's about average in everything. Her work habits are good. She' very neat and quiet . . . no problem at all. She can take care of herself. She usually doesn't have much to say." Only one Black girl was labeled by her teacher as "one of my brightest students," an accolade usually given only to White students.

Also reflected in the evaluations was a concentration on social skills ("neat and quiet"), even when teachers were asked to discuss academic skills. Delby's comments about Nancy are another example: "She's an average student, I would say, but oh, what a helper. She always keeps her eyes on things, picks things up, helps out other [students] who don't understand work or are having some problem. She is always asking: 'What can I do to help?' "

Teachers sometimes suggested that Black girls' social rather than academic skills might be most critical to success in school, as was apparent in Todd's comments about the low-achieving Doris: "It takes her longer to learn things than most children. . . . Other children help her out a lot because Doris is such a pleasure to have in the class. She is always smiling, always trying, always being kind to other people. [Classmates] have a lot of patience with her. . . . They don't treat her the way they treat [other low achievers]. I think that will be pretty important to her later on."

Teachers' responses to the questions about academic skills were coded point by point for each child, and ratios of academic to nonac-

LINDA GRANT

ademic criteria mentioned for various race-gender children were compared. Examples of academic criteria were "He's very good in science" and "She has trouble reading." Examples of nonacademic criteria were "She's always beautifully dressed" and "He's got a strong rebellious streak." Some teachers (for example, Horton) made mostly academic comments about students, while others (for example, Delby) relied more heavily on nonacademic criteria. Nevertheless, every teacher used higher ratios of nonacademic criteria when evaluating Black females than other groups. This suggested that for this group, teachers were more attentive to students' nonacademic behaviors and attributes than their academic skills. Assessments of White girls in most rooms relied on nearly equal proportions of academic and nonacademic criteria, while assessments of boys of both races stressed academic criteria.

Teachers made the most extensive comments about the academic skills of unusually high achievers (mostly White students) or unusually low achievers (predominantly Black males). They viewed high achievers as reflecting favorably upon teachers, while low achievers threatened to expose them as poor instructors or to disrupt the class. The average, shy, quiet Black females fell outside these groups, and they attracted only limited teacher attention, a pattern observed in other studies (Byalick and Bershoff 1974; Irvine 1985).

## SOCIAL SKILLS RATINGS

Teachers commented that Black girls were mature, self-sufficient, and helpful. They also identified White girls as mature, labeling them cognitively mature and "ready for school." For Black girls the assessment of maturity did not translate into expectations of high academic performance in the same way that it did for White girls. Teachers did not see Black girls as cognitively mature. Instead, they described them as having a precocious social maturity that was detrimental to academic performance. Douglas praised six-year-old Edna for feeding and dressing three preschool siblings each morning so that her mother, a nurse working the night shift, could sleep. But Douglas added: "Of course, all that responsibility doesn't give her much time to concentrate on [school work]."

Teachers pointed to Black girls' preoccupation with adult roles, viewed by teachers as a distraction from work. At recess these children played house, portraying family members, cooking and cleaning, and primping for dates with imaginary boyfriends. At sharing time they bragged of assuming adultlike roles, such as preparing a large meal. Maxwell noted that a group of Black girls often were inattentive to lessons because "they're passing around lipstick or giggling about who kissed whom on the bus yesterday."

The precocious maturity of Black girls also was observed by Joyce Ladner (1971) in a study of Black teenagers living in a housing project. She found that most Black girls lived in adult worlds at young ages. Parents gave them adult-level knowledge and responsibilities, the first to shield them from harsh realities of their environment and the second to provide help to parents in meeting their own multiple roles. Rather than seeing these qualities as assets, teachers in this study viewed them as impediments to learning.

Teachers identified fourteen of the twenty-six Black girls as generous and helpful to teachers and peers. These qualities were noted twice as often in reference to Black girls as to other students. Such attributes seemed to be the most reliable means for Black girls to capture teachers' favorable attention.

## TEACHER–STUDENT INTERACTIONS

There were two components to teacher–student interactions: behaviors initiated by teachers and behaviors initiated by students.

**Teacher Behaviors.** As was the case for all race-gender students, teachers' behaviors toward students were partially consistent, and partially inconsistent, with their evaluations of them. In subtle ways teachers encouraged Black girls to pursue social contacts rather than press toward high academic achievement. This was observable through track placements, responses to academic work, and feedback for behavior.

All teachers in the Midwest schools used ability groups for reading instruction. After the first two weeks of observation, groups became quite stable, with less than 4 percent of students (none of them Black females) changing groups. In the Southern schools 5 percent of students changed groups. The three Black girls involved all moved downward. Midwestern teachers identified groups as composed of students reading above, at, and below grade level. Black females most often were placed in at-grade-level groups (48 percent); 21 percent were in above-grade-level groups, and 31 percent were below grade level. These distributions closely paralleled placements for all students, regardless of race-gender status, except that Black girls were more often in at-grade-level and less often in above-grade-level groups. Consistent with teachers' assessments of ability, Black girls were placed lower than White girls, higher than Black boys, and similarly to White boys. Black girls had very similar group placements in the Southern school. Group placements usually paralleled teachers' assessments of students' skills, but often White girls—and occasionally also a few Black girls—were placed in higher groups in doubtful cases because teachers believed they behaved well. Avery, uncertain whether Diana (Black) belonged in an average or a lower group, decided on the former because "She tries hard, helps other children, obeys, and sets a good example."

Counts of teachers' praise and criticism for academic work showed no particular pattern of favoritism for any race-gender group across the six Midwestern rooms. Black girls received average, and in some rooms slightly greater than average, amounts of praise for day-to-day work. The three Black teachers were somewhat more apt to praise Black girls' academic work than were the White teachers. In comparison with other students, Black girls received slightly more qualified praise, suggesting that work fell short of the best in the room (e.g., "That's a fine printing paper, much better than yesterday's."). Black girls in most rooms received less criticism for academic work than most students, although teacher criticism sometimes is important in pressing students to do their best work.

Black girls never received a significant type of praise reserved almost exclusively for White girls. Teachers assigned white girls high-responsibility academic tasks, such as tutoring or orienting a new student to class work. Of twenty-two such special assignments, eighteen went to White girls. Designating White girls as trusted aides may have overridden routine praise and marked these children as particularly competent in the eyes of peers. Such assignments often were mentioned by children when discussing which peers were "smart." The qualification of praise, and the exclusion of Black girls from special tasks implying academic competence, suggested that teachers did not view them as the most able students in the room.

Feedback patterns suggested that teachers were especially sensitive to the social behaviors of Black females. Behavioral feedback was defined as teacher praise or criticism for actions unrelated to academic work (e.g., "I like the way Rhonda [Black] is standing quietly in the lunch line."). In three rooms (Maxwell's, Horton's, Avery's) Black girls received substantially more behavioral praise than other students. In Delby's and Douglas's rooms they received considerably fewer reprimands for behavior than other student groups. In all rooms they received substantially fewer reprimands for behavior than Black males did. There were no systematic relationships between teacher race and feedback patterns to Black girls for behaviors. Black girls received disproportionately high ratios of praise for behavior from most teachers.

**Student Behaviors.** Teachers' behaviors toward Black females created certain opportunities for some Black girls to gain visibility and teacher praise via social actions. Teachers' behavioral praises were asymmetrically distributed among Black girls. In each White teacher's classroom in the Midwest, one Black girl received the most praise. This child was the go-between. The go-betweens who emerged in the four Southern classrooms also had atypically high ratios of teacher praise. Black teachers' classrooms in the Midwestern schools (Horton's, Todd's, and Douglas's) did not have go-betweens, although they contained identifiable enforcers and helpers.

Black girls were uniquely situated in their classes for the go-between role. Their position in what Bruce Hare (1975) terms the "psychological and academic middle ground" gave them experiences in common with those of all other race-gender groups. Their relative freedom from teacher monitoring, in comparison with Black males, gave them both opportunity and motivation to play the role. For some, peer involvements were alternative sources of reward. The go-between had ready access to the teacher's sphere of influence and to peer networks but was probably not perceived as having exclusive allegiance to either. The role also is consistent with themes in parental socialization of Black daughters (Ladner 1971; Lewis 1975; Lightfoot 1979; Reid 1972).

By playing the go-between role, Black females likely made important contributions to the social integration of desegregated classrooms. By avoiding exclusive commitments to tight peer groups but maintaining weaker ties with many peers, the go-between wove a pattern of loose connections that Mark Granovetter (1973) argues contributes to social integration of a collectivity.

The enforcer role also is logically related to Black girls' locations vis-à-vis teachers and peers. Enforcement was an alternative to high academic achievement for teacher recognition. Since teachers only rarely counted Black girls among the highest achievers in their classes, enforcement was the most successful means for garnering teacher praise. Enforcement also could benefit peers if it kept them out of trouble with the teacher. It worked only when students had substantial social power in peer networks and were willing to risk retaliation from classmates. As I have reported elsewhere, Black girls were less likely than White girls to be intimidated by aggression or threats of aggression from peers (L. Grant, 1983). This meant that Black girls were more likely to enforce rules on peers directly. White girls either ignored classmates' infractions or told teachers about their misbehaviors.

It is unclear to what extent teachers in the Midwestern and Southern classrooms encouraged helper, enforcer, and go-between roles and to what extent they evolved from parental socialization and preschool experience stressing social skills and loyalty to peers. Both likely are important. Since this study collected no data on preschool socialization, consideration of the issue can be only speculative. Teachers seemed to reinforce the roles. Five of the six teachers in the Midwestern schools called on Black girls almost twice as frequently as any other race-gender group to help peers in nonacademic matters, whereas White girls were their usual choice for help with academic tasks, such as tutoring. All teachers in the Southern school except Parker also overselected Black girls as helpers. Parker was equally likely to select Black and White girls (relative to enrollments in her room) as helpers and chose Black girls as tutors slightly more often than White girls. Critical in the go-between and enforcer roles was Black girls' orientations toward teachers. These ranged from apple-polishing to wary avoidance, but mostly fell in between. Although generally compliant with teacher rules, Black females were less obviously tied to teachers than White girls and contacted teachers only when they had reason to do so. In each room a contingent of White girls spent a great deal of time with teachers, prolonging questions into chats. Black girls' contacts were briefer, more task-oriented, and often on behalf of a peer rather than self. Black girls risked reprimands in many cases to get aid for peers. Overall, in the Midwestern rooms from 32 to 47 percent of Black girls' approaches to teachers (depending on room) were on behalf of peers. This compared with no more than 17 percent for children of other race-gender groups in any room. Black girls' tendency to interrupt their academic work to seek aid for peers was a behavior rarely observed in other students.

Black girls spontaneously took on aspects of the three roles, especially that of the go-between. When Camille was ill for a week, another Black girl attempted to become the go-between—Camille's role. Teacher Maxwell rebuffed Helene's efforts, however. When Camille returned, she resumed her duties with no apparent communication with Maxwell about the matter.

## BLACK GIRLS' RELATIONSHIPS WITH PEERS

Black girls' ties with classmates were logically related to their relationships with teachers and to themes in preschool socialization. These children's peer relationships also were critical to their assumption of the distinctive classroom roles.

Black girls had the most extensive, most egalitarian peer ties of any race-gender group (L. Grant 1983). Although they rarely instigated physical or verbal aggression, they were less apt than White girls to be intimidated by aggression or threats. Black girls thus appeared more powerful and less exploited in peer networks than other students.

**Extent of Contacts.** In all the Midwestern rooms except Delby's, Black girls had more extensive peer contacts than any other race-gender group. Most Black females crossed race and gender lines more readily than did other students. This finding is contrary to some research with older students, which suggests that Black girls are more isolated than other students (D'Amico 1986; DeVries and Edwards 1977; Patchen 1982; Schofield 1982). Although this study cannot wholly account for the discrepancy, some speculation is possible.

Janet Schofield found that emerging romantic and sexual interests and normative patterns of male–female recreational activities limited cross-racial ties of female junior high students more so than those of boys. Sexuality was not an issue for first graders. Furthermore, first-grade girls played in large groups. They had not yet moved into the tight, small cliques that Schofield found most common among the teenagers. Larger-group activities encourage cross-racial interaction.

Second, many previous studies have been conducted in schools where Blacks and Whites differed markedly in social class and achievement. In schools used in this study, Black and White students were of common social class origins, and Black girls were most often in middle academic tracks, where they had contacts and common experiences with diverse peers.

Third, these rooms had greater-than-token proportions of minority students, and their dynamics thus probably differed from rooms where one racial group was an extreme majority. James Rothenberg (1982) has suggested that nearly equal proportions and multiple status lines diminish the importance of any one characteristic, such as race or gender, as an interaction barrier.

**Helping Behaviors.** Black girls gave substantial academic help to peers. Academic aid was given and received in nearly equal proportions. This contrasted to patterns for White girls, who gave much more academic aid than they received. Black girls gave somewhat more care than they received in return, but their caring activities were more likely to be reciprocated than were those of White girls. Also, as noted earlier, Black girls helped diverse race-gender peers, rather than concentrating on close friends, as other students did. These activities likely maintained the extensive social ties and social influence needed to carry out the distinctive classroom roles. Unlike White girls, Black females received nearly as much aid and care as they dispensed. These variations resulted from different patterns of within-race, cross-gender interactions. Black males and females aided one another reciprocally. However, White girls gave from 62 to 75 percent of help and 68 to 75 percent of care (depending on room) when interacting with White males.

**Aggression.** All Midwestern teachers forbade physical and verbal aggression, but each room had its share of pushings, name-callings, and hair-pullings. Depending on the room, from 58 to 89 percent of physical aggression involved males only. Black males were only slightly more likely than White males to be involved in these incidents. Less than 4 percent of physical aggression involved girls only. Thus, most physical aggression involving girls was cross-gender. Males initiated from 59 to 90 percent of physical aggression (depending on the room).

In most rooms Black girls were only slightly more likely than White girls to be involved in aggression, but the responses of Black girls were different. White girls usually backed down, complied, withdrew, or—very occasionally—complained to the teacher. Aggression or threats thus were used by other students to exercise power over them. Such tactics were less effective with Black girls, who fought back verbally or physically against more than half the aggression they encountered. Their retaliation rate was far above the 14–25 percent rate for White girls in the six rooms, but far below that for boys of either race.

**Racist and Sexist Remarks.** Black girls were the sole victims of the six racist remarks by White males recorded in five Midwestern rooms. A Black girl was the target of the only racist remark recorded in the Southern school. Although such remarks were rare, they were dramatic and captured the attention of all classroom actors when they occurred. Five of the six came in nearly identical circumstances. After the teacher had complimented a Black girl for her work, a White boy of lower achievement made a racist remark. Just after Avery's compliment to Diana (Black) for her work, Bruce (White) asked her, "When are you going to fatten up, like most Black ladies?" Black girls also were targets of four of eight sexist remarks, a slight overrepresentation.

The pattern seemed an example of what Schofield (1982) termed "appealing to one's strong suit." White boys, perhaps threatened by the Black girls' academic skills, appealed to their seemingly irrelevant statuses of whiteness and maleness to put Black females in their place. Thus, Black girls sometimes risked sanctions from peers for high academic achievement.

Overall, however, Black girls had more egalitarian peer relationships than did White girls. This might have resulted from teacher practices, norms that evolved among peers, or preschool socialization. The latter probably was the strongest influence, although this study cannot directly address the issue. Peers influenced Black girls to give aid and care, for example, by asking them to do so more often than other children. Peers were important supporters of the go-between role by looking to Black girls to take messages to teachers. Black girls' reputation among peers for not backing down probably contributed to successful performance of the enforcer role. The patterns also are consistent with themes in parental socialization of Black girls, including helping peers and fighting to protect one's interests. In these rooms peer interchanges, as well as teacher–student contacts, put a premium on Black girls' social, rather than academic, skills.

## Implications of Classroom Roles

I have drawn a complex, not always consistent, portrait of Black girls' experiences in desegregated classrooms. Conclusions must be cautious, since I studied only a limited number of classrooms. Many of the issues raised—such as the genesis, prevalence, and maintenance of the go-between role—deserve further research attention.

This study provides evidence that Black girls' classroom roles differ from those of other children. In schools Black girls occupy a "place" that is established by the interaction of multiple forces, including parents, teachers, peers, and societal norms about appropriate roles for persons of certain race-gender statuses. The "place" Black girls occupy is, in Goffman's terms, "not a material thing to be possessed and then displayed" but, rather, "a pattern of appropriate conduct, coherent, embellished, and well articulated" (1959:75).

The roles probably contribute to classroom social order. The go-between, and to a lesser extent the helper and the enforcer, weave ties between many peers, enhancing social integration. The cost may be enhancement of social skills at the expense of academic development. While social skills sometimes give Black girls academic benefits (for example, placement in higher reading groups in doubtful cases), they are learning relational modes of achievement and social skills. In schools and societies that reward individual achievement, they may be disadvantaged in the long run.

Since my research to date has covered only the first and second grades, implications for adult roles are less clear. Emphasis on Black girls' social rather than academic skills, which occurs particularly in White-teacher classrooms, may point to a hidden cost of desegregation for Black females. Although they usually are the top students in all-Black rooms, they lose this position to White students in desegregated rooms. Their development seems to become less balanced, with emphasis on social skills. These skills assuredly are helpful in high-status adult roles, but the lesser attention to Black girls' academic work may discourage them from gaining credentials to enter such positions. Black girls' everyday schooling experiences seemingly do more to nudge them toward stereotypical roles of Black women than toward alternatives. These include serving others and maintaining peaceable ties among diverse persons rather than developing one's own skills.

Schools are by no means the only contributors to Black girls' socialization. There are important overlaps in Black girls' experiences in school and in other spheres of social life, such as parental socialization. Nonetheless, classroom life supports the channeling of Black girls toward stereotypical roles. This occurs through selective reinforcement of students' entering predispositions. Actions of teachers and peers, and responses of Black girls, seem only minimally influenced by students' abilities and aptitudes or by teacher ideologies. Rather, they are products of teachers' and students' transmission of societal expectations. Blocking infiltration of such expectations from society requires, first, a recognition of the subtle ways in which they filter into school life and, second, intervention in aspects of school life that limit rather than enhance options for students of all race-gender groups.

## Note

*Acknowledgments*: Parts of the research for this chapter were supported by funding from the following sources: a National Institute of Mental Health grant in Sociology and Social Policy, the Institute of Behavioral Research at the University of Georgia, and the Spencer Foundation Small Grants program. The interpretations in this paper do not necessarily reflect those of the funding agencies. I appreciate the aid of the following persons in preparing this chapter: Maxine Baca Zinn, Steven T. Bossert, Mark A. Chesler, Bonnie Thornton Dill, Carl Glickman, Judith Preissle, Wayne K. Myers, and James Rothenberg.

# References

Allen, Walter. 1979. "Family Occupational Status and Achievement Orientations Among Black Females in the U.S." *Signs* 4: 670–680.

Bowles, Samuel, and Herbert Gintis. 1976. *Schooling in Capitalist America.* New York: Basic Books.

Byalick, Robert, and Donald Bershoff. 1974. "Reinforcement of Black and White Teachers in Integrated Classrooms." *Journal of Educational Psychology* 66: 473–480.

Chesler, Mark, and William Cave. 1981. *A Sociology of Education: Access to Power and Privilege.* New York: Macmillan.

Crain, Robert, and Rita Mahard. 1978. "Desegregation and Black Achievement: A Review of Research." *Law and Contemporary Society* 42: 17–56.

Crain, Robert, Rita Mahard, and Ruth Narot. 1982. *Making Desegregation Work: How Schools Create Social Climates.* Cambridge, Mass.: Ballinger.

D'Amico, Sandra. 1986. "Cross-Group Opportunities: Impact on Interpersonal Relationships in Desegregated Middle Schools." *Sociology of Education* 59: 113–123.

Davis, Angela. 1971. "The Black Woman's Role in the Community of Slaves." *Black Scholar* 3 (4): 2–15.

DeVries, William, and Keith Edwards. 1977. "Student Teams and Learning Games: Their Effects on Cross-Sex Interaction." *Journal of Educational Psychology* 69: 337–343.

Goffman, Erving. 1959. *The Presentation of Self in Everyday Life.* Garden City, N.Y.: Anchor Doubleday.

Granovetter, Mark. 1973. "The Strength of Weak Ties." *American Journal of Sociology* 78: 1360–1380.

Grant, Carl, and Christine A. Sleeter. 1986. *After the School Bell Rings.* London: Falmer Press.

Grant, Linda. 1983. "Gender Roles and Status in Elementary Children's Peer Interactions." *Western Sociological Review* 14 (Fall): 58–76.

———. 1984. "Black Females' 'Place' in Desegregated Classrooms." *Sociology of Education* 57: 98–111.

———. 1985. "Race-Gender Status, System Attachment, and Children's Socialization in Desegregated Classrooms." Pp. 57–77 in *Gender Influences in Classroom Interaction,* edited by Louise Cherry Wilkinson and Cora Bagley Marrett. New York: Academic Press.

Guttentag, Marcia, and Helen Brag. 1976. *Undoing Sex Stereotypes.* New York: McGraw-Hill.

Hare, Bruce. 1985. "Black Girls: A Comparative Study of Self-Perception and Academic Achievement by Race, Sex, and Socioeconomic Background." In *Beginnings: The Social and Affective Development of Black Children,* ed. Margaret B. Spencer et al. Hillsdale, N.J.: Erlbaum.

Irvine, Jacqueline Jordan. 1985. "Teacher–Student Interactions: Effects of Student Race, Sex, and Grade Level." *Journal of Educational Psychology* 78: 14–21.

Ladner, Joyce. 1971. *Tomorrow's Tomorrow: The Black Woman.* Garden City, N.Y.: Anchor Doubleday.

Lewis, Diana. 1975. "The Black Family: Socialization and Sex Roles." *Phylon* 36: 221–237.

Lightfoot, Sara. 1979. *Worlds Apart: Relationships Between Families and Schools.* New York: Harper Colophon.

Luttrell, Wendy. 1989. "Working-Class Women's Ways of Knowing: Effects of Gender, Race, and Class." *Sociology of Education* 62: 33–46.

Murray, Paule. 1975. "The Liberation of Black Women." Pp. 351–363 in *Women: A Feminist Perspective,* edited by Jo Freeman. Palo Alto, Calif.: Mayfield.

Ogbu, John. 1978. *Minorities and Caste.* New York: Academic Press.

Patchen, Martin. 1982. *Black-White Contact in Schools.* West Lafayette, Ind.: Purdue University Press.

Reid, Inez. 1972. *"Together" Black Women.* New York: Emerson Hall.

Rothenberg, James. 1982. "Peer Interactions and Classroom Activity Structures." Ph.D. dissertation, University of Michigan.

Sadker, Myra, and Nancy Frazier. 1973. *Sexism in School and Society.* New York: Harper & Row.

Schofield, Janet. 1982. *Black and White in School.* New York: Praeger.

Scott-Jones, Diane, and Maxine Clark. 1986. "The School Experiences of Black Girls: The Interaction of Gender, Race, and Socioeconomic Status." *Phi Delta Kappan* 67: 520–526.

# 4

## Hiring Immigrant Women:
## Silicon Valley's "Simple Formula"

### Karen J. Hossfeld

*I have a very simple formula for hiring. You hire right, and managing takes care of itself. Just three things I look for in hiring [entry-level, high-tech manufacturing operatives]: small, foreign, and female. You find those three things and you're pretty much automatically guaranteed the right kind of work force. These little foreign gals are grateful to be hired—very, very grateful—no matter what.*
—a White male production manager and hiring supervisor in a
   Silicon Valley printed circuit board assembly shop

*Trainers and employment agencies around town have this story we tell that explains why we prefer to invest our resources in groups with a good track record.*

*If you tell people that there's a job call Monday morning downtown at nine, this is what happens: the Chinese and the Koreans show up the night before and camp outside the door, so they'll be the first in line. The Iranians used to show up at seven, but now they own everything so they don't need the jobs. Between eight and nine, the Whites show up. The Mexicans come in the afternoon, after their siesta, and the Blacks roll by—maybe—sometime the next day.*
—a White male industrial training program and employment
   agency director in Silicon Valley

California's famed high-tech industrial region, Silicon Valley, is renowned for the great opportunities it has provided to live out the American dream. Since the 1970s, thousands have flocked there in hopes of getting rich quick by hitching their wagons (computerized ones, of course) to the lucrative high-tech revolution. In fact, thousands have indeed become millionaires in the process. Thousands more have successfully turned to the industry in search of new and exciting professional careers, at a time when most other industries in the country are declining. But not every group has had equal access to the preponderance of riches fueled by the region's rapid industrial growth. In fact, shoring up the simple formula of the American dream is another "simple formula" that is actually quite complex: many employers' predilection for basing hiring on gender, race, and nationality. This chapter examines this predilection on the "low-tech" side of high-tech industry: manufacturing assembly work. I explore the factors that peg workers who are "small, foreign and female" in the lowest paid jobs—factors that are not quite as obvious as they might appear.

The findings draw from my larger study of the lives and labors of Third World[1] immigrant women workers in Silicon Valley's semiconductor manufacturing industry (Hossfeld 1988, 1992). Empirical data come from conversations I had between 1982 and 1990 with over 200 workers, as well as with many of their family members, employers, managers, labor organizers, and community leaders. Extensive in-depth interviews were conducted with eighty-four immigrant women representing twenty-one nationalities, and with forty-one employers and managers who represented twenty-three different firms. All but five of these management representatives are white men born in the United States. All of the workers and managers are employed at Santa Clara County, California, firms engaged in some aspect of semiconductor chip manufacturing assembly. I directly observed production at fifteen of these firms.

Silicon Valley's high-tech production labor force includes immigrants from at least thirty Third World nations. The primary informant sampling in the study reflects this diversity. Approximately 40 to 50 percent of the workers, in both the study and the larger labor force, are from Mexico, with other sizable groups representing Vietnam, the Philippines, South Korea, and Taiwan. Smaller numbers come from Cambodia, Laos, Thailand, Malaysia, Indonesia, India, Pakistan, Iran, Ethiopia, Haiti, Cuba, El Salvador, Nicaragua, Guatemala, and Venezuela. There is also a very small group of Southern European workers, mainly from Portugal and Greece, who are not considered in this study.

All of the women workers were first interviewed informally, in small groups, and then individually, following a formal interview schedule that lasted at least three hours. None of the workers were approached on the job or interviewed at the job site. Additional in-depth, open-ended interviews were conducted with thirty-six of the women at their homes, and were accompanied by group interviews with their household members. Access to worker informants was gained by three methods: through my established contacts in immigrant communities; by attending social, church, and neighborhood functions within these communities; and by attending advertised job calls at high-tech manufacturing firms. Many of my initial informants introduced me to their friends and coworkers. In order to ensure a broad sample, I did not interview more than five people who were introduced by the same source or who worked at the same plant.

In addition to interviews, many worker informants were also visited several times over an eight-year period. During these visits, I participated in household functions and helped deal with family, immigration, and work concerns. By far the most revealing data, from managers and workers alike, were gathered during informal conversations in homes or other social environments.

Managers and employers were identified and approached through personal contacts in the local high-tech industry. The three largest semiconductor manufacturing firms that dominate the industry are all represented in the management sample, as are the majority of the middle-sized firms that employ assembly workers. Managers and employers were formally interviewed for a minimum of one hour at their work site; most also were interviewed informally away from the work site for at least an hour.

## Hiring Dynamics: The Continuing Significance of Race

Silicon Valley high-tech manufacturing companies' propensity to recruit and hire primarily Asian and Latina women for operative jobs has been documented by several researchers (Green 1980; Katz and Kemnitzer 1984; Siegel and Borock 1982; Snow 1986). It is well recognized that this pattern is not exclusive to the region but applies to the high-tech industry globally (Ehrenreich and Fuentes 1981; Grossman 1979; Lim 1978; Women Working Worldwide 1991). The microelectronics industry is, in fact, at the forefront of corporate capital's trend to relocate manufacturing production in peripheral and semi-peripheral areas where cheap, often state-controlled, women's labor is plentiful, particularly in Southeast Asia but also in Mexico, Puerto Rico, and other locations in Asia, Central America, South America, and Europe (Siegel 1980). Since the 1960s, large U.S. microelectronics manufacturers have been shifting the bulk of their production facilities to offshore locations but have maintained factories in core regions, such as Silicon Valley, in order to facilitate prototypic, custom-design, and short-term manufacturing.

Employers and labor market analysts frequently argue that individuals who are women and/or people of color and/or immigrants take low-paying jobs either because they are content with them, or because they are unqualified for and sometimes even undeserving of better-paying jobs. I refer to these ideologies—and the hiring strategies that accompany them—as racial, immigrant, and gender "logic." Whether employers are conscious of it or not, each of these logics serves as a form of "capital logic," that is, as strategies that increase profit maximization. Specifically, hiring patterns that are informed by racism, national chauvinism, and sexism increase class stratification and labor control, and decrease potential unity among workers.

White employers' use of racism to help establish a hierarchical and exploitative division of labor is not a new phenomenon, nor is it specific to high-tech industry. The contemporary textile industry, for example, also draws heavily on Third World women workers, an increasing trend in global capitalist development. In textiles, as in high-tech industry, employers have used sexist and racist stereotypes to help establish an international division of labor. For example, textile employers tell indigenous textile workers in Western Europe and North America that wage cuts and layoffs should be blamed on Third World women who are "naturally" willing to work for less and to tolerate more exploitative conditions than workers in the core, not on the skewed capitalist international division of labor (Chapkis and Enloe 1983).

Another aspect of racism and the division of labor is explored by Ralph Fevre in his case study of wool textile firms in West Yorkshire, Britain (Fevre 1984). He found that Indians and Pakistanis were recruited and hired in this low-paid manufacturing sector mainly because their labor had already been categorized by a racially discriminatory society as being worth less than White workers'—before they were ever hired. Employers set low wages not only because of cost and profit dictates but also because they "regarded low wages as the basic, immutable condition of wool textile production" (Fevre 1984:11), and as all that Asian workers deserved. Employer respondents in Fevre's study believed that Indian and Pakistani male workers were "intellectually limited," and that they possessed racially specific characteristics suiting them to the monotonous work. As one of these British employers put it: "Asians are plodders so you put them in combing where you need plodders" (Fevre 1984:111). These same groups of workers were denied the opportunity to demonstrate other work abilities because employers refused to hire them for "non-plodding" jobs.

William Julius Wilson, one of the most widely read sociological scholars of contemporary racial dynamics, argues that since World War II, race has played a diminishing role in the structuring of the aggregate capitalist labor force in the United States (Wilson 1978, 1988). Wilson's work focuses specifically on Black Americans, but his thesis that class has replaced race as the most significant determinant of Blacks' economic condition in the United States has influenced the way sociologists look at race and racism in general. Critics such as Manning Marable have challenged Wilson's emphasis, arguing that although socioeconomic class may indeed have an increasing significance for middle-class Blacks, this does not decrease the significance of race and racism for most Blacks in the United States, who are not middle class. Part of the danger of Wilson's insistence on the diminishing impact of racism, Marable argues, is that it legitimates social policy aimed at cutting affirmative action, and implies that capitalist economic development, left unhindered, can and will rid itself of racism (Marable 1980:215–217). My research in Silicon Valley suggests that at least within the particular industrial sector I studied, capitalist economic development utilizes and thrives on racism as a method of labor division and control. Precisely because it is a major indicator of class, race remains a significant determinant in the Silicon Valley division of labor.

Two other contemporary scholars of racism's relationship to employment, Michael Omi and Howard Winant, argue that racism was actually resurgent in the 1980s, and that race relations have the capacity to shape class relations in the contemporary United States (Omi and Winant 1983, 1986). They note that most traditional sociological interpretations of the relationships between workers and employers, such as those of Marx, were based on White males. Thus, these theories do not fully consider how women and people of color may be treated differently by employers and managers. In fact, Omi and Winant argue, racism serves employers as an effective tool to divide workers, and the class system functions to serve White privilege (1983:40).

"Model minority" theory is another interpretation of race-employment dynamics currently in vogue both in mainstream social sciences (Wong 1985) and in many corporate personnel offices. The findings of my study challenge model minority theory's explanation of why different racial minority groups have had different economic "success" rates, and the theory's corollary prescription for how "less successful" minority groups might better succeed. Model minority theory posits that lifestyle patterns and cultural values of some racial minority groups (Asians) are more conducive to successful integration into the mainstream U.S. economy than those of other groups (African Americans and Latinos). Model minority theorists in previous decades took Japanese and Chinese Americans as models for other groups to emulate. In the 1980s, model minority theorists pointed to Vietnamese and Koreans as economic success models.

Model minority theory tends to overlook structural barriers, such as institutionalized racism, that restrict economic opportunities for people of color. One of its dangerous implications is that it facilitates blaming the comparatively low income levels of African Americans, Latinos, Native Americans, and unaffluent Asians on their cultural values. The theory also has been used to argue that affirmative action and equal opportunity programs are unnecessary, because "some" racial minorities have "made it on their own." It can be used to validate excluding all Asians from affirmative action, including the many Asians and Pacific Islanders who are not wealthy or privileged (Wong 1985).

The idea that all Asians have "made it" in the United States, and that they have done so because of racial or cultural superiority, is, as Eugene Wong points out, a true American myth (Wong 1985). It is also a myth that is damaging to all minority groups, including Asian ones, who are now being lumped together and attacked by Whites for being "too successful" (Omi and Winant 1986). Omi and Winant have argued against simplistic explanations that posit Asians as lesser victims of racism because they are seen by Whites as "closer" to Whites in color and culture. It is not that Whites are "less racist" to Asians than to other people of color but, rather, that racism against different groups takes different forms in different historical periods.

Asian workers have historically been among the most exploited in the United States, which may make it appear that employers have preferred to hire Asians. But Whites' designation of Asians as favored workers has been conflictual and frequently hostile, as California's anti-Filipino riots of the 1930s and long history of anti-Chinese legislation illustrate. More recently, in the mid-1980s, a nationwide anti-Japanese backlash, blaming the Japanese for loss of American jobs and cheaper foreign products, helped create the climate for a series of violent racial hate crimes (including murder) by Whites against anyone the perpetrators thought "looked Japanese." Since the 1980s, Asian immigrants and their U.S.-born children have become disproportionately high achievers in American schools. If this trend continues, and if U.S. Asian populations continue to grow dramatically, Whites' professed admiration for Asians' cultural values as a path to upward mobility may turn increasingly to resentment.

## Silicon Valley's Division of Labor

Silicon Valley, as California's Santa Clara County is commonly referred to, is famed for its microelectronics industry and for the technological revolution it helped to generate. The region is renowned for its computer wizards and for the high-tech fortunes made and lost by venture capitalists and entrepreneurs. But behind Silicon Valley's celebrity is a less-known feature both of the specific region and of the world's fastest-growing industry in general. The microelectronics industry is predicated on a division of labor that is more sharply stratified by class, gender, race, and nationality than almost any other contemporary industry. The high-profile, high-paid engineers, executives, and investors are overwhelmingly White, male U.S. citizens. On the opposite end of the occupational spectrum, the majority of low-paid manufacturing workers are Third World women.

Close to 200,000 people, or 25 percent of employees in the San Jose Metropolitan Statistical Area labor force, work in Silicon Valley's microelectronics industry.[2] There are over 800 manufacturing firms that hire ten or more people each, including 120 large firms that each count over 250 employees. In addition, an even larger number of small firms hire fewer than ten employees apiece. Approximately half of this high-tech labor force—100,000 employees—are in production-related work.[3] An estimated one-quarter of all high-tech industry employees, or half of production-related workers (50,000–70,000), work in semiskilled operative jobs (Siegel and Borock 1982). This contrasts sharply with the majority of other manufacturing industries, where the workers directly engaged in production average from 70 to 80 percent of total employees (Gregory 1984). Semiconductor manufacturing, the industrial sector that is the focus of this study, involves the production of integrated circuits, the silicon "chips" that serve as the basic building block of microelectronics technology. Production includes a complex combination of engineering processes that are performed by highly skilled technicians, as well as finishing and assembly work that is classified as unskilled or semiskilled work. The division of labor within the industry is highly skewed by gender and race. Although women account for close to half of the total Santa Clara County paid labor force both within and outside the industry, only 18 percent of managers, 17 percent of professional employees, and 25 percent of technicians in the industry are female. Conversely, women account for at least 68 percent, and by some reports as much as 85–90 percent, of the operative jobs in high-tech work (California Department of Development 1983).

Similar disparities exist vis-à-vis minority employment, although there are established bourgeoisies among the immigrant communities in the region who have achieved financial prosperity.[4] According to the 1980 census, 73 percent of all employees in Santa Clara County are non-Hispanic White; 15 percent are Hispanic (all races); 7.5 percent are Asian or Pacific Islander; 3 percent are Black; and 0.5 percent are Native American (California Department of Development 1983:96–97). These work force figures are roughly equivalent to each group's regional population percentage, according to census estimates. However, the census does not adequately measure the county's thousands of undocumented residents. In addition, since the census, the region has seen a steady increase in the number of Third World immigrants arriving each year, due in part to influxes of refugees. The number of Indochinese living in Santa Clara County is thought to have quadrupled between 1980 and 1984 alone. It is in these groups of recent immigrants that high-tech employers find much of their production labor force.

Within the microelectronics industry, 12 percent of managers, 16 percent of professionals, and 18 percent of technicians are minorities, mainly concentrated at the lower-paying and less powerful ends of these categories. An estimated 50–75 percent of operative jobs are held by racial minorities, according to state estimates (California Department of Development 1983). Employers and industry analysts estimate that in the industry as a whole, approximately half of all operatives are Third World immigrants.

## Findings

Findings indicate that race, national origin, and gender have major significance in determining the class structure and division of labor of Silicon Valley's high-tech industry. High-tech industry managers still use race and nationality, in addition to gender, as primary categories in designating the division of labor. At each of the subcontracting firms I observed, between 80 and 100 percent of workers are Third World immigrants. These firms tend to specialize primarily in unskilled and semiskilled assembly work, which is subcontracted out from other firms. Subcontractors usually pay lower wages and offer fewer benefits than the larger, more vertically integrated, better-known semiconductor firms, such as Silicon Valley's "Big Three": Intel, National Semiconductor, and Advanced Micro Devices. Subcontractors provide an easily expandable and expendable labor force for the very volatile industry. These assembly shops, where immigrant women were the most highly concentrated, have the lowest job security in the business.

Both employers and workers interviewed in this study agree that the lower the skill and pay level of the job, the greater the proportion of Third World immigrant women tends to be. Assembly work, which is classified as the lowest skilled and is the lowest-paid production job, has the highest concentration of these workers. Entry-level electronics production workers, in job categories such as semiconductor processing and assembly, earn an average of from $4.50 to $5.50 an hour; experienced workers in these jobs earn from $5.50 to $8.50. At each of the small (less than 250 employees) subcontracting assembly plants directly observed, immigrant women account for at least 75 percent and up to 100 percent of the assembly labor force. At only one of these plants do White males account for more than 2 percent of the production workers. By contrast, 90 percent of managers and owners at these businesses are White males. The proportion of nonimmigrant women of all races and of immigrant and nonimmigrant minority men increases in skilled production work. Men are concentrated in higher-paying specialties, such as machine and tool operating and technician work. The nonimmigrant women who work in production tend to do semiskilled labor, such as semiconductor processing. This pays slightly more than assembly work but less than jobs where men are concentrated.

The large nonsubcontracting firms I observed have higher percentages of male and nonimmigrant women assemblers and operatives than do smaller subcontracting firms. But even at the big firms, Third World immigrant women typically account for at least 50 percent of the workers. Men are always in a minority on the assembly line, and White men are rare. The presence of some men, however, and of larger numbers of nonimmigrants at larger firms is probably related to the greater opportunities for advancement there. A personnel manager who had worked both at a subcontracting firm and at one of the Big Three told me that the larger, vertically integrated semiconductor firms, unlike subcontractors, try to hire "a certain percentage of 'regular' American workers." This, he says, enables personnel departments to have "an educated, more permanent, in-house work force that we can draw on for training and promotion for more skilled work."

# Gender Logic

The employers interviewed indicated that they prefer to hire immigrant women, as compared to immigrant men, for assembly work because of beliefs shared by workers and employers alike that women can afford to work for less. None of the employers had any concrete knowledge about their workers' families or arrangements. Yet almost all of the employers stated that they assumed that their women workers were attached to male workers who were earning more than the women were. In fact, 80 percent of the women workers I interviewed were the main income earners in their families.[5]

Approximately 75 percent of the managers and employers interviewed stated that immigrant women are better suited to high-tech assembly work than immigrant men. Their jobs are characterized by assembly line-style repetition of a small set of tasks. According to workers, the work is extremely tiring because it requires constant concentration and intensive eye–hand coordination to manipulate the tiny, intricate circuitry. Employers and managers consistently claimed that Third World immigrant women are particularly suited to the work because of their supposedly superior hand–eye coordination and their patience. One male manager claimed that the "relatively small size" of many Asian and Mexican women "makes it easier for them to sit quietly for long periods of time, doing small detail work that would drive a large person like [him] crazy." The workers this man supervised, however, thought he preferred to hire physically small women because he could then feel superior and intimidating, "more like a big man," as a Filipina employee put it.

## "Immigrant Logic" in Hiring

*If I had to pay higher wages, I wouldn't stay in business here. It's not that I couldn't "afford" it per se, but the profit margin would be smaller, obviously. In Singapore, labor costs one-fifth of what it does here.*
—a White male employer, subcontracting assembly plant

According to employers, low-level production jobs in Silicon Valley probably would not exist unless there were workers available to work cheaply at insecure nonunionized jobs. Without such a reserve army of labor to call on, manufacturers might very well have developed the industry differently, with an even greater emphasis on automation and overseas location. An engineer in charge of production technology at a semiconductor manufacturing firm observed: "We already have the technology to fully automate everything we do here—it's just more expensive. We could definitely automate every step of the process if it ever becomes cheaper to do that than use human labor. Because of the large supply of unskilled immigrants in the area, labor is still cheaper for doing certain jobs than machines are." He later commented that two major factors could tip the balance in this equation: a curtailed immigration flow and unionization.

Employers interviewed in Silicon Valley electronics plants explain their penchant for hiring large numbers of immigrants in terms typical of employers everywhere who hire immigrants: they are more willing than nonimmigrants to work for low pay in "bad" jobs (i.e., jobs that are unsafe, monotonous, uncomfortable, and unsteady). Immigrants are seen—and see themselves—as being more desperate for work at any wage, because of lack of language, employable skills, or education.

Fifty percent of the employers interviewed offered some form of unsolicited moral legitimation for why they pay such low wages. The following remark from a assembly shop owner typifies this: "I don't want you to think I'm some kind of heartless ogre—my people really do seem to manage quite well on what they earn." The remaining 50 percent offered no personal legitimation: they simply indicated that their wage structures are the result of market supply and demand. This comment from an employer at a subcontracting assembly plant is unusually straightforward:

> Beats me how [entry level operatives] survive: they can't possibly do much more than eke by on these wages. But if they don't know the language, and some of them are illiterate even in their own language, and let's suppose, hypothetically of course, that they're not exactly here [in the U.S.] legally—just how many options have they got? We [employers] take advantage of this, but I'm not here to apologize for capitalism.

Employers (as well as the nonimmigrant White and African American workers with whom I talked) argue that immigrants from industrializing countries are better able to survive on very low wages than nonimmigrants. They surmise this is for two reasons. First, people from poor countries are viewed as skilled at and "used to" living on scant resources. Several employers and managers believed that "poverty management skills," as one assistant personnel manager termed it, are one of the "cultural values" that render certain minority groups more likely to succeed. A White male owner of a disk drive manufacturing facility reported:

These people from Third World countries really are incredible: they're so resourceful! I have this one woman who works for me—she's Filipino, or from somewhere around there—and she supports three kids and her parents on $5.65 an hour. Not only that, but she always makes the best of the situation, and she's always bringing in cakes and things for everyone. We only have one kid, and my wife says she can't make ends meet. And believe me, I make more than $5.65 an hour!

A second explanation several employers offered in explaining immigrant workers' willingness and ability to live on low wages is that such workers' family members are probably still living in their countries of origin, to which the immigrants themselves are planning to return. What might seem like meager savings in the United States, these employers pointed out, stretch much farther in poorer countries.

Historically, employers and the public in the United States have viewed Third World immigrant workers as being able to survive on substandard wages because the immigrants' families were living "back home," where U.S. dollars went farther. Immigrants are seen as people—usually men—who live frugally now in order to live well when they return to their countries of origin. For some immigrants, this scenario is indeed true, but the majority of immigrants to the United States never return to their native countries to live. Today's immigrants to Silicon Valley are rarely planning to save money in order to return home: over 95 percent of the immigrant workers I interviewed reported that they plan to stay in the United States permanently. The great majority also came with families: the low wages they earn must support them on U.S, not Third World, prices. And although many are helping to support relatives in their countries of origin, all had immediate family members living in the United States.

Employers stressed that they are doing immigrant workers a favor by supplying them with any job at all, as the following quotes from two board shop owners reveal:

I don't really prefer to hire immigrants, but they're usually the only ones willing to do the job. Most Americans would find it kind of boring work, but the Mexicans and the rest of them are grateful for whatever they can get. It beats welfare—both from their point of view, and from ours.

Actually, it's a good deal all around. A lot of these people were starving before they came to the States, so to them this job is a real step up. They haven't got many skills and they don't speak much English, so they can't expect to be paid much. They're grateful for whatever they get, and I feel we're providing a service by employing them.

In general, employers feel that immigrants are not taking jobs away from U.S. citizens, because relatively few citizens apply for such low-paid and "boring" jobs. That U.S. citizens do not, by and large, take these jobs does indeed suggest that they do not want them, as long as they can get better-paying ones. Yet White North American workers of both sexes, and often men of color, are discouraged by management from applying for entry-level manufacturing jobs, and are more likely to be denied such jobs when they do apply. This was openly confirmed by the majority of hiring personnel interviewed, who claim that most men and White women are not well suited for these jobs.

All of the subcontracting employers interviewed think American-born workers, and particularly American men, would be so frustrated at the lack of mobility opportunity in assembly shops that they would soon quit. One of them explained: "I've had White guys come in here—mainly college kids on breaks wanting to pick up money for the summer. One of them I put in management, but I won't put them on the line. They wouldn't last a week, it's so boring."

When I applied for assembly jobs at various plants, I was repeatedly told by personnel directors that the work wouldn't suit me and that I'd be much happier at a professional job or in a training program, because I was "an American." Naomi Katz (like me, a college-educated, White, North American woman) told me she had the same experience when she looked for assembly work during her study of Silicon Valley workers (Katz and Kemnitzer 1984). While investigating *maquiladora* work in southern California, Maria Patricia Fernandez-Kelly, who speaks both Spanish and English fluently, found that when she made phone inquiries for production jobs in Spanish, she was told there were openings, but when she inquired in English, she was told there were not (Fernandez-Kelly 1985).

Adapting Fernandez-Kelly's technique, I had a team of nationally diverse male and female students call plants and inquire about entry-level production job openings. Female students with Asian, Pacific Islander, or Latino "accents" were told there might be jobs available for them three times more often than male students with Anglo accents.[6] One of the reasons for this bias, a personnel director told me, is that managers think the only educated Americans who would take such jobs must be either journalists or union organizers who were trying to get a story or stir up trouble.

Managers typically exclude American workers of color from their rationale that U.S. citizens are not appropriate for assembly jobs. The hiring personnel I interviewed tended to lump all applicants within a broad racial or ethnic grouping together in their hiring evaluation, whether the individuals were U.S. citizens, native-born or not, especially if the applicants speak with any kind of accent that managers perceived as "foreign." Thus, a third-generation Chicana worker who speaks with a "Spanish" accent may be classified with recent Mexican immigrants in terms of managers' racial and nationality categorizations about who is appropriate for a job.

One of the central reasons that employers "prefer" to hire immigrants rather than available nonimmigrants for low-skill, low-paid, and precarious jobs is that their worth is less valued in society in general. This is clearly expressed by one of the factory owners I interviewed: "This industry is very volatile: the market demand is constantly fluctuating. One month I may have to let a third of my production people go, and the next month I may need to double my work force. Let's face it, when you have to expand and contract all the time, you need people who are more expendable. When I lay off immigrant housewives, people don't get as upset as if you were laying off regular [sic] workers."

Employers also prefer Third World immigrants because they are often newly proletarianized, with little organizing experience in an industrialized setting. And as people who are insecure in their residential status, whether documented or not, immigrants are seen as unlikely to "make waves" against any part of the American system for fear of jeopardizing their welcome. Many of the production processes in semiconductor manufacturing involve the use of highly toxic chemicals, and the rate of reported occupational illnesses in the industry in California is three times the average for all industries (Olson 1984:71). Labor organizers interviewed believe that one of the reasons management prefers to hire immigrants is that they are less familiar with occupational health and safety laws than other workers, and less likely to seek their enforcement.

## Racial Logic

As the quote about job trainers' racial hiring preferences at the beginning of this paper suggests, Silicon Valley employers and their colleagues distinguish not only between immigrants and nonimmigrants but also between different immigrant groups. A clear racial, ethnic, and national pecking order of management's hiring preferences emerges from interview findings. Most employers have a difficult time clearly distinguishing the myriad diverse races, ethnicities, and nationalities represented in their labor force. Yet this did not prevent many of them from making stereotypic assumptions about very broadly and usually incorrectly categorized groups. The two such broadly defined "groups" most prevalent in the immigrant work force, and thus most often compared by employers, are Asians and Pacific Islanders, to whom employers variously refer as "Asians" or "Orientals"; and Latinos, to whom employers variously refer as "Hispanics," "Latins," "South Americans," or, generically, "Mexicans." Asian immigrant women are clearly management's preferred production workers. Eighty-five percent of the employers and 90 percent of the managers interviewed stated that they believe Asian women make the best assembly-line workers in high-tech manufacturing.

Because employers tend to ascribe specific work characteristics to entire groups, they assign each group to jobs that emphasize these characteristics, thereby fulfilling their own prophecies. I observed hiring practices that appeared to be based on employers' racial and gender pecking orders. The training and employment agency director quoted at the beginning of this article assumes that different work characteristics exist according to race, and that members of some racial groups always show up late, and some always early, to job calls—not only to job calls, he implies, but also to work. Yet at none of the five large job calls I attended at high-tech manufacturing plants was this the case: Blacks, Whites, Latinos, and Asians all showed up early.

At the two job calls where I was able to obtain the relevant data, Asians were the most likely to obtain entry-level assembly jobs requiring no previous experience, and Whites and Blacks the least likely, regardless of nationality. Of those applying, approximately 20 percent of Asians, 12 percent of Latinos, 5 percent of Whites, and 5 percent of Blacks were hired. Although over 25 percent of the applicants for entry-level assembly jobs were male, they received only approximately 10 percent of the jobs. Three men who came specifically to apply for assembly jobs were hired as technicians, jobs for which they did not originally apply. Although data collection at these job calls did not control for other important factors—such as age, education, immigration status, language skills, and job experience—the heavily skewed hiring preferences clearly suggest racial discrimination.

Most managers interviewed consider African Americans to be the least desirable workers, not because they are believed to be too good for the jobs, as Whites are generally considered, but because they are not considered dependable enough for employment in general. Managers were mixed in their evaluation of Black immigrants: one production manager commented that Black Caribbean immigrants are "not usually as cocky" as African Americans. Management attitudes toward entry-level African American applicants are more negative than toward any other group. For working-class African Americans in Silicon Valley, this suggests, Wilson's prognosis of the declining significance of race in the labor market is not applicable. However, Silicon Valley hiring personnel repeatedly commented that there is a shortage of African American applicants at the professional level. I was told by several that they would like to find and hire well-credentialed African American engineers or programmers.[7] This suggests that White racism against Blacks may indeed be partially mitigated by Blacks' class and educational status, as Wilson proposes (Wilson 1978), but I was unable to find African American high-tech professionals who could confirm or deny this. My impression from talking with both managers and workers is that White racism against Blacks is a strong factor in the structuring of the Silicon Valley labor force but that, unsurprisingly, it is more intensely (although certainly not exclusively) experienced by and directed toward working-class Blacks.

Three of the firms I talked with were considering opening plants in U.S. localities with large Mexican populations (Brownsville, Texas; Albuquerque, New Mexico; and Watsonville, California). When I suggested locations characterized by large reserve labor pools of Black workers, such as nearby Oakland and East Palo Alto, spokespersons at all three firms indicated that these areas did not have suitable labor climates. Black workers are hired by high-tech production facilities in North Carolina's Research Triangle, however. An organizer whose union was conducting an organizing campaign in the high-tech manufacturing industry at the time suggested that Silicon Valley firms would not consider locating in Oakland because of union strength in that largely Black area. A leader in a different union that was targeting a large local semiconductor manufacturing company believed the industry's avoidance of the region was directly rooted in racism.

Four employers who had no direct experience—either negative or positive—with hiring Blacks and Latinos in skilled positions told me that they would prefer not to do so unless no one else was available. Their preferences, according to the respondents, were not based on comparative productivity reports from colleagues but on what they had personally concluded about these groups outside of the workplace. "Blacks are troublemakers," explained one administrator. "I found that out when I was at [the University of California at Berkeley]. They don't like Whites and they don't like authority—and

I'm both." Only two of the employers interviewed reported that they had no racial preferences in hiring for entry-level jobs. Only one of the two claimed to have absolutely no racial preference for hiring at any level, but even he amended his claim by adding, "as long as the secretaries are pretty, and personally, I don't find most Black women that attractive."

I was told several times by employers and managers that they prefer not to put Blacks and Hispanics in jobs that require much training, because, as one White manager worded it, "that would be throwing good money after bad—they tend to quit faster, so why invest in them?" Yet at none of the companies I observed was management able to provide me with a racial breakdown of turnover rates. A Black Jamaican woman who worked in the plant of the manager just quoted confided: "More Blacks would be likely to stick around if they gave us a chance at the better jobs, but they never do. So of course you're going to leave if you find a better offer, or if you just get tired knowing you'll stay at the bottom, no matter what you do."

Guadalupe Friaz's in-depth study of a large Silicon Valley electronics firm provides another example of how what appears to be a race distinction between workers may actually be a result of managers' racism. Friaz found that Asians had the lowest turnover rate of any group at the firm, and that Blacks and Latinos had the highest. She suggests that one possible explanation for this difference is the bias of racist supervisors, who treat workers differently and recommend promotions according to race (Friaz 1985).

Certainly not all employers and managers I interviewed and observed displayed blatant racism. Even those who admitted to personal racial preferences in hiring typically indicated that they knew it was illegal to institutionalize such preferences, as this executive's words illustrated: "It would be fine with me if I could simply advertise that I only wanted to hire certain groups. But nobody's that stupid—you'd get your butt sued off. But it's not against the law to choose where you post jobs—and where you don't. . . . I resent anybody telling me who I should hire, regardless of who does the best work, but I'm a stickler about doing everything by the law."

Less than 10 percent of the managers and employers in my study reported that they were aware of the Equal Employment Opportunity Commission (EEOC) investigating or reviewing their firms' hiring practices. One employer, however, pointed out that if his firm were being investigated, he probably would not admit it. An EEOC staff worker who was contacted for this study clarified that the agency mainly dealt with professional-level jobs and/or firms with government contracts. Even if someone filed a discrimination complaint, she explained, the regional office was backlogged well over a year in its investigations.

Interviews with White employers and administrators suggested that they are most comfortable when their workplace colleagues and office staff are also White, and their production work force is not. This makes it easier for management to construct an "us" and a "them" to help solidify the division of labor. It protects the white-collar Whites from having to confront their own racism, enabling them to view work relationships as occupationally, rather than racially, based. This is certainly not a unique situation. As a union organizer phrased it, "Historically, it has always been easier for bosses to exploit people they don't identify with."

## Are Asians "Better" Workers?

Over 80 percent of employers and managers interviewed referred to Asian immigrant workers as one collective category, rarely distinguishing between ethnic and nationality groups. All but one thought Asians make the best production workers. The reasons Silicon Valley employers and managers gave for preferring Asian workers typically paralleled model minority theory analysis. The theory was directly applied in several Silicon Valley personnel offices, and was mentioned by name by personnel staff at three different plants. A personnel director at one of the fifteen largest semiconductor manufacturing firms in Silicon Valley said she approaches her job (making most of the firms' hiring decisions) with the assumption that Asians are "better" production workers than other racial groups. She explained that the basis for her assumption was theoretical, not experiential: her master's thesis in industrial psychology was a review of model minority literature about "the Asian success story." She cited "uniquely Asian cultural values" as being "especially well-suited to the American free market system." According to this manager, these Asian values explain comparatively high income levels for Asian Americans and Asian immigrants, and include the following traits: investment in and commitment to higher education, even at the cost of financial hardship; dedication to hard work and willingness to work unusually long hours; a frugal lifestyle; putting aside small sums of capital until investment in a small business is possible; employing [apparently unpaid or low-paid] family members to keep labor costs down; and "a cultivated tradition of perseverance, coupled with cultural identification with, and a strongly positive feeling towards, the American dream."[8]

KAREN J. HOSSFELD

Employers' explanatory schemata for why Asians are the best workers ignore two interrelated critical factors: class origins and racism. In terms of class origins, several of the earlier waves of Indochinese, Koreans, and Chinese who worked in Silicon Valley production shops were originally from college-educated, middle-class, professional backgrounds. Although they temporarily lost that status upon immigration, particularly in the case of political refugees, who frequently fled with only the clothes they wore, eventually many of them were able to reestablish it, at least to some extent. White American employers who saw this reestablishment of upper-middle-class origins often seemed to confuse it with some innate racial ability. By comparison, few Mexican immigrant workers come from middle-class, college-educated backgrounds. Because earlier waves of Asian immigrants, particularly from Indochina, include substantial numbers of the ruling class and professionals, later groups of immigrants from these countries, who are from poorer backgrounds, have had both role models and, often, sponsors. This is another reason why Asians are perceived as working harder than Mexicans: they may in fact work faster and more carefully because they believe there will be a payoff greater than their paycheck. They have more examples in their communities who suggest that hard work can indeed result in class mobility. In addition, employers, trainers, educators, and social service workers may have formed opinions of Asians based on interaction with or exposure to the middle- and upper-class sectors of the population.

Today, the class background of Asian immigrant communities is rapidly shifting. The later waves of Indochinese refugees are not entrepreneurs and professionals fleeing socialist nationalization of private property but "boat people" who are poor, destitute, unskilled at industrialized jobs, and comparatively unlikely candidates for upward mobility. With this class and demographic change, the dominant White culture's perception of Asian communities may also change, and with it employers' preference for Asian workers. Social service workers I interviewed in Asian communities suggest this is already occurring. Vietnamese residents of Silicon Valley report that an escalating racist backlash is accompanying the growth in the number of Vietnamese-owned businesses and the political and religious clout of the Vietnamese population in the Silicon Valley city of San Jose. San Jose's Vietnamese population grew from an estimated 11,700 in 1980 to 75,000 in 1987. Jim McEntee, director of human relations for the Human Relations Commission of Santa Clara County, reports that racism against the Vietnamese is on the rise, due to "paternalistic" attitudes in the mainstream population about the proper place of minority groups. "It was fine as long as [the Vietnamese] were nice and quiet. Then they were 'nice' people" (*San Jose Mercury News*, July 26, 1987:1B).

In general, although employers and managers express resentment of upper- and middle-class Asians and Asian Americans whom they view as competitors, they continue to prefer Asian workers. One manager, who refers to his Mexican workers as "bean eaters," said, "I've just never liked Mexicans. They rub me wrong." He explained that he finds Mexicans both lazy and insubordinate on the job. When asked for specifics, he replied: "Well, it's not anything they do or don't do. It's not like there have been any incidents. I just pick up on their attitude. Once a grape picker, always a grape picker."

Many of the White managers interviewed resent Mexicans and Chicanos because they think Mexican immigrants are "ripping off" the United States. Several of the production and other midlevel managers grew up in California agricultural regions where battles between White farm owners and the predominantly Mexican United Farm Workers have been bitter. They interpret the union's organizing as a racial problem, not as class struggle. Most seem to have no idea that similar battles had been waged between Whites and Asians in earlier generations (Filipino farm workers, for example, were also active in forming the United Farm Workers), and that White hostility to Asian workers was once just as vehement.

Although employers claim that certain racial groups are more productive or responsible workers, none of the employers or managers interviewed could provide any comparative productivity data to back up such claims. Categorical judgments about particular racial groups may indeed be borne out in reality, but they also may be based on stereotyping that results in self-fulfilling prophecy. One employer, for example, admitted that since the start of his company, he has channeled Blacks and Latinos into monotonous and dangerous jobs where high turnover is expected and comparatively unimportant, since "those people have a propensity to quit sooner and be less reliable workers anyway." As to why he hires workers he believes are inferior, he commented, "I'm not prejudiced—I hire every color of the rainbow here. We're a regular affirmative action paragon of virtue." Indeed, his production force is composed entirely of minority groups. In contrast, his office staff is entirely White, which he explains by saying that race is not a factor; he simply hires the most qualified who apply for each job. His company, he claims, passed EEOC guidelines with "flying colors," and thus is eligible to obtain government contracts.

Another example of self-fulfilling racist prophecies is shown in the story of two neighbors who, unbeknownst to each other, called about the same job openings as packers (typically a job filled by men) at a high-tech manufacturing assembly plant. One, a Chinese immigrant who speaks English with a very discernible Chinese accent, was told to show up on the following morning at 8 A.M. sharp. The other, a U.S. citizen whose voice patterns as an African American are also very discernible, was told to "come by sometime tomorrow morning." When the Black man arrived at 9 A.M., he was told the job had already been filled, on a first-come, first-served basis. The Chinese man, who got one of the positions, later reported that at the end of the first day of work, employees were told that there were still two openings available, in case they knew anyone who might be interested. He told the White employer that his neighbor, who was "like a brother" to him, might want the job and was told, "Chinese are good workers; bring him by." The neighbor, the same Black man who had tried earlier to apply, accompanied the Chinese man to work the next day, where he was again told there were no openings. The employer later told the Chinese employee, "I thought you said you were bringing your brother." The next week, two other Asian immigrants were hired. On a separate occasion, the White personnel director at this firm told me that the reason so few Blacks worked at her firm was because so few applied. "Personally, I think because [Blacks] have lived here longer [than Asian immigrants] they know how to scam better." She added, "They don't need to get regular jobs in order to survive."

## Immigrant Women Workers' Consciousness

*It takes time . . . sometimes even years, before many Third World immigrants realize that racism stands in their way. . . . They tend to think their slow economic progress is just because they are new in this country, just as the Irish and the Italians and the Jews once were. It takes a while for them to realize the ramifications of the fact that although accents and citizenship and cultural customs can change in one or two generations, skin color does not. That is the main way that today's immigrants differ from yesterday's. When their newness wears off, they will still be non-Whites in a world dominated by Whites.*
—a Chinese American social worker in San Francisco's Asian
   immigrant communities

Cross-nationally, working-class immigrants interviewed for this study concurred with employers' "immigrant logic" that all immigrants who arrive in the United States with little or no material wealth, and with little or no English or easily transferable job skills, will have to work their way up from near the bottom of the job and class ladders. Even those who arrive with transferable job skills do not expect to compete on an equal footing with nonimmigrant workers in the short run. There is a strong sense that as new immigrants, they must pay their dues by taking unpreferred jobs and living close to the poverty margin. Most do not view this as unfair or exploitative. It does not make them like their jobs, but they see their situation as something every family or ethnic group must go through upon immigration. They view their position in the U.S. labor force as part of a cycle of economic assimilation. They believe that any new immigrants who work hard and pay their dues will eventually move into the middle or upper middle class, or at least the stable working class, and that their low-level jobs will be filled by new waves of immigrants, who in turn can work their way up and be replaced by even newer waves. This is described by many as the "American way." Almost all believe that their families will be economically assimilated by their second genera- tion in the United States, if not sooner.

The ideology that Third World immigrants "deserve less" is cut from a cloth similar to the ideology that devalues women's labor, and the two are often intertwined in the workplaces where immigrant women are employed. There is a major difference between the two ideologies, though. Immigrant status can be overcome, at least within one generation, but gender status is more permanent. And even in terms of immigrant status, the reality of U.S. society is that not every immigrant group has made equal inroads into the middle- and upper- class strata, even with time. Although most White groups have done so, many Third World groups have not.[9]

Many of the immigrant informants confirmed that they are indeed better off than they would be if they had stayed in their countries of origin. A Vietnamese community leader explained that my questions about the "quality of work" and "standard of living" are not very relevant to refugees who have brushed death so closely. The majority of immigrants interviewed were grateful to the United States and to their employers, an attitude I did not expect to find among such a low-paid work force. Even the immigrant workers who did not feel particularly grateful, mainly Latinos but also some Asians, agreed that whatever the shortcomings of their lives in the United States, they were economically worse off before they came here. A Mexican woman told me: "I don't earn enough here to support my family. If there weren't three of us working in our household, we wouldn't get by. But what choice do I have? [In Mexico] I had no job at all, and three babies to feed."

Regardless of how long they have been at their current jobs, all of the women workers interviewed believed that they would move on to better jobs within a few years. I found numerous workers who had been doing the same or similar work for over five years, yet still maintained that their jobs were temporary. Even individuals who had been on the job for as long as ten years still tended to view the job as a temporary stop, as a stepping-stone to somewhere else. Although this may prove to be the case, they have spent a substantial portion of their work lives "not getting involved" in trying to change unfavorable conditions because of this view. A union organizer commented:

> Six years ago, when we approached workers at [a large semiconductor firm], I met this very bright, articulate Mexicana who seemed pretty feisty, who I thought would be an excellent union advocate on the floor. I approached her about it, and she said no, that she believed in unions but she was going to be out of that place soon and didn't want to make any commitments there. This year I ran into her again—she's now at [a competitor firm] doing the same job, and she said the exact same thing. Maybe she'll go for it in another five years—if there's any jobs left here to be "about to quit" in the first place.

Excerpts from an interview with a young Filipina fabrication operator also illustrate this predicament. Asked about her attitudes toward unions, she replied: "Most of the women here are not interested in organizing a union. The work is pretty bad for the health, and we'd like to see that changed, and better benefits, but most of us don't expect to be here too long. Union drives take a long time—sometimes a couple of years—and I'll be gone by then." This statement takes on a new perspective when juxtaposed to an earlier part of the interview:

*Interviewer (I)*: How long have you been in this line of work?

*Respondent (R)*: Four years.

*I*: How long did you plan on staying when you took the job?

*R*: A year.

*I*: When do you plan on leaving?

*R*: Within a year. (laugh) This time I mean it!

*I*: What kept you from leaving sooner?

*R*: I was trying to save up enough to go to school to get a beautician's license.

*I*: Have you saved almost enough?

*R*: No, nothing. I spent it all on things my family needed.

*I*: What will you do when you leave?

*R*: Something more interesting—I don't know. Maybe we'll win the lottery! (laughter)

I later showed this woman her two sets of statements, and asked her to compare them. After reading her own words, she explained:

> You're probably thinking that in four years I could have worked to organize a union, or at least filed a grievance about the allergies I developed from the [processing chemicals]. But even though I didn't leave, I was ready to at any time, in case something else came along. And I want to stay ready to leave at any time—I don't want to feel committed and sucked in at a job I don't like. . . . this year I'm leaving for sure.

Two years later, this same woman was working at another semiconductor plant after being temporarily unemployed due to a layoff at her old plant.

Although small groups of immigrants suffered racial or ethnic oppression in their homelands, most of the immigrant workers interviewed were accustomed to being members of the majority racial group in their countries of origin. Thus, most of them did not grow up subject to internalized racial oppression, as Erica Sherover-Marcuse (1986) suggests is the case for people of color born and raised in the United States. This may help to explain why managers often make a pretense of disguising their racism as immigrant logic when dealing directly with workers. Many of the more recent immigrants deny the existence of discrimination and prejudice against their racial or national group in the United States. Informants who have been in the United States five years or less are much more likely to explain their experiences with discrimination as being based in their ignorance as, or others' ignorance of, foreigners rather than as race related. This is true for close to 70 percent of the Asian immigrants interviewed but for only 30 percent of the Mexican immigrants. Mexican immigrants are more likely to have heard explicit accounts of racism in the United States before immigrating, from friends and relatives who migrated back and forth between the two countries. A recently arrived, undocumented Mexican worker commented: "I already knew that 'gringos' don't like

Mexicans before we came here, because my cousin lived in the States. But I also knew they would hire us for certain jobs, so we came anyway." Her observation is typical of those made by her compatriots. Latinos in general, as well as the few Black immigrants among the informants, are more likely than Asians to expect racism to deter their access to equitable jobs and incomes.

Most of the Asian immigrants were not very knowledgeable about U.S. racism when they immigrated, or at least did not realize it extends to Asians. A woman from India commented: "I knew that Americans [sic] did not like the Blacks, but I was surprised they don't like Indians too much, either." Remarks from a recently immigrated Chinese worker suggest that she is shocked by derogatory racial slurs when they are directed at her own national/racial group, but not when they are directed at certain others: "Why do they say these things to us?" she asked. "People treat us bad, like they do the Blacks or Mexicans. I don't understand. I thought Chinese culture is very respected here."

## Conclusion

The main source of legitimation of both gender and racial hierarchy within the high-tech industry in Silicon Valley lies, obviously, in the existence of occupational and social stratification. Every day workers and managers view the gender-, class-, and race-tiered structure of the industry, and although some may consider it unfair, most believe that it is inevitable. As a Chicana who worked as a bonder in a large firm said of the company's racial and gender hierarchy: "Of course I don't like it, but there's nothing I can do about it—it's like that everywhere." An African American woman coworker agreed: "It's a White man's world—just look around the plant. I take the job I can get and I do it." The few who did challenge the hierarchy, during conversation, were mainly not immigrants: some of the White women workers questioned sexual hierarchies, and some nonimmigrant women of color questioned both sexual and racial boundaries. In general, though, as with sexism, employers can use "immigrant-specific" logic because it corresponds to workers' own consciousness of their limited options.[10]

In conclusion, the racial division of labor in the Silicon Valley high-tech manufacturing work force originates in the racially structured labor market of the larger economy, and in the "racial logic" that employers use in hiring. This "racial logic" is based on stereotypes—both observed and imagined—that employers have about different racial groups. One of the effects of this racial logic, vis-à-vis workers, is to reproduce the racially structured labor market and class structure that discriminates against minorities and immigrants. Another effect is that within the workplace, racial categories and racism become tools for management to divide and control workers. These are dynamics that individuals and organizations interested in social change must become more familiar with—not just in Silicon Valley but elsewhere. As for the situation in highly "innovative" Silicon Valley itself, to date, neither labor, women's, nor ethnic organizations have made major inroads in challenging the hiring hierarchy (Hossfeld 1991). But challenge it we must. Equality of opportunity, both at work and away from it, cannot be achieved unless we learn to recognize and reject practices that are based on "simple formulas" about gender, race, and nationality.

## Notes

1. As many recent scholars and activists have noted, the term "Third World" is problematic and imprecise. Yet so, too, are currently available substitute terms such as "postcolonial," "industrializing," and "developing." For references to the terminology debate from a feminist perspective, see Mohanty, Russo, and Torres, 1991. In this article, the term "Third World immigrants" refers to individuals who have migrated (in this case to the United States) from world regions with a history of colonial domination.

2. Statistical references in this study have not been updated to reflect the 1990 census because the research was conducted, and refers to conditions, during the 1980s.

3. These production jobs include the following U.S. Department of Labor occupational titles: semiconductor processor, semiconductor assembler, electronics assembler, and electronics tester. Entry-level wages for these jobs in Silicon Valley are $4.00–$5.50; wages for workers with one to two years' experience or more are $5.50–$8.00 an hour, with testers sometimes earning up to $9.50. California Department of Employment Development 1983.

4. This is especially true of Asian communities. The Vietnamese, for example, have founded several business associations, and own several blocks of businesses in downtown San Jose. Hispanic groups have a much smaller business ownership base, although there is a Hispanic Chamber of Commerce in the area.

5. For a more extensive discussion of how gender ideologies are used as the basis of both labor control and labor resistance in this work force, see Hossfeld 1990.

6. The student team was composed of University of California at Santa Cruz undergraduates, aged eighteen to twenty-five.

7. In Silicon Valley, the low proportion of Black workers correlates to the low proportion of Blacks in the overall county labor force, 3.11 percent.

8. The association of a "frugal lifestyle" with the consumeristic American dream is perplexing.

9. Japanese Americans are among the top income earners in the United States, while Blacks and Hispanics are among the lowest in income. For evidence that Japanese and other Asian Americans have had to work harder for relatively lower economic status than whites, see Woo 1985.

10. For discussion of how immigrant women workers resist managers' efforts to use racism and sexism as forms of labor control, see Hossfeld 1990. For discussion of barriers to labor organizing around these issues, see Hossfeld 1991.

# References

California Department of Employment Development. 1983. *Annual Planning Information: San Jose Standard Metropolitan Statistical Area 1983–1984*. San Jose.

Chapkis, Wendy, and Cynthia Enloe. 1983. *Of Common Cloth: Women in the Global Textile Industry*. Amsterdam: Transnational Institute.

Ehrenreich, Barbara, and Annette Fuentes. 1981. "Life on the Global Assembly Line." *Ms.*, January, pp. 52–59.

Fernandez-Kelly, Maria Patricia. 1983. *For We Are Sold, I and My People: Women and Industry in Mexico's Frontier*. Albany: State University of New York Press.

———. 1985. "Advanced Technology, Regional Development and Hispanic Women's Employment in Southern California." Paper presented at the Women, High Technology and Society Conference, University of California, Santa Cruz, June 1.

Fevre, Ralph. 1984. *Cheap Labour and Racial Discrimination*. Aldershot, U.K.: Gower.

Friaz, Guadalupe. 1985. "Race and Gender Differences in Mobility and Turnover in a Large Electronics Firm." Paper presented at the Women, High Technology and Society Conference, University of California, Santa Cruz, June 1.

Green, Susan S. 1980. *Silicon Valley's Women Workers: A Theoretical Analysis of Sex-Segregation in the Electronics Industry Labor Market*. Honolulu: Impact of Transnational Interactions Project, Cultural Learning Institute, East-West Center.

Gregory, Kathleen. 1984. "Signing-up: The Culture and Careers of Silicon Valley Computer People." Ph.D. dissertation, Northwestern University. Ann Arbor, Michigan: University Microfilms International.

Grossman, Rachel. 1979. "Women's Place in the Integrated Circuit." *Southeast Asia Chronicle* 66 and *Pacific Review* 9 (joint issue): 2–17.

Hossfeld, Karen. 1988. "Divisions of Labor, Divisions of Lives: Immigrant Women Workers in Silicon Valley." Ph.D. dissertation, University of California, Santa Cruz. Ann Arbor, Michigan: University Microfilms International.

———. 1990. " 'Their Logic Against Them': Contradictions in Sex, Race and Class in Silicon Valley." In Kathryn Ward, ed., *Women Workers and Global Restructuring*. Ithaca, N.Y.: ILR Press.

———. 1991. "Why Aren't High-Tech Workers Organized?" In Women Working Worldwide, eds., *Common Interests: Women Organizing in Global Electronics*. London: Women Working Worldwide.

———. 1992. *Small, Foreign, and Female: Immigrant Women Workers in Silicon Valley*. Berkeley: University of California Press.

Katz, Naomi, and Davis S. Kemnitzer. 1984. "Women and Work in Silicon Valley: Options and Futures." In Karen Brodkin Sacks and Dorothy Remy, eds., *My Troubles Are Going to Have Trouble with Me: Everyday Trials and Triumphs of Women Workers*. New Brunswick, N.J.: Rutgers University Press.

Lim, Linda. 1978. *Women Workers in Multinational Corporations: The Case of the Electronics Industry in Malaysia and Singapore*. Michigan Occasional Papers in Women's Studies no. 9. Ann Arbor: University of Michigan.

Marable, Manning. 1980. *From the Grassroots: Social and Political Essays Toward Afro-American Liberation*. Boston: South End Press.

Mohanty, Chandra, Ann Russo, and Lourdes Torres, eds. 1991. *Third World Women and the Politics of Feminism*. Bloomington: Indiana University Press.

Olson, Lynne. 1984. "The Silkwoods of Silicon Valley." *Working Woman* (July): 71–72, 106, 108, 110–111.

Omi, Michael, and Howard Winant. 1983. "By the Rivers of Babylon: Race in the United States." *Socialist Review* 13, no. 5 (September–October): 31–66.

———. 1986. *Racial Formation in the United States from the 1960's to the 1980's*. New York: Routledge and Kegan Paul.

Sherover-Marcuse, Erica. 1986. *Emancipation and Consciousness*. London: Basil Blackwell.

Siegel, Lenny. 1980. "Delicate Bonds: The Global Semiconductor Industry." *Pacific Research* 1.

Siegel, Lenny, and Herb Borock. 1982. *Background Report on Silicon Valley*. Prepared for the U.S. Commission on Civil Rights. Mountain View, Calif.: Pacific Studies Center.

Snow, Robert. 1986. "The New International Division of Labor and the U.S. Workforce: The Case of the Electronics Industry." In June Nash and Maria Patricia Fernandez-Kelly eds., *Women, Men and the International Division of Labor.* Albany: State University of New York Press.

Wilson, William Julius. 1978. *The Declining Significance of Race: Blacks and Changing American Institutions.* Chicago: University of Chicago Press.

———. 1987. *The Truly Disadvantaged.* Chicago: University of Chicago Press.

Women Working Worldwide, eds. 1991. *Common Interests: Women Organizing in Global Electronics.* London: Women Working Worldwide.

Wong, Eugene F. 1985. "Asian American Middleman Theory: The Framework of an American Myth." *The Journal of Ethnic Studies* 13, no. 1 (Spring): 51–88.

Woo, Deborah. 1985. "The Socioeconomic Status of Asian American Women in the Labor Force: An Alternative View." *Sociological Perspectives* 28, no. 3 (July): 307–338.

# 5

## Inside the Work Worlds of Chicana and Mexican Immigrant Women

### Denise A. Segura

C hicanas (Mexican American women) and Mexicanas (immigrant women from Mexico)[1] confront many barriers to employment and job advancement. Securing decent jobs and promotions can be a difficult, if not impossible, task, considering structural features of the labor market (e.g., occupational segregation), social aspects of work, family responsibilities, and individual characteristics. This chapter brings the human dimension of this problem to life through an analysis of in-depth interviews with forty Chicana and Mexicana workers. I argue that labor market structure, particularly occupational segregation by race-ethnicity and gender, shapes Chicanas' and Mexicanas' experiences at work as well as their chances for job mobility. Within these confines, Chicanas and Mexicanas actively seek to develop strategies to maximize their social and economic betterment.

I organize my analysis first to provide a larger picture of Chicana and Mexicana employment and occupational segregation. Usually occupational segregation refers to the disproportionately large concentration of women in low-paying occupations (Harkess 1985). In this chapter, however, occupational segregation by gender is taken one step further to distinguish between jobs where the work force is primarily White women (White-female-dominated jobs) or primarily racial-ethnic minority women (minority-female-dominated jobs). This analytic separation is based on the perceptions of my study informants.[2] Second, I discuss the process whereby the women I interviewed became employed in jobs associated with their gender, or their gender/race-ethnicity, in the San Francisco Bay area of northern California. Third, I use three representative case studies to illustrate key features of the different labor market segments in which the respondents worked, and discuss their implications for occupational mobility. This analysis of the experiences of Chicana and Mexicana workers contributes new research on workplace features and dynamics that reinforce occupational segregation.

## Chicanas and Occupational Segregation

Chicanas and Mexican immigrant women have historically worked in jobs that have been filled by racial-ethnic minorities (Barrera 1979; Segura 1984), women (Blau and Ferber 1987), and/or women of color (Malveaux and Wallace 1987; Dill et al. 1987). Current employment patterns point to a cumulative effect of race-ethnicity and gender that limits Chicanas' access to better-paying jobs. Table 5.1 illustrates that in 1990, relatively few Chicano men and Chicana women, vis-a-vis non-Hispanic men and women, worked in the relatively better-paying, prestigious managerial and professional occupations.[3]

Like non-Hispanic women, Chicanas are occupationally segregated in female-dominated technical, sales, or administrative support occupations (see Table 5.1). In 1990, about 38 percent of Chicana and Mexicana women worked in these jobs. Fewer Chicanas and Mexicanas were employed in these female-dominated jobs, however, than non-Hispanic women. Moreover, research indicates that when Chicanas and Mexicanas work in these female-dominated occupations, they tend to occupy the lower levels (e.g., file clerk rather than supervisor) (Malveaux and Wallace 1987). Also, like other women of color, but unlike White women or Chicano men, Chicanas are overrepresented in low-paying, low-status jobs susceptible to seasonal fluctuations, such as domestic workers, cannery workers, and garment factory seamstresses.

There are other differences in employment between Chicanas/ Mexicanas and non-Hispanic men and women. In 1990, the unemployment rate for Chicanas and Mexicanas was 9.8 percent, as opposed to 5.7 percent and 4.9 percent for non-Hispanic men and women, respectively (U.S. Department of Commerce, 1991). In 1989, the median earnings of Chicana/Mexicana workers were $8,874 as opposed to $22,081 for non-Hispanic men and $11,885 for non-Hispanic women. This employment and unemployment profile suggests that Chicanas encounter a unique situation in the labor market, one characterized by jobs that mirror a combination of two sets of statuses—race-ethnicity and gender.

Human capital theory (e.g., Becker 1980) posits a different view,

DENISE A. SEGURA

**Table 5.1.** Occupational Distribution of Men and Women of Mexican and Non-Hispanic Origin, Sixteen Years and Over, March 1990[a]

| Occupation | Mexican Origin[b] | | Non-Hispanic | |
| --- | --- | --- | --- | --- |
| | Male | Female | Male | Female |
| Managerial and professional | 8.3% | 14.2% | 27.4% | 27.1% |
| Tech., sales, admin. support | 12.6 | 38.1 | 21.0 | 45.3 |
| Services | 5.1 | 23.9 | 9.2 | 16.9 |
| Farming, forestry, fishing | 11.2 | 1.8 | 3.6 | 1.0 |
| Precision production, craft, repair | 21.2 | 3.2 | 19.3 | 2.1 |
| Operators, fabricators, laborers | 31.7 | 18.8 | 19.5 | 7.5 |
| Total number (thousands) | 3,335 | 2,006 | 58,235 | 49,759 |

[a]All numbers in this table are estimates.
[b]Includes both Chicano/a and Mexicano/a people.
*Source:* U.S. Department of Commerce, Bureau of the Census, *The Hispanic Population in the United States, March 1990.* Current Population Reports, Series P-20, no. 449 (Washington, D.C.: U.S. Government Printing Office, 1991).

one that emphasizes the importance of individual characteristics for employment and mobility. According to this perspective, wages and mobility reflect an individual's level of educational attainment and job skills. Thus, Chicanos' lower earnings result from their lower levels of human capital relative to White males. In addition, as women, Chicanas and Mexicanas have family roles that may lessen the time they can make available for their jobs and severely hamper their chances to advance on the job (Becker 1985; Polachek 1979). Theoretically, then, women "choose" less prestigious jobs (e.g., clerical) because they are relatively easy to enter and exit, thereby offering a good fit with women's gender roles and expectations (Becker 1985; Mincer 1985). What is problematic in this perspective is the assumption that all workers enjoy equal opportunities to acquire or augment their human capital, have the same access to job information, and act in rational, self-interested ways that are only minimally affected by social relations (Granovetter 1985). Human capital theory also tends to accept uncritically gender ideology and expectations as given rather than socially constructed (Sokoloff 1980; Berk 1985).

Other research highlights structural barriers to job entry and mobility for Chicanas and Mexicanas. They are occupationally segregated in operative jobs and lower-level service and clerical jobs (Dill et al. 1987; Segura 1984). These jobs tend to be located in what many labor economists and sociologists call the "secondary labor market" of semiskilled and unskilled jobs, where high turnover of personnel, instability, low wages, and few avenues for advancement predominate (e.g., garment workers, child care workers). Such occupational segregation can be viewed as a structural feature of the labor market. As such, it is regarded by many as the major barrier to good pay, good working conditions, and job advancement that women of color experience.

Occupational segregation is sustained by a range of social forces. Employer discrimination (by race and gender) is one dynamic that reinforces occupational segregation by limiting Chicanas' and Mexicanas' access to better jobs in the primary labor market, and favoring their entry into jobs traditionally associated with minorities and women (Barrera 1979; Braddock and McPartland 1987; Segura 1986b). Racial-ethnic-, class-, and/or gender-segregated social networks can also reproduce occupational segregation (Duncan 1984; Granovetter 1974; Braddock and McPartland 1987). Insofar as workers rely on family and friends for job information, they become limited to jobs traditionally filled by these groups—which, in the case of the working class, intensifies the occupational segregation of racial-ethnic minorities (Braddock and McPartland 1987; Segura 1986a).

The organization of the workplace and the work environment also plays a key role in maintaining workers in low-paying jobs. For example, some lower-level (or "secondary") jobs are organized hierarchically in ways that provide a limited degree of mobility to workers. Gradations within lower-level jobs can offer workers a degree of mobility (e.g., moving from sorting fruit to packing fruit, or from piecework wages to hourly wages). While the degree of this mobility may not always be statistically significant, it is qualitatively distinct and important when it helps keep workers in an occupationally segregated work world. When actual job advancement is not likely, positive social relations may reinforce the occupational segregation of Chicana and Mexicana workers, as this paper will illustrate.

## Forty Women of Mexican Descent

For this study, I interviewed twenty Chicanas and twenty resident Mexican immigrant women in 1984–85. All the women were selected from the 1978–79 or 1980–81 CETA (Comprehensive Employment Training Act) cohorts of an adult education and employment training program in the San Francisco Bay area.[4] This program was designed to increase the job skills of participants through educational, language,

DENISE A. SEGURA

and specialized vocational training. Participants were usually placed by the program, or found employment via their social networks, in clerical, operative, and service jobs often filled by women and racial-ethnic minorities. Forty-nine Chicanas and Mexicanas had participated in this program during the targeted years. While I tried to contact all forty-nine women, I could locate and interview only forty. Each interview lasted from three to four hours. The interviews were informal and usually took place in the respondent's home. I talked with six women at the training program at their own request. The interviews were open-ended, and were based on an interview guide I developed early in the research. I did not administer a questionnaire but asked general questions that became more specific in the course of the interview. The questions were designed to gather in-depth life and work histories from the Chicana and Mexicana informants to explore (1) why they entered and exited from their jobs, (2) how they perceived and experienced occupational mobility in the labor market, and (3) the barriers to mobility they were experiencing. I defined occupational mobility as an increase in wages and job status, from the first job after leaving the training program to their last/current job.

From their life histories, I discovered that all but one Mexicana and one Chicana grew up in families they described as poor or working class. Forty percent of the Mexicanas had less than a primary school education, and 60 percent had finished elementary school. All but three of the Mexicanas had obtained a high school equivalency diploma by the time they finished the training program. Slightly over half of the Chicanas had not finished high school. By the time they finished the training program, only five did not have either a high school diploma or its equivalent.

Of the forty respondents, thirty-one had been involved in a conjugal relationship (either legal marriage or informal cohabitation with a partner) at some point in their lives before being interviewed. At the time of the interviews, six Chicanas and fourteen Mexicanas were married. Seven Chicanas and four Mexicanas were single parents. All but ten respondents had children.

## Employment and Mobility

When the women discussed the dynamics of job choice, I ascertained they were essentially channeled into female-dominated jobs. This finding is an important critique of human capital's emphasis on individual rational choice. Women in this study framed their initial employment not as a matter of choice but as part of a fluid process that was continuously being constructed and reconstructed, depending on institutional practices, family economic need, gender ideology, and other social influences. The women who had attended high school had participated in youth employment programs that had placed them in female-dominated jobs (e.g., clerical aide). None of the women reported being encouraged to consider nontraditional jobs either by secondary school counselors or by family members. In fact, the respondents relied on their social networks and/or the training program for job placements.

The program provided access to male-dominated jobs (paint packer, venetian blind maker, mail carrier) to only three women. Only one woman accepted such a job. Her economic need was acute (her husband was unemployed), whereas the other two women had husbands who were employed and did not want their wives working in male-dominated jobs.[5] The combination of institutional dynamics and family needs and preferences led thirty-nine of the forty respondents (nineteen Mexicanas and twenty Chicanas) to enter jobs where their coworkers were mostly women. This initial job placement reinforced the respondents' occupational segregation in female-dominated jobs and upheld traditional conceptions of gender within this community.

Another critical finding that emerged in the interviews concerned racial-ethnic segregation within the female-dominated jobs held by the respondents (see Table 5.2). Seventeen respondents (thirteen Chicanas and four Mexicanas) reported working in jobs where a majority of their coworkers were White women. Twenty-two respondents (fifteen Mexicanas and seven Chicanas) worked in jobs where nearly all of their coworkers were women of color.

In the course of the interviews, it became apparent that the jobs where the majority of the work force consisted of White women corresponded to better working conditions, higher salaries, and more advancement opportunities vis-à-vis jobs where a majority of workers were women of color.[6] Salaries were much higher in male-dominated jobs. Of the fourteen women who had become occupationally mobile, ten secured promotions within White-female-dominated clerical occupations. One Mexicana became upwardly mobile within a minority-female-dominated occupation (she went from hotel maid to assistant housekeeping manager). One Chicana and one Mexicana switched from White-female-dominated occupations to a male-dominated occupation. They moved from clerical jobs to mail carriers. The last upwardly mobile woman, a Mexicana, was promoted within a male-dominated occupation (from paint packer to line foreman). This

DENISE A. SEGURA

**Table 5.2.** Study Informants' Employment

| Male-Dominated Jobs | White-Female-Dominated Jobs | Minority-Female-Dominated Jobs |
| --- | --- | --- |
| Mail carrier | Clerical | Hotel maid |
| Line foreman | | Bilingual child care worker |
| Paint packer | | Bilingual teacher's assistant |
| | | Seamstress |
| | | Operative (e.g., tool packer) |
| | | Assistant housekeeping manager |
| | | Waitress |

*Note:* Race-ethnic and gender job descriptions are based on informants' reports of the gender and race-ethnicity of coworkers. For male-dominated jobs, less than 10 percent of coworkers were female. For White-female-dominated jobs, less than 10 percent of coworkers were men or women of color. For minority-female-dominated jobs, less than 10 percent of coworkers were White women or men.

mobility profile suggests that the local labor markets accessed by the respondents reinforced larger racial-ethnic and gender hierarchies.

Women's opportunities for occupational advancement often hinged upon the degree to which they felt attached to their jobs. A woman's relationship with her coworkers and the quality of her interaction with supervisors were critical in this regard. The better a woman felt about the social relations at work, the more likely she would be to call on others to devise strategies to manage problematic aspects of the job or to seek out the means for promotion. At the same time, if a woman felt alienated at work, her attachment to her job typically suffered, resulting in her exit from the job as soon as her economic circumstances allowed.

Racial-ethnic and class differences between the respondents and their coworkers/supervisors shaped the contours of the social relations at work. Moreover, the structure of the labor market—the occupational segregation of the respondents into White-female-dominated jobs or minority-female-dominated jobs—restricted their chances to realize occupational mobility in a number of ways. To illustrate in more concrete terms the impact of labor market structure and interactional dynamics at work among Chicana and Mexicana workers, I present three cases: Norma, Laura, and Angela. Each represents women in a different job situation who confronted and managed structural, individual, and social barriers to occupational mobility.

# Case 1: Norma

The first case is Norma, a Mexicana who became occupationally mobile in a clerical job. At the time of her interview, Norma was twenty-nine years old and married, with two preschool-aged children. She was promoted from clerical trainee to data entry clerk II in a large research firm. Norma entered her first job through a 1980 affirmative action program that targeted racial-ethnic minorities.

Norma recalled that gaining access to her job had been difficult and stressful. She told me that during her initial job interview, a supervisor told her that her English was inadequate. Norma reported this incident to her job counselor at the training program. The counselor called the supervisor's manager to inform him of Norma's high written and oral English proficiency test scores and to suggest that refusing her employment based on language might be discriminatory. Norma went for a second interview and was hired. While Norma was pleased to obtain the job, she felt that her assertive pursuit of it had made her anathema to some of the supervisory staff. This troubled her, but she maintained that if she had not fought for her employment rights, she would not be working in a "good" clerical job.

Norma contended that her predominantly White female coworkers and supervisors have never accepted her. After five years on the job, she still experiences a sense of social isolation at work:

> It has been difficult to get used to working here. The atmosphere is very different [than Mexico]. The customs are different. There is little conversation beyond "hi." Only with their friends do they say more. I realize that these feelings usually happen when one enters a new job. But usually the novelty wears off. For me it has never worn off. The atmosphere still seems very cold. I have thought that perhaps it is the language. But I don't know . . . perhaps it's being Latina. The few Latinos they've had there—all of them leave.

Norma told me that she had nearly quit her job after eleven months. She had felt socially isolated from coworkers and had not received much direction, training, or support from her immediate supervisor. Like the other respondents in White-female-dominated clerical jobs, Norma understood that becoming informed about the opportunities for advancement on the job was a critical prerequisite to becoming occupationally mobile. The respondents maintained that jobs posted on bulletin boards were not the best sources of information for promotions. Rather, supervisors, and often coworkers, were key informants in distinguishing jobs that were "really open" from jobs that were already filled. To receive this kind of information, women had to be part of a social network.

After eleven months, Norma despaired of achieving social acceptance at work or getting ahead in her job. Then, she took a six-month maternity leave. Norma returned to her job as scheduled because of her husband's recent job loss. When she returned, she had a new unit supervisor (or manager), a Chicano male. He gave her additional training, advised her to attend specific classes at the local community college, and gave her moral support when she was harassed by coworkers regarding certain small but critical details, such as the pictures she chose to decorate her corner of the office, her makeup, and her accent. He recommended her for the one promotion she obtained. Recently, this manager told her that he would be leaving his job within a year. He advised Norma to start looking for another job while he could still help her.

Norma averred that she was taking this manager's advice to look for a better job. She believed that her painful experiences in her current job will help her do better in subsequent jobs. Norma laughed as she told me that she was no longer "verde" (green) and now understood "more how things work." When I asked her to elaborate on what she had learned, she discussed the importance of "patience," "seeking out people who will help one," and "understanding that there's a lot of racism out there."

Like many of the Mexicana respondents, Norma was initially reluctant to designate problems at work as possible manifestations of racism. Chicanas, on the other hand, were usually quick to identify and condemn racism in the labor market and in society generally. This difference probably reflects Chicanas' experiences and perceptions of themselves as members of a racial-ethnic minority in the United States, whereas Mexicanas were typically unused to characterizing themselves as "minorities." Instead, the Mexicana respondents focused on being immigrants in search of better lives. They rationalized cold or hostile treatment as part of the immigrant experience that would abate as they became culturally and linguistically proficient in English and the American way of life. To Norma and the other Mexicanas, adhering to this rationalization was part of being "green" or a novice in the labor market. The Mexicanas in this study typically lost this idealized view by the end of their first year in their first job in the United States.

## Case 2: Laura

The second example is Laura, a Chicana who became occupationally mobile by leaving a clerical job and entering a male-dominated job, mail carrier. Laura was twenty-five years old, single, with one year of college education. As part of an intensive affirmative action campaign at a local college, she was hired as a receptionist in its engineering department. There were about seven other clerical workers in her unit, all but one of them White women. Laura's account was similar to Norma's with respect to the sense of social isolation experienced. But while Norma focused on the ways her racial-ethnic or cultural background separated her from her coworkers, Laura emphasized how class differences separate workers socially:

> With my coworkers it was difficult. It was a very stuffy environment there at the college. . . . Everyone there, they were from a totally different class. They were more into themselves and others like them—you know, more upper class. So I guess I couldn't relate to them. They used to talk about things I didn't know anything about. I felt really out of place. . . . After I'd been there about three years, I'd reached the top level—for me. Then I got called to the post office. When I told my supervisor that I was leaving, she was shocked. [She laughs with a wicked gleam in her eye.] She said, "Why don't we try for a promotion?" I said, "It's kind of late for that." You see, I'd been trying to transfer and be promoted for about two years.

Laura felt that her working-class background set her apart from her coworkers. When I asked her what she meant by this, she said that the kinds of movies she liked, the jokes she found amusing, and her dress were different from those of her coworkers. In addition, she felt uncomfortable when they used "big" words or discussed events she believed formed part of "White, upper-class culture." Her words suggest that occupational mobility can be problematic if a woman's bearing, including her choice of words, mannerisms, and dress, vary significantly from the workplace norm. Both Norma and Laura discussed the major modifications they had made in their makeup, hairstyles, and dress. But their less obvious qualities—in particular, their social mannerisms—were much more difficult to modify. Thus, persistently, they felt out of place.

The tensions Laura, Norma, and other respondents felt in White-female-dominated jobs lessened only slowly. Some women, like

Norma, adapted to the work environment under the auspices of a supportive supervisor. Others, like Laura, did not receive this kind of support and left the job in search of greener pastures. According to Laura, her supervisor did not regard her as an able worker worthy of additional training and promotion, both of which she had repeatedly asked for. This lack of support, coupled with her social distance from coworkers, contributed to Laura's disengagement from her job. So Laura enrolled in a night course to prepare for the post office exam—a job that was opening up to Hispanics due to a recent consent decree. After three unsatisfactory years as a clerical worker, she entered the high-paying, male-dominated world of the mail carrier.

Laura, Norma, and the other respondents differed with respect to how long a time should elapse before they might reasonably "give up" on establishing rapport with supervisors and coworkers. If a woman felt a great deal of hostility directed at her, she generally left within a year. Other women stayed in White-female-dominated jobs even though they had not been promoted. Their job attachment hinged on two factors: (1) their earnings were critical for their economic survival or that of their families—particularly if they were single parents; and (2) they perceived clerical work as "better" than the low-level factory or service jobs they knew about and had connections to.

## Case 3: Angela

The third example is Angela, a Mexicana garment worker who is not occupationally mobile. Angela is thirty-one years old, married, with a ten-year-old child. Her husband works irregularly as a janitor. Angela left the training program in 1980 with a job as a tool packer in a small, local factory. This job paid the minimum wage and offered health benefits to workers but not to their families. After about six months, Angela left this job due to health problems. She quickly found employment as a seamstress in a small shop. That job offered similar wages and benefits, but ended eighteen months later. In 1983, Angela obtained her current job as a seamstress in a medium-sized factory. When I asked her why she chose employment in garment factories, Angela replied, "Here Mexican women are appreciated mainly for their work in the kitchen, taking care of children, and in factories because they are very patient. In other jobs—I'm not so sure."

Although Angela had received clerical training, she was not able to find either a clerical job or a service job that paid her as much as piecework wages in a sewing factory. When I asked her how long she had looked for a different job, she admitted she had applied to only two or three places.

What was drawing Angela to the sewing factory was a combination of her prior experience as a seamstress, the sense that she would have relatively easy access to a sewing job, and the knowledge that she would work with women she would feel comfortable with. Her current job is sewing small stuffed animals. Because of the extensive detailing on the animals, the job was difficult to learn, but Angela's coworkers assisted her. She described this process warmly: "At the beginning, it [the job] was very difficult for me and I was very slow. My coworkers helped me sometimes so that I could make more money and my quota. We get along well together. Thanks to their support I stayed there, even though my supervisor sometimes says, 'You must hurry yourself up!' "

Angela enjoys a good relationship with her coworkers but feels tense due to pressure from her supervisor to exceed current production levels. She does not feel this is discriminatory harassment, however, since the supervisor urges everyone to increase production. In fact, Angela gave high marks to her supervisor for her evenhanded treatment of employees: "She [the supervisor] has more than enough experience and a lot of patience. But when we don't produce the minimum [production level], she tells us we have to hurry—but in a good way."

Angela's supervisor is a Mexican woman, and her coworkers are Latina or Asian immigrant women. Like other women employed in minority-female-dominated jobs in factories, hotels, child care centers, and bilingual classrooms, Angela and her coworkers socialize during lunchtimes, and sometimes after work as well. Angela indicated that she enjoys being able to speak Spanish on the job with her Latina coworkers and Mexican supervisor. She practices her English skills with her Asian coworkers, who are also interested in speaking English. Angela told me that she feels a part of her workplace, and has not been avoided, isolated, or harassed in any way by her coworkers. The warm social relations she described contrasted sharply with the alienation felt by the Chicana and Mexicana respondents in clerical jobs where their coworkers were predominantly White women and men.

Angela and the other respondents understood the unstable nature of factory, hotel, and child care jobs. Nor did they expect to get promoted in these jobs. But economic need and feeling comfortable socially at work enhanced their job attachment. These feelings impeded the respondents' chances to realize occupational mobility because they discouraged them from leaving what they termed "decent-paying jobs" for more lucrative jobs that involved (in their view) a high risk of failure. Moreover, they provided one form of compensation for harsh physical conditions and lack of promotional opportunities.

## Conclusion

The experiences of the women in this study point to important structural and experiential barriers to employment and mobility. Each case has profound implications for racial-ethnic, class, and gender segregation at work and in society. First, occupational segregation by gender, and by gender/race-ethnicity, was actively created and re-created at the macro and micro levels. Second, occupational segregation limited women's job attachment and mobility. Third, social relations at work played a key role in women's employment options. Fourth, social relations at work were shaped by the social class, race-ethnicity, and gender of coworkers and supervisors.

Occupational segregation was reinforced by a channeling process. Respondents described schooling that did not impart a sense of employment options outside those traditionally ascribed to women. Similarly, the employment training program rarely provided them with access to jobs outside of those occupied by women and/or women of color in the community. Family dynamics (economic need, husband's dislike of wives working with men) also upheld women's participation in female-dominated jobs. This intersection of macro/micro social dynamics posed strong barriers to women's job attachment and mobility.

Employment in jobs occupationally segregated by gender and race-ethnicity restricted the type of occupational mobility the respondents could attain or aspire to. Among the respondents, promotional opportunities were greater in White-female-dominated clerical jobs than in minority-female-dominated service and operative jobs. The quality of social relations at work often intensified existing patterns of occupational segregation. That is, the racial-ethnic and social class background of the respondents often separated them from coworkers and supervisors. It was difficult for both the respondents and their coworkers to establish a rapport if they were from different social worlds.

Social relations within minority-female-dominated jobs typically were much warmer. The relative absence of conflict based on race or class differences in these jobs often attracted and held the respondents to this structurally unstable arena. In this fashion, positive social relations at work reinforced the occupational clustering of the respondents in low-paying jobs.

Another dilemma many of the respondents faced was disaffection on the part of some coworkers and supervisors, triggered by their recruitment through affirmative action hiring programs. Women usually did not address this predicament directly but tried to outlast the resentment—a task rendered somewhat easier as the respondents adapted to the culture of their work environments or the workplace became more diversified (e.g., Norma's supportive Chicano supervisor). This problem points to the need to prepare workers and managers for a diverse workplace.

It is important to remember that while heterogeneity may promote intergroup relations (Blau 1977), moving beyond homogeneity is a difficult and often painful process, as this study has demonstrated. Continuing to explore the human dimensions of this dilemma is essential. As we become more knowledgeable of the ways in which structural forces and micro dynamics uphold class, racial-ethnic, and gender segregation in the labor market, we will be that much closer to developing strategies to promote intergroup relations and erode labor market inequality.

## Notes

1. In this chapter, the term "Chicana" refers to Mexican American women, women of Mexican descent born in the United States (n = 18) or who emigrated to the United States as preschool children (n = 2). "Mexicanas" were women born and raised in Mexico who emigrated as young women or adults (over sixteen years of age). "Hispanic" and "Latino/a" are broader terms that refer to men and women of Spanish origin (both native and foreign born) living in the United States.

2. A job usually is "female-dominated" when women constitute more than their proportion (43 percent) of the labor force. Chicanas and Mexicanas are overrepresented in a job when their participation exceeds that of their proportion in the labor force (2.5 percent). In this chapter, jobs are considered to be female-dominated if the respondents report that nearly all of their coworkers are women. However, an important finding in this study was that several of the women worked in racial-ethnic/gender-segregated jobs. This means that in several instances nearly all of their coworkers were White women, whereas others reported that all of their coworkers were women of color. This finding led me to subdivide typically female jobs into "White-female-dominated jobs" (jobs filled primarily by

White women) and "minority-female-dominated jobs" (jobs filled by women of color), as reported by the study respondents. I present distinguishing features from each segment of the female labor market for their impact on job attachment and occupational mobility.

3. Although this discrepancy is substantial, it actually reflects a modest level of improvement for Chicana/Mexicana women. In 1977, 9.1 percent of Chicanas and Mexicanas were professional, technical, or managerial workers (U.S. Bureau of the Census 1977).

4. For additional information on the methods and sample selection, see Segura, 1986a.

5. I explore in-depth husbands' influences on their wives' employment decisions as part of a larger system of patriarchy and Chicano/Mexicano familism in Segura 1989.

6. The overall average monthly wages of the eleven women working in White-female-dominated jobs from January 1984 to January 1985 was $896.54. The fourteen women employed during the same time period who worked in minority-female-dominated jobs earned an average of $772.85 per month, and the three women working in male-dominated jobs earned $1,920.00. If we consider full-time job status, women in White-female-dominated jobs earned an average $1,122.00, while women in minority-female-dominated jobs earned $849.00 and women in male-dominated jobs earned $1,920.00.

# References

Barrera, Mario. 1979. *Race and Class in the Southwest: A Theory of Racial Inequality.* Notre Dame, Ind.: University of Notre Dame Press.

Becker, G. S. 1975. *Human Capital.* 2d ed., 1980. Chicago: University of Chicago Press.

———. 1985. "Human Capital, Effort, and the Sexual Division of Labor." *Journal of Labor Economics* 3, no. 1 (suppl): 533–558.

Berk, Sarah Fenstermaker. 1985. *The Gender Factory: The Apportionment of Work in American Households.* New York: Plenum Press.

Bielby, W. T., and J. N. Baron. 1984. "A Woman's Place Is with Other Women: Sex Segregation Within Organizations." In *Sex Segregation in the Workplace: Trends, Explanations, Remedies,* edited by B. F. Reskin. Washington, D.C.: National Academy Press.

Blau, F. D., and M. A. Ferber. 1987. "Occupations and Earnings of Women Workers." In *Working Women: Past, Present, Future,* edited by K. S. Koziara, M. H. Moskow, and L. D. Tanner. Washington, D.C.: Bureau of National Affairs.

Blau, P. M. 1977. *Inequality and Heterogeneity: A Primitive Theory of Social*

*Structure*. New York: Free Press.

Braddock, J. H., and J. M. McPartland. 1987. "How Minorities Continue to Be Excluded from Equal Employment Opportunities: Research on Labor Market and Institutional Barriers." *Journal of Social Issues* 43, no. 1 (Spring): 5–39.

Dill, B. T., L. W. Cannon, and R. Vanneman. 1987. *Pay Equity: An Issue of Race, Ethnicity, and Sex*. Washington, D.C.: National Commission on Pay Equity.

Duncan, G. 1984. *Years of Poverty, Years of Plenty*. Ann Arbor, Mich.: Institute for Social Research, University of Michigan.

Granovetter, M. S. 1974. *Getting a Job: A Study of Contacts and Careers*. Cambridge, Mass.: Harvard University Press.

———. 1985. "Economic Action and Social Structure: The Problem of Embeddedness." *American Journal of Sociology* 91, no. 3 (November): 511–521.

Harkess, S. 1985. "Women's Occupational Experiences in the 1970's: Sociology and Economics." *Signs: Journal of Women in Culture and Society* 10, no. 31 (Spring): 495–516.

Malveaux, Julianne, and Phyllis Wallace. 1987. "Minority Women in the Workplace." In *Working Women: Past, Present, Future*, edited by K. S. Koziara, M. H. Moskow, and L. B. Tanner. Washington, D.C.: Bureau of National Affairs.

Mincer, J. 1985. "Intercounty Comparisons of Labor Force Trends and of Related Developments: An Overview." *Journal of Labor Economics* 3 (suppl): 501–532.

Polachek, S. W. 1979. "Occupational Segregation Among Women: Theory, Evidence, and a Prognosis." In *Women in the Labor Market*, edited by C. Lloyd. New York: Columbia University Press.

Reich, M., D. M. Gordon, and R. C. Edwards. 1973. "A Theory of Labor Market Segmentation." *American Economic Review* 63, no. 2 (May): 359–365.

Segura, D. A. 1984. "Labor Market Stratification: The Chicana Experience." *Berkeley Journal of Sociology* 29 (Spring): 57–91.

———. 1986a. "Chicanas and Mexican Immigrant Women in the Labor Market: A Study of Occupational Mobility and Stratification." Ph.D dissertation, University of California, Berkeley.

———. 1986b. "Chicanas and Triple Oppression in the Labor Force." In *Chicana Voices: Intersections of Class, Race, and Gender*. Conference Proceedings, National Association for Chicano Studies, Austin, Texas. Austin: Center for Mexican American Studies, University of Texas.

———. 1989. "The Interplay of Familism and Patriarchy on the Employment of Chicana and Mexican Immigrant Women." In Renato Rosaldo

Lecture Series Monograph 5, pp. 35–53. Tucson: Mexican American Studies Center, University of Arizona.

Sokoloff, N. J. 1980. *Between Money and Love: The Dialectics of Women's Home and Market Work.* New York: Praeger.

U.S. Department of Commerce, Bureau of the Census. 1991. *"The Hispanic Population in the United States, March 1990."* Current Population Reports, Series P-20, no. 449. Washington, D.C.: U.S. Government Printing Office.

———. 1977. *Persons of Spanish Origin in the United States, March 1977.* Current Population Reports, Series p. 20, no. 317. Washington, D.C.: U.S. Government Printing Office.

U.S. Department of Labor, Women's Bureau. 1987. *Women of Hispanic Origin in the United States Labor Force.* Fact Sheet no. 85–11. Washington, D.C.: U.S. Government Printing Office.

# 6

## Black Professional Women: Job Ceilings and Employment Sectors

### Elizabeth Higginbotham

**M**yths and stereotypes about the success of educated Black women, many promoted by misleading news reports of major trends, mask important employment problems faced by members of this group (Sokoloff 1992). The limited social science research on the plight of middle-class Black women makes fertile ground for myths about their success and stereotypes about their abilities to handle all situations. In reality, this is not a population exempt from problems on the job. Research on the employment status of educated Black women can be important in addressing the nature of contemporary racism in America and how it impacts people of color who are members of the middle class.

This chapter explores the employment status of Black professional women.[1] Throughout the twentieth century, there has been a tiny elite of educated Afro-American women employed in professional and managerial positions. Since the 1970s, this population has experienced significant growth. In 1984, 14.3 percent of full-time, year-round employed Black women were in professional, technical, and kindred specialties, and 5.4 percent were managers, officials, and proprietors (U.S. Department of Labor 1984). They constituted nearly a fifth of all full-time, year-round employed Black women sixteen years and older. They are employed in a variety of occupations, but the majority—even today—are primary and secondary teachers, social workers, librarians, school counselors, and nurses. Since the 1970s, the number of Black women in traditionally male professions, such as attorney, accountant, physician, dentist, and minister, has increased, but the majority continue to be clustered in traditionally female professional and managerial positions (Kilson 1977; Sokoloff 1987, 1992; Wallace 1980).

The more education a woman has, the more likely she is to be employed. Thus, while a minority of Black women have college educations—about 5 percent of Black women over twenty-five years of age—this is the group most likely to be in the labor force (Jones 1986).

Some scholars might argue that the size of this group of Black women in professional and managerial positions is evidence that racial and sexual barriers can be scaled by the talented. From another perspective, educated Black women's employment patterns reveal a history of racial discrimination. During most of this century, the majority of employed professional and managerial Black women have worked either in the public sector (city, county, state, and federal government) or for small independent agencies and employers in the Black community (Higginbotham 1987; Hine 1989).

This chapter provides details of the contemporary employment patterns of Black and White women to illustrate segmentation or clustering of professional and managerial women along racial lines. It addresses the question: What form does racial stratification take in this post–Civil Rights era? The concepts of job ceilings and employment sectors are used to illustrate shifting patterns of racism in the labor market options of professional and managerial Black women. These concepts are useful in evaluating the recent progress made by Black women.

## The Black Middle Class

The traditional social science practice is to view social class as status rankings. New scholarship offers a definition that views social class as opposing structural positions in the social organization of production. Different social classes do not represent different ranks in a social hierarchy but denote shared structural positions with regard to ownership of the means of production, level and degree of authority in the workplace, or the performance of mental or manual labor. From this perspective, the middle class is defined to include the small traditional groups of self-employed shopkeepers and independent farmers, and the numerically larger group of professionals, managers, and administrators. This group, frequently referred to as the professional-managerial class (see Walker 1979), performs the mental labor necessary to control the labor and lives of the working class. In the modern industrial capitalist state, it is designated as middle class because of its position between labor and capital. The primary role of the middle class is to plan, manage, and monitor the work of others. Its members have greater incomes, prestige, and education than other workers, but the social relations of dominance and subordination are key in defining their social class position (Braverman 1974; Poulantzas 1974; Ehrenreich and Ehrenreich 1979; Vanneman and Cannon 1987).

While Black women and men in middle-class positions enjoy many class advantages, they are still members of a racially devalued group. Understanding the middle class of a racially oppressed group requires a perspective that can investigate how both race and class interact to shape the lives of males and females. Racial oppression may be shared within the racial minority community but mediated by one's position within the class hierarchy (Barrera 1979). Both working-class and middle-class Afro-Americans are segmented and limited to the least remunerative and prestigious occupations, relative to Whites within their social class. Working-class Black men and women were denied access to many industrial, clerical, and sales jobs because these positions were reserved for Whites. Black men and women were readily able to find work in jobs that White people did not want. In the case of Black women, in the first half of the century they were employed primarily as domestics, and later gained access to service work, factory work, and some clerical and sales jobs (Amott and Matthaei 1991; Jones 1984).

Historically, Black middle-class men and women who occupied professional positions served their racial communities. These positions are often shunned by White professionals. Even today, most middle-class Black people teach and provide health and human services, and professional and managerial services to other Black people. The size and affluence of the Black community is a factor in the growth of the Black middle class (Drake and Cayton 1970; Landry 1987). Gender also plays a significant role in access to professional occupations.

## Gender Differences in Job Ceilings for Black Americans

As noted above, patterns of discrimination are evident in the history of employment for educated Black women and men. The concept of job ceilings helps clarify practices prior to the 1960s. Contrasting employment patterns between the public and private sectors best describes discriminatory patterns after the passage of Civil Rights legislation.

Job ceilings are the racially specific caps or ceilings placed on the occupational mobility of targeted groups. This form of economic oppression can be maintained by formal or informal practices. The results are the same. Black people are denied the opportunity to fill certain jobs, even if they are qualified, because employers have decided that this particular work is closed to Black Americans. Over the years, Black Americans have learned to watch for subtle changes or cracks in this ceiling.

Job ceilings, institutionalized early in this century, were instrumental in excluding Black people from many industrial jobs—both positions they might have held in the past and new jobs that were opening up. Job ceilings were very effective means of keeping Black people in low-wage manual jobs—the lowest of all working-class employment.

In *Black Metropolis*, St. Clair Drake and Horace Cayton (1970) talked in detail about the job ceiling in Chicago in the 1920s and 1930s:

> Between the First World War and the Depression, the bulk of the Negro population became concentrated in the lower-paid, menial, hazardous, and relatively unpleasant jobs. The employment policy of individual firms, trade-union restrictions, and racial discrimination in training and promotion made it exceedingly difficult for them to secure employment in the skilled trades, in clerical and sales work, and as foremen and managers. Certain entire industries had a "lily-white" policy—notably the public utilities, the electrical manufacturing industry, and the city's banks and offices. (p. 112)

The job ceiling was not unique to Chicago. It was a fundamental part of the labor market in urban and rural communities, both in the North and in the South (Hine 1989). Its existence prohibited Black males and females from following occupational mobility patterns open to both native-born White Americans and White immigrants. Over time, even first- and second-generation White immigrants were able to move from menial jobs into unskilled and semiskilled factory work. The next generation might proceed into skilled industrial work and sometimes eventually into white-collar positions.

With this established channel closed to them, Black American men and women had to find alternative routes out of the low-wage jobs in private household work, janitorial and custodial services, laundry work, and the other positions in which they could seek employment. A few Black men and women, with the support of their families or through their own efforts, were able to carve out an alternative course to better employment. They struggled to get an education, most often in traditionally Black institutions.

Acquiring a college education was often a route around the job ceiling for Black males and females. An education gave the credentials to qualify for middle-class positions. In this way, some Black people could bypass the ceiling and move to the next floor. That floor consisted of white-collar professional and managerial positions, primarily within the minority community.

For Black women, a college education did not guarantee a better livelihood than domestic or other low-wage service work. The Black females who obtained a college education, even an advanced degree, found another layer of obstacles in front of them. In a racially segmented society, even middle-class occupational positions are shaped by racism (and in the case of women, also sexism). So Black women who had the education to merit employment in middle-class professional jobs still faced race and sex barriers to securing satisfying and economically rewarding work in the middle class.

Prior to World War II, gender restrictions shaped the professions for which Black women could prepare and practice. Black women seeking higher education were steered into primary and secondary school teaching, nursing, social work, and library sciences (Hine 1989; Jones 1985). Gender also shaped the options of Black men. They were directed into medicine and dentistry, the ministry and business, as well as teaching. These gender-specific trends were noted by earlier social science researchers (Cuthbert 1942; Johnson 1969; Noble 1956). Black males and females were expected to practice their gender-specific professions within a racially segregated society.

On the whole, educational training equipped Black men for professional occupations in which they could be self-employed or work within Black institutions. With medical or dental training, they could set up independent or joint practices as physicians and dentists, in which they saw mostly Black patients—and in large communities, they were able to develop successful enterprises. As ministers, Black men were directly responsible to a congregation—if it was a large congregation, they could gain economic security. Some Black men moved into providing insurance and other services to the Black population. And other Black men found employment in traditionally Black educational institutions, where they were somewhat removed from the racist policies and practices in the White-dominated labor market.

College-educated Black women faced a different prospect. They were discouraged from pursuing traditionally male occupations and directed into developing female professions (Hine 1989). Thus, Black women were not educated for professions that enabled them to set up their own businesses or independent practices. Nurses do not set up individual practices; they are hired to work for doctors or employed in hospitals or clinics. Teachers do not recruit their own students; they are hired by public or private school systems. Librarians do not run their own institutions; they are hired to work in libraries operated by the city, the county, or an educational facility. And social workers do not go into business for themselves; they are hired by human service agencies in the private or public sector. Gender barriers, along with race and class obstructions in both educational institutions and the labor market, complicated Black women's securing professional employment (Higginbotham 1987; Hine 1989; Jones 1985). A college education often prepared them for occupations where they still faced a racial job ceiling.

And Black women did confront rigid job ceilings. Many Northern cities did not hire Black people for professional positions in their schools, clinics, hospitals, libraries, and other agencies. In the South, some public sector jobs were set aside for Black people, because Jim Crow policies dictated segregated facilities. This was particularly the case in the teaching field, where Afro-Americans had a monopoly on positions in Black schools, and during the Depression in public health and voluntary health operations (Hine 1989). North of the Mason-Dixon Line, city and county employment policies regarding Black professionals were very mixed. De facto segregation was usually the rule for designating where children were schooled, but cities differed in whether they would hire Black teachers to staff the facilities used to educate Black children (Tyack 1974). Black nurses could not find employment outside of Black hospitals and private homes. Because they were not trained for professions that could be translated into independent entrepreneurial practices, Black females were dependent on salaries and wages. Thus, employment prospects for educated Black women were contingent upon city and county hiring policies to staff public institutions.

For these reasons, the numbers of Black professional and managerial women remained small and lagged behind the percentages of White women in these occupations. The percentage of Black women employed as professional, technical, or kindred workers increased from 4.3 in 1940 to 5.3 in 1950, 7.7 in 1960, and to 15.3 percent by 1980. Despite the increase among professionals, the number of Black women in managerial positions did not exceed 1.4 percent until 1980, when it reached 4.2 percent (Higginbotham 1987).

# Employment Sectors:
## Black Professional Women's Place

Legislation against race and sex discrimination challenged many of the arbitrary practices, such as job ceilings. Since the mid-1960s, more educated Black people have found jobs in the professions for which they have credentials. This has meant an increase in the numbers of Black women in professional and managerial positions, as well as their employment in a wider range of occupations (Kilson 1977; Sokoloff 1992; Westcott 1982). Yet, Civil Rights legislation did not dismantle the racism that is a critical part of the labor market. Empirical research indicates that the occupational positions of educated Black women are still problematic (Higginbotham 1987; Sokoloff 1987, 1988, 1992). They continue to face employmentt barriers, but the discrimination has taken a new form. Now Black women find themselves limited to employment in certain sectors of the labor market.

Recent scholarship, especially work by Sharon Collins (1983), indicates that Black employees in professional and managerial positions are concentrated in the public sector. When they are in the private sector, Black middle-class employees are in the marginal areas of production (such as personnel, public relations, and the like). These observations are supported by reports from Black managers in the private sector (Bascom 1987; Fulbright 1986).

In an earlier work (Higginbotham 1987), I discussed how contemporary professional Black women remain concentrated in the traditionally female professions of teacher, social worker, nurse, librarian, and so forth. Recently, a significant number of Black women, as well as their White sisters, have broken into new occupations—those traditionally dominated by males. Today, there are more Black and White women who are physicians, dentists, lawyers, accountants, and managers in both small and large firms. Indeed, if one looks at broad occupational categories, the degree of sex segregation in the professional labor market has declined since the 1970s (Sokoloff 1987, 1988, 1992). If one looks below the surface, one can identify how racism remains embedded in the social structure. Instead of being evenly split between the private and public sectors, the majority of professional and managerial Black women are employed in the public sector. Census data reveal that in fourteen of the fifteen Standard Metropolitan Statistical Areas (SMSAs) with the largest Black populations, the majority of Black professional and managerial women are employed in the public sector (see Table 6.1).[2] In each of the same fifteen metropoli-

**Table 6.1.** Sectoral Distribution of Women Managerial and Professional Specialty Workers for Fifteen SMSAs, 1980

| SMSA | Black | | | | Non-Black | | | |
|---|---|---|---|---|---|---|---|---|
| | N | Public (%) | Private (%) | Other (%)[a] | N | Public (%) | Private (%) | Other (%) |
| Atlanta | 18,479 | 55.7 | 42.5 | 1.8 | 81,998 | 34.8 | 60.3 | 4.9 |
| Baltimore | 19,902 | 72.3 | 26.9 | 0.8 | 79,351 | 40.4 | 55.1 | 4.4 |
| Chicago | 44,066 | 53.8 | 44.8 | 1.4 | 268,359 | 26.6 | 69.0 | 4.4 |
| Cleveland | 10,835 | 53.8 | 44.0 | 2.1 | 65,049 | 30.0 | 65.9 | 4.1 |
| Dallas | 11,308 | 54.8 | 42.6 | 2.6 | 122,666 | 32.2 | 62.0 | 5.8 |
| Detroit | 24,257 | 59.3 | 39.1 | 1.5 | 127,661 | 33.7 | 62.1 | 4.2 |
| Houston | 19,418 | 55.5 | 42.4 | 2.1 | 114,954 | 30.8 | 63.5 | 5.7 |
| Los Angeles | 36,119 | 47.6 | 49.3 | 3.1 | 299,395 | 27.3 | 64.9 | 7.9 |
| Memphis | 9,040 | 71.7 | 27.0 | 1.3 | 26,633 | 34.6 | 60.3 | 5.1 |
| Miami | 9,679 | 60.3 | 38.2 | 1.5 | 59,261 | 26.7 | 66.9 | 6.4 |
| Newark | 14,208 | 55.2 | 43.6 | 1.2 | 78,532 | 33.5 | 62.1 | 4.4 |
| New Orleans | 11,446 | 65.8 | 32.8 | 1.4 | 36,259 | 31.5 | 63.7 | 4.9 |
| New York | 67,026 | 49.3 | 48.8 | 1.8 | 697,395 | 34.4 | 59.8 | 5.8 |
| Philadelphia | 25,273 | 56.0 | 42.2 | 1.8 | 164,890 | 29.2 | 65.6 | 4.6 |
| St. Louis | 12,939 | 58.2 | 40.3 | 1.4 | 81,959 | 29.3 | 66.3 | 4.4 |
| Mean Percentage | 15.4 | 57.9 | 40.3 | 1.7 | 84.6 | 31.7 | 63.2 | 5.1 |

[a]Includes self-employed and unpaid family workers.
Source: U.S. Bureau of the Census, *Census of Population 1980*, vol. 1, *Characteristics of the Population* (Washington, D.C.: U.S. Government Printing Office, 1983), ch. D, "Detailed Population Characteristics," Table 220.

tan areas, the majority of White professional and managerial women were employed in the private sector.[3]

For example, in the Memphis metropolitan area, Black women are about 25.3 percent of the females employed in professional and managerial occupations, and 71.7 percent are employed in the public sector; only 34.5 percent of White professional and managerial women are so employed. Likewise, 60.4 percent of White professional and managerial women work in the private sector, while only 27 percent of Black women in those same occupations do so. This is a common pattern for both Northern and Southern cities.

In the metropolitan area of Newark, New Jersey, Black women constitute 15 percent of women employed in professional and managerial occupations. In 1980, 55.2 percent of these Black women worked in the public sector, while only 33.7 percent of White professional and managerial women did so. And 61.8 percent of White women worked in the private sector, while only 43.6 percent of the Black professional and managerial women did. This is very interesting, in light of the fact that about the same percentages of Black and White professional and managerial women in the Newark metropolitan area are teachers, counselors, and librarians (34 percent)—they are just employed in different sectors. While 82.1 percent of the Black teachers, librarians, and counselors in Newark are employed in the public sector, 70.3 percent of the White women in the same occupations are employed there (Higginbotham 1987).

In the New York City metropolitan area, Black professional women are more evenly distributed in public (49.3 percent) and private (48.8 percent) sector work. With many corporate headquarters and larger numbers of private schools, social service agencies, and hospitals, one might expect that Black women would have more options in the private sector than might be found in either Newark or Memphis. But White women also have these options. In the Big Apple, only 26.6 percent of White professional and managerial women were employed in the public sector and 66.5 percent were in the private sector. New York ranks third, behind Chicago and Miami, in the concentration of White professional and managerial women in the private sector. The figures for other cities in the nation are similar, with only a slight regional variation—Southern cities have somewhat higher concentrations of Black professional women in public sector employment. Los Angeles is the only city where the majority of Black professional women are in the private sector.

The 1980 census indicates that many educated Black women are working as professionals and managers, but they are mostly likely to be public school teachers, city and county health advocates, city welfare workers, public librarians, city attorneys, public defenders, city and county managers and administrators, and faculty members of public community, and four-year colleges and universities. Professional Black women are less likely to work for major corporate law firms, teach at private educational institutions on any level, or serve on the medical staff of private hospitals than are their White counterparts. These data encourage us to ask questions about the nature and extent of progress for Black professional women.

The search for explanations of the continued clustering of Black professional and managerial women in the public sector reveals two major factors. First, educated Black women continue to be concentrated in traditionally female occupations—jobs that are primarily dependent upon the public sector for employment. Indeed, the majority of our teachers, librarians, social workers, and so forth are employed by city, state, and county governments. In Southern cities, outside of Atlanta and Miami, professional and managerial women, both Black and White, are clustered in traditionally female occupations, especially primary and secondary school teaching.

The second factor is racism—a racism that persists from an earlier era but takes on new forms in this post–Civil Rights age (Omi and Winant 1987). The distribution of employed Black and White professional and managerial women in public and private sectors provides the means for examining differences in the structural barriers women face in the labor market.

## A Decade of Progress?

An examination of 1970 census data on the sector distribution of Black and non-Black women for the same fifteen SMSAs reveals that in fourteen of the fifteen SMSAs used in the previous analysis, the majority of Black professional women were employed in the public sector, while the majority of non-Black women were found in the private sector (see Table 6.2). In 1970, it was New York, not Los Angeles, that was the exception. For the same fifteen SMSAs, the mean percent of Black women in the public sector was 61.5, 3.6 percentage points higher than the 1980 mean. In 1970, the mean percentage of non-Black professional and managerial specialty women in the public sector was 37.8, 6.1 percentage points higher than the 1980 figures for non-Blacks. Thus a comparison of the 1970 and 1980 census figures, even with the limitations of the data, indicates that a smaller percent-

**Table 6.2.** Sectoral Distribution of Women Managerial and Professional Workers for Fifteen SMSAs, 1970

| SMSA | Black | | | | Non-Black | | | |
|---|---|---|---|---|---|---|---|---|
| | N | Public (%) | Private (%) | Other (%)ᵃ | N | Public (%) | Private (%) | Other (%) |
| Atlanta | 6,973 | 68.5 | 29.0 | 2.5 | 37,105 | 43.0 | 50.6 | 6.1 |
| Baltimore | 10,461 | 72.6 | 24.4 | 2.9 | 45,591 | 45.0 | 49.2 | 5.8 |
| Chicago | 21,239 | 59.2 | 38.0 | 2.7 | 162,771 | 34.3 | 60.5 | 5.2 |
| Cleveland | 6,390 | 59.4 | 36.2 | 4.4 | 45,162 | 37.3 | 57.6 | 5.1 |
| Dallas | 4,709 | 51.8 | 42.9 | 5.3 | 40,668 | 34.9 | 56.8 | 8.4 |
| Detroit | 12,920 | 57.8 | 39.2 | 3.0 | 80,224 | 41.3 | 53.3 | 5.4 |
| Houston | 7,516 | 53.0 | 41.1 | 5.9 | 47,090 | 35.7 | 55.4 | 8.9 |
| Los Angeles | 17,429 | 58.0 | 37.4 | 4.6 | 194,433 | 36.2 | 54.8 | 9.0 |
| Memphis | 4,772 | 76.8 | 20.0 | 3.2 | 14,742 | 43.1 | 49.5 | 7.4 |
| Miami | 3,120 | 68.9 | 27.7 | 3.4 | 30,161 | 34.0 | 57.8 | 8.2 |
| Newark | 6,550 | 55.9 | 40.7 | 3.4 | 46,450 | 40.4 | 53.9 | 5.7 |
| New Orleans | 5,450 | 68.5 | 28.6 | 2.9 | 21,331 | 34.4 | 57.1 | 8.5 |
| New York | 41,131 | 49.2 | 47.5 | 3.3 | 317,389 | 36.5 | 57.1 | 6.3 |
| Philadelphia | 14,772 | 58.7 | 38.3 | 3.1 | 106,796 | 35.2 | 58.4 | 6.4 |
| St. Louis | 7,357 | 63.8 | 33.2 | 3.0 | 54,666 | 36.0 | 56.0 | 5.9 |
| Mean Percentage | 13.7 | 61.5 | 34.9 | 3.6 | 86.3 | 37.8 | 55.2 | 6.8 |

ᵃIncludes self-employed and unpaid family workers.
Source: U.S. Bureau of the Census, Census of Population 1970, vol. 1, Characteristics of the Population (Washington, D.C.: U.S. Government Printing Office, 1973), "Detailed Population Characteristics," Table 173.

age of professional and managerial women, both Black and White, are employed in the public sector.

Table 6.3 reports the percentage point change in the sector distribution of women in professional and managerial specialty occupations between 1970 and 1980 for the fifteen SMSAs. The last column reveals that there have been small but significant gains in the percentage of Black women employed in professional and managerial positions. These data reinforce other findings about the progress Black women made during the decade (Sokoloff 1988, 1992; Westcott 1982). But a closer look at the percentage increases and decreases in the public and private sectors indicates that change is not uniform for all professional and managerial women.

In the majority of the metropolitan areas, the percentages of non-Black women (the majority of this population is White, but it includes Asian American, Latina, and Native American women) in the private sector have grown considerably. This progress is due to the entrance of women into traditionally male occupations, which are more likely to be found in the private sector, and increasing opportunities to perform traditionally female work in the private sector (private schools, private hospitals, and private colleges and universities).

Even in Memphis, private sector employment for White professional and managerial women increased by 10.8 percentage points.[4] A few other cities also witnessed significant growth in the percentages of non-Black women in the private sector: 10.3 percentage points for St. Louis, 11.1 percentage points for Miami, 8.8 in Detroit, and in many other metropolitan areas, increases in the range of five to nine percentage points. The mean percentage point increase in private sector employment for non-Black women across the fifteen SMSAs was 8.15.

Black professional and managerial women have also made serious inroads into the private sector since 1970. Yet, in all but two metropolitan areas, their progress lags behind their non-Black sisters. Only in Atlanta and Los Angeles did Black women have larger percentage point increases in private sector employment than did non-Black women. Both of these are Sunbelt cities where there were large increases in private sector employment for non-Black women as well.

The more common pattern saw smaller changes for Black women than non-Black women. Houston, another Sunbelt city, had a small increase for Black women (1.3 percentage points), but a significant shift of 8.1 percentage points for non-Black women. In Baltimore, Newark, New York, and Philadelphia, Black professional and managerial women had percentage point increases below 4. In the metropolitan areas of Chicago, Memphis, and Cleveland, Black professional women

**Table 6.3.** Percent Change in the Sectoral Distribution of Women Managerial/Professional Specialty Workers for Fifteen SMSAs, 1970–1980

| SMSA | Public | | Private | | Other[a] | | Total Change |
|---|---|---|---|---|---|---|---|
| | Black | Non-Black | Black | Non-Black | Black | Non-Black | Black[b] |
| Atlanta | -12.8 | -8.2 | +13.5 | + 9.7 | -0.7 | -1.2 | +2.6 |
| Baltimore | - 0.3 | -0.6 | + 2.5 | + 5.9 | -2.1 | -1.4 | +1.3 |
| Chicago | - 5.4 | -7.6 | + 6.8 | + 8.3 | -1.3 | -0.8 | +2.6 |
| Cleveland | - 5.6 | -7.3 | + 7.8 | + 8.3 | -2.3 | -1.0 | +1.9 |
| Dallas | + 3.0 | -2.7 | - 0.3 | + 5.2 | -2.7 | -2.6 | -0.7 |
| Detroit | + 1.5 | -7.6 | - 0.1 | + 8.8 | -1.5 | -1.2 | +2.1 |
| Houston | + 2.5 | -4.9 | + 1.3 | + 8.1 | -3.8 | -3.2 | +0.6 |
| Los Angeles | -10.4 | -8.9 | +11.9 | +11.1 | -1.5 | -1.1 | +2.6 |
| Memphis | - 5.1 | -8.5 | + 7.0 | +10.8 | -1.9 | -2.3 | +0.9 |
| Miami | - 8.6 | -7.3 | +10.5 | +11.1 | -1.9 | -1.8 | +4.6 |
| Newark | - 0.7 | -6.9 | + 2.9 | + 8.2 | -2.2 | -1.3 | +2.9 |
| New Orleans | - 2.7 | -2.9 | + 4.2 | + 6.6 | -1.5 | -3.6 | +3.7 |
| New York | + 0.1 | -2.1 | + 1.3 | + 2.7 | -1.5 | -0.5 | -2.7 |
| Philadelphia | - 2.7 | -6.0 | + 3.9 | + 7.2 | -1.3 | -1.8 | +1.1 |
| St. Louis | - 5.6 | -6.7 | + 7.1 | +10.3 | -1.6 | -1.5 | +1.7 |
| Mean Percentage | - 3.2 | -5.9 | + 5.4 | + 8.2 | -1.8 | -1.6 | +1.7 |

[a]Includes self-employed and unpaid family workers.
[b]Represents percentage point change in Black/non-Black composition of all women managerial and professional specialty workers.

increased their percentages in private sector employment by 6.8, 7.0, and 7.8, respectively. Table 6.3 provides evidence that Black women are moving out of public sector employment in many metropolitan areas, but that movement is slower than that of their non-Black counterparts. The mean percentage point increase in private sector employment for Black women across the fifteen SMSAs is 5.4, considerably lower than the figure for non-Black women of 8.2

In two SMSAs, the concentration of Black managerial and professional specialty women in the private sector declined. In Dallas, the percent of Black women in these occupations who were employed in the private sector declined by 0.3 percentage point while non-Black women increased by 5.2 percentage points. In Detroit, Black women's concentration in the private sector declined by 0.1 percentage point while non-Black women's concentration in the private sector increased by 8.8 percentage points. It is evident that educated White women made more significant progress than educated Black women. Racism does not disappear when one gets an education and a middle-class occupation. These data provide one means of detailing the racial constraints faced by Black women in professional and managerial employment.

## Conclusion

Black women as well as White women are gaining access to education in traditionally male fields. Once they finish this training, they enter a racist and sexist labor market. With only one major discriminatory barrier, more White than Black women are able to enter the private sector. Thus, some research indicates that dominant culture women are moving into the upper levels of the middle class while Black women are lagging behind (Landry 1987). Black women, even with advanced degrees, still struggle with racial discrimination and informal barriers to occupational advancement. Instead of the myth of the advantages of being a double minority, both Black and female (Epstein 1972), Fulbright's (1986) research indicates that there are no advantages to being both Black and female for managers; instead, there are additional constraints. The case can also be made for Black women in traditionally female fields. Even when women remain in traditionally female occupations, White women are able to practice these professions in the private sector, especially private schools and agencies (Higginbotham 1987).

Both gender and racial discrimination play a role in the occupational distribution of Black women. First, Black women continue to be steered into training for traditionally female occupations and discouraged from attempting innovative careers. Thus, their professional training keeps them dependent upon the public sector for employment as teachers, social workers, nurses, and librarians. Second, rigid racial barriers that limit Black people's employment options in the private sector, in both male- and female-dominated occupations, keep their numbers in the private sector low. Therefore more Black women, even those trained in traditionally male fields, find jobs in the public sector because there is less discrimination in hiring in this segment of the labor market.

These data prompt many other questions about the quality of work life for Black professional and managerial women. What does it mean to be employed in the public sector in metropolitan areas today? In the light of city, county, and state fiscal problems and reduced commitments to human services, the prospects appear grim. Many public school teachers are demanding more police protection in the schools and the institutionalization of faculty and student identification cards, as well as insisting upon smaller class sizes and more materials. In many urban communities there are additional demands to raise teachers' salaries and provide greater fringe benefits, but on the whole, working conditions are equally critical work issues for many primary and secondary public school faculty members.

In the light of these tensions and the decreasing desirability of public schools as places to work, many Black teachers are finding they have few alternatives in the labor market. Many are returning to universities for retraining to increase their employment options. Others are redefining their goals and planning to work their twenty, twenty-five, or thirty years until retirement—with the hope that the financial cushion of a pension will enable them to begin second careers.

Similar issues confront human service workers in health and social service agencies. Budget cuts have resulted in significant reductions in staffing—leaving the remaining employees with high caseloads and impossible tasks. Such individuals are lucky to be able to keep their jobs during an era when the delivery of services to poor and working-class people is not a priority. Yet they face daily frustrations on the job. As the data suggest, many of professional and managerial people working under such conditions are Black women and other people of color.

These current realities suggest that public sector professional employment, especially for women in traditionally female occupations, is not the prize it appeared to be in the 1950s and 1960s (Block et al. 1987). In an earlier age, women employed as teachers, social workers, and nurses in public schools and city agencies had excellent salaries, decent fringe benefits, and vacations. They also could easily return to their professions after their childbearing years. Even where professional public sector employees have been able to keep their wages on a par with private sector employees in their metropolitan areas, the conditions of work have deteriorated. These realities may provide the motivation to leave the public sector. If so, we must ask if each public sector professional employee has the same chance of securing comparable work in the private sector. These data suggest that White women might be more successful in seeking new employment options outside the public sector.

These data should encourage detailed investigations of the progress of Black, White, Latina, Asian American, and Native American professional and managerial women in the private sector. As a nation, we celebrate the impact of the Civil Rights and women's movements and the passage of federal guidelines in opening corporate doors for women and racial minorities, yet these gains are fragile in the face of indifferent federal administrations (Collins 1983). Given these shifts, how do professional and managerial women survive in the private sector? Perhaps a major obstacle for many is gaining access to private sector jobs.

The racial barriers faced by educated Black women are different from the blanket opposition to hiring Black people in professional and managerial positions that characterized the early part of this century. There has been significant progress in both access to higher education and employment options. The persistence of racism can result in a middle class that is segmented along racial lines. Black professionals, managers, and administrators are clustered in the public sector. In their positions they serve clients in public schools, local welfare agencies, public hospitals, public defender's offices, and other human service agencies. Many of these clients are poor and working class, and many are Black people or other people of color. Meanwhile, non-Black women (especially White women) are increasing their numbers in private sector employment. Are Black professionals, particularly women, trapped in public sector employment? In these middle-class positions, are they professionals relegated to jobs, wages, and working conditions that mirror the racial segmentation in traditional working-class occupations?

I addressed the persistence of racial restrictions in the employment options for Black professional and managerial women. Indeed, the findings suggest that one way to explore racial discrimination is to observe racial differences in access to jobs in employment sectors. There are many other issues that merit exploration, especially the day-to-day experiences of Black and other women of color in professional and managerial positions in different occupations and sectors.

With a grounding in theory—especially a theoretical approach that recognizes that racism is still with us—and with solid empirical tools, we can build an exemplary scholarship of people of color across social class lines. Armed with both theory and data, we can uncover evidence that highlights the intersection of race, gender, and class. This scholarship can praise the diligence and persistence of female and male members of the Afro-American community. It can also portray the costs of racism for this population. Knowledge such as this will help us know ourselves and understand the larger problems that we confront as we continue to struggle against racism and sexism in all their forms.

## Notes

*Acknowledgments*: I wish to thank Lynn Weber, Betty Wiley, Jobe Henry, Jr., and Sandra Marion for their help in preparing this chapter. I would also like to acknowledge the comments of the editors, Maxine Baca Zinn and Bonnie Thornton Dill.

1. This discussion does not include Black women who are in the middle class solely by virtue of marriage. Black women married to professional and managerial men but are not employed in the labor force, faced different circumstances.

2. This study does not include the District of Columbia because it is a major metropolitan area where a significant number of all residents are employed in the public sector.

3. In 1970, the data on occupational distribution by SMSA categorized workers as either Black or non-Black; thus, the non-Black figures included Asian American, Latina, and Native American women as well as White women. This makes the status of non–racially oppressed White women difficult to ascertain. Better data on White and Black women are available for 1980 and those data are used here in the text. In Table 6.1, data for Black and non-Black women are used to facilitate comparisons with 1970 data.

4. Memphis has a small Asian American, Latino, and Native American population; thus we can assume that the vast majority of the non-Black population is White.

## References

Amott, Teresa, and Julie A. Matthaei. 1991. *Race, Gender and Work: A Multicultural Economic History of Women in the United States.* Boston: South End Press.

Barrera, Mario. 1979. *Race and Class in the Southwest*. Notre Dame, Ind.: University of Notre Dame Press.

Bascom, Lionel. 1987. "Breaking Through Middle-Management Barrier." *Crisis*, April/May, pp. 13–16, 61, 64.

Block, Fred, Richard Cloward, Barbara Ehrenreich, and Frances Fox Piven. 1987. *The Mean Season: The Attack on the Welfare State*. New York: Pantheon.

Braverman, Harry. 1974. *Labor and Monopoly Capital*. New York: Monthly Review Press.

Collins, Sharon. 1983. "The Making of the Black Middle Class." *Social Problems* 30 (April): 369–382.

Cuthbert, Marion. 1942. *Education and Marginality*. New York: Stratford Press.

Davis, George, and Glegg Watson. 1982. *Black Life in Corporate America*. Garden City, N.Y.: Anchor Press/Doubleday.

Drake, St. Clair, and Horace Cayton. 1970. *Black Metropolis*. New York: Harper Torchbooks.

Ehrenreich, Barbara, and John Ehrenreich. 1979. "The Professional and Managerial Class." Pp. 5–25 in *Between Labor and Capital*, Pat Walker, ed. Boston: South End Press.

Epstein, Cynthia F. 1973. "The Positive Effect of the Multiple Negative: Explaining the Success of Professional Black Women." *American Journal of Sociology* 78 (January): 912–933.

Fulbright, Karen. 1986. "The Myth of the Double-Advantage: Black Female Managers." Pp. 33–45 in *Slipping Through the Cracks: The Status of Black Women*, Margaret C. Simm and Julianne Malveaux, eds. New Brunswick, N.J.: Transaction Press.

Higginbotham, Elizabeth. 1987. "Employment for Black Professional Women in the Twentieth Century." Pp. 73–91 in *Ingredients for Women's Employment Policy*, Christine Bose and Glenna Spitze, eds. Albany: State University of New York Press.

Hine, Darlene Clark. 1989. *Black Women in White: Racial Conflict and Cooperation in the Nursing Profession, 1890–1950*. Bloomington: Indiana University Press.

Johnson, Charles. 1969. *The Negro College Graduate*. College Park, Md.: McGrath.

Jones, Barbara A. P. 1986. "Black Women and Labor Force Participation: An Analysis of Sluggish Growth Rates." Pp. 11–31 in *Slipping Through the Cracks: The Status of Black Women*, Margaret C. Simm and Julianne Malveaux, eds. New Brunswick, N.J.: Transaction Press.

Jones, Jacqueline. 1985. *Labor of Love, Labor of Sorrow: Black Women, Work and the Family from Slavery to the Present*. New York: Basic Books.

Kilson, Marion. 1977. "Black Women in the Professions." *Monthly Labor Review* 100 (May): 38–41.

Landry, Bart. 1987. *The New Black Middle Class.* Berkeley: University of California Press.

Noble, Jeanne. 1956. *The Negro Women's College Education.* New York: Teachers College, Columbia University.

Omi, Michael, and Howard Winant. 1987. *Racial Formation in the United States.* New York: Routledge.

Poulantzas, Nicos. 1974. *Classes in Contemporary Society.* London: New Left Books.

Sokoloff, Natalie. 1987. "Black and White Women in the Professions: A Contradictory Process." Pp. 53–72 in *Ingredients for Women's Employment Policy.* Christine Bose and Glenna Spitze, eds. Albany: State University of New York Press.

———. 1988. "Evaluating Gains and Losses of Black and White Women and Men in the Professions, 1960–1980." *Social Problems* 35 (February): 36–53.

———. 1992. *Black Women and White Women in the Professions.* New York: Routledge.

Tyack, David B. 1974. *The One Best System: A History of American Education.* Cambridge, Mass.: Harvard University Press.

United States Bureau of the Census. 1973. *Census of Population 1970.* Vol. 1, *Characteristics of the Population.* Washington, D.C.: U.S. Government Printing Office.

———. 1983. *Census of Population 1980.* Vol. 1, *Characteristics of the Population.* Washington, D.C.: U.S. Government Printing Office.

United States Department of Labor, Bureau of Labor Statistics. 1984. *Employment and Earnings* 31 (December). Washington, D.C.: U.S. Government Printing Office.

Vanneman, Reeve, and Lynn Weber Cannon. 1987. *The American Perception of Class.* Philadelphia: Temple University Press.

Walker, Pat, ed. 1979. *Between Labor and Capital.* Boston: South End Press.

Wallace, Phyllis. 1980. *Black Women in the Labor Force.* Cambridge, Mass.: MIT Press.

Westcott, Diane Nilsen. 1982. "Blacks in the 1970's: Did They Scale the Job Ladder?" *Monthly Labor Review* 105 (June): 29–38.

# 7

## Puerto Rican Families
## and Social Well-Being

### Ruth E. Zambrana

This chapter provides a brief overview of the sociocultural and historical conditions contributing to the health status of Puerto Rican women living in the mainland United States. It specifically examines quality-of-life indicators such as educational attainment, housing conditions, reproductive health, and related concerns in the Puerto Rican population. The primary sources used are empirical data collected by federal, state, and local agencies.[1] Since data are limited for this population group, I also draw from my own experiences, observations, and related work in the field on poverty and racial-ethnic women to discuss major areas of concern for this group, particularly in reference to family functioning, health behaviors, and survival strategies.

### Profile of Puerto Rican Women
### in the United States

The largest numbers of Puerto Ricans migrated to the mainland United States in the 1950s and 1960s. This was unlike the earlier period of the arrival of European immigrants, when industry was expanding (Sandis 1973).

The Puerto Rican migration to the United States has created a Puerto Rican diaspora or a "divided nation." By 1970, one out of every three Puerto Ricans was living in the mainland United States (Almquist 1979:81). The situation has been further compounded by the back-and-forth migration of those who become disillusioned with living in the mainland United States. Many women returned to Puerto Rico because of difficulty finding employment and suitable child care.[2] Clara Rodriguez, Virginia Sanchez Korrol, and Jose Alers (1980:2) suggest that this back-and-forth migration "reflects repeated ruptures and renewals of ties, dismantling and reconstructions of familial and communal networks in old and new settings." All these factors contribute to a sense of rootlessness and have implications for a community's ability to build leadership and a strong institutional base. Thus the lack of stability and the depressed economic situation among Puerto Rican women and their families contribute significantly to adverse health conditions.

Puerto Rican women, who represent 13.1 percent of Latina women, are distinguished by several economic, historical, and political conditions that have influenced their status and shaped their experiences in the mainland United States. Characteristics that distinguish Puerto Rican women from other groups are that the majority are very young (half the population is below the age of twenty-five) and in their reproductive years. High fertility rates have contributed to the growth of this population because Puerto Rican females, much like Mexican women, tend to have their children at an earlier age than non-Latinos. Puerto Ricans are second to Mexicans in having a larger-than-median family size, 3.62 (U.S. Bureau of the Census 1988). Except for Cubans, Puerto Rican women are the most highly urbanized of all minority groups. Over 75 percent of Puerto Rican women live in the Northeast, primarily in New York City (50.5 percent) and urban New Jersey (12.1 percent). Overall, 65 percent of all Puerto Ricans in the continental United States live in the tristate region of New York, New Jersey, and Connecticut.

An analysis of the sociodemographic characteristics of Puerto Rican women quickly reveals that as a group they are characterized as a vulnerable or an "at risk" population for unfavorable health status. As a group, Puerto Ricans have the lowest income level of any Latino group (median family income is $12,371), the highest poverty rate (41.9 percent, which exceeds that of the Black community), and the lowest labor force participation rates for males (66.9 percent) and females (39 percent). In fact, between 1959 and 1984, the Puerto Rican mean family income decreased by approximately 25 percent, a rate twice that of Blacks and higher than any other Latino group (Tienda and Jensen 1988:47).

Forty-four percent of Puerto Rican households are headed by single females, the highest rate of all groups living in the United States; 74 percent of these women are living below the poverty level (U.S. Bureau of the Census 1985). Joan Moore and Harry Pachon (1985:104) listed problems such as language barriers, newly arrived status, and cultural norms that regulate women's roles to remain mothers and homemakers, but state that these explanations ignore the fact that the condition of Puerto Rican women has gradually worsened since the 1970s.

## DECLINING DEMAND FOR LABOR

The decreased labor force participation and subsequent low socio-economic conditions are due in great part to structural factors. New York City has suffered the greatest decline in industries in which Puerto Rican women historically have been employed. The reduction in the continental United States of light manufacturing industry, such as the garment industry, where Puerto Rican women have traditionally been employed, has contributed greatly to decreased work opportunities for these women. Urban flight and automation have had a profound impact on the economic condition and work status of Puerto Rican women. This downward spiral of job availability in the manufacturing sector has continued into the 1980s (Gray 1978; Cooney 1979; Ortiz 1986).

## EDUCATIONAL ATTAINMENT AND EMPLOYMENT

The educational profile of Puerto Rican women helps to explain their concentration in the lowest-paying and least stable sectors of the economy. The two groups with the lowest levels of schooling in the United States are foreign-born Mexicans, who average approximately eleven years, and Puerto Ricans, who average approximately eight years (Mare and Winship 1988:181). Puerto Ricans have relatively low high-school completion rates, with only 54.3 percent of men and 52.7 percent of the women achieving high school graduation. These rates are well below the average for American Indian women (71.1 percent), Black women (74.7 percent), and White women (87.6 percent) (Mare and Winship 1988:182).

Puerto Ricans attend highly segregated schools. Minority student enrollment in New York, New Jersey, and Connecticut systems may be as high as 90 to 100 percent. In 1984, the schools in these three states educated 12 percent of the nation's Latino children but accounted for only 9 percent of the high school graduates (Latino Commission of Tri-State 1988:24).

Changing requirements of the labor market from industrial sector to service sector favor more educated groups, thereby limiting Puerto Rican women's access to jobs. Upgrading of work-related educational requirements makes it difficult for Puerto Ricans with low educational attainment to compete in the job market. Lower educational levels limit upward mobility and access to even low-income housing.

## HOUSING IN NEW YORK CITY

Puerto Ricans are clustered in some of the worst housing in the city. Housing availability has been connected to the need for a labor pool. In the 1950s, when labor demands were high, subsidized and public housing was available to Puerto Ricans. This situation changed with the decreasing demand for unskilled labor as industries moved to the suburbs, to the South, or abroad for a cheaper labor pool in the 1960s. In the future New York City will be dependent on a racial labor pool (Rodriguez 1989).

## Poverty, Gender, and Health: An Overview

Low income is related to poor health status. Health, defined as the physical and mental well-being of an individual, has been found to be highly related to education, income, coping behaviors, and lifestyle factors (including nutritional status, environmental conditions, use of alcohol and drugs, smoking behaviors, and social-support networks).

Latinos, like other low-income people, experience more illness, higher death rates, and more accidents and injuries than nonpoor people (Perales and Young 1987). Fernando Trevino, Eugene Moyer, Robert Burciago-Valdez, and Christine Stroup-Benham (1991) found that Blacks, Puerto Ricans, and Cuban Americans were almost twice as likely as Whites not to have health insurance; Mexican Americans were three and one-half times as likely not to have health insurance. Latinos who more frequently report poor health usually do not have a regular source of health care.

### REPRODUCTIVE HEALTH

Latino women, who tend to have higher fertility rates, have children at a younger age than the rest of the U.S. population. They also have larger families. Many do not have adequate health care, especially during pregnancies. Prenatal care can be very important to the health of the mother and child because it provides screening, assessment of risk conditions, and information on appropriate health practices, self-care, and nutrition. Health professionals find that prenatal care is a cost-effective intervention.

Delayed prenatal care (its initiation in the third trimester) represents a major risk because medical problems, if they exist, cannot be identified early enough to prevent infant mortality and morbidity.

Puerto Rican women, who have the highest rate of delayed prenatal care (16 percent) among Latino groups, four times the rate of White women (4 percent), have less access to prenatal care. The infant mortality rate for Puerto Rican women is 9.1 per 1000, almost double the rate for White and Mexican American women.

Furthermore, one out of every ten Puerto Rican infants is born with low birth weight (LBW), 5.5 pounds or less (Ventura 1988). LBW infants are twenty times more likely to die in the first year of life. If they survive the first year, they are at significantly greater risk of developing long-term disabilities such as cerebral palsy, autism, developmental lags, and mental retardation (Children's Defense Fund 1987).

Numerous studies suggest that a combination of social risk factors contributes to delayed prenatal care (Brown 1988; Institute of Medicine 1985; Alan Guttmacher Institute 1987). Social risk factors pertinent to Puerto Rican women include low educational levels, single parent-hood, and psychosocial conditions such as frequent stressful life events and low social support from the baby's father. Among Puerto Rican women, additional factors, such as poor nutrition and use of drugs, alcohol, and cigarettes, may negatively influence the health of mother and infant.

Early childbearing can have serious consequences for many women. Katherine Darabi and Vilma Ortiz (1987) report that women's life chances are seriously impeded by early childbearing. Among Puerto Rican women close to 20 percent have children before they reach twenty years of age. Young Puerto Rican adolescent females have less access to institutional and family resources. As a result, they are least likely to return to school or to afford child care in order to work. Adolescent childbearing and other reproductive health issues, such as cervical cancer and a lack of access to health care services, constitute serious health concerns among Puerto Rican women.

Iris Lopez (1987) found that among adult Puerto Rican women, sterilization has historically been a serious concern due to institutional abuse and lack of options. By 1982 the rate of sterilization among Puerto Rican women in Puerto Rico was 39 percent (Vasquez-Calzada 1988). In New York City, Puerto Rican women had a sterilization rate seven times greater than White women and almost three times greater than Black women (Lopez, 1987).

Further, Puerto Rican women were used as experimental subjects in early clinical trials of birth control pills, intrauterine devices, and Emko contraceptive cream in the 1950s. A long-range consequence of this experimentation has been a high rate of cervical cancer. The risk of cervical cancer appears to be further increased due to childbearing at an earlier age coupled with a high fertility rate.

Historically Puerto Rican women have been at a disadvantage in their interaction with a medical system that is predominantly male, upper middle class, and White. Their vulnerability in the medical care system has been compounded by their low educational levels, limited English-language proficiency, and low levels of knowledge of medical protocols. These characteristics have increased barriers to their access to health services—that is, they are less likely to obtain a preventive annual checkup for themselves or their children. Furthermore, Puerto Ricans have experienced negative interactions with providers in the health care system. For example, Marsha Hurst and Ruth E. Zambrana (1980) found that urban Puerto Rican mothers perceived health care providers as treating them poorly, not understanding their needs, and not being sensitive to sociocultural behaviors.

## UTILIZATION OF HEALTH SERVICES

Researchers have begun to refocus their work from a "blaming the victim" approach to "blaming the system." In this view, population characteristics do not provide explanations for low utilization of health care services among Latinos. Rather, this approach focuses on "institutional barriers" that occur at the level of the provider but are influenced by features of the larger society, such as discrimination, poverty, and immigration law. For example, the high cost of medical care, accessibility difficulties, language barriers, undocumented immigrant status, long waiting lines, lack of transportation, lack of evening and weekend services, lack of child care, and lack of knowledge of available resources are central to understanding health issues among Latino families.

Rosina Becerra and Milton Greenblatt (1983) point out that "intraorganizational" factors, such as the "growing bureaucratization of medical organizations," affect utilization in ways, such as decreased "personalized" medical care, that discourage the use of health services by low-income minority populations.

Aida Giachello (1988) emphasizes that the lack of "usual source of care" for Latinos is related to the ineligibility of this population to access government-sponsored medical programs or private insurance. She explains that social class, rather than cultural and ethnicity factors, is the reason for lower utilization rates among the Latino population. Further, the pattern of low use of health services, as a result of limited access to these services, is especially problematic during pregnancy.

At present, limited information is available on the health needs of Puerto Rican women and their families. Researchers continue to neglect this group's needs. Evidence suggests that individual attributes of Puerto Rican women do not account for their patterns of health care use. Rather, significant barriers associated with the current health care system—such as lack of health insurance and poor provider–patient communication—strongly influence the patterns of health care use among women. Current knowledge in this area suggests that the health of Puerto Rican women seriously affects, and is affected by, their socioeconomic position in society.

## LIFESTYLE PRACTICES AND COMMUNITY HEALTH

Positive lifestyle practices, defined as individual and collective behaviors that promote and sustain favorable health status, receive limited attention among most low-income racial and ethnic populations. Positive lifestyle behaviors include six to eight hours of sleep, regular exercise, abstinence from cigarettes and drugs, a low-cholesterol diet, increased intake of fruits and vegetables, and limited alcohol intake. Among Puerto Ricans, limited economic means and a lack of knowledge in these areas may contribute to poor health status. Furthermore, among Puerto Rican women, the lifestyle behaviors of children, extended kin, and partners may be significant factors contributing to family stress.

Many Puerto Rican women may be dealing with alcohol and drug problems because of alcohol and drug consumption among Puerto Rican men. Raul Caetano (1986) found strong evidence that Puerto Rican men exceed the general population in alcohol and drug abuse. The stresses of poverty and cultural changes, combined with disruption of family, language barriers, and discrimination, may lead to heavy drinking and alcoholism. Nine percent of Latino men report that drinking has had harmful effects on home life, whereas only 6 percent of Black men and 4 percent of White men report this problem. These data suggest that a number of Puerto Rican women may be living with alcohol- and drug-related problems. For many women this represents living in a chronic state of stress.

In the United States, 20 percent of all women who are HIV positive are Latinas. These women are concentrated in New York, New Jersey, Florida, and Puerto Rico (where the majority of the Latino population is Puerto Rican). Eighty-eight percent of Latinas with AIDS have sex partners who are intravenous drug users, bisexual, or HIV infected (Centers for Disease Control 1988). A direct health consequence of substance use and abuse is the transmission of AIDS from partner to mother and mother to child at birth. The risk to the future generation of Puerto Rican children is very high, with an estimated 30–50 percent probability of mother–child transmission of HIV infection in cases where the mother is HIV positive (Centers for Disease Control 1988).

## RESISTANCE AND SURVIVAL

Factors previously mentioned cannot totally explain the status of Puerto Ricans because they fail to acknowledge the contribution that racial prejudice makes to occupational stratification under capitalism (Sotomayor 1988). Many Puerto Ricans are of mixed ancestry—White, Black, and Native American—as a result of the colonial and racial history of the island (Rodriguez 1989). The author suggests that perceptual incongruence results when a racially mixed, culturally homogeneous group enters a larger, culturally and racially distinct and divided group (Rodriguez 1989). Though racial diversity and economic conditions have greatly influenced the status of Puerto Rican women and their families, many Puerto Rican families have strong natural support systems.

## NATURAL SUPPORT SYSTEMS

"Natural-support system" is used to differentiate such systems from the professional care-giving systems of the community. Natural support systems include family and friendship groups, local, informal caregivers, voluntary service groups not directed by caregiving professionals, and mutual-help groups (Delgado and Humm-Delgado 1982; De La Rosa, 1988).

Melvin Delgado and Denise Humm-Delgado's (1982) comprehensive examination of natural support systems reveals four important ones in the Latino community: (1) the extended family, (2) folk healers, (3) religious institutions, and (4) merchants and social clubs that function totally or partially to help individuals in distress.

The extended family is defined as the primary social support system within the Latino family. Extended family systems, which include relatives and the *compadrazgo* system, represent a critical social support network. Puerto Ricans "are more likely to seek initial assistance from family, friends, or people with special expertise who are known informally through social networks, not an institutional representative" (McGowan 1988:57). The Latino family consists of "blood relatives" and a wide-ranging constellation of "adoptive relatives" who fulfill either formal or informal functions within the extended family. Informal members consist of close family friends and neighbors who, over a period of years, prove their willingness to be involved in important family matters and events. The term *como familia* (like family) has been used to describe these individuals.

The ritual kinship process within the Latino family, known as *compadrazgo*, formally includes friends, key neighbors, and distant relatives. It serves to widen and enhance the individual's primary

RUTH E. ZAMBRANA

group by transforming outsiders into family members or more distant relatives into particularly close associates. This ritual kinship process is achieved through an individual's formal participation in one of the following ceremonies: (1) baptism, (2) first Communion, (3) confirmation, or (4) marriage. In many cases religious ceremonies bring families, extended kin, and neighbors together.

A natural support system for Latino individuals in crisis has been organized religion. Roman Catholicism is regarded as the primary religion of Latinos, although its influence has not been as great with some Latino groups, particularly Puerto Ricans. The church has served to channel frustration and aggression that otherwise could not be resolved satisfactorily in situations of emotional stress and life crisis.

Although the church represents a link to the community and community members, folk religion (spiritism) represents an informal natural support system that is an integral part of the infrastructure of the community (Delgado 1988). Its dominant role has been to help individuals and families deal with psychosocial problems such as marital difficulties, intergenerational problems between parent and child, and culturally specific issues, such as auditory or visual experiences.

Among Puerto Ricans in the United States, Melvin Delgado (1988) identifies four types of folk or spiritual healers: (1) spiritists, (2) *santeros*, (3) herbalists, and (4) *santiguadores*. Each healer addresses particular needs experienced by individuals in distress and uses unique, culture-specific methods to diagnose and treat ailments. The spiritist and the *santero* focus primarily on emotional and interpersonal problems; the herbalist and the *santiguador* focus on physical ailments.

These spiritual or cultural healers maintain a balance between the physical and the mental spheres. They may be incorporated into existing mental health and health care systems to enhance the effectiveness of the service and build on the cultural institutions of the community.

Community-based organizations such as mutual-aid associations, merchant organizations, and social clubs offer resources to meet the needs of the communities in which they are located. The three most common merchant and social clubs are (1) *botanicas*, (2) *bodegas*, and (3) *club sociales*. *Botanicas* provide a wide range of herbs and healing paraphernalia, as well as consultations on certain ailments and referrals to local healers. *Bodegas* (grocery stores) meet a variety of Latinos' needs. Some refer people to formal and informal resources such as folk healers. *Club sociales*, predominantly found in Puerto Rican communities, function to provide recreation, orientation for individuals new to the community, and social services such as linkages to housing, employment, and other institutions (Delgado and Humm-Delgado 1982).

These support systems offer intrinsic strength and acceptability in the community. The presence and use of natural support systems reveal sociocultural-based strengths in the Puerto Rican community. However, these inherent strengths should not hinder the development of a delivery system that is culturally sensitive to this population group. Such natural support systems should be encouraged and studied further, to assure that they are reinforced rather than debilitated.

## Research and Policy Implications

A major framework for understanding the lives of Puerto Rican women and their families requires an examination of the denial of civil and legal rights to a group—barriers to societal resources. Puerto Ricans, like other racial-ethnic groups, have been denied quality education and have been given jobs with little opportunity for advancement and upward mobility. Limited options in both the educational and the work setting greatly curtail economic viability and contribute to what has been labeled the urban underclass (Moore 1988). The urban underclass can be most simply interpreted as a group unable to achieve economic viability, which results in a persistent multigenerational cycle of poverty. Some Puerto Ricans have experienced success in some areas, but a significant portion of the group still experiences significant barriers to advancement in this society.

The first step in the solving of any problem is to identify its nature and extent. Surprisingly, little research attention has been directed at the interactive effects of psychosocial factors, socioeconomic status, and consequent health problems that Puerto Rican women experience in both the mainland United States and Puerto Rico.

Researchers need to reframe the questions so as to examine influential changes in the political economy, technology, job opportunities in urban areas, quality of the school system, health, and accessibility to health insurance more effectively. Underlying assumptions regarding racial-ethnic groups, especially Puerto Ricans, need to be examined and challenged in order to assure their more accurate representation. One approach should be a cultural-strength model that focuses on the positive attributes of the culture and its fit with the environment. Researchers need to explore family life as multidimensional, giving attention to how individuals and families develop in response to societal cues.

Researchers must give immediate attention to factors that influence pregnancy outcomes among Puerto Rican women, especially early childbearing among adolescent girls, and to assess chronic disease problems such as diabetes and hypertension—and how the presence of these diseases influences family functioning. Research inquiry also needs to include the health of children and youth: compliance with immunization recommendations/requirements, exposure to AIDS and other communicable diseases, medical care, and related matters.

National and state policies must be geared to enhance the basic quality of life for the group by redressing the inequities in the social structure that persistently deny Puerto Ricans access to basic social welfare services, such as adequate housing, health care, and quality education. Increased social welfare resources would contribute to expanding the life chances of this group. Subsidized housing, a national health insurance program, and the allocation of monetary resources to the school system would certainly initiate a new cycle of opportunity for Puerto Rican women and their families.

# Notes

*Acknowledgments:* I gratefully acknowledge the assistance of Dr. Marilyn Aguirre-Molina for information included in this chapter. I also acknowledge the support of the Agency for Health Care Policy and Research (formerly known as National Center for Health Services Research) (HS/HD #05518–01A1).

1. Latinos, who number 19.4 million, make up 8.1 percent of the U.S. population. From 1980 to 1988, the entire Latino population living in the United States increased by 34 percent (about five million people), compared with 7 percent for the rest of the population (U.S. Bureau of the Census 1988). The Latino population is expected to grow at a rate more than three times that of the total population, reaching twenty-five million by the year 2000, making Latinos the largest racial-ethnic group in the country.

Puerto Ricans are the second largest subgroup of Latinos living in the United States, with an estimated population of 2.5 million. They are also one of the youngest racial minority groups (U.S. Bureau of the Census 1988). The growth of the Latino population in the 1990s has been heralded by some as the "Decade of the Hispanic," but this has been a meaningless phrase for the more than 1.3 million Puerto Rican women living in the continental United States. They make up more than half of the Puerto Rican population (53.3 percent) and comprise the highest percentage of females among any population group (U.S. Bureau of the Census 1985).

2. In 1900, the Foraker Act granted citizenship to all individuals of Puerto Rican birth. At the time, Puerto Rico became a U.S. territory. The island of Puerto Rico is plagued by high rates of poverty (62 percent) and unemployment.

## References

Alan Guttmacher Institute. 1987. *Blessed Events and the Bottom Line: Financing Maternity Care in the United States.* New York: AGI.

Almquist, Elizabeth McTaggert. 1979. *Minorities, Gender and Work.* Lexington, Mass.: Lexington Books.

Becerra, Rosina, and Milton Greenblatt. 1983. *Hispanics Seek Health Care: A Study of 1,000 Veterans of Three War Eras.* Lanham, Md.: University Press of America.

Brown, Sarah S., ed. 1988. *Prenatal Care: Reaching Mothers, Reaching Infants.* Washington, D.C.: National Academy Press.

Caetano, Raul. 1986. "Patterns and Problems of Drinking Among U.S. Hispanics." In U.S. Department of Health and Human Services, Report of the Secretary's Task Force on Black and Minority Health, *Chemical Dependency and Diabetes,* vol. 7, pp. 142–186. Washington, D.C.: U.S. Government Printing Office.

———. 1987. "Acculturation, Drinking and Social Settings Among U.S. Hispanics." *Drug and Alcohol Dependence,* 19 (4): 279–311.

Centers for Disease Control. 1988. "Leading Major Congenital Malformations Among Minority Groups in the United States, 1981–1986." In CDC, *Surveillance Summaries. Morbidity and Mortality Weekly Report* 37 (355): 1755–2455.

Children's Defense Fund 1987. "Health." In *A Children's Defense Budget: An Analysis of FY 1987 Federal Budget and Children,* pp. 100–125. Washington, D.C.: Children's Defense Fund.

Cooney, Rosemary. 1979. "Intercity Variations in Puerto Rican Female Participation." *Journal of Human Resources* 14: 222–235.

Darabi, Katherine, and Vilma Ortiz. 1987. Childbearing Among Young Latino Women in the United States." *American Journal of Public Health,* 77 (1): 25–28.

De La Rosa, Mario. 1988. "Natural Support Systems of Puerto Ricans: A Key Dimension for Well-being." *Health and Social Work* 13 (3): 181–190.

Delgado, Melvin. 1988. "Groups in Puerto Rican Spiritism: Implications for Clinicians." In Carolyn Jacobs and Dorcas D. Bowles, eds., *Ethnicity and Race: Critical Concepts in Social Work*, pp. 34–47. Silver Spring, Md.: National Association of Social Workers.

Delgado, Melvin, and Denise Humm-Delgado. 1982. "Natural Support Systems: A Source of Strength in Hispanic Communities." *Social Work* 27: 81–89.

Falcon, Angelo, Minerva Delgado, and Gerson Borrerro, eds. 1989. *Toward a Puerto Rican-Latino Agenda for New York City*. New York: Institute for Puerto Rican Policy.

Giachello, Aida L. 1985. "Hispanics and Health Care." In Pastora Cafferty and William McCready, eds., *Hispanics in the United States: A New Social Agenda*, pp. 159–194. New Brunswick, N.J.: Transaction Books.

Gray, Lois. 1978. "The Jobs Puerto Ricans Hold in New York City." *Monthly Labor Review* 98: 12–16.

Hurst, Marsha, and Ruth Zambrana. 1980. "The Health Careers of Urban Women: A Study in East Harlem." *Signs: Journal of Women in Culture and Society* 5 (3): S112–126.

Institute of Medicine, Division of Health Promotion and Disease Prevention. 1985. *The Prevention of Low Birthweight*. Washington, D.C.: National Academy Press.

Latino Commission of Tri-State. 1988. *Outlook—The Growing Latino Presence in the Tri-State Region*. New York: United Way of Tri-State.

Lopez, Iris O. 1987. "Sterilization Among Puerto Rican Women in New York City: Public Policy and Social Constraints." In Leith Mullings, ed., *Cities of the United States: Studies in Urban Anthropology*. New York: Columbia University Press.

McGowan, Brenda G. 1988. "Helping Puerto Rican Families at Risk: Responsive Use of Time, Space, and Relationships." In Carolyn Jacobs and Dorcas D. Bowles, eds., *Ethnicity and Race: Critical Concepts in Social Work*, pp. 48–70. Silver Spring, Md.: National Association of Social Workers.

Mare, Robert, and Christopher Winship. 1988. "Ethnic and Racial Patterns of Educational Attainment and School Enrollment." In Gary Sandefur and Martha Tienda, eds., *Divided Opportunities: Minorities, Poverty and Social Policy*. New York: Plenum Press.

Melendez, Edwin, and Clara Rodriguez. 1988. "Puerto Ricans in the Northeast and the Changing Economy: A Summary of Research Issues." *Dialogo—A Newsletter of the National Puerto Rican Policy Network* no. 5 (Fall): 1.

Moore, Joan. 1988. "Is There a Hispanic Underclass?" *Social Science Quarterly* 70 (2): 265–284.

Moore, Joan, and Harry Pachon. 1985. *Hispanics in the United States*. Englewood Cliffs, N.J.: Prentice-Hall.

Ortiz, Vilma. 1986. "Changes in the Characteristics of Puerto Rican

Migrants from 1955 to 1980." *International Migration Review* 20 (3): 612–623.

Perales, Cesar A., and Lauren S. Young, eds. 1987. *Women, Health and Poverty.* New York: Haworth Press.

Rodriguez, Clara. 1989. *Puerto Ricans: Born in the U.S.A.* Winchester, Mass.: Unwin Hyman.

Rodriguez, Clara, Virginia Sanchez Korrol, and Jose Alers, eds. 1980. *The Puerto Rican Struggle: Essays on Survival in the U.S.* Maplewood, N.J.: Waterfront Press.

Sandis, Eva E. 1973. "Characteristics of Puerto Rican Migrants to, and from, the United States." In Francesco Cordasco and Eugene Bucchioni, eds., *The Puerto Rican Experience: A Sociological Sourcebook*, pp. 127–149. Towota, N.J.: Rowman and Littlefield.

Sotomayor, Maria. 1988. "Federalism and People of Color." In Carolyn Jacobs and Dorcas D. Bowles, eds., *Ethnicity and Race: Critical Concepts in Social Work*, pp. 6–18. Silver Spring, Md.: National Association of Social Workers.

Tienda, Martha, and Leif Jensen. 1988. "Poverty and Minorities: A Quarter-Century Profile of Color and Socioeconomic Disadvantage." In: Gary D. Sandefur and Martha Tienda, eds., *Divided Opportunities: Minorities, Poverty and Social Policy.* New York: Plenum Press.

Trevino, Fernando, Eugene Moyer, Robert Burciaga-Valdez, and Chrisine A. Stroup-Benham. 1991. "Health Insurance Coverage and Utilization of Health Services by Mexican-Americans, Mainland Puerto Ricans and Cuban Americans." *Journal of the American Medical Association* 265 (2): 233–237.

U.S. Bureau of the Census. 1985. *Persons of Spanish Origin in the United States (Advance Report).* Series P-20. Current Population Survey. Washington, D.C.: U.S. Government Printing Office.

———. 1988. *The Hispanic Population in the United States: March 1988 (Advance Report).* Current Population Reports, 1988. series P-20, no. 431. Washington, D.C.: U.S. Government Printing Office.

U.S. Department of Health and Human Services. 1986. Report on the Secretary's Task Force on Black and Minority Health. *Infant Mortality and Low Birth Weight*, vol. 4. Washington, D.C.: U.S. Government Printing Office.

Vasquez Calzada, Jose L. 1988. *La Poblacion de Puerto Rico y su Trajectoria Historica.* San Juan: Escuela Graduada de Salud Publica, Recinto de Ciencias Medicas, Universidad de Puerto Rico.

Ventura, Stephanie. 1988. "Births of Hispanic Parentage, 1985." *NCHS Monthly Vital Statistics Report* 36 (11).

RUTH E. ZAMBRANA

# III

# SOCIAL AGENCY: CONFRONTING THE "WALLS"

# 8

## Fictive Kin, Paper Sons, and Compadrazgo: *Women of Color and the Struggle for Family Survival*

### Bonnie Thornton Dill

R ace has been fundamental to the construction of families in the United States since the country was settled. People of color were incorporated into the country and used to meet the need for cheap and exploitable labor. Little attention was given to their family and community life except as it related to their economic productivity. Upon their founding, the various colonies that ultimately formed the United States initiated legal, economic, political, and social practices designed to promote the growth of family life among European colonists. As the primary laborers in the reproduction and mainte-nance of families, White[1] women settlers were accorded the privileges and protection considered socially appropriate to their family roles. The structure of family life during this era was strongly patriarchal: denying women many rights, constraining their personal autonomy, and making them subject to the almost unfettered will of the male head of the household. Nevertheless, women were rewarded and protected within patriarchal families because their labor was recognized as essential to the maintenance and sustenance of family life.[2] In addition, families were seen as the cornerstone of an incipient nation, and thus their existence was a matter of national interest.

In contrast, women of color experienced the oppression of a patriarchal society but were denied the protection and buffering of a patriarchal family. Although the presence of women of color was equally important to the growth of the nation, their value was based on their potential as workers, breeders, and entertainers of workers, not as family members. In the eighteenth and nineteenth centuries, labor, and not the existence or maintenance of families, was the critical aspect of their role in building the nation. Thus they were denied the societal supports necessary to make their families a vital element in the social order. For women of color, family membership was not a key means of access to participation in the wider society. In some instances racial-ethnic families were seen as a threat to the efficiency and exploitability of the work force and were actively prohibited. In other cases, they were tolerated when it was felt they might help solidify or expand the work force. The lack of social, legal, and economic support for the family life of people of color intensified and extended women's work, created tensions and strains in family relationships, and set the stage for a variety of creative and adaptive forms of resistance.

## African American Slaves

Among students of slavery, there has been considerable debate over the relative "harshness" of American slavery, and the degree to which slaves were permitted or encouraged to form families. It is generally acknowledged that many slave owners found it economically advantageous to encourage family formation as a way of reproducing and perpetuating the slave labor force. This became increasingly true after 1807, when the importation of African slaves was explicitly prohibited. The existence of these families and many aspects of their functioning, however, were directly controlled by the master. Slaves married and formed families, but these groupings were completely subject to the master's decision to let them remain intact. One study has estimated that about 32 percent of all recorded slave marriages were disrupted by sale, about 45 percent by death of a spouse, about 10 percent by choice, and only 13 percent were not disrupted (Blassingame 1972). African slaves thus quickly learned that they had a limited degree of control over the formation and maintenance of their marriages and could not be assured of keeping their children with them. The threat of disruption was one of the most direct and pervasive assaults on families that slaves encountered. Yet there were a number of other aspects of the slave system that reinforced the precariousness of slave family life.

In contrast to some African traditions and the Euro-American patterns of the period, slave men were not the main providers or authority figures in the family. The mother–child tie was basic and of greatest interest to the slave owner because it was essential to the reproduction of the labor force.

In addition to the lack of authority and economic autonomy experienced by the husband–father in the slave family, use of rape of

BONNIE THORNTON DILL

women slaves as a weapon of terror and control further undermined the integrity of the slave family.

> It would be a mistake to regard the institutionalized pattern of rape during slavery as an expression of white men's sexual urges, otherwise stifled by the specter of the white womanhood's chastity. . . . Rape was a weapon of domination, a weapon of repression, whose covert goal was to extinguish slave women's will to resist, and in the process, to demoralize their men. (Davis 1981: 23–24).

The slave family, therefore, was at the heart of a peculiar tension in the master–slave relationship. On the one hand, slave owners sought to encourage familiarities among slaves because, as Julie Matthaei (1982:81) states, "These provided the basis of the development of the slave into a self-conscious socialized human being." They also hoped and believed that this socialization process would help children learn to accept their place in society as slaves. Yet the master's need to control and intervene in the family life of the slaves is indicative of the other side of this tension. Family ties had the potential to become a competing and more potent source of allegiance than the master. Also, kin were as likely to socialize children in forms of resistance as in acts of compliance.

It was within this context of surveillance, assault, and ambivalence that slave women's reproductive labor[3] took place. They and their menfolk had the task of preserving the human and family ties that could ultimately give them a reason for living. They had to socialize their children to believe in the possibility of a life in which they were not enslaved. The slave woman's labor on behalf of the family was, as Angela Davis (1971) has pointed out, the only labor in which the slave engaged that could not be directly used by the slave owner for his own profit. Yet, it was crucial to the reproduction of the slave owner's labor force, and thus a source of strong ambivalence for many slave women. Whereas some mothers murdered their babies to keep them from being slaves, many sought autonomy and creativity within the family that was denied them in other realms of the society. The maintenance of a distinct African American culture is testimony to the ways in which slaves maintained a degree of cultural autonomy and resisted the creation of a slave family that only served the needs of the master.

Herbert Gutman (1976) gives evidence of the ways which slaves expressed a unique African-American culture through their family practices. He provides data on naming patterns and kinship ties among slaves that fly in the face of the dominant ideology of the period, which argued that slaves were immoral and had little concern for or appreciation of family life. Yet Gutman demonstrates that within a system that denied the father authority over his family, slave boys were frequently named after their fathers, and many children were named after blood relatives as a way of maintaining family ties. Gutman also suggests that after emancipation a number of slaves took the names of former owners in order to reestablish family ties that had been disrupted earlier. On plantation after plantation, Gutman found considerable evidence of the building and maintenance of extensive kinship ties among slaves. In instances where slave families had been disrupted, slaves in new communities reconstituted the kinds of family and kin ties that came to characterize Black family life throughout the South. The patterns included, but were not limited to, a belief in the importance of marriage as a long-term commitment, rules of exogamy that excluded marriage between first cousins, and acceptance of women who had children outside of marriage. Kinship networks were an important source of resistance to the organization of labor that treated the individual slave, and not the family, as the unit of labor (Caulfield 1974).

Another interesting indicator of the slaves' maintenance of some degree of cultural autonomy has been pointed out by Gwendolyn Wright (1981) in her discussion of slave housing. Until the early 1800s, slaves were often permitted to build their housing according to their own design and taste. During that period, housing built in an African style was quite common in the slave quarters. By 1830, however, slave owners had begun to control the design and arrangement of slave housing and had introduced a degree of conformity and regularity to it that left little room for the slaves' personalization of the home. Nevertheless, slaves did use some of their own techniques in construction, often hiding them from their masters.

> Even the floors, which usually consisted of only tamped earth, were evidence of a hidden African tradition: slaves cooked clay over a fire, mixing in ox blood or cow dung, and then poured it in place to make hard dirt floors almost like asphalt. . . . In slave houses, in contrast to other crafts, these signs of skill and tradition would then be covered over. (Wright 1981:48)

Housing is important in discussions of family because its design reflects sociocultural attitudes about family life. The housing that slave owners provided for their slaves reflected a view of Black family life consistent with the stereotypes of the period. While the existence of slave families was acknowledged, they certainly were not nurtured. Thus, cabins were crowded, often containing more than one family, and there were no provisions for privacy. Slaves had to create their own.

> Slave couples hung up old clothes or quilts to establish bounda-
> ries; others built more substantial partitions from scrap wood.
> Parents sought to establish sexual privacy from children. A few
> ex-slaves described modified trundle beds designed to hide pa-
> rental lovemaking. . . . Even in one room cabins, sexual segrega-
> tion was carefully organized. (Wright 1981:50)

Perhaps most critical in developing an understanding of slave women's reproductive labor is the gender-based division of labor in the domestic sphere. The organization of slave labor enforced considerable equality among men and women. The ways in which equality in the labor force was translated into the family sphere is somewhat specula-tive. Davis (1981:18), for example, suggests that egalitarianism be-tween males and females was a direct result of slavery: "Within the confines of their family and community life, therefore, Black people managed to accomplish a magnificent feat. They transformed that negative equality which emanated from the equal oppression they suffered as slaves into a positive quality; the egalitarianism characteriz-ing their social relations."

It is likely, however, that this transformation was far less direct than Davis implies. We know, for example, that slave women experi-enced what has recently been called the "double day" before most other women in this society. Slave narratives (Jones 1985; White 1985; Blassingame 1977) reveal that women had primary responsibility for their family's domestic chores. They cooked (although on some planta-tions meals were prepared for all the slaves), sewed, cared for their children, and cleaned house after completing a full day of labor for the master. John Blassingame (1972) and others have pointed out that slave men engaged in hunting, trapping, perhaps some gardening, and furniture making as ways of contributing to the maintenance of their families. Clearly, a gender-based division of labor did exist within the family, and it appears that women bore the larger share of the burden for housekeeping and child care.

In contrast to White families of the period, however, the division of labor in the domestic sphere was reinforced neither in the relation-ship of slave women to work nor in the social institutions of the slave community. The gender-based division of labor among the slaves existed within a social system that treated men and women as almost equal, independent units of labor.[4] Thus Matthaei (1982:94) is probably correct in concluding that whereas . . . the white homemaker interacted with the public sphere through her husband, and had her work life determined by him, the enslaved Afro-American homemaker was directly subordinated to and determined by her owner. . . . The equal enslavement of husband and wife gave the slave marriage a curious kind of equality, an equality of oppression.

Black men were denied the male resources of a patriarchal society and therefore were unable to turn gender distinctions into female subordination, even if that had been their desire. Black women, on the other hand, were denied support and protection for their roles as mothers and wives, and thus had to modify and structure those roles around the demands of their labor. Reproductive labor for slave women was intensified in several ways: by the demands of slave labor that forced them into the double day of work; by the desire and need to maintain family ties in the face of a system that gave them only limited recognition; by the stresses of building a family with men who were denied the standard social privileges of manhood; and by the struggle to raise children who could survive in a hostile environment.

This intensification of reproductive labor made networks of kin and fictive kin important instruments in carrying out the reproductive tasks of the slave community. Given an African cultural heritage where kinship ties formed the basis of social relations, it is not at all surprising that African American slaves developed an extensive system of kinship ties and obligations (Gutman 1976; Sudarkasa 1981). Research on Black families in slavery provides considerable documentation of participation of extended kin in child rearing, childbirth, and other domestic, social, and economic activities (Gutman 1976; Blassingame 1972; Genovese and Miller 1974).

After slavery, these ties continued to be an important factor linking individual household units in a variety of domestic activities. While kinship ties were also important among native-born Whites and European immigrants, Gutman (1976:213) has suggested that these ties

were comparatively more important to Afro-Americans than to lower-class native white and immigrant Americans, the result of their distinctive low economic status, a condition that denied them the advantages of an extensive associational life beyond the kin group and the advantages and disadvantages resulting from mobility opportunities.

His argument is reaffirmed by research on African American families after slavery (Shimkin et al. 1978; Aschenbrenner 1975; Davis

1981; Stack 1974). Niara Sudarkasa (1981:49) takes this argument one step further, linking this pattern to the African cultural heritage.

> Historical realities require that the derivation of this aspect of Black family organization be traced to its African antecedents. Such a view does not deny the adaptive significance of consanguineal networks. In fact, it helps to clarify why these networks had the flexibility they had and why they, rather than conjugal relationships, came to be the stabilizing factor in Black families.

In individual households, the gender-based division of labor experienced some important shifts during emancipation. In their first real opportunity to establish family life beyond the controls and constraints imposed by a slave master, Black sharecroppers' family life changed radically. Most women, at least those who were wives and daughters of able-bodied men, withdrew from field labor and concentrated on their domestic duties in the home. Husbands took primary responsibility for the fieldwork and for relations with the owners, such as signing contracts on behalf of the family. Black women were severely criticized by Whites for removing themselves from field labor because they were seen to be aspiring to a model of womanhood that was considered inappropriate for them. The reorganization of female labor, however, represented an attempt on the part of Blacks to protect women from some of the abuses of the slave system and to thus secure their family life. It was more likely a response to the particular set of circumstances that the newly freed slaves faced than a reaction to the lives of their former masters. Jacqueline Jones (1985) argues that these patterns were "particularly significant" because at a time when industrial development was introducing a labor system that divided male and female labor, the freed Black family was establishing a pattern of joint work and complementarity of tasks between males and females that was reminiscent of preindustrial American families. Unfortunately, these former slaves had to do this without the institutional supports given white farm families and within a sharecropping system that deprived them of economic independence.

## Chinese Sojourners

An increase in the African slave population was a desired goal. Therefore, Africans were permitted and even encouraged at times to form families, as long as they were under the direct control of the slave master. By sharp contrast, Chinese people were explicitly denied the right to form families in the United States through both law and social practice. Although male laborers began coming to the United States in sizable numbers in the middle of the nineteenth century, it was more than a century before an appreciable number of children of Chinese parents were born in America. Tom, a respondent in Victor Nee and Brett de Bary Nee's book, *Longtime Californ'*, says: "One thing about Chinese men in America was you had to be either a merchant or a big gambler, have lot of side money to have a family here. A working man, an ordinary man, just can't!" (1973:80).

Working in the United States was a means of gaining support for one's family with an end of obtaining sufficient capital to return to China and purchase land. This practice of sojourning was reinforced by laws preventing Chinese laborers from becoming citizens, and by restrictions on their entry into this country. Chinese laborers who arrived before 1882 could not bring their wives and were prevented by law from marrying Whites. Thus, it is likely that the number of Chinese American families might have been negligible had it not been for two things: the San Francisco earthquake and fire in 1906, which destroyed all municipal records, and the ingenuity and persistence of the Chinese people, who used the opportunity created by the earthquake to increase their numbers in the United States. Since relatives of citizens were permitted entry, American-born Chinese (real and claimed) would visit China, report the birth of a son, and thus create an entry slot. Years later, since the records were destroyed, the slot could be used by a relative or purchased by someone outside the family. The purchasers were called "paper sons." Paper sons became a major mechanism for increasing the Chinese population, but it was a slow process and the sojourner community remained predominantly male for decades.

The high concentration of males in the Chinese community before 1920 resulted in a split household form of family. As Evelyn Nakano Glenn observes:

> In the split household family, production is separated from other functions and is carried out by a member living far from the rest of the household. The rest—consumption, reproduction and socialization—are carried out by the wife and other relatives from the home village. . . . The split household form makes possible maximum exploitation of the workers. . . . The labor of prime-age male workers can be bought relatively cheaply, since the cost of reproduction and family maintenance is borne partially by unpaid subsistence work of women and old people in the home village. (1983:38–39)

The Chinese women who were in the United States during this period consisted of a small number who were wives and daughters of merchants and a larger percentage who were prostitutes. Lucia Cheng Hirata (1979) has suggested that Chinese prostitution was an important element in helping to maintain the split household family. In conjunction with laws prohibiting intermarriage, it helped men avoid long-term relationships with women in the United States and ensured that the bulk of their meager earnings would continue to support the family at home.

The reproductive labor of Chinese women, therefore, took on two dimensions primarily because of the split household family. Wives who remained in China were forced to raise children and care for in-laws on the meager remittances of their sojourning husband. Although we know few details about their lives, it is clear that the everyday work of bearing and maintaining children and a household fell entirely on their shoulders. Those women who immigrated and worked as prostitutes performed the more nurturant aspects of reproductive labor, that is, providing emotional and sexual companionship for men who were far from home. Yet their role as prostitutes was more likely a means of supporting their families at home in China than a chosen vocation.

The Chinese family system during the nineteenth century was a patriarchal one and girls had little value. In fact, they were considered temporary members of their father's family because when they married, they became members of their husband's family. They also had little social value; girls were sold by some poor parents to work as prostitutes, concubines, or servants. This saved the family the expense of raising them, and their earnings became a source of family income. For most girls, however, marriages were arranged and families sought useful connections through this process. With the development of a sojourning pattern in the United States, some Chinese women in those regions of China where this pattern was more prevalent would be sold to become prostitutes in the United States. Most, however, were married to men whom they saw only once or twice in the twenty- or thirty-year period during which he was sojourning in the United States. A woman's status as wife ensured that a portion of the meager wages her husband earned would be returned to his family in China. This arrangement required considerable sacrifice and adjustment by wives who remained in China and those who joined their husbands after a long separation.

Maxine Hong Kingston tells the story of the unhappy meeting of her aunt, Moon Orchid, with her husband, from whom she had been separated for thirty years: "For thirty years she had been receiving money from him from America. But she had never told him that she wanted to come to the United States. She waited for him to suggest it, but he never did" (1977:144). His response to her when she arrived unexpectedly was to say: " 'Look at her. She'd never fit into an American household. I have important American guests who come inside my house to eat.' He turned to Moon Orchid, 'You can't talk to them. You can barely talk to me.' Moon Orchid was so ashamed, she held her hands over her face" (1977:178).

Despite these handicaps, Chinese people collaborated to establish the opportunity to form families and settle in the United States. In some cases it took as long as three generations for a child to be born on U.S. soil.

> In one typical history, related by a 21 year old college student, great-grandfather arrived in the States in the 1890s as a "paper son" and worked for about 20 years as a laborer. He then sent for the grandfather, who worked alongside great-grandfather in a small business for several years. Great-grandfather subsequently returned to China, leaving grandfather to run the business and send remittance. In the 1940s, grandfather sent for father; up to this point, none of the wives had left China. Finally, in the late 1950s father returned to China and brought his wife back with him. Thus, after nearly 70 years, the first child was born in the United States. (Glenn 1981:14)

## Chicanos

Africans were uprooted from their native lands and encouraged to have families in order to increase the slave labor force. Chinese people were immigrant laborers whose "permanent" presence in the country was denied. By contrast, Mexican Americans were colonized and their traditional family life was disrupted by war and the imposition of a new set of laws and conditions of labor. The hardships faced by Chicano families, therefore, were the results of the U.S. colonization of the indigenous Mexican population, accompanied by the beginnings of industrial development. The treaty of Guadalupe Hidalgo, signed in 1848, granted American citizenship to Mexicans living in what is now called the Southwest. The American takeover, however, resulted in the gradual displacement of Mexicans from the land and their incorporation into a colonial labor force (Barrera 1979). Mexicans who immigrated into the United States after 1848 were also absorbed into that labor force.

Whether natives of northern Mexico (which became part of the United States after 1848) or immigrants from southern Mexico, Chicanos were a largely peasant population whose lives were defined by a feudal economy and a daily struggle on the land for economic survival. Patriarchal families were important instruments of community life, and nuclear family units were linked through an elaborate system of kinship and godparenting. Traditional life was characterized by hard work and a fairly distinct pattern of sex-role segregation.

> Most Mexican women were valued for their household qualities, men by their ability to work and to provide for a family. Children were taught to get up early, to contribute to their family's labor to prepare themselves for adult life. . . . Such a life demanded discipline, authority, deference - values that cemented the working of a family surrounded and shaped by the requirements of Mexico's distinctive historical pattern of agricultural development, especially its pervasive debt peonage. (Saragoza 1983:8)

As the primary caretakers of hearth and home in a rural environment, Chicanas' labor made a vital and important contribution to family survival. A description of women's reproductive labor in the early twentieth century may be used to gain insight into the work of the nineteenth-century rural women.

> For country women, work was seldom a salaried job. More often it was the work of growing and preparing food, of making adobes and plastering houses with mud, or making their children's clothes for school and teaching them the hymns and prayers of the church, or delivering babies and treating sickness with herbs and patience. In almost every town there were one or two women who, in addition to working in their own homes, served other families in the community as *curanderas* (healers), *parteras* (midwives), and schoolteachers. (Elasser et al. 1980:10)

Although some scholars have argued that family rituals and community life showed little change before Word War I (Saragoza 1983), the American conquest of Mexican lands, the introduction of a new system of labor, the loss of Mexican-owned land through the inability to document ownership, and the transient nature of most of the jobs in which Chicanos were employed resulted in the gradual erosion of this pastoral way of life. Families were uprooted as the economic basis for family life changed. Some people immigrated from Mexico in search of a better standard of living and worked in the mines and railroads. Others, who were native to the Southwest, faced a job market that no longer required their skills. They moved into mining, railroad, and agricultural labor in search of a means of earning a living. According to Albert Camarillo (1979), the influx of Anglo[5] capital into the pastoral economy of Santa Barbara rendered obsolete the skills of many Chicano males who had worked as ranch hands and farmers prior to the urbanization of that economy. While some women and children accompanied their husbands to the railroad and mining camps, many of these camps discouraged or prohibited family settlement.

The American period (after 1848) was characterized by considerable transiency for the Chicano population. Its impact on families is seen in the growth of female-headed households, reflected in the data as early as 1860. Richard Griswold del Castillo (1979) found a sharp increase in female-headed households in Los Angeles, from a low of 13 percent in 1844 to 31 percent in 1880. Camarillo (1979:120) documents a similar increase in Santa Barbara, from 15 percent in 1844 to 30 percent by 1880. These increases appear to be due not so much to divorce, which was infrequent in this Catholic population, as to widowhood and temporary abandonment in search of work. Given the hazardous nature of work in the mines and railroad camps, the death of a husband, father, or son who was laboring in these sites was not uncommon. Griswold del Castillo (1979) reports a higher death rate among men than women in Los Angeles. The rise in female-headed households, therefore, reflects the instabilities and insecurities introduced into women's lives as a result of the changing social organization of work.

One outcome, the increasing participation of women and children in the labor force, was primarily a response to economic factors that required the modification of traditional values. According to Louisa Vigil, who was born in 1890, "The women didn't work at that time. The man was supposed to marry that girl and take care of her. . . . Your grandpa never did let me work for nobody. He always had to work, and we never did have really bad times" (Elasser et al. 1980:14).

Vigil's comments are reinforced in Mario Garcia's (1980) study of El Paso. In the 393 households he examined in the 1900 census, he found 17.1 percent of the women to be employed. The majority of this group were daughters, mothers with no husbands, and single women. In Los Angeles and Santa Barbara, where there were greater work opportunities for women than in El Paso, wives who were heads of household worked in seasonal and part-time jobs, and lived from the earnings of children and relatives in an effort to maintain traditional females roles.

Slowly, entire families were encouraged to go to railroad work camps and were eventually incorporated into the agricultural labor market. This was a response both to the extremely low wages paid to Chicano laborers and to the preferences of employers, who saw family labor as a way of stabilizing the work force. For Chicanos, engaging all family members in agricultural work was a means of increasing their earnings to a level close to subsistence for the entire group and of keeping the family unit together. Camarillo provides a picture of the interplay of work, family, and migration in the Santa Barbara area in the following observation:

> The time of year when women and children were employed in the fruit cannery and participated in the almond and olive harvest coincided with the seasons when the men were most likely to be engaged in seasonal migratory work. There were seasons, however, especially in the early summer when the entire family migrated from the city to pick fruit. This type of family seasonal harvest was evident in Santa Barbara by the 1890s. As walnuts replaced almonds and as the fruit industry expanded, Chicano family labor became essential. (1979:93)

This arrangement, while bringing families together, did not decrease the hardships that Chicanas had to confront in raising their families. We may infer something about the rigors of that life from Jesse Lopez de la Cruz's description of the workday of migrant farm laborers in the 1940s. Work conditions in the 1890s were as difficult, if not worse.

> We always went to where the women and men were going to work, because if it were just the men working it wasn't worth going out there because we wouldn't earn enough to support a family. . . . We would start around 6:30 a.m and work for four or five hours, then walk home and eat and rest until about three-thirty in the afternoon when it cooled off. We would go back and work until we couldn't see. Then I'd clean up the kitchen. I was doing the housework and working out in the fields and taking care of two children. (Quoted in Goldman 1981:119–120)

In the towns, women's reproductive labor was intensified by the congested and unsanitary conditions of the barrios in which they lived. Garcia described the following conditions in El Paso:

> Mexican women had to haul water for washing and cooking from the river or public water pipes. To feed their families, they had to spend time marketing, often in Ciudad Juarez across the border,

as well as long, hot hours cooking meals and coping with the burden of desert sand both inside and outside their homes. Besides the problem of raising children, unsanitary living conditions forced Mexican mothers to deal with disease and illness in their families. Diphtheria, tuberculosis, typhus and influenza were never too far away. Some diseases could be directly traced to inferior city services. . . . As a result, Mexican mothers had to devote much energy to caring for sick children, many of whom died. (1980:320–321)

While the extended family has remained an important element of Chicano life, it was eroded in the American period in several ways. Griswold del Castillo (1979), for example, points out that in 1845 about 71 percent of Angelenos lived in extended families, whereas by 1880, fewer than half did. This decrease in extended families appears to be a response to the changed economic conditions and the instabilities generated by the new sociopolitical structure. Additionally, the imposition of American law and custom ignored, and ultimately undermined, some aspects of the extended family. The extended family in traditional Mexican life consisted of an important set of family, religious, and community obligations. Women, while valued primarily for their domesticity, had certain legal and property rights that acknowledged the importance of their work, their families of origin, and their children. In California, for example,

> equal ownership of property between husband and wife had been one of the mainstays of the Spanish and Mexican family systems. Community-property laws were written into the civil codes with the intention of strengthening the economic controls of the wife and her relatives. The American government incorporated these Mexican laws into the state constitution, but later court decisions interpreted these statutes so as to undermine the wife's economic rights. In 1861, the legislature passed a law that allowed the deceased wife's property to revert to her husband. Previously it had been inherited by her children and relatives if she died without a will. (Griswold del Castillo 1979:69)

The impact of this and similar court rulings was to "strengthen the property rights of the husband at the expense of his wife and children" (Griswold del Castillo 1979:69).

In the face of the legal, social, and economic changes that occurred during the American period, Chicanas were forced to cope with a series of dislocations in traditional life. They were caught between conflicting pressures to maintain traditional women's roles and family customs, and the need to participate in the economic support of their families by working outside the home. During this period the preservation of traditional customs—such as languages, celebrations, and healing practices—became an important element in maintaining and supporting familial ties.

According to Alex Saragoza (1983), transiency, the effects of racism and segregation, and proximity to Mexico aided in the maintenance of traditional family practices. Garcia has suggested that women were the guardians of Mexican cultural traditions within the family. He cites the work of anthropologist Manuel Gamio, who identified the retention of many Mexican customs among Chicanos in settlements around the United States in the early 1900s.

> These included folklore, songs, and ballads, birthday celebrations, saints' days, baptisms, weddings, and funerals in the traditional style. Because of poverty, a lack of physicians in the barrios, and adherence to traditional customs, Mexicans continued to use medicinal herbs. Gamio also identified the maintenance of a number of oral traditions, and Mexican style cooking. (Garcia 1980:322)

Of vital importance to the integrity of traditional culture was the perpetuation of the Spanish language. Factors that aided in the maintenance of other aspects of Mexican culture also helped in sustaining the language. However, entry into English-language public schools introduced the children and their families to systematic efforts to erase their native tongue. Griswold del Castillo reports that in the early 1880s there was considerable pressure against speakers of Spanish in the public schools. He also found that some Chicano parents responded to this kind of discrimination by helping support independent bilingual schools. These efforts, however, were short-lived.

Another key factor in conserving Chicano culture was the extended family network, particularly the system of *compadrazgo* (godparenting). Although the full extent of the impact of the American period on the Chicano extended family is not known, it is generally acknowledged that this family system, though lacking many legal and social sanctions, played an important role in the preservation of the Mexican community (Camarillo 1979). In Mexican society, godparents were an important way of linking family and community through respected friends or authorities. Participants in the important rites of passage in the child's life, such as baptism, first Communion, confirmation, and marriage, godparents had a moral obligation to act as guardians, to provide financial assistance in times of need, and to substitute in case of the death of a parent. Camarillo (1979) points out that in traditional society these bonds cut across class and racial lines.

The rite of baptism established kinship networks between rich and poor, between Spanish, mestizo and American Indian, and often carried with it political loyalty and economic-occupational ties. The leading California patriarchs in the pueblo played important roles in the *compadrazgo* network. They sponsored dozens of children for their workers or poorer relatives. The kindness of the *padrino* and *madrina* was repaid with respect and support from the *pobladores* (Camarillo 1979:12–13).

The extended family network, which included godparents, expanded the support groups for women who were widowed or temporarily abandoned and for those who were in seasonal, part- or full-time work. It suggests, therefore, the potential for an exchange of services among poor people whose income did not provide the basis for family subsistence. Griswold del Castillo (1979) argues that family organization influenced literacy rates and socioeconomic mobility among Chicanos in Los Angeles between 1850 and 1880. His data suggest that children in extended families (defined as those with at least one relative living in a nuclear family household) had higher literacy rates than those in nuclear families. He also argues that those in larger families fared better economically and experienced less downward mobility. The data here are too limited to generalize to the Chicano experience as a whole, but they do reinforce the actual and potential importance of this family form to the continued cultural autonomy of the Chicano community.

## Conclusion

Reproductive labor for African American, Chinese American, and Mexican American women in the nineteenth century centered on the struggle to maintain family units in the face of a variety of assaults. Treated primarily as workers rather than as members of family groups, these women labored to maintain, sustain, stabilize, and reproduce their families while working in both the public (productive) and private (reproductive) spheres. Thus, the concept of reproductive labor, when applied to women of color, must be modified to account for the fact that labor in the productive sphere was required to achieve even minimal levels of family subsistence. Long after industrialization had begun to reshape family roles among middle-class White families, driving White women into a cult of domesticity, women of color were coping with an extended day. This day included subsistence labor outside the family and domestic labor within the family. For slaves, domestics, migrant farm laborers, seasonal factory workers, and prostitutes, the distinctions between labor that reproduced family life and labor that economically sustained it were minimized. The expanded workday was one of the primary ways in which reproductive labor increased.

Racial-ethnic families were sustained and maintained in the face of various forms of disruption. Yet the women and their families paid a high price in the process. High rates of infant mortality, a shortened life span, and the early onset of crippling and debilitating disease give some insight into the costs of survival.

The poor quality of housing and the neglect of communities further increased reproductive labor. Not only did racial-ethnic women work hard outside the home for mere subsistence, they worked very hard inside the home to achieve even minimal standards of privacy and cleanliness. They were continually faced with disease and illness that resulted directly from the absence of basic sanitation. The fact that some African women murdered their children to prevent them from becoming slaves is an indication of the emotional strain associated with bearing and raising children while participating in the colonial labor system.

We have uncovered little information about the use of birth control, the prevalence of infanticide, or the motivations that may have generated these or other behaviors. We can surmise, however, that no matter how much children were accepted, loved, or valued among any of these groups of people, their futures were precarious. Keeping children alive, helping them to understand and participate in a system that exploited them, and working to ensure a measure—no matter how small—of cultural integrity intensified women's reproductive labor.

Being a woman of color in nineteenth-century American society meant having extra work both inside and outside the home. It meant being defined as outside of or deviant from the norms and values about women that were being generated in the dominant White culture. The notion of separate spheres of male and female labor that developed in the nineteenth century had contradictory outcomes for the Whites. It was the basis for the confinement of upper-middle-class White women to the household and for much of the protective legislation that subsequently developed in the workplace. At the same time, it sustained White families by providing social acknowledgment and support to women in the performance of their family roles. For racial-ethnic women, however, the notion of separate spheres served to reinforce their subordinate status and became, in effect, another assault. As they increased their work outside the home, they were forced into a productive labor sphere that was organized for men and "desperate" women who were so unfortunate or immoral that they could not confine their work to the domestic sphere. In the productive sphere, racial-ethnic women faced exploitative jobs and depressed wages. In the reproductive sphere, they were denied the opportunity to embrace the dominant ideological definition of "good" wife or mother. In essence, they were faced with a double-bind situation, one that required their participation in the labor force to sustain family life but damned them as women, wives, and mothers because they did not confine their labor to the home.

Finally, the struggle of women of color to build and maintain families provides vivid testimony to the role of race in structuring family life in the United States. As Maxine Baca Zinn points out:

> Social categories and groups subordinate in the racial hierarchy are often deprived of access to social institutions that offer supports for family life. Social categories and groups elevated in the racial hierarchy have different and better connections to institutions that can sustain families. Social location and its varied connection with social resources thus have profound consequences for family life. (1990:74)

From the founding of the United States, and throughout its history, race has been a fundamental criterion determining the kind of work people do, the wages they receive, and the kind of legal, economic, political, and social support provided for their families. Women of color have faced limited economic resources, inferior living conditions, alien cultures and languages, and overt hostility in their struggle to create a "place" for families of color in the United States. That place, however, has been a precarious one because the society has not provided supports for these families. Today we see the outcomes of that legacy in statistics showing that people of color, compared with whites, have higher rates of female-headed households, out-of-wedlock births, divorce, and other factors associated with family disruption. Yet the causes of these variations do not lie merely in the higher concentrations of poverty among people of color; they are also due to the ways race has been used as a basis for denying and providing support to families. Women of color have struggled to maintain their families against all of these odds.

# Notes

*Acknowledgments:* The research in this study was an outgrowth of my participation in a larger collaborative project examining family, community, and work lives of racial-ethnic women in the United States. I am deeply indebted to the scholarship and creativity of members of the group in the development of this study. Appreciation is extended to Elizabeth Higginbotham, Cheryl Townsend Gilkes, Evelyn Nakano Glenn, and Ruth Zambrana (members of the original working group), and to the Ford Foundation for a grant that supported in part the work of this study.

1. The term "White" is a global construct used to characterize peoples of European descent who migrated to and helped colonize America. In the seventeenth century, most of these immigrants were from the British Isles. However, during the time period covered by this article, European immigrants became increasingly diverse. It is a limitation of this chapter that time and space do not permit a fuller discussion of the variations in the White European immigrant experience. For the purposes of the argument being made herein and of the contrast it seeks to draw between the experiences of mainstream (European) cultural groups and those of racial-ethnic minorities, the differences among European settlers are joined and the broad similarities emphasized.

2. For a more detailed discussion of this argument and the kinds of social supports provided these families, see an earlier version of this paper: "Our Mothers' Grief: Racial-Ethnic Women and the Maintenance of Families," *Journal of Family History* 13 (4) (1988): 415–431.

3. The term "reproductive labor" is used to refer to all of the work of women in the home. This includes, but is not limited to, the buying and preparation of food and clothing, provision of emotional support and nurturance for all family members, bearing children, and planning, organizing, and carrying out a wide variety of tasks associated with socialization. All of these activities are necessary for the growth of patriarchal capitalism because they maintain, sustain, stabilize, and reproduce (both biologically and socially) the labor force.

4. Recent research suggests that there were some tasks assigned primarily to males and some others to females. Whereas some gender-role

distinctions with regard to work may have existed on some plantations, it is clear that slave women were not exempt from strenuous physical labor.

5. This term is used to refer to White Americans of European ancestry.

# References

Aschenbrenner, Joyce. 1975. *Lifelines: Black Families in Change.* New York: Holt, Rinehart, and Winston.

Baca Zinn, Maxine. 1990. "Family, Feminism and Race in America." *Gender and Society* 4 (1) (March): 68–82.

Barrera, Mario. 1979. *Race and Class in the Southwest.* Notre Dame, Ind.: Notre Dame University Press.

Blassingame, John. 1972. *The Slave Community: Plantation Life in the Antebellum South.* New York: Oxford University Press.

———. 1977. *Slave Testimony: Two Centuries of Letters, Speeches, Interviews, and Autobiographies.* Baton Rouge: Louisiana State University Press.

Camarillo, Albert. 1979. *Chicanos in a Changing Society.* Cambridge, Mass.: Harvard University Press.

Caulfield, Mina Davis. 1974. "Imperialism, the Family, and Cultures of Resistance." *Socialist Review* 4 (2) (October): 67–85.

Davis, Angela. 1971. "Reflections on the Black Woman's Role in the Community of Slaves." *Black Scholar* 3 (4) (December): 2–15.

———. 1981. *Women, Race, and Class.* New York: Random House.

Degler, Carl. 1980. *At Odds.* New York: Oxford University Press.

Elasser, Nan, Kyle MacKenzie, and Yvonne Tixier Y. Vigil. 1980. *Las Mujeres.* New York: The Feminist Press.

Garcia, Mario T. 1980. "The Chicano in American History: The Mexican Women of El Paso, 1880–1920—A Case Study." *Pacific Historical Review* 49 (2) (May): 315–358.

Genovese, Eugene D., and Elinor Miller, eds. 1974. *Plantation, Town, and County: Essays on the Local History of American Slave Society.* Urbana: University of Illinois Press.

Glenn, Evelyn Nakano. 1983. "Split Household, Small Producer, and Dual Earner: An Analysis of Chinese-American Family Strategies." *Journal of Marriage and the Family.* 45 (1) (February): 35–46.

Goldman, Marion S. 1981. *Gold Diggers and Silver Miners.* Ann Arbor: University of Michigan Press.

Griswold de Castillo, Richard. 1979. *The Los Angeles Barrio: 1850–1890.* Los Angeles: University of California Press.

Gutman, Herbert. 1976. *The Black Family in Slavery and Freedom, 1750–1925.* New York: Pantheon.

Hirata, Lucia Cheng. 1979. "Free, Indentured, Enslaved: Chinese Prostitutes in Nineteenth Century America." *Signs* 5 (Autumn): 3–29.

Jones, Jacqueline. 1985. *Labor of Love, Labor of Sorrow*. New York: Basic Books.

Kennedy, Susan Estabrook. 1979. *If All We Did Was to Weep at Home: A History of White Working-Class Women in America*. Bloomington: Indiana University Press.

Kessler-Harris, Alice. 1981. *Women Have Always Worked*. Old Westbury, N.Y.: The Feminist Press.

———. 1982. *Out to Work*. New York: Oxford University Press.

Kingston, Maxine Hong. 1977. *The Woman Warrior*. New York: Vintage Books.

Matthaei, Julie. 1982. *An Economic History of Women in America*. New York: Schocken Books.

Nee, Victor G., and Brett de Bary Nee. 1973. *Longtime Californ'*. New York: Pantheon Books.

Saragoza, Alex M. 1983. "The Conceptualization of the History of the Chicano Family: Work, Family, and Migration in Chicanos." In *Research Proceedings of the Symposium on Chicano Research and Public Policy*. Stanford, Calif.: Stanford University, Center for Chicano Research.

Shimkin, Demetri, E. M. Shimkin, and D. A. Frate, eds. 1978. *The Extended Family in Black Societies*. The Hague: Mouton.

Spruill, Julia Cherry. 1972. *Women's Life and Work in the Southern Colonies*. New York: W. W. Norton. (First published Chapel Hill: University of North Carolina Press, 1938).

Stack, Carol S. 1974. *All Our Kin: Strategies for Survival in a Black Community*. New York: Harper & Row.

Sudarkasa, Niara. 1981. "Interpreting the African Heritage in Afro-American Family Organization." Pp. 37–53 in *Black Families*, edited by Harriette Pipes McAdoo. Beverly Hills, Calif.: Sage.

White, Deborah Gray. 1985. *Ar'n't I a Woman? Female Slaves in the Plantation South*. New York: W. W. Norton.

Wright, Gwendolyn. 1981. *Building the Dream: A Social History of Housing in America*. New York: Pantheon.

Zaretsky, Eli. 1978. "The Effects of the Economic Crisis on the Family." Pp 209–218 in *U.S. Capitalism in Crisis*, edited by Crisis Reader Editorial Collective. New York: Union of Radical Political Economists.

# 9

## Black Women in Prison: The Price of Resistance

### Regina Arnold

I n this chapter, I examine processes of criminalization experienced by young Black girls and explanations for sustained criminal involvement by adult Black women. I argue that (1) the process of criminalization for many young Black girls is initiated by gender oppression and class oppression in conjunction with a criminal justice system that blames the victim, and that (2) sustained criminal involvement, continuing from girlhood into adulthood, is a rational coping strategy, a response to alienation and structural dislocation from the primary socializing institutions of family, education, and work. The chapter is informed by scholarship on female criminality in general (Price and Sokoloff 1982), theoretical work that emphasizes the need for empirical data on initial and sustained criminal involvement of women (Leonard 1982), and empirical research on women in prison (Chesney-Lind and Rodriguez 1983; Arnold 1979; Shakur 1978), which suggests a systematic process of criminalization unique to women that magnifies the relationship between victimization and entrapment in the criminal justice system. The findings enlarge and enhance our understanding of an emerging issue in the study of women and crime: the relationship between the experience of having been victimized and subsequent offending (Rafter 1986; Chesney-Lind and Rodriguez 1983). Utilizing data from participant observation, interviews, and questionnaires administered to Black female prisoners serving sentences in a city jail (Arnold 1979) and a state prison (Arnold 1986), I discuss how females, as young girls, are labeled and processed as deviants, and subsequently as criminals, for refusing to participate in their own victimization. Second, I show how this refusal results in structural dislocation from family and education, and leads to entry into the criminal life. Third, I reveal how crime becomes a rational choice in the face of dislocation from family, education, and work in the paid labor force, and how drugs are used to dull the pain of reality.

## Criminalization of Young Black Girls

An examination of the lives of Black female prisoners as young girls revealed the processes of defining deviance and labeling deviants through a complex of reinforcements involving societal reaction to gender, class, and race. Factors operating in this process of criminalization ranged from sexual and other physical abuse, and a lack of monetary and other resources associated with an impoverished status, to racial discrimination and structural dislocation from two of the primary socializing institutions of the society: the family and the educational institution. This factor of structural dislocation has been discussed in the context of homeless women, for whom displacement often occurs as a consequence of domestic violence, abuse, or the breakup of extended family households (Hope and Young 1986). In the face of structural dislocation and the absence of a strong family substitute, deviance and criminality became the modus operandi very early in the lives of these young Black girls. Thus, the process of criminalization included elements of sexual or other physical abuse, poverty, and miseducation. Running away from home, stealing, and leaving school were ways of resisting oppression that subsequently led to being labeled a status offender, and finally a criminal.

As the interviewees discussed their childhoods, three issues emerged that targeted structural dislocation from family, education, and work: running away from home, dropping out of school, and stealing as a means of helping to support an impoverished family. Girls who ran away from home usually had experienced some form of sexual abuse within the family. Girls who dropped out of school had experienced overwhelming problems connected with school (including racial discrimination) and with a home environment that did not support the continuation of their education. Girls who stole were from economically marginal families that were unable to make ends meet. These three issues often coalesced in the life of an individual woman. Thus, it was not unusual for a runaway, because of her homeless status, to become dislocated from school, and subsequently from work in the paid labor force.

A process of criminalization involving gender oppression, victim-blaming, and structural dislocation from the family is manifest in the case of Barbara G., who was serving time in a state prison for a felony offense.

Barbara was sexually molested by her stepfather when she was thirteen; unlike most girls who experience sexual assault, she confided in her mother. Although her mother expressed disbelief, Barbara was sent to live with one aunt and then with another. The aunts were sympathetic and permitted her to stay awhile, but they eventually sent her home to "patch things up" with her mother. At home, while her mother worked the night shift as a nurse, Barbara's stepfather tried to molest her again. This time, she hit him over the head with one of her school sports trophies, leaving a huge gash. When she told her mother, her stepfather's explanation was that he had been "working under the hood of his car when the hood fell on his head." He explained that Barbara was "just a chronic liar." This time, Barbara ran away from home. She says:

> My stepfather molested me twice. My mother didn't believe it. I was angry, I was hurt, I was afraid. I was going through a lot of things then. Eventually I ran away from home. I met a man, a much older man. I was almost fourteen. He used to lock me up in his apartment, so I was like a runaway prisoner. My stepfather found me and brought me back home. Before my fifteenth birthday, I ran away again, and I've been on my own ever since. I felt like my only alternatives were either stay at home and deal with this man or leave and deal with the world the best way you know how. And dealing with the world at that time seemed a lot better than to stay there dealing with this.

Since her immediate and extended families of women were unable to assist her, Barbara ran away from the family, into the streets. Picked up by the police for vagrancy and running away from home, she was processed and labeled a status offender. Her stepfather, however, was never arrested for his crimes against her. She was now a person to whom the label "deviant" had been successfully applied. In Barbara's case, it was a label imposed by the criminal justice system. Although she continued her education for a short time thereafter, once her ties to the family were severed, the mechanics of getting to school became increasingly impossible. This is not unlike the situation of women who, experiencing homelessness, try to hold on, as long as possible, to their conventional roles in society. Barbara stated:

> I slept in hallways for about a week, and I was going to school. I washed my clothes out in the bus station and I'd still go to school, rough-dry but clean. The truant officer had to notify my parents for something I did, fighting or whatever, and my mother admitted I didn't live there [i.e., at home]. So the school called the authorities, and the authorities had me arrested for vagrancy.

This process of criminalization, beginning with victimization and running away, and culminating in structural dislocation and being labeled a status offender, can be observed as well in the case of Harriette D., also serving time for a felony offense. As an infant, Harriette was placed in foster care by her mother. She was sexually abused by her foster father, ran away from home, and dropped out of school prior to being institutionalized. As in the case of Barbara G., it was Harriette, and not her abuser, who was arrested, labeled a status offender, and institutionalized. Harriette said:

> I was with this foster lady who was very cruel. She was abusive, and I was no more than a maid as a child. That was my purpose. She received welfare for foster kids, that was her purpose. I stayed there 'til I was thirteen, then ran away. I was tired of the physical abuse. I ran to my mother's. The man she lived with sexually abused me, and I ran away again. I was in the street. I got arrested for shoplifting. I was picked up for vagrancy when I was almost fifteen. The judge gave my mother an option to take me home or he would have no other choice but to send me away. She says, "Send her away, I don't want her." So they sent me away. I went to a state home for girls.

Many of the interviewees who were abused and institutionalized as girls were homeless upon entry into prison. Their idea of what it meant to be part of a family included abuse, victimization, rejection, and ultimately running away or structural dislocation. Some victims became runaways as a way out of the abuse situation, only to find themselves homeless and in even more precarious situations. This link between conditions of abuse and escape (running away) has been documented by researchers working in the area of juvenile delinquency (Gutierres and Reich 1981; Rhoades and Parker 1981). The literature reaffirms the tendency for abused children to be more involved in escape behaviors such as running away. This is most frequent with victims of sexual abuse. As Sara Gutierres and John Reich (1981) point out, running away may be a coping mechanism in response to child abuse rather than a delinquent behavior. In research on incest in the lives of girls and women, Diana Russell (1986) warns that millions of American girls are being socialized into victim roles that lead to future self-destructive behavior. The connection between physical abuse of young girls and their subsequent entry into the juvenile justice system has been well documented (Chesney-Lind and Rodriguez 1983; Davidson 1982; Smith et al. 1980).

In the 1980 report of the National Juvenile Justice Assessment

Center, Smith and his colleagues concluded that although most abused and neglected children are referred to the juvenile court because they are victims, they leave the system defined as offenders. For status offenses, or such noncriminal acts as truancy, ungovernability, incorrigibility, sexual activity or promiscuity, and running away from home, girls specifically are referred to family court as persons in need of supervision (Chesney-Lind 1982). The very children who are abused are referred to court by the abusive parent; females are more than twice as likely as males to be turned in by their parents (Rosenberg and Zimmerman 1982; Chesney-Lind 1982). Girls are usually referred to the courts with greater frequency than are boys (Chesney-Lind 1978). They are locked up more often, and for longer periods, than are boys (Sarri 1976).

Female prisoners discussing their family backgrounds, and what it was like for them to grow up as young Black girls, often made the connection between being abused, running away from home, and initial entry into the criminal justice system. For young Black girls who resisted sexual oppression by running away from home and family, and subsequently dropping out of school, crime became a way of surviving on the streets. Such was the case of Harriette D. discussed above. Once she left home and dropped out of school, she was on her own at the age of fifteen, with no institutional support. She stated:

> I was in the street and I couldn't work. I had no skills. I was a kid with a record, so I started stealing, and I would steal for my food. I would go in restaurants and order food and not pay for it, and things like that. A lady introduced me to another way of making money. All I had to do was what had been done, have sex. At sixteen, I was arrested for prostitution. I started using drugs—heroin, cocaine. Not only was I selling my body to support the habit, I was doing robberies, burglaries, whatever I had to do. Within a six-month period I was back in jail, and it didn't faze me because I was secure there. I had a home, had a roof over my head, had three hot meals. I had clean clothing. I didn't have to sleep in hallways, and I didn't have to sell my body for a chicken dinner.

A system of male dominance and control was operative in the lives of these young girls, a set of social relations of power wherein males were controlling their sexuality. As young girls, many of the interviewees acted against their oppressors by running away rather than fighting. This was consistent with both their age and their gender role socialization. Indeed, the combination of size, age, and gender made fleeing the more rational response and fighting the least feasible. Unlike so many young girls similarly situated, these girls were unwilling to accept domination and abuse passively. Yet, in their nonacceptance, it was they who were snared subsequently in another patriarchal web—that of the criminal justice system. In a study of 200 street prostitutes in San Francisco, Mimi Silbert and Ayola Pines (1981) found that about two-thirds of the women had run away from home to escape sexual or other brutality. Meda Chesney-Lind (1978) suggests that the police, the courts, and other criminal justice personnel sanction women as much for violating gender role expectations as for committing illegal behavior.

In the case of Harriette D., and in the cases of many other recidivists who were dislocated from family, prison became their home and other criminals and prisoners became their family. They spoke of drug addicts as their family, and of using drugs as a way of blotting out what they had to do to survive on the streets. Once they were addicted, the drugs became an end in themselves, and crime a way of supporting the drug habit.

However, gender oppression was only one of the precipitating factors pushing girls out of the family and into the streets. Class oppression and racial oppression were also salient factors in the process of criminalization (Balkan et al. 1980). Both the *National Study* (Glick and Neto 1977) and the San Francisco jail study (Lewis and Bresler 1981) indicated that as children, Black women came from a more impoverished socioeconomic background than did White women, and that they were more than twice as likely to have been on welfare when arrested. To be young, Black, poor, and female is to be in a high-risk category for victimization and stigmatization on many levels. Class oppression was alluded to in the women's comments about growing up poor and turning to deviant behavior as a way of helping themselves and their families.

For some Black women, the process of criminalization began when, as young girls, they decided to assist the family financially, by stealing. They were helping to meet the needs of an economically depressed family for whom welfare was insufficient. Mable P. discusses the economic situation of her family and its impact on her behavior: "There were eight children in the family. My father had a mover's job, but we also got welfare. We moved from hotel to hotel and ended up in the projects. I needed things, so I had no choice but to steal. I've been stealing since I was ten."

Similarly, Clara R. comments on how the socioeconomic situation of her family, and the hardships endured by her mother, affected her behavioral choices. She says that what frustrated her most was

the living situation my family was in. My father beat my mother and neglected his children. He could have taken care of us, but he left. We were on welfare. I began stealing when I was twelve. I hustled to help feed and clothe the other [twelve] kids and help pay the rent. [Crime is] a trade to one that knows nothing else.

Mable and Clara took it upon themselves to fulfill adult role responsibilities, but they did this through deviant means. Considering their youth, inexperience, and lack of skills and education, the deviant route became the choice for assisting other family members and for helping themselves. They chose an assertive, nontraditional course of action, out of step with the cultural mandates for young girls in the society. Such action would exact a costly toll upon their lives. And yet, as Joyce Ladner (1972) revealed in her research on young Black girls, when few options are available for meeting basic human needs for food and clothing, thus forcing one to steal, this becomes the necessary proof that the social system can and should be violated.

In many cases, economic need interfered with a young Black girl's ability to continue her education or to concentrate on schoolwork. Responding to open-ended questions about school and teachers, some of the women commented as follows on the connection between their socioeconomic circumstances and their schooling: "[My teachers] tried talking to me, but talk didn't buy my clothes"; "I was a good student, but other things were on my mind, like cash money"; "I dropped out of school to work." Although school was a refuge for many of the women, it was not a sufficient counterbalancing force for the severe damage to personhood and self-esteem that occurred within the family. Without support from the family and the educational institution, one's life chances are severely stunted, and such was the case for these women. Once they were structurally dislocated from the very institutions responsible for socializing them into lawful and legitimate activities, street crime and association with criminals became a reality. As Dara T. succinctly put it, "I hated myself as I grew older, but I'm not ashamed. I'm just the reflection of what my past was."

Racial oppression in the school was also a factor in alienating some of the women from the educational institution. Women spoke of going to school every day and still not learning anything, of teachers who had their education but who didn't see to it that they got theirs, of teachers who were just there to pick up a paycheck. Jan D. commented in the following manner about the teachers in her school: "It was hard for me to get along with the teachers. Some were prejudiced, and one had the nerve to tell the whole class he didn't like Black people." If racial oppression in the schools is offset by parents who take an activist role in their children's education, children are more likely to remain in school, coping as best they can. However, for the women discussed here, such parental or other support was not available, and so most took it upon themselves to leave alienating school environments and teachers who denigrated them as Black girls.

A few Black women alluded to racial factors in discussions of their criminal behavior. Responses to the open-ended statement "Crime is . . ." included "[Crime is] Black people's support, if they're not working for a living—and that's bad"; "[Crime is] the ultimate source of survival in the world of those who are Black." The intersection of race, gender, and crime was manifested in a particularly striking way as Cheryl J. described her criminal activity:

> I don't mess with Black women. And the reason for that is because I'm Black myself, okay. I look at it like this: I know we struggle. We're struggling for whatever we get, we earned it. So, you know, leave them alone. But the White people, like, they've always had. That's the way I've always looked at it. Taking these White people's money made me feel good inside.

On the one hand, Cheryl considers herself assertive, good at her trade—"a professional," in her words, who is rarely arrested. On the other hand, she stays with the man who taught her the con game and who now abuses her regularly, a man she is afraid to leave, living out a victim role along with her children.

## Sustained Criminal Involvement by Black Women

Although the majority of women arrested and imprisoned are first offenders, a large number are repeat offenders, or recidivists—women for whom the cycle of crime-arrest-imprisonment has become a way of life. These recidivists are disproportionately poor and Black. They are women who have rarely worked in the paid labor force, who are essentially unskilled, undereducated, and structurally dislocated from the labor market. Many were abused as girls and institutionalized at an early age. The life of Alicia R. is a case in point.

Alicia was reared by a father who raped her at the age of eleven. She says his action was meant to punish her for being "too attracted to girls." At age twelve, she ran away from home and has been on her own ever since—between institutions and foster homes. She began using drugs as a way of blotting out the pain of the past, and became an addict. Subsequently she was involved in criminal activity to support a growing habit. She is in prison more than she is out, and her friends and newly constituted family are fellow criminals and prisoners.

Similarly, if we assess the case of Harriette D., it becomes clear how sustained criminal involvement became a way of life. Once she had run away from the sexual abuse she experienced at home, and was institutionalized through actions taken by the family court with her mother's permission, the stage was set for her to fend for herself by whatever means were necessary or available to a young girl with little education, no skills, and no social network. Structurally dislocated from the family, school, and work opportunities, Harriette had others in similar situations as her socializing agents. Deviant and criminal behavior was learned through association with people in the criminal life, and sustained criminal involvement was supported by a "family" of other drug addicts and criminals. Harriette gave a glimpse of what her life of sustained criminal activity was like:

> There was really nowhere for me to go. So I went up on the corner, hung out, and reverted back to selling myself and doing stickups or robberies or burglaries, whatever I needed to do. I ended up living in a shooting gallery—where dope fiends go to get high—sleeping on a chair. And I'm sitting in there, and I sleep in there, and I eat in there, and I get high in there. I wasn't changing my clothes. I had long hair—I wasn't combing it. All I wanted to do was stay high. . . . Drug addicts accept you. This was your family, you know. And I don't care what time of night it was, if you needed one of 'em, they were there. And in my mind, I always had a place to go. The average drug addict is a very lonely person, with a low self-esteem.

Repeat offenders are usually drug addicts who engage in illegal activities that yield monetary rewards which can be used to sustain their lifestyle. In the larger cities, over 50 percent of the female jail population are convicted prostitutes (Mann 1984). Research on females involved in prostitution and drug sales has revealed that the stated motivations for such crimes are economic (Silbert and Pines 1981; James 1976). As Jane Chapman's (1980) work shows, drug abuse is associated directly with economic need and therefore relates directly to economic crime.

Marsha Rosenbaum (1981) and Meda Chesney-Lind and Noelie Rodriguez (1983) have documented the connection between female addicts and female criminals. Initially, the female addict tries to hold onto her job with drug use as an aside or pastime, but eventually the job is relinquished as the addiction takes over. The chaos and uncertainty of the addict lifestyle make routine tasks extremely difficult, and the daily habits of work almost impossible to maintain. Being "in the life" or involved in the drug world is, as Rosenbaum and others have revealed, especially attractive to poor women who are jobless and unable to reap many of the advantages society has to offer.

Josey, Edna, and Ann are three young women for whom drug addiction and crime have become a persistent reality. Josey B., who is twenty-six, has been addicted to heroin since age nineteen. Initially she would get high between jobs. However, less than a year after she began using drugs, she was arrested and charged with petty larceny and forgery. The cycle of drug addiction and crime persists for Josey. Like Josey, Edna P., who is twenty-seven, worked in the paid labor market until she became addicted to drugs (in her case, heroin). Edna thinks her life took a turn for the worse when she reunited with her husband and started using drugs. Since that time, she has been arrested often for a variety of crimes including forgery, burglary, larceny, possession of stolen property, and prostitution. Similarly, Ann T., who says she was introduced to heroin by her husband at age twenty-four, became involved in prostitution as a way of earning money for "the bare necessities."

The women interviewed often spoke of being introduced to drugs by their lovers or husbands, and of having worked in low-skilled, low-paying jobs prior to becoming addicted. When dislocation from the occupational structure is combined with dislocation from the family, and when one has a drug habit to support, crime, which is an illegal form of work, becomes inevitable for survival. It is the alternative available to impoverished women who are removed from normative social networks and, at the same time, addicted to drugs.

Most of the interviewees periodically held low-paying, part-time jobs such as waitress, short-order cook, factory worker, typist, file clerk, cashier, or maid. In their discussions about work and drug use, two women stated: "I worked awhile at an A&P supermarket wrapping meat, and at the Associated Food Store, but had to leave due to drugs" and "For two years I did filing and general office work at [a university], but left due to drugs."

Other women, with little education and few skills, commented simply on the relationship between lack of employment and their criminal behavior. Mary W. said, "I'm not proud of what I'm doing. It's just that I need these things. I had a job at one time and was doing good. It kept me out of trouble. I'd take any kind of job as long as I got some way to get some money. Now it's hard to get a job." In the words of three other women: "I know crime is not something to get involved in, but I get nervous when I don't have money"; "Prior to coming to jail, I supported myself by prostitution and stealing"; "Crime nowadays seems to be a necessity."

Female recidivists suffer from chronic disabilities (alcoholism, drug use), from personal crises (physical/sexual abuse), and from economic difficulties (unemployment/poverty). People who are homeless have been similarly described (Hope and Young 1986). Prior to becoming involved in crime, a sexually abused girl may run away from home, abuse drugs, drop out of school, and occupy a marginal role in the paid labor force. Similarly, a young girl may begin stealing to augment the family welfare check, become addicted to drugs, and, having learned no other skill or trade, persist in this behavior as an adult woman.

The typical contemporary woman in prison is young, poor, a member of a minority group, a high school dropout, unmarried, and the mother of two or more children for whom she is the sole support. Economic pressures, particularly on the poor, and the spread of drugs throughout the population are playing a major role in increasing the number of imprisoned women. The majority of women in prison have been charged with economic crimes, not with murder or manslaughter. Since the 1980s, the rate of increase in property crimes and drug crimes among women has been greater than the rate of increase for violent crimes without economic motives. Economic crimes consist of property crimes, forgery, counterfeiting, fraud, embezzlement, possession of stolen property, and prostitution. These women can be counted among the hard-core unemployed, the homeless, the drug addicted, and the sexually abused.

Women comprise approximately 4.9 percent of the total prison population, up from 4.2 percent in 1981 (Applebome 1987), and Black women comprise a disproportionately high percentage of that female population. Studies conducted by other researchers (Owens 1980; Owens and Bell 1977; Bell 1973) reveal that racial bias affects Black offenders at each stage of the criminal justice cycle, and that Black women are more severely sanctioned than Black men by the criminal justice system.

# Summary

This chapter has attempted to integrate the importance of gender relations with race and class factors in highlighting the process of criminality for young Black girls and the sustained criminal involvement of adult Black women. The habitual Black female criminals discussed here were women who were abused as children. They had no advocates nor social networks to assist them in overcoming physical, sexual, or emotional abuse, so they experienced a profound sense of normlessness and isolation. It was inevitable that they would become disaffected first from two primary socializing institutions—the family and the school—and subsequently from the occupational structure. They ran away from home, dropped out of school, and attempted to make it on their own without structural supports, skills, or training—and usually without a high school diploma. They were also involved in privatized forms of self-destructive behavior not normally considered criminal—alcoholism, drug addiction—as a rebellion against their subordinate, powerless status.

Women who are structurally dislocated from the primary institutions of the society, and who adopt criminal behavior as a coping strategy, are eventually resocialized within criminal networks and relocated structurally within the prison. Once incarcerated, habitual criminals form prison families and kinship networks, and identify more with other criminals and prisoners because they have few ties to the conventional world. Thus, in order to intervene in the process of criminalization for habitual female criminals—a process that begins with early victimization and subsequent dislocation from social institutions—the criminal justice system must assist, rather than further penalize and stigmatize, young girls who have been systematically oppressed within the society, and who are resisting that oppression. The present findings on the criminogenic aspects of oppression and victimization may suggest ways to break the insidious cycle in which victimization and crime feed upon one another. Further examination of the relationship between macrostructures of control (family, school, criminal justice system) and microstructures of resistance (accommodation and resistance) by girls and women is essential.

# References

Applebome, Peter. 1987. "Women in U.S. Prisons: Fast-Rising Population." *New York Times*, June 16, p. A16.

Arnold, Regina. 1979. "Socio-structural Determinants of Self-Esteem and the Relationship Between Self-Esteem and Criminal Behavioral Patterns of Imprisoned Women." Ph.D. dissertation, Bryn Mawr College.

————. 1986. Unpublished focused oral history interviews with women in a state prison, New York.

Balkan, Sheila, Ronald Berger, and Janet Schmidt. 1980. *Crime and Deviance in America: A Critical Approach.* Belmont, Calif.: Wadsworth.

Bell, Derrick A. 1973. *Race, Racism and American Law.* Boston: Little Brown.

Chapman, Jane Roberts. 1980. *Economic Realities and the Female Offender.* Lexington, Mass.: Lexington Books.

Chesney-Lind, Meda. 1978. "Chivalry Reexamined: Women and the Criminal Justice System." In Lee Bowker, ed., *Women, Crime, and the Criminal Justice System.* Lexington, Mass.: D. C. Heath.

————. 1982. "Introduction" and "From Benign Neglect to Malign Attention: A Critical Review of Research on Female Delinquency." Pp. 51–71 in Sue Davidson, ed., *Justice for Young Women.* Tucson, Ariz.: New Directions for Young Women.

Chesney-Lind, Meda, and Noelie Rodriguez. 1983. "Under Lock and Key: A View from the Inside." *Prison Journal* 63(2): 47–65.

Davidson, Sue, ed. 1982. *Justice for Young Women.* Tucson, Ariz.: New Directions for Young Women.

Glick, Ruth, and Virginia Neto. 1977. *National Study of Women's Correctional Programs.* Washington, D.C.: U.S. Government Printing Office.

Gutierres, Sara E., and John W. Reich. 1981. "A Developmental Perspective on Runaway Behavior: Its Relationship to Child Abuse." *Child Welfare* 60 (2): 89–94.

Hope, Marjorie, and James Young. 1986. *The Faces of Homelessness.* Lexington, Mass.: Lexington Books.

James, Jennifer. 1976. "Motivation for Entrance into Prostitution." Pp. 125–139 in Laura Crites, ed., *The Female Offender.* Lexington, Mass.: D. C. Heath.

Ladner, Joyce. 1971. *Tomorrow's Tomorrow: The Black Woman.* Garden City, N.Y.: Doubleday.

Leonard, Eileen. 1982. *Women, Crime and Society: A Critique of Criminology Theory.* New York: Longman.

Lewis, Diane K. and Laura Bresler. 1981. *Is There a Way Out? A Community Study of Women in San Francisco County Jail.* San Francisco: Unitarian-Universalist Service Committee.

Mann, Cora R. 1984. *Female Crime and Delinquency.* Tuscaloosa: University of Alabama Press.

Owens, Charles E. 1980. *Mental Health and Black Offenders.* Lexington, Mass.: Lexington Books.

Owens, Charles E., and Jimmy Bell. 1977. *Blacks and Criminal Justice.* Lexington, Mass.: Lexington Books.

Price, Barbara R., and Natalie J. Sokoloff. 1982. *The Criminal Justice System and Women*. New York: Clark Boardman.

Rafter, Nicole Hahn. 1986. "Left out by the Left: Crime and Crime Control." *Socialist Review* 16 (89): 7–23.

Rhoades, Philip W., and Sharon L. Parker. 1981. *The Connections Between Youth Problems and Violence in the Home: Preliminary Report of New Research*. Portland: Oregon Coalition Against Domestic and Sexual Violence.

Rosenbaum, Marsha. 1981. *Women on Heroin*. New Brunswick, N.J.: Rutgers University Press.

———. 1982. "Work and the Addicted Prostitute." Pp. 131–150 in Nicole Hahn Rafter and Elizabeth A. Stanko, eds., *Judge, Lawyer, Victim, Thief: Women, Gender Roles and Criminal Justice*. Boston: Northeastern University Press.

Rosenberg, Debby, and Carol Zimmerman. 1982. "Listen to Me." In Sue Davidson, ed., *Justice for Young Women*. Tucson, Ariz.: New Directions for Young Women.

Russell, Diana E. H. 1986. *The Secret Trauma: Incest in the Lives of Girls and Women*. New York: Basic Books.

Sarri, Rosemary C. 1976. "Juvenile Law: How It Penalizes Females." In Laura Crites, ed., *The Female Offender*. Lexington, Mass.: D. C. Heath.

Shakur, Assata (Joanne Chesimard). 1978. "Women in Prison: How We Are." *Black Scholar* 9 (April): 8–15.

Silbert, Mimi, and Ayola Pines. 1981. "Occupational Hazards of Street Prostitutes." *Criminal Justice and Behavior* 8 (December): 395–399.

Smith, C. P., and O. J. Berkman, and W. M. Fraser. 1980. *Report of the National Juvenile Justice Assessment Centers*. Washington, D.C.: American Justice Institute.

# 10

## Cultural Survival and Contemporary American Indian Women in the City

### Jennie R. Joe
### Dorothy Lonewolf Miller

**P**rior to their conquest and subsequent colonization, Indian women in most tribes held important positions as healers, teachers, and leaders. Moreover, because of their resourcefulness and ability to gather and store seeds, roots, and berries, and to hunt small game, they were able to feed their families when big game was scarce and hunting was poor. In some tribes, the women were the agriculturists and thereby provided the major food source for their families. The European conquest, however, greatly altered the world of most Native Americans.

The erosion of the role and position of Indian women began with missionization and education. Indian girls were forced to go to school to learn to be homemakers or handmaidens for non-Indian families. Others who dared to return to the reservations found themselves alienated until they either had to relearn traditional skills for survival and/or return to the non-Indian world to find work. This loss of values among Indian peoples was accelerated as more and more tribes were forced into a paternalistic or wardship position with the federal government. The fabric of many tribal cultures, however, survived because in many instances women of the tribe used whatever means were available to protect their children and their men. Unfortunately, they were no match against the powerful arm of the federal government, an institution that was bent on "civilizing" the Indians. Tribes may have been able to save some elements of their language or their cultural traditions, but these efforts did not stem the tide of other changes, which have resulted in poverty and the loss of psychological well-being.

Various forms of oppression and poverty continue today for many

Indian women and their families. Forced by public outcry to improve the lot of American Indians, the federal government over the years has periodically initiated programs to deal with some of these problems. One economic alternative was the relocation of young Indian women and men to urban areas where the federal government had arranged contracts with trade schools and employment agencies for job placement. Jobs were primarily unskilled or semiskilled, and resettlement was in urban ghettos. Thus, other than when World War II manpower shortages permitted Indian women to be recruited to work in war plants (the first large-scale out-migration), the federal relocation program of the 1950s and 1960s was the second major out-migration of Indian women from the reservations. The relocation program, however, favored single young adults, which meant that many of the young women had to leave their children behind with grandparents or other extended family members. Once settled, they could arrange child care and other services; then women brought their children to the city and/or started their family in the city.

The government-sponsored relocation program uprooted many single young Indian women as well as young married women. Although the relocation was necessary for the economic survival of many women and their families, that policy, along with the push toward wage labor, began to erode the traditional extended family units that had acted as a buffer against many of the daily stresses of poverty and other hardships. Since the move to the city left them lacking the psychological support of kin and friends, many young women and their children were forced either to seek out other Native Americans in the city or to save enough money to finance frequent trips home. Frustrations and stresses in the city were compounded by problems of discrimination and loneliness. In addition, poverty and unemployment continued to plague many of the families—a situation that continually undermined the economic roles of men and, in some instances, shifted the burden of family support to the women. Because they were far from the reservation, many Indian women who had children had to assume sole responsibility for maintaining cultural continuity and tribal identity for their children.

Today, the future of Indian culture continues to be threatened by the increased migration to the cities. For example, the move to the city often breaks down the geographical boundaries of a reservation that help maintain tribalism and/or continuity of culture. This is not to say that reservation life remains unaffected by modernization and culture change. The erosion of cultural values and beliefs has been and continues to be widespread, so that the geographic boundaries are not enough. With time, the pressures toward assimilation have bred a number of "marginal" individuals, those who have no firm footing in either the Indian or the non-Indian world. The marginal existence has wrought devastation intergenerationally, and the scars from this experience continue to surface in various self-destructive behaviors: alcoholism, suicide, homicide, and/or permanent disability associated with other forms of "careless" behavior. Given these past experiences and their devastating consequences for many Indian families, the cultural strengths that kept tribal identity and families together have centered on the role of women in most tribes. For example, one Navajo woman leader (Wauneka 1987:2) posits that "When Indian women move to the city or marry a non-Indian, the continuity of the tribal culture is threatened. . . . most of us learn about our 'Indianness' from our mothers."

Thus, continuity of culture and tribal identity is of paramount concern for most Native American communities. For example, many legal and policy debates today focus on such issues as tribal membership and degree of Indian blood of the membership. As a result of this interest, there is an increased concern about whom an Indian woman marries and whether her children will be eligible for tribal membership. Urbanization, because it often results in marrying out and detribalization, is seen as a real threat to tribal and cultural continuity. How the responsibility for cultural continuity is accentuated for women in the city is explored in this chapter by examining the lives and experiences of a small sample of American Indian women in Tucson, Arizona, who have found ways to promote or construct cultural and tribal linkages for their children in the urban world.

## Urbanization

Today, over half of the 1.9 million American Indians and Alaska Natives live in off-reservation communities, especially cities such as Los Angeles, Denver, San Francisco, and Chicago (U.S. Department of Commerce, 1991).[1] As stated before, relocation to urban centers is viewed by many tribal leaders as one of the major threats to cultural continuity. Their fears are not unfounded. For example, these leaders point to the increasing number of intertribal and interracial marriages among the Indian population residing in the cities, and the increasing number of Indian children born and reared in the cities who have little or no knowledge of their tribal traditions or languages. One American Indian demographer has confirmed the tribal leaders' prediction by indicating that by the year 2080, the percentage of urbanized American

Indians with one-half or more Indian blood will decrease from the present (1980 census) 87 percent to 8 percent (Thornton 1987:237).

In 1970 only one-third of all American Indians were married to non-Indians, but by 1980 this percentage increased to 50 percent (Thornton 1987:236). As a result of intertribal and interracial marriages, the tribal identification among urbanized Indians appears to have become more generic over time. For example, Indians living in the cities are more likely than those living on the reservation to identify themselves generically as American Indians rather than as members of a specific tribe. It also is not uncommon to find an Indian child claiming lineage from more than one tribe because his or her parents also claim lineage from more than one tribe. In addition, because these Indian children are reared in ethnically diverse urban neighborhoods, they may not speak their tribal language and are less likely to hear their tribal language spoken.

Although there is no information yet available from the 1990 census as to how many urbanized Indians speak their tribal language, in 1970, 26 percent of urbanized Indians and 32 percent of Indians on the reservation indicated a tribal language as the first language learned (Thornton 1987:238). In Los Angeles, where there is a sizable Indian population, 23 percent of the 54,569 American Indians interviewed in 1979 reported English as their second language (UCLA 1987). Matthew Snipp and Gary Sandefur (1988) found that 18 percent of the urban-dwelling Indians and 41 percent of the reservation Indians use their native language in their homes.

## American Indian Women in Tucson

The Indian women who are subjects of this study either were born in the city of Tucson or have lived in Tucson for a number of years. Unlike the Indian women in Los Angeles, whose family history may include involuntary relocation, most of these women have always lived in Tucson or voluntarily moved there from nearby reservation communities. Yet, despite voluntary relocation and prolonged urbanization, most of these women have acculturated but not assimilated. They are bicultural and bilingual. It could be said that for most of these women and their families, the walls of their houses, apartments, or mobile homes serve as psychological boundaries that help them maintain their cultural and tribal identity. These psychological boundaries therefore serve to encapsulate against assimilation.

Tucson, the second largest urban center in Arizona, is home to 6,868 American Indians, mostly Tohono O'odham, Pima, and Yaqui tribal members (Tucson Planning Department 1985). These three tribal groups constitute 89 percent of all Indians living in the city (Evaneshko 1988). The city sprawl is adjacent to the vast desert homelands of the Tohono O'odham (formerly Papago). One Tohono O'odham community and the two Yaqui villages (one on a new reservation) are within Tucson city limits. The Indian families in the city therefore live close to relatives and friends, and thus most familial and other social ties are maintained.

The urban experiences of these Indian women in Tucson afford an opportunity to examine some of the explanations regarding the forces present in their lives that help them maintain or foster cultural traditions and tribal identity for their children and themselves. This study therefore examines data from two tribal groups of women who were selected from a sample of clients—twenty-three Tohono O'odham and ten Yaqui women—who utilize the urban Indian health clinic in Tucson. These women were part of a larger study that began with a sample of 100 Indian clients utilizing the Tucson urban Indian clinic.[2]

## TOHONO O'ODHAM

The Tohono O'odham were residing in southern Arizona when the Spanish explorers first entered the region, and the O'odham view the valley of Tucson as part of their ancestral homeland. Their reservation is vast, covering a large part of southwestern Arizona, and a few tribal members live below the Mexican border in the state of Sonora. There exists a considerable ethnographic literature of the O'odham people (Densmore 1929; Underhill 1939; Spicer 1949, 1962; Shaw 1968; Bahr 1969).

The O'odham have undergone three major waves of invasion and conquest, the first by Spain, followed by Mexico and the United States. The Spanish and Mexican regimes introduced Catholicism into tribal life, beginning with construction of missions and winning of souls for the church. As a result, for a number of decades Tohono O'odham children were largely educated in Catholic schools that dotted the reservation. Yet, as is true throughout the Southwest, Catholicism was modified by the O'odham to mesh with their traditional religious beliefs. The cycles of conquest resulted in loss of vast lands, the depletion of water resources, and the influx of a large non-Indian population that grew into the city of Tucson. Under Anglo colonization, Tohono O'odham children were sent to government schools both on and off the reservation while their parents were forced into wage labor. With few or no job skills, most began to follow seasonal work, picking cotton or fruit in nearby areas. Other adults, because of poor health, age, or lack of job skills, became increasingly dependent upon public welfare programs.

## YAQUIS

Unlike the Tohono O'odham, the Yaquis are newcomers to Tucson. They fled from northern Mexico in the late nineteenth and early twentieth centuries, and settled in a number of small villages and enclaves between Tucson and Phoenix. Historically and culturally, the Yaquis have remained distinct from their neighbors of northern Mexico and from their new neighbors, the Tohono O'odham (Chaudhuri 1974). After years of work and countless efforts, the Yaquis were officially granted federal recognition in 1978 as an American Indian tribe (Locust 1987:4). Although not all Yaquis are enrolled as members of this newly recognized tribe, today, there is nevertheless a strong sense of tribal identity, and the new reservation of New Pascua serves as headquarters for the Yaqui tribal government.

Like the Tohono O'odham, the Yaquis have experienced diverse conditions since the 1890s. The Mexican Revolution and its aftermath divided the Yaqui communities in Mexico. Some Yaquis were captured and sent to Yucatan, others served in the Mexican Revolutionary armies, and still others fled to southern Arizona. Since the Spanish conquest of Mexico, Catholicism has been deeply embedded among the Yaquis. Despite their conflicts with the Mexican government, they became heavily Mexicanized, adopting many Mexican customs of food, dress, and social activities during their two centuries under Mexican government (Spicer 1949; Kelley 1978). Despite their Mexican-ization, many Yaquis claim loyalty to the Yaqui culture. Yaqui women, for example, are especially sensitive to the accusation that they may "become Mexican." For example, one Yaqui woman, referring to her former daughter-in-law who was now married to a Mexican, observed, that "She is not a Yaqui anymore—she became Mexican." Older Yaqui women are very deeply religious, as is shown by their collections of *santos* (religious statues) and religious pictures.

## The Subjects: A Statistical Portrait

The statistical profile of the Indian women in this study indicates that Tohono O'odham women were younger, had a few more years of education, and had slightly more children than the Yaqui women. Table 10.1 summarizes the average ages, education, and family size.

Thirty percent of these women from both tribes were head of their

**Table 10.1.** Average Age, Education, and Number of Children of Tohono O'odham and Yaqui Mothers ($N = 33$)

| Tribe | Age | Education (years) | Number of Children |
|---|---|---|---|
| Tohono O'odham | 34.7 | 9.6 | 2.7 |
| Yaqui | 45.4 | 6.9 | 2.3 |

household, a somewhat higher number in comparison to the 23 percent found among the Indian households in Los Angeles County (UCLA 1987). In addition, all ten Yaqui women in the sample were born and reared in the city of Tucson, compared to 30 percent of the Tohono O'odham women.

Although a majority of both groups were members of the Catholic Church and said that marriage in the church was desirable, about 30 percent indicated that they had been married more than once, often outside the church. Over 44 percent declared themselves single on public documents, but some were living with a mate who may or may not be the father of their children. Only 18 percent of these Indian mothers were married to a man from their tribe, 40 percent were single parents, and others had companions who were from other tribes or who were Mexicans. Only one reported that an Anglo man resided with her. Perhaps as a result of the Catholic religion, there are not many divorces. Some of the fathers of their children had either deserted the family or had never legitimized the children by marriage. Thus some of these women were financially dependent on Aid to Families with Dependent Children (AFDC) and whatever cash they could obtain from domestic or other part-time work.

Nearly half of these mothers were born on their reservation or in their village. Tohono O'odham women were more likely to be born in their reservation communities than were Yaqui women (52 percent vs. 30 percent). One-third of these Indian mothers speak their native language (many are trilingual: English, Spanish, and their native language). Fifteen percent of their children speak their native language. In addition, 82 percent of all the children are enrolled in their mother's tribe, a crucial element in maintaining tribal ties and continuity of Indian identity. Tribal enrollment becomes very crucial in obtaining health and education benefits as well as providing a structural basis for deeper psychological definitions of the self.

An examination of the cultural identities of the sample population is presented in Table 10.2. The women from the Tohono O'odham and

**Table 10.2.** Tribal Identity of Urban O'odham and Yaqui Mothers

| | Yaqui (N = 10) N (%) | O'odham (N = 23) N (%) | Total (N = 33) N (%) |
|---|---|---|---|
| Mother born on reservation | 3 (30) | 12 (52) | 15 (47) |
| Mother speaks native lang. | 3 (30) | 8 (35) | 11 (33) |
| Child speaks native lang. | 3 (30) | 2 (9) | 5 (15) |
| Child enrolled in tribe | 8 (80) | 19 (83) | 27 (82) |
| Married, same tribe | 3 (30) | 3 (13) | 6 (18) |
| Use medicine people | 4 (40) | 9 (39) | 13 (39) |
| Use Indian remedies | 6 (60) | 7 (30) | 13 (39) |

Yaqui communities, for the most part, identify themselves as either O'odham or Yaqui. Children likewise speak of themselves as O'odham or as Yaqui, although in school, their non-Indian teachers and school-mates frequently refer to them as "Indians." At home, specific tribal identity is more common. For example, when asked about cultural values and identity, some of the responses were "To be O'odham is to be good. To be special. To do things in a certain way. . . ." To be Yaqui is to "live the Yaqui way. . . ." In many instances, for the women as well as for their children, language and skin color provide two dimensions of the variations of their view of the non-O'odham or non-Yaqui world. Although language and skin color may be most visible, proximity to the reservation and age are also factors. Younger women place less emphasis on tribal identity than do older women. This observation parallels that of Jane Kelley (1978), who posits that Tohono O'odham can be expected to adhere less precisely to indige-nous beliefs when they are away from members of their social group or away from their family life. On the other hand, Kelley also notes that there comes a time in life (middle age) when old beliefs reappear and are reinforced by that social group.

In addition, the cultural ties to traditional medicine and Indian lifestyles of these women is indicated by the fact that nearly 40 percent used medicine people and Indian remedies during times of illness. Thus the blending of secular and sacred medicine for illnesses is common among both groups.

The Tohono O'odham and Yaqui women share many characteris-tics that are relevant to their adaptation to urban life. First, these women tend to be welfare mothers, often separated from stable incomes or enduring relationships with an employed man; second, the core of their cultural life is the Catholicism–native belief system that they practice in their daily lives; and third, they live separate from the mainstream of Tucson urban life—they reside in segregated residential areas, they know Tucson Anglos "look down" upon Indians, and they avoid confrontation or do not expect equal employment or economic opportunities. Thus, these women are forced to maintain their native identities as best they can (often without viable structural tribal support).

Public welfare and Anglo racism, on the one hand, and tribal identity and relationships, on the other, keep these Yaqui and O'odham women bound to the rapidly changing cultural remnants of their indigenous lifestyles. However, using Catholicism, tribal religious activities, and extended family networks, these women manage to socialize their children to be bicultural and to have a tribal identity.

The tribal identification of these women is important and is underscored by the actions of each tribe. For example, in their battle to obtain federal recognition as an Indian tribe, the Yaquis kept reemphasizing that despite the overshadowing Mexican influence, they were nevertheless Yaqui, an Indian tribe. Similarly, the Tohono O'odham fought to have their tribal name changed from Papago, a Spanish word with a derogatory connotation, to Tohono O'odham, which means the Desert People, the name by which they have historically called themselves. Table 10.3 lists how these women described the cultural orientation of their families.

Because they have had prolonged exposure to the Mexican culture, the Yaquis, more so than the O'odham, have often been described as being tricultural, and many still continue to blend the three cultures. And because the Spanish language is more functional in dealing with the outside world, many of the children of these women learned Spanish instead of Yaqui (Chilcott et al. 1979). Since the mid-1980s, however, the Yaqui community has aggressively supported a Yaqui–English bilingual education program for their children.

The Tohono O'odham children in the city are predominantly taught their native language by their mothers and grandmothers. Sometimes the children are placed in boarding schools on the reservation so that they may be with other O'odham children, in order to retain or learn the O'odham language. In the Tucson public schools, Indian bilingual teachers are employed to work with the Indian children. The Indian committees that oversee these programs are usually made up of women—mothers of some of the children enrolled in these schools.

Although not all the Yaquis are enrolled as members of their tribe,

**Table 10.3.** Cultural Orientation of Subjects

| Cultural Orientation | Tohono O'odham (%) | Yaqui (%) |
|---|---|---|
| Mostly Indian | 40 | 30 |
| Bicultural | 43 | 40 |
| Mostly non-Indian | 17 | 30 |

most of the mothers carefully guard birth certificates and other records so that their children will not be counted as non-Indian by the schools. Most of the Tohono O'odham mothers also said that their children are enrolled in the tribe, and enrollment information is kept in a safe place.

These women said they pass on their "Indianness" or tribalism by giving their children Indian names, allowing their children to live with their grandmothers or other relatives on the reservation, taking their children to native healers, teaching their children some of the stories and customs of the tribe, and teaching them to appreciate "Indian food" and "Indian music." Some of the mothers who work hired other Indian women to care for their young children so that their children would be with Indian people.

In the larger urban arena, these women participate in activities that are Indian-oriented. The Indian Center in Tucson is directed by a woman, as is the urban Indian health program. A majority of the women employed in these facilities are Indian. They also advise and serve on cultural enrichment programs such as the Johnson-O'Malley and Title IV Indian Education Programs.[3] They usually help hire Indian tutors and assist with other cultural programs in the Tucson community.

Similarly, in Los Angeles, the major urban Indian health program is directed by an Indian woman, and, as in Tucson, a majority of the human service workers in this agency are women. They help organize the powwows, arrange special outings for the elders and the youth, and serve on committees advising various agencies on how best to serve the Indians in the city. They also help support the popularity of Indian arts and crafts by buying from Indian craftspeople.

This description of Indian women residing in the city represents those who are most often married to Indians and who continue consciously and unconsciously to be the culture bearers. Indian women who are married to non-Indians, on the other hand, are less likely to be actively involved in types of activities that are designed for the Indian clients, although they may support the cultural survival activities in other ways. They may, for example, attend fund-raising

**Table 10.4.** Urban Yaqui and O'odham Mothers: Social Problems

| Social Problem | Yaqui N(%) | O'odham N(%) | Total N(%) |
|---|---|---|---|
| On public assistance | 5 (50) | 17 (74) | 22 (67) |
| Single parent | 4 (40) | 15 (65) | 19 (58) |
| Child school problem, dropout | 4 (40) | 7 (30) | 11 (33) |
| Alcohol, drug problem in family | 3 (30) | 5 (22) | 8 (24) |

functions. Because they often keep themselves marginal to the world of other Indian women, most remain invisible to the Indian network unless their children, upon finding that they have Indian heritage, begin to frequent the Indian center or participate in some of the programs.

Life in the city is complicated by a variety of problems. Table 10.4 summarizes some of these problems, as reported by the women in the study. As indicated, poverty is an important factor in the daily life of Indian women and their families; nearly two-thirds of them were receiving public assistance as their primary source of financial support. Although public welfare funds provide a safety net against economic collapse, the level of support guarantees a life trapped in a culture of poverty. That, combined with a mother-headed household (58 percent) and the impact of alcohol and drugs on the family (24 percent), undoubtedly contributes to the high dropout and school problem rate (33 percent) of the children of these women. The combination of being Indian, being poor, and living in the segregated neighborhood pockets of Tucson presents Indian mothers with many structural barriers to survival or to rising in the mobile Anglo world, but their tribally oriented, encapsulated world helps them survive psychologically and culturally. But these women's survival in the city is not without psychological cost, as the levels of stress in Table 10.5 show.

These subjects took the Health Opinion Survey (HOS), a self-reporting mental health scale that has been used with other tribes. HOS helped to gauge the degree of stress among these Indian mothers. As shown in Table 10.5, 70 percent scored in the moderate-high range of stress; 70 percent stated they often "get discouraged" and are in "poor spirits." One-third reported they frequently have "bad dreams." These psychological symptoms are serious for women who are less acculturated and who hold to forces of positive power, avoiding states of discouragement and of being in poor spirits. "Bad

**Table 10.5** Psychological Effects of Urban Living on Yaqui and O'odham Mothers

| Psychological Effects | Yaqui N (%) | O'odham N (%) | Total N (%) |
|---|---|---|---|
| Moderate-high stress score | 8 (80) | 15 (65) | 23 (70) |
| Bad dreams | 3 (30) | 8 (35) | 11 (33) |
| Gets discouraged | 8 (80) | 15 (65) | 23 (70) |
| In poor spirits | 8 (80) | 15 (65) | 23 (70) |

dreams" are often perceived as serious warnings of forthcoming disaster that require the services of medicine people to lift the negative forces at work in one's life.

Other data indicate how these Indian mothers deal with these serious social and psychological pressures. They turn to medicine people (30 percent); they turn to families and relatives on the reservation (27 percent); they turn to family and friends in the city for help (39 percent). All these help-seeking patterns provide coping strategies as well as messages and behaviors that strengthen the women's sense of identity.

## Summary

The cultural endurance and encapsulation of Indian women and their families in the city are the consequences of poverty and racism, two negative structural properties of American life. On one hand, Indian women bring to the city a strong sense of identity with their tribal life and land base, and on the other hand, they are assigned to a separate status as a lower caste and class group, living in segregated communities, largely dependent on some form of welfare. Thus both poverty and racism work to keep American Indians from melting into American urban life.

By maintaining cultural boundaries, some women seek ways to avoid racial assignment within the urban culture. Thus they remain predominantly tribally oriented rather than take on the more generic identification of "Indian," as they are commonly referred to by their non-Indian neighbors. By encapsulating themselves within their tribal identity, these women may become culturally pluralistic but rarely are assimilated. There are several explanations offered as to why American Indians have not become totally assimilated over hundreds of years of conquest and governmental pressures. Among these are four major explanations.

1. Indians have been isolated geographically and have not been given the necessary opportunity for education and resources that would enable them to integrate fully into the American mainstream. This is the "taken-for-granted" view held widely by the public and by social and political planners.

2. Forced acculturation has resulted in high degrees of resistance to change in Indian cultural patterns (Dozier 1955). This resistance has been aided by the "draining off" of the most acculturated segment of the reservation population, leaving a residue of those Indians who hold more firmly to their culture and increase their resistance to "forced change" (Vogt 1957). Edward Spicer spoke of the acculturation admixture as follows: "Political domination stimulated the Indians in a variety of ways to resist submergence in the conquering societies. Moreover, in the dominant nation, the tendency was ultimately reinforced by the recognition of the Indian entities and even encouraged their continued existence as distinct ethnic groups" (1962: 157).

3. It is the nature of culture that while material aspects of a culture change, family and kinship institutions are more persistent, so those aspects of a way of life, the implicit values of the core culture, and the cultural orientations and personality types are even more persistent (Linton 1936; Vogt 1957; Spicer 1962; Hallowell 1945; Bruner 1956).

4. The organized communal structure, such as that found on many reservations, preserves Indian cultural beliefs and functions in the urban environment (Wolf 1955).

This study of Tucson Indian women revealed an acculturative strategy of encapsulation. Four adaptive strategies utilized by these women are especially evident: (1) strong tribal identity, (2) cultural beliefs, (3) American racism, and (4) welfare lifestyle, that is, institutionalized poverty. All four of these factors operate to prevent total assimilation of these Tohono O'odham and Yaqui mothers residing in Tucson, Arizona. These "push" and "pull" forces stalemate the assimilative process and serve as counterweights to aid the women in their tribally oriented life way.

As mothers, most of these women translate their cultural heritage within the framework of their everyday life, particularly as they socialize their children into the values and behaviors of their tribal culture. As mothers they also see to it that their tribal affiliations are kept intact by making certain that their children are registered with their tribe and that the tribal identity is maintained from one generation to the next. In contrast, the man's role, under conquest, has deteriorated and has become devalued in contemporary urban society. Although forced cultural change has meant that their men are often unable to be fathers, these women as mothers maintain their role as caretakers of the children.

As mothers, these women face the racism of segregated housing and must struggle to keep their family ties intact (Blumer 1958). They comfort their children when other children ridicule them as "Injuns" or "savages," or beat them up at school. As mothers, they protest and defend their Indian children against racism and, indirectly, against assimilation into the broader non-Indian world.

Some of these women are welfare mothers. Public assistance programs such as AFDC have always relied on mothers to hold their families together, albeit at a level of financial assistance that assured they would live in a culture of poverty. Thus, despite a history of government programs aimed at assimilating them into the mainstream, these women have clung to their cultural identities as tribal members. The reasons for the failure of the rapid assimilation are complex, and include the struggles of these women to maintain their cultural continuity and tribal identity for themselves and their children, despite the powerful forces of racism and poverty.

Sometimes, these women worry more about losing their men and their children to the ravages of alcoholism and drugs than to losing their offspring to mainstream society. As long as they themselves identify with their tribal heritage, they find ways to manipulate the home and social environment as much as possible to ensure that their children do not forget "who they are." They may not speak the language or share all the beliefs and teachings of the tribe, but these women do instill in their children information and identification about their tribal roots.

In the field of women's studies, we need to note the contributions of Indian women not only in terms of the strategies they use to foster tribalism and "Indianness" but also of the ways in which they define these important concepts within their contemporary worldview and self-identity.

# Notes

*Acknowledgments*: This study was supported by a grant from the National Institute on Disability and Rehabilitation Research (NIDRR), U.S. Department of Education (#G0083C0094). We would also like to thank our colleague, Robert Young, for his valuable suggestions, and Trudie Narum, who helped with this study.

1. It should be noted that although the relocation was often viewed as a major urbanization experience for Indian people, migration to the cities was not a new phenomenon for some, especially those who were among the first to be dispossessed from their land and those whose homelands were near the urban growth centers. In fact, social and other problems of Indians in the city were mentioned in the 1928 Meriam Report (Meriam 1928).

2. The study was intended to be an assessment of the health needs and problems of the clients utilizing the urban clinic (Joe et al. 1988).

3. The Johnson-O'Malley Act, enacted in 1934, permitted the federal government to contract with public schools to educate Indian children. Title IV of the Indian Education Act. (P.L. 92-318).

# References

Agar, Lynn P. 1980. "The Economic Role of Women in Alaskan Society." Pp. 305–318 in E. Bourguigan, ed., *A World of Women*. New York: Praeger.

Albers, Patricia C. 1983. "Introduction: New Perspective on Plains Indian Women." Pp. 1–26 in Patricia Albers and Beatrice Medicine, eds., *The Hidden Half: Studies of Plains Women*. Lanham Park, Md.: University Press of America.

———. 1985. "Autonomy and Dependency in the Lives of Dakota Women: A Study in Historical Change." *Review of Radical Political Economics* 17: 109–134.

———. 1989. "From Illusion to Illumination: Anthropological Studies of American Indian Women." Pp. 132–170 in Sandra Morgen, ed., *Gender and Anthropology*. Washington, D.C.: American Anthropological Association.

Albers, Patricia C., and Beatrice Medicine. 1983. "The Role of Sioux Women in the Production of Ceremonial Objects: The Case of the Star Quilt." Pp. 123–142 in Patricia Alberts and Beatrice Medicine, eds., *The Hidden Half: Studies of Plains Indian Women*. Lanham Park, Md.: University Press of America.

Allen, Paula Gunn. 1986. *The Sacred Hoop: Recovering the Feminine in American Indian Traditions*. Boston: Beacon Press.

Bahr, Donald. 1969. "Pima Shamanism: The Sickness." Ph.D. dissertation, Harvard University.

Bataille, Gretchen, and Kathleen M. Sands. 1984. *American Indian Women Telling Their Lives*. Lincoln: University of Nebraska Press.

Black, Mary. 1984. "Maidens and Mothers: An Analysis of Hopi Corn Metaphors." *Ethnology* 23: 279–288.

Blackwood, Evelyn. 1984. "Sexuality and Gender in Certain Native American Tribes: The Case of Cross-Gender Females." *Signs: Journal of Women in Society and Culture* 10: 27–42.

Blumer, Hubert. 1958. "Race Prejudices as a Sense of Group Position." *Pacific Sociology Review* 1: 3–7.

Bruner, Edward M. 1956. "Cultural Transmission and Cultural Change." *Southwest Journal of Anthropology* 10: 191–199.

Buckley, Thomas. 1982. "Menstruation and the Power of Yurok Women: Methods in Cultural Reconstruction." *American Ethnologist* 32: 37–56.

Bysiewicz, Shirley, and Ruth Van de Mark. 1977. "The Legal Status of Dakota Women." *American Indian Law Review* 3: 255–312.

Chaudhuri, Joystpul. 1974. *Urban Indians of Arizona: Phoenix, Tucson, and Flagstaff*. Tucson: University of Arizona, Institute of Government Studies.

Chilcott, John, Barbara Buchanan, Felipe Molina, and James Jones. 1979. *An Education-Related Ethnographic Study of a Yaqui Community*. Tucson: University of Arizona Press.

Conte, Christine. 1982. "Ladies, Livestock, Land and Lucre: Women's Network and Social Status on the Western Navajo Reservation." *American Indian Quarterly* 6: 105–124.

Cruikshank, Julie. 1975. "Becoming a Woman in Athapaskan Society: Changing Traditions in the Upper Yukon River." *Western Canadian Journal of Anthropology* 5: 1–14.

Densmore, Frances. 1929. *Papago Music*. Bureau of American Ethnology, Bulletin 90. Washington, D.C.: U.S. Government Printing Office.

Downs, James. 1972. "The Cowboy and the Lady: Models as Determinant of the Rate of Acculturation Among the Pinon Navajos." Pp. 275–290 in Howard M. Bahr, Bruce A. Chadwick, and Robert E. Day, eds., *Native Americans Today*. New York: Harper & Row.

Dozier, Edward. 1955. "Forced and Permissive Acculturation." *The American Indian* 7: 38–41.

Evaneshko, Veronica. 1988. *Demographics of Native Americans in the Traditional Indian Alliance Catchment Area*. Tucson: University of Arizona, College of Nursing.

Green, Rayna. 1980. "Native American Women." *Signs: Journal of Women in Society and Culture* 7: 248–267.

————. 1983. *Native American Women: A Contextual Bibliography*. Blooming-ton: Indiana University Press.

Hallowell, A. I. 1945. "Socio-psychological Aspects of Acculturation." Pp. 171–200 in Ralph Linton, ed., *The Science of Man in the World Crisis*. New York: Columbia University Press.

Joe, Jennie R. 1982. "Cultural Influences on Navajo Mothers with Disabled Children." *American Indian Quarterly* 6: 170–190.

Joe, Jennie R., Dorothy Lonewolf Miller, and Trudie Narum. 1988. *Traditional Indian Alliance: Delivery of Health Care Services to Arizona Indians*. Tucson: University of Arizona, Native American Research and Training Center, Monograph Series, No. 4.

Kehoe, Alice. 1976. "Old Woman Had Great Power." *Western Canadian Journal of Anthropology* 6: 68–76.

————. 1983. "The Shackles of Traditions." Pp. 53–76 in Patricia Albers and Beatrice Medicine, eds., *The Hidden Half: Studies of Plains Indian Women*. Lanham Park, Md.: University Press of America.

Kelley, Jane H. 1978. *Yaqui Women: Contemporary Life Histories*. Lincoln: University of Nebraska Press.

Keohane, Nannerl, Michelle Zimbalist Rosaldo, and Barbara Gelpi, eds. 1982. *Feminist Theory: A Critique of Ideology*. Chicago: University of Chicago Press.

Kidwell, Clara Sue. 1979. "The Power of Women in Three American Indian Societies." *Journal of Ethnic Studies* 6: 113–121.

Klein, Alan. 1983. "The Plains Truth: The Impact of Colonization on Indian Women." *Dialectical Anthropology* 7: 299–313.

Knack, Martha. 1980. *Life Is with People: Household Organization of the Contemporary Southern Paiute Indians*. Anthropological Papers 19. Socorro, N.M.: Ballena Press.

Lamphere, Louise. 1977. *To Run After Them*. Tucson: University of Arizona Press.

Landes, Ruth. 1971. *The Ojibwa Woman*. New York: W. W. Norton.

Lincoln, Kenneth. 1983. *Native American Renaissance*. Berkeley: University of California Press.

Linton, Ralph. 1936. *The Study of Man*. New York: Appleton-Century.

Locust, Carol. 1987. *Yaqui Indian Beliefs About Health and Handicap*. Tucson: University of Arizona, Native American Research and Training Center, Monograph Series.

Lurie, Nancy. 1961. *Mountain Wolf Woman: Sister of Crashing Thunder, a Winnebego Indian*. Ann Arbor: University of Michigan Press.

Lynch, Robert. 1986. "Women in Northern Paiute Politics." *Signs: Journal of Women in Society and Culture* 11: 253–266.

Medicine, Beatrice. 1978. *The Native American Woman: A Perspective*. Austin, Tex.: National Educational Laboratory Publications.

———. 1987. "Indian Women and the Renaissance of Traditional Religion." Pp. 159–171 in Raymond J. DeMallie and Douglas R. Parks, eds., *Sioux Indian Religion: Tradition and Innovation*. Norman: University of Oklahoma Press.

Meriam, Lewis. 1928. *The Problem of Indian Administration*. Baltimore: Johns Hopkins University Press.

Metcalf, Ann. 1979. "Reservation Born—City Bred: Native American Women and Children in the City." Pp. 21–34 in Ann McElroy and Carolyn Matthiasson, eds., *Sex Roles in Changing Cultures: Occasional Papers in Anthropology*. Buffalo: State University of New York Press.

Schlegel, Alice. 1973. "The Adolescent Socialization of the Hopi Girl." *Ethnology* 12: 449–462.

Shaw, Daniel R. 1968. "Health Concepts and Attitudes of the Papago Indians." Master's thesis, University of Arizona.

Snipp, C. Matthew, and Gary D. Sandefur. 1988. "Earnings of American Indians and Alaska Natives: The Effects of Residence and Migration." *Social Forces* 66: 994–1008.

Spicer, Edward H. 1949. *Pascua, a Yaqui Village of Arizona*. Chicago: University of Chicago Press.

———. 1962. *Cycles of Conquest*. Tucson: University of Arizona Press.

Thornton, Russell. 1987. *American Indian Holocaust and Survival: A Population History Since 1492*. Norman: University of Oklahoma Press.

Tucson Planning Department. 1989. "1985 Computer Printout of Tucson Census Data." Tucson: Tucson City Government.

UCLA Ethnic Studies Center. 1987. *Ethnic Groups in Los Angeles: Quality of Life Indicators*. Los Angeles: UCLA, Ethnic Studies Center.

Underhill, Ruth. 1939. *Social Organization of the Papago Indians*. New York: Columbia University Press.

U.S. Department of Commerce. 1991. *1990 Census: National and State Population Counts for American Indians, Eskimos, and Aleuts*. Washington, D.C.: Bureau of the Census.

Vogt, Evon Z. 1957. "The Acculturation of American Indians." *Annals of the American Academy of Political and Social Science* 311: 137–146.

Wauneka, Annie D. 1987. "Navajo Women." A keynote presentation given at the Navajo Nation Conference on Women, Tsaile, Arizona.

Weaver, Sally. 1972. *Medicine and Politics Among the Grand River Iroquois*. Ottawa, Canada: National Museum of Man.

Williams, Walter. 1986. *The Spirit and the Flesh: Sexual Diversity in American Indian Cultures*. Boston: Beacon Press.

Wolf, Eric R. 1955. "Types of Latin-American Peasantry: A Preliminary Discussion." *American Anthropologist* 57: 456–457.

# 11

## Asian American Women at Work

### Esther Ngan-Ling Chow

The workplace is an important social setting, one that closely links the macro level of labor market and work organization with the micro process of personal interaction, and one that demonstrates how the interlocking of race, class, and gender affects the work lives of Asian working women in particular and of women of color in general. On the one hand, the hierarchical nature of the workplace provides structural conditions that often determine opportunities, job options, and work dynamics for the workers. On the other hand, it institutionalizes discrimination of various forms in the work process to which people of color, women, and people of the working class are particularly subjected. Thus the workplace often becomes what Richard Edwards (1979) calls a contested terrain; it is a place where workers confront discriminatory practices by selecting from their cultural repertoires in such a way as to give ideas and meanings to their effort to survive, resist, and cope with a variety of work situations.

Placing Asian American women, a very much neglected research population, as a central focus of analysis, this chapter specifically examines how the social context of the work bureaucracy has shaped the labor experience of this group of minority women and has specified their coping strategies when they encounter discrimination. The chapter first briefly describes these women's location and condition in the current labor market. Then the focus turns to the nature of work organization as central to these women's subjugation and oppression, conditions under which they learn to cope with their place in the work structure. Finally, this study demonstrates ways in which Asian American women use different strategies to deal with and resist unfair treatment in the workplace as they seek to assure family survival, affirm personal dignity, and raise collective consciousness of their place in the work setting.

## The Study

This study is based on a cross-sectional survey that investigated the effect of major social and psychological factors on occupational outcomes for 161 employed Asian American women.[1] Women who identified themselves as members of one of the four largest Asian American subgroups (Chinese, Filipino, Japanese, and Korean) and who resided in the Washington, D.C., metropolitan area at the time of the study were included in the sample selection.[2] Because over half of the Asian American population in the United States was foreign-born, the sample of this study consisted of half foreign-born and half U.S.-born Asian American women. In order to make adequate subgroup comparisons, variations in occupational level (high or low in terms of Duncan's occupational code) were considered in selecting the sample. In-depth interviews were the primary method of data collection, supplemented by questionnaires and field observations. Most of the interviews were conducted bilingually by the author with some help from trained interviewers who had command of the native languages of the respondents. All respondents volunteered to be involved in the study and enthusiastically agreed to be interviewed. While Asian American women of U.S. birth were easily able to express their thoughts in English, women of foreign birth, who were interviewed bilingually, took much longer to complete the interviews.[3] Before the bureaucratic experience of these Asian American women in the workplace is discussed, the sociohistorical contexts and the conditions under which they participated in the paid labor market are briefly described.

## Local Labor Conditions

The first chapter of the immigration history of Asian Americans begins with the arrival of Chinese in the United States in the mid-nineteenth century. After many Chinese laborers completed the transcontinental railroad in 1869, a considerable number remained in California, while some began moving gradually eastward and to other regions in search of better economic opportunities. According to *The Evening Star* (Cohen 1927), Chiang Kai became the first Chinese resident of Washington, D.C., settling on Pennsylvania Avenue in 1851. Many more Chinese later arrived to work as laundry personnel, domestic servants, tailors, cooks, "coolies" (unskilled laborers), construction workers, and merchants. Other Asian groups began to come to the Washington area in the early part of the twentieth century, but Asian American communities grew very slowly prior to World War II. Exclusionary U.S. immigration laws barring first Chinese and later other Asians (the Chinese Exclusion Act of 1882 and the Exclusion Act of 1924) discouraged family formation by Asians for more than half a century. The relative absence of female immigrants resulted in a highly skewed sex ratio of Asian men to Asian women, establishment of bachelor communities, stagnant population growth, and limited family lives (Chow 1987; Yung 1986). After 1943, when the repressive immigration laws were repealed, the Chinese community regained its vitality and other Asian American communities eventually developed, concentrating in various localized areas within metropolitan areas (e.g., Chinatown and "Little Saigon") in the 1960s and 1970s.

The Washington, D.C., metropolitan area, though it is not climatically appealing to many Asians, provides job opportunities and security for many Asian American women and their families because of its proximity to the federal government and its tourism industries. In the absence of manufacturing and heavy industries, many Asian American women entered typically female and minority jobs, working in hotel and food industries, sales, and other service sectors. Like other immigrant women and women of color, Asian American women in the Washington area participated in the labor market in greater numbers than their White counterparts. With some ethnic variations, their occupational pattern is characterized by a bimodal distribution, with approximately one-fourth in the professional and technical categories and close to two-thirds concentrated in clerical, service, crafts, operative, and nonfarm jobs (U.S. Bureau of the Census 1983, 1988). The Asian American women in this study reflect this wide spectrum of job attainments. They had been employed for an average of 11.34 years and generally had held two to three jobs in their work history.

Their location in the economic structure is primarily the result of the intersection of class, gender, and race/ethnicity affecting their "place" in the labor market rather than the result of one factor alone. Like other immigrant groups and people of color, Asian men and women, particularly the foreign-born, have provided cheap and exploitable sources of migrant labor to meet the needs of an expanding capitalist economy in the United States (Cheng and Bonacich 1984; Glenn 1986). The decision to immigrate to this country has subjected them, voluntarily or involuntarily, to a segmented labor market composed of two tiers, a primary sector and a secondary one, that basically reflect the class structure. Those who are from middle-class backgrounds, with better education and training, are more likely to enter the primary sector, finding jobs mainly in professional, technical, and administrative categories with relatively high wages, good working conditions, chances of advancement, and relative employment stability. Those who come from class backgrounds that have fewer education and training resources are more likely to have jobs in the semiskilled, unskilled, service, and nonfarm areas of the secondary sector that tend to be low paying, with poor working conditions, little chance of advancement, job instability, and high turnover (Piore 1972). People of color, women, and immigrants tend to occupy jobs in the secondary sector even after several generations in the United States, and Asian American women are no exception (Dill 1988b; Glenn 1986; Segura 1984).

Class differences also are a consequence of U.S. immigration policies, which selected certain classes of Asian women to come at different times. Most of the Asian immigrant women of the pre-World War II era were of working-class origin and acquired jobs primarily in the secondary sector, whereas those of the post-World War II era came from heterogeneous class backgrounds and entered a wide range of occupational fields. Recent immigration policies favoring those with professional skills, high levels of education, and vocational training have allowed more Asian American women to acquire jobs in the primary sector than before. Consequently, a bifurcated occupational pattern that clearly distinguishes job opportunities, conditions, and mobility for the workers in the primary and secondary sectors has emerged, markedly for the Chinese and Filipino women, and to a lesser extent for the Japanese and Korean women, in this study.[4]

Furthermore, the patriarchal principle, rooted in both traditional Asian culture and family structure and in the American system, clearly defines gender roles for women in the home as well as in the labor market (Chow and Berheide 1988; Hartmann 1981). The "typically female" jobs in the labor market are extensions of women's domestic roles. Women workers tend to concentrate in "female jobs" (e.g., secretary and file clerk) located in the secondary labor market. When gender is compounded with race and ethnic factors, Asian American women, like other women of color, tend to have "minority female jobs" that are characterized by lower pay, lower rank, more limited job ladders for mobility, and less desirable working conditions than the "typically female" jobs (Segura 1984). In this study, it is clearly evident that Asian women of foreign birth are concentrated in considerable numbers in "minority female jobs" (e.g., waitresses in ethnic restaurants, beauticians, fast food workers, and domestic help). Asian American women who are U.S.-born, highly educated, trained in job skills, and have a good command of English have attained a much higher occupational level than those who are foreign-born, have less education and skill training, and speak little English.

For many Asians, immigration has devastating effects on their labor process and work experience. Encountering status loss, difficulties in searching for or changing jobs, problems of skill transferability, language differences, state licensing requirements (including examinations) unfamiliar work environments, and discrimination affects their job prospects regardless of class and even of gender. The experience of Sau Ling, a Chinese immigrant woman with a high school diploma who worked as a waitress in a Chinese restaurant downtown, typified the kinds of job prospects interviewees found in the Washington, D.C., area.[5] She explained, "Immigrating to the United States seemed to be a dream for me at the beginning. It was my husband who insisted on coming to the U.S.A. and whose decision I do not regret when I think about it now. It is all for the good future of our four kids. We both sweat working in this pit, my husband as a cook and I as a waitress. Day after day, we earn the minimum to get by. When I asked about her chances of getting a better job, she said, "For a Chinese woman like me, it has become a vanishing hope to get out of this place. I am not a Lao Fan (Cantonese for an American). Suk Han, who spoke some broken English, found herself a slightly better-paying job working at the cafeteria in a big hotel nearby. I guess that I am not as lucky as she is after all."

Veronica, a Filipino doctor working in a local hospital, mentioned difficulties, such as barriers to obtaining licenses for foreign-trained professionals, male dominance, occupational segregation, and professional subordination, that educated Asian women overcome in order to break into jobs in the primary sector:

> I worked as a surgeon for twelve years in my country before I and my children came here to join my husband, who arrived earlier for his import-export business. For the first six years, I could only work as a nursing aide because I had a hell of a time getting a state license. Finally I obtained a medical license to practice community medicine in the District. I don't think that I will have much chance of breaking into the white- and male-dominated medical institution to be a surgeon again.

The employment experiences of these two Asian American women illustrate how sexism, meshed with racism and economic oppression, results in barriers that are quite different from the forms of sexism with which white women contend.

## Work Bureaucracy as an Organization of Inequality

Almost all (98 percent) of the Asian American women in the survey sample were salaried or wage workers employed in bureaucratic settings that were hierarchically structured into many layers of positions with rank, authority, duties, and privileges clearly specified. Work bureaucracy penetrates social life along many interrelated dimensions, integrating atomized individuals from the private sphere into the public domain of work and linking the macro level of social institutions with the micro level of workers' activities. Within the bureaucratic setting, Asian American women experienced cooperation as well as contradictions that generally served the interests of the organization. On the one hand, they were rewarded socioeconomically for their labor and services to the organization; on the other hand, they often were politically victimized by it. To understand how the work bureaucracy operates to create a particular set of problems for Asian American women workers, an analysis of the nature of work organization is in order.

Work bureaucracy is basically a social organization of inequality, reflecting the social context of late capitalist society, in which social relations among classes, races, and genders are fundamentally unequal (Foucault 1972; Ferguson 1984). Since Max Weber, many scholars have pointed out that advanced capitalism needs the administrative structure of the work organization to impose predictability, efficiency, and stability on the economic sector for profit maximization and capital accumulation (Braverman 1974; Edwards 1979; Scott 1987). Radical analyses conceptualize work organization as both a structure and a process set up as a mechanism of social control to maintain domination, to reproduce inequality, and to suppress opposition. Thus the work organization becomes one of the primary sources of exploitation and oppression of the working class, people of color, and women— including Asian American women.

This organization of social inequality has several distinctive characteristics. First, the authority structure of the work organization is simultaneously class-based, gendered, and racially segregated. It possesses the persistent power relations of domination and subordination between capitalists and workers, men and women, and the white majority and the nonwhite minority. This bureaucracy consists of

ESTHER NGAN-LING CHOW

many institutionalized sets of roles, activities, and events in a division of labor along lines of class, race, and gender at different hierarchical levels that put individual members in their proper "places" within the organization. The bureaucracy uses an ideology of efficiency, meritocracy, and seniority to explain social differentiations in roles, activities, and events and to justify the system that creates them. To the question "Who benefits from the work organization?" Ferguson's (1984:84) answer is that very few do. She explains that, excluding the top elites, who benefit from, and to some extent exercise control over, the organizational network, all others are embedded in a system that is colonized at different levels within the organization.

The consequences of bureaucratic control are complex and political, with far-reaching effects. A few of the Asian American women interviewed gave vivid descriptions of their organizational experience. One of the logical outcomes is that bureaucratic control tends to intensify the polarized power relationship between the dominant and subordinated groups and among the subordinated groups, attempting to justify the adversarial nature of these power relationships in the name of administration. Control is accomplished through task routinization and depersonalization of relationships within the bureaucracy. Routinization creates fragmentation in the division of labor and cheapens the worth of workers, deskilling them and making them easily replaceable (Braverman 1974; Glenn and Feldberg 1989). The bureaucratic requirement of depersonalization, by imposing rule-governed relationships, produces alienation that isolates workers from one another, threatening group identity and discouraging meaningful social interaction among individuals. One Korean American woman, Kim, who worked as a file clerk in a government agency, was delighted to be interviewed in the middle of her workday so that she could get away from her monotonous, dull, and repetitive filing tasks. She said,

> I began my day early in the morning by putting files, old or new, back into the filing cabinet. It was so boring a job that I was occasionally daydreaming about other things, so that my mind is occupied while my hands are busy. It is an easy job, but very boring. . . . I am not that proud of what I am doing for a living. I guess that I shouldn't complain after all because I get pay, though quite cheap, for doing this kind of lousy job. If I quit, my boss will have no trouble finding someone to replace me.

While Kim did not identify highly with her job, Setsuko, a Japanese clerk-typist in a law firm, achieved dignity by having excellent typing and word-processing skills. However, her competence, while an asset to her supervisor, was a threat to her coworkers in the typing pool, which frequently worked below the output norms regarding time, pace, punctuality, and quality of production. In order to bring the output level up to par, her supervisor imposed a rule forbidding talking about any nonjob-related matters during core office working hours. The supervisor gave Setsuko more typing assignments than others, stationing her in an isolated corner of the office so that she would get more work done and making it more difficult for her to socialize with others.

Moreover, the seemingly obedient and submissive character of Asian American women makes them good candidates for bureaucratic control; their strong task orientation, high achievement motivation, and hard work qualify them as reliable instruments of production. Setsuko was a typical example in her readiness to accept whatever directives she received from her supervisor, even though this involved taking on a disproportionate share of task assignments. Thus, many administrators see Asian American women (as well as men) as ideal candidates for treatment as tokens. Administrators tend to label them a "model minority," a designation many of those so labeled reject or even despise (Cabezas 1986). Tokenism is a powerful and divisive tactic often used by a dominant group to pit individuals or minority groups against each other. Treated as tokens who were visibly different from the mainstream, some Asian Americans in the sample experienced great pressure toward conformity and performance in order to live up to the image the organization created for them.

These images were, in many respects, in conflict with the racial/ethnic backgrounds, cultural expectations, and social practices of these women. A few of the women found it difficult to internalize fully the organizational values of control and to convince others, as well as themselves, of the appropriateness of these values for the organization (Kanter 1977; Laws 1975). For instance, Yang, a Korean woman employed as a social worker, commented, "If I do something well, people will recognize me readily. If I do it poorly, people will think about me as a Korean who is easily to be singled out for bad performance. Then, people don't forgive me that easily. . . . Sometimes I wonder whether I fit in the office. I was shocked that country of origin can affect me that much."

Kang, a Korean doctor, also explained this situation:

At the professional level, it is hard for a woman or a foreigner to take an important position as a chairman or a director of a department or an association. First of all, people don't feel comfortable with anyone who is different. They tend to think of difference as inferiority before I even have a chance to say anything. . . . White people do not like to see or be examined by Korean doctors. . . . People will question: Why is she here? and what does she know? I did not get fair treatment at the beginning. I had to work hard to get my position. It took a long time for them to accept me as one of them.

For an organization to maintain itself, it needs to reproduce itself with "like kind and like mind" (Whyte 1957). Are Asian American women the "right" persons to fit into the organizational network? The answers are rather ambivalent, indicating the grim reality of the workplace. Their job was very important to many of these women, for it provided a major source of income to support the family and a sense of economic security and independence. To some extent, due to the discrimination that some encountered, their job experience was quite negative. Most bureaucratic jobs, especially those in the higher ranks, are middle class in nature and require not only middle-class literacy and educational credentials but also the "cultural resources" (e.g., values, mannerisms, lifestyle, language, and symbols) of the middle class that many Asian American women, especially immigrant ones, have not acquired or cannot easily obtain through acculturation. Sometimes upward mobility occurs, partly on merit and partly to co-opt a few "tokens" into managerial ranks. But even when middle-class cultural resources were obtained, as Shui King (a Chinese American scientist) pointed out, "Possession of good things in life does not necessarily guarantee that the chemistry of all the ingredients will work, and the network of the inner group is so tight that it is not possible to break into it."

Furthermore, the double jeopardy of Asian American women as females and as members of a racial minority adds immense difficulties if they seek to break into the administrative ranks, because sexual and racial stereotypes Whites hold about them generally inhibit the possibility of their presenting a positive image. The women are seen as childlike, possessing little managerial potential (Wright and Delorean 1979), and feminine, possessing weak qualities of the "second sex" (Acker 1987; Ferguson 1984; Kanter 1977; Martin 1989). Yang, a Korean social worker, perceived that Americans tend to have a low opinion of Korean Americans. A Japanese cafeteria assistant, Mieko, confirmed that observation:

Some people have positive views about Japanese women, but some don't. Although the Americans generally have a high opinion of Japanese, we still do not have an equal footing with the

Whites. When it comes to job competition, I was not picked for managerial training sessions, but Clark, a male coworker with less seniority, was selected. I strongly believe that I am a better worker than he is. . . . This society is not ready for accepting Orientals as a whole in the job market.

Frequently work organization creates contradictions of its own that, on the one hand, demand control and conformity and, on the other hand, generate disciplinary and personnel problems (e.g., low morale, absenteeism, lateness, sabotage, and high turnover). Organizational response to these problems is to increase close supervision and rule adherence, which further generates workers' resentment, lessens their ability to engage in collective bargaining, decreases sociability between and within ranks, and diminishes work efficiency of the organization by diverting its resources from actual production (Garson 1975). Kim, the Korean file clerk, told me that all the workers in her office disliked the supervisor, who paced back and forth in the office, keeping them under surveillance most of the time. "The Mystery Cases of Missing Files" was a game that irritated workers created for the offensive supervisor, who later discovered that some files were intentionally misplaced and unfiled, left lying in different parts of the office.

In addition, the depersonalization of the organization is an alien element in the cultural experience of many Asian American women, a number of whom come from societies placing high values on collective interest and striving for harmonious interpersonal relations. To some extent, the impersonal nature of the bureaucratic setting has modified the women's view of work, which they see as a necessary means to achieving other life goals and personal interests beyond the public work domain, which subsequently may increase their dependence on their patriarchal family. As Azucena, a Filipino health administrator, succinctly summed up the situation:

> I think that I am an unassimilated kind. After more than ten years of living in the United States, I am still not used to the impersonal, uncaring, and rigid work environment in America and long for the intimate and caring relationships in the workplace which I experienced before I immigrated to this country. . . . I dislike those token bees pretending that they have made it to the top of the world. I have refused to be treated as such. By not subscribing myself to the values of others, I have to pay a price. I was bypassed, quite a few times, for promotion to the managerial position. . . . Supervisors think Asians are different, knowing nothing. . . . Now I prefer to spend more time with my family.

# Resistance and Coping in the Workplace

Resistance is an inseparable part of oppression in all forms of power relationships. "Those who resist organizational oppression do so from within the very structure that creates that oppression" (Ferguson 1984:116). Thus, work bureaucracy provides a unique social context in which resistance is manifested in the process of work dynamics. This study presents some interesting results that demonstrate how the Asian American women interacted with supervisors and coworkers when experiencing unfair treatment at work, and reveal how they felt subjectively toward the work dynamics they experienced. Their coping and resistance show struggles against patriarchal rule, racial domination, class exploitation, and cultural barriers.

## DEALING WITH SUPERVISORS

Being brought up in a tradition of deferring to authority, many Asian American women sometimes found themselves in situations that caused difficulties in dealing with supervisors who, in their mind, represented figures with such omnipotent authority that they were not easy to challenge. Given the fact that workers, mostly powerless, depended on the goodwill of the supervisors or bosses, conformity and compliance became important concepts for these women to follow.

Many women in the study were employed in racially mixed settings; however, the fact that almost all of them had White men and women rather than racial-ethnics as their direct supervisors is an indicator of how workers were racially stratified in the work hierarchy. The kinds of work problems that the women faced with supervisors related, for the most part, to the supervisors' perception of their inabilities, disrespect for Asian women, unreasonable work assignments, unfair performance evaluation, accusation of job errors, inappropriate decisions regarding promotion, intolerance of language accents, and suspicion of discrimination. When interviewees reported confronting such problems with supervisors, they were asked how frequently they had any difficulties in expressing their displeasure, showing their anger, or insisting on their fair share. While slightly more than half of the women reported that they "seldom" or "rarely" had difficulty in expressing their displeasure to a supervisor, 47 percent of them "always" or "usually" had difficulty in expressing anger, and 62 percent of them "always" or "usually" had difficulty in demanding their fair share from supervisors. Analysis has revealed some variations in these responses according to occupational level, ethnicity, and nativity.

One major finding was that women of high occupational status reported having a more difficult time expressing their anger about job problems with their supervisors, especially in demanding a fair share. Those of lower occupational status seemed to have little to lose if they chose to resist and rebel, even when they knew that they could easily be replaced, whereas those of higher occupational status tended to be more concerned with job security and mobility, and were generally afraid of personal repercussions if they were often at odds with their bosses. Onyoung, a Korean woman working in the housekeeping department of a hotel chain, told me that she occasionally found that other workers took cleaning supplies and equipment home for personal use. When her White female supervisor and male assistant manager investigated the situation, she said, "I learn not to rock the boat, you know. I was not the one who 'squealed' because I knew we were all together on this floor. Many of us depend on this job to support our families. When I am blamed for the things that I do not do and have no part of it, I will yell my guts out to protest. At most I will lose this job. I want my dignity, to be an honorable person, which my parents taught me."

Her case resembles the experience of Black domestic workers (Dill 1988a; Rollins 1985), Chicana private housekeepers (Romero 1988), and Japanese domestic helpers (Glenn 1986), demonstrating how those placed in a low-status occupation can construct personal dignity in managing employer–employee relationships and gain mastery over a situation in which they are socially defined as objects. Fighting back is one of the main keys to survival at work (Dill 1988a).

For professional women, Betty Harragan (1977) and others (Henning and Jardin 1976; Kennedy 1980) advise following Rule No. 1: "absolute deference to the authority invested in your immediate boss." It is important for women workers, especially those aspiring to high positions, to attune carefully to the moods and attitudes of the superior, to present themselves in an approved way, and to shape their image in such a way as to approximate that of their supervisor. Deniz Kandiyoti (1988), describing women in the Far East, points out the strategic nature of women's choices in bargaining with the patriarchy in the classic patriarchal system. Using impression-management techniques, some Asian American professional women have learned to embrace unequal power relations with ease and to attribute work difficulties to the ways in which they failed to manage their feelings and images by not being "assertive" rather than to the work conditions that created these problems. For example, "anger desensitization" is a technique that Arlie Hochschild (1983) vividly describes as essential for

ESTHER NGAN-LING CHOW

flight attendants; it requires them to imagine acceptable reasons for unacceptable behavior in dealing with unreasonable passengers. Anger desensitization, tolerance of hostility, and collective shame control are cultural responses to which Asian American women are accustomed in their socialization and responses that are reinforced by their acculturation experience in America. Ichi, a Japanese researcher-scientist, recognized that

> People in hiring do not necessarily see Asian women in authority positions, and therefore they do not treat them as seriously as men. When a problem occurs, I will try to put up with it as much as possible, so that my apparent anger will not bring a bad name to Japanese women [in general]. I will wait until my supervisor is in a good mood; then I will discuss with him and suggest a way in which he could rectify the problem and alter the situation.

Ethnicity and nativity also account for some of the variations in the women's responses to supervisors. While more Korean women than Chinese, Filipino, and Japanese women reported always finding themselves having difficulty in expressing anger, Japanese women reported the fewest problems in demanding their fair share at work. Foreign-born Asian American women were more likely than U.S.-born ones to have difficulty in expressing displeasure about their work problems and in insisting on their fair share with supervisors. Sook Choi, a Korean immigrant who worked as an account correspondent, cited her accent and the language barrier as the major reasons for her being unable to express her anger. Unfamiliarity with the work world in the United States due to limited job experience, White and male dominance at work, lack of career information, conflicting work ethics and values, problems of transferable job skills, and language barriers in communication all contributed, directly or indirectly, to problems associated with the immigrant women's work transplantation to American soil.

Belying their apparently docile and demure appearance, however, some of the Asian American women clearly evidenced inner strength, tenacity, and courage. For these women, resistance was used to undermine organizational tyranny. A firm believer in hard work as a key to success, Bih-Chun, a Chinese computer specialist, described her ways of dealing with her situation:

> I work doubly hard at doing my job, to perform at the top of the whole division, and trying to fit into the system in order to overcome the initial problems of being a woman and an Asian American. I got an outstanding achievement award for my excep-

tional performance. Because of my superiors' dependency on me to do my job as well as theirs, I can be obnoxious sometimes, being critical about how the company works and about how workers are unfairly treated.

This is what Robert Presthus (1962) calls the "artist," the one who rises above the organizational values through exceptional productivity and whose nonconformity is accepted as merely idiosyncratic.

Lina, a Filipino executive administrator working in a business firm, presented another view of corporate success, pointing out the naïveté of the "Horatio Alger" myth, which equates hard work with success:

> Much of the career advice to women that emphasizes deference to authority, dressing for success, and self-improvement does not always work. To some extent, this career advice is irrelevant to the ways in which the system operates. I see a corporation sometimes promotes incompetence rather than competence, depending on whether one plays the right game or not. My VP is a typical case. I often serve as his scapegoat, being blamed for things that go wrong. For me to keep my job, a lot of energy goes toward covering his mistakes and protecting his incompetence. This is not to deny that my boss does not appreciate my work. . . . However, the system is such that breaking into it is just like hitting your head against the wall.

## DEALING WITH COWORKERS

Work bureaucracies are political arenas in which struggles for power, status, values, personal autonomy, and survival are endemic, even among workers in subordinate positions. Almost all the Asian American women attempted to develop congenial working relationships with people located at different levels of their work organizations. They were asked questions dealing particularly with discrimination from white female and white male coworkers.[6] For instance, they were asked, "If a White male coworker is blatantly unfair, do you find it difficult to say something about it to him? Would you please tell me what you might say to him?" Similar questions were asked about their responses to White female coworkers whom they considered to have treated them with blatant unfairness. Two-thirds of the women reported not having much difficulty in protesting unfair treatment by their White coworkers. Degree of difficulty was reportedly lesser in dealing with White male than with White female coworkers, the most frequent reason given involving strong gender identification. Interviewees viewed White women as their allies at work and as having more in common with them than White men did. While some were more willing to tolerate ill treatment from White women than from White men, others thought that oppression from White women was harder for them to handle because they did not expect women workers to mistreat other women.

Coping strategies used in handling blatant discrimination from coworkers reveal Asian American women's attempts to gain a sense of autonomy, control, and self-worth in situations in which they were socially defined as objects or machines, good only for getting the work done for others. Suffering from unfair treatment helped the women to develop a range of innovative approaches to dealing with oppressive situations. Based on content analysis of the qualitative data, coping strategies used by these women are classified into four main types: confrontational, assertive, affiliative, and indirect/situational adjustment. While some of these coping strategies could be characteristic of almost any group of women, the social and cultural meanings the women attributed to the content and style of their coping are to some extent uniquely their own.

The confrontational style, a rather aggressive way of opposing racist, sexist, class-biased circumstances at work, involved head-on protest against those coworkers the women viewed as insensitive and threatening to their survival. The confrontational style was used to fight back in the face of seemingly overwhelming obstacles, to protect one's work rights, and to show unwillingness to compromise oneself when others' wishes were deemed unreasonable. For example, Reiko, a Japanese salesperson in a department store, experienced sexual harassment when a White male customer made sexual remarks and advances toward her. But her White female coworker commented, "Isn't that what a Japanese geisha girl is good for?" Anger was a natural response to this sexually and racially oppressive situation in dealing with her coworker as well as the patron. She recalled angrily,

> How others perceive me stereotypically as a geisha girl is beyond me. I asked her [the female coworker] to get off my back. Women tend to be more emotional than men. Once emotion is built up, it might blast off once in a while. White male colleagues are easier to talk to because they handle emotions better than White women. Although I am a U.S.-born Japanese, my ability to speak perfect "American" English has not helped me earn full status as a real American.

Protesting could go as far as quitting one's job rather than putting up with being pushed around. Quitting was the ultimate form of resistance; the worker walked out of a domination relationship, affirming the importance of her self-respect and of human dignity over job security. The case of Bih-Chun partly illustrates this style. She knew that people in her office called her "dragon lady" behind her back because she could not be replaced easily. When jealousy and back stabbing occurred, she felt compelled to say or to do something to those who treated her unjustly. She made it very clear that "I owe nothing to my employer. I either own the job or am owned by it."

The assertive style was a direct approach by which Asian American women exercised their work rights and independence by negotiating their time, effort, intellect, commitment, and personal involvement with other workers. Perhaps this style represents a combination of the Asian mode of adaptation by tolerance or modesty with the American value placed on internal control. Regardless of ethnicity, nativity, and occupation, about half the women studied chose the assertive coping style, and they were more likely to do so when they dealt with White male workers than with White female ones. The majority reported that they expressed their viewpoints and judgment of the situation, demanded explanations from offensive workers, and focused their efforts on problem solving. In this way, they portrayed themselves as active agents and goal-oriented actors, capable of taking charge of their own lives. In an explicit way, they showed unwillingness to suppress their needs in favor of those of the employer or coworker. They openly elected to acknowledge coworkers' humanness and to show concern for them by using equity principles to guarantee fairness and justice for all involved.

Alicia, a Filipino procurement clerk, explained the racial politics in her office, where she sometimes was caught in the crossfire. She was regarded by others as a good troubleshooter because of her assertive, interpersonal, and diplomatic skills:

> Being too emotional will not work out for me in my office because people will back off and don't focus on what I want to talk about. Once they avoid the subject, they tend to be uncooperative as a result. Let me give you an example of liberal leave in the office. Other workers took advantage of it and left earlier without getting their jobs done. I was asked to see the supervisor, who demanded me to be responsible for the situation. First I calmed her down and then gave her a reasonable explanation. Now she respects me and gives me support from time to time.

The principle of reciprocity was also applied here; women using the assertive approach expected mutual agreement and reinforcement in the process of negotiation. When the spillover racial effects were such that Alicia was not able to handle them, she would establish clear boundaries between work and personal life, between coworkers and herself, setting limits on how far a job was allowed to absorb or infringe upon her life outside of work. She admitted that the strength, courage, and support from her extended family sustained her and helped her to survive in the workplace.

The affiliation style was sometimes used to show the importance of collegial congeniality in approaching problem solving at the workplace. Personal consideration, friendliness, and candidness were mentioned as primary approaches in achieving some kind of parity with coworkers. Asian American women employing this approach tended to emphasize their racial/ethnic and/or gender identification (e.g., consciousness of one's own kind, sisterhood, and "all are fresh from the boat") in order to form an alliance with those in question, to dispel issues of inequity, and to neutralize feelings of injustice.

The women in the study reported that they were more prone to utilize the affiliative style, justified as sex/gender alliance, with White female workers than with male workers. For instance, Veronica, a Filipino executive administrator, acknowledged that Jewish women, even though they were White, suffered from anti-Semitism as well as sexism, a way for her to justify her problematic working relationship with a Jewish executive secretary. Shui-King, a Chinese scientist doing medical research in a public hospital, reported that when there was a misunderstanding between her and a White female pathologist, she purposely invited her colleague to a Chinese restaurant to clear up their mutual misperception about the work situation and worked out an acceptable alternative. "After all, we are all women and I assume that we understand each other well," she said. But, she added, "It turned out that she was the one who sold me out at the end."

The last style of coping, indirect/situational adjustment, was basically an indecisive and seemingly passive way of dealing with work problems and with coworkers involved. Instead of tackling the prob-lem directly, some Asian American women chose to take a defensive stand, thereby protecting themselves from the hurt by pushing their tolerance to the limit. Some avoided the problematic situations as much as they possibly could, doing very little about them or hoping that the problems would subside eventually. Some women sought to use the indirect style by writing to or telling the supervisor about an offensive coworker or making an impersonal telephone call to the coworker in question, with the hope that they could discuss the matter and find a solution to the problem. Rizalina, a Filipino program planning assistant, explained, "I was asked to design a system for a project. Janet [White, female] thought that she has the sole privilege to do it. It seems there is a ring of protection around her so that I have difficulty to confront her directly. I went to tell the supervisor about it instead of approaching her. As a rule, I'll try to avoid awkward situations as much as possible."

Their passive resistance sometimes involved not clear-cut coping strategies but indirect strategies of adjusting to situations and personalities as problems occurred. Onyoung, the Korean hotel service worker, while quite aggressive in dealing with the supervisor, in fact protected the interest of her colleagues even though she knew some had transgressed against job norms. Facing interrogation by her supervisors, she narrowly redefined honesty as only applying to herself, but she tried to cover up what other coworkers had blamed her for. "As far as I am concerned, I am an honest person. I didn't do it," she said. But her resistance tended to crystallize around the feeling that her rights were subject to violation, that she was often taken advantage of by others, and that she ought to be prepared to defend herself in order to make her work situation bearable.

For those women who felt trapped, under tremendous tension in an unbridgeable gulf between themselves and other coworkers, quitting was the ultimate weapon in fighting unfair treatment. Job resignation represented a decisive act of resistance against those who denied these women's humanity when this tactic was coupled with use of the assertive style. However, quitting was a defeatist option for those who used the indirect style. They blamed themselves for what happened rather than affirming their self-respect.

Chinese people often say "Silence is golden." Surprisingly, only 6 percent of the Asian American women in the sample said that they elected not to say anything to a problem instigator or to make any statement at all about an incident they perceived to be unfair. Perhaps American acculturation has taught Asian American women to stand up for their rights more readily. Chinese American women in the sample were more likely than the other three groups to use silence, a legitimate response in Chinese culture, to deal with problem situations. Silence means willingness, by choice or by circumstance, to submit oneself to poor treatment and even to domination. Acquiescence may indicate co-optation that results from fear of job loss. It may simply mean that one feels powerless, incapable of coping. More important, silence is a typical means of passive resistance, a way of finding meaning in one's action, of neutralizing negative feelings, and of resigning oneself to a situation, temporarily or permanently, in order to place oneself with a self-defined "proper" perspective and remain independent. As a Chinese paralegal assistant, Wai Lan, described her behavior, "I do not share things in common with that worker. It is meaningless to lower myself to his level. I don't want to be a troublemaker in my office. What I want to do is try to put up with him as much as possible, so that I will be left alone."

Silence may be a temporary reaction in the process of coping. It was not uncommon to find some Asian American women changing strategies from indirect/situational adjustment to other styles of coping. Those who carried the burden of a job problem to the limit of their tolerance might readily resort to direct confrontation, transforming passive into active, radical resistance (Lordes 1984).

## Conclusion

Studies of resistance have done much to counter the tendency of social research to portray women as passive and submissive rather than active, goal-oriented doers. Building on the insights of previous studies on women of color (Asian American Women United of California 1989; Caulfield 1974; Chai 1987; Chow 1987; Dill 1983, 1988a; Gilkes 1983, 1988; Lordes 1984; Romero 1988; Segura 1984; Baca Zinn 1987), this study explores a neglected dimension of organizational resistance in the workplace and links it to the labor conditions and work adaptation of Asian American women. It specifically examines the ways in which Asian American women struggle at work to ensure family survival and to cope with racist oppression, patriarchal domination, and economic exploitation within the work bureaucracy.

Exploration of the organizational dimension of resistance shed theoretical light on reconceptualizing the nature of work bureaucracy as a social organization of inequalities central to the subjugation and oppression of many people, including Asian American women. Organization has a great capability to control its members and to reproduce its victims. However, organizational analyses tend to overlook the very real struggle for personal dignity, autonomy, and self-respect among the interacting personalities within work bureaucracy. The articulation of the submerged voices of many of the invisible Asian American women interviewed echoes the concerns of the radical and feminist critiques presented earlier in this chapter that recently engendered a rethinking about organizations. New knowledge about this submerged voice of women is thus produced outside the mainstream of conventional thought, allowing human life to be comprehended in its totality, and organizational alternatives to be explored for redesigning a humanitarian and egalitarian work world of the future.

This rethinking about organization has transformed understanding about the political nature of organizational life and about how an individual's political experience is linked to the social structure that is rooted in the race, gender, and class stratification system. Asian American women, suffering from multiple oppressions, have employed various coping strategies not only to foster short-term social adaptation but also, in the long run, to enhance their ability to negotiate the complex relationships in the context of oppression and exploitation at work. The four coping styles identified in this study are by no means unique to Asian American women. However, some of the contents and contexts of each coping style used, and the meaningful justifications given by these women, are distinctively Asian. To some extent, their coping responses seem to represent the product of their Asian cultural learning and acculturation experience in America.

More specifically, in the face of discrimination many of these women challenge supervisors and coworkers who threaten their survival. This is clearly the case when half of the women studied utilized the assertive style, one thought to be rather uncommon among Asian women. It is also surprising to find that only 6 percent of them chose silence as a response, one that might be expected to be common in adverse work conditions. Utilizing assertive interpersonal skills, fighting back to protect one's work rights, setting boundaries to maintain personhood, and even keeping silent are meaningful responses that symbolize the inner strength, resourcefulness, and perseverance of Asian American women. The social referents to whom these women applied their coping strategies reflect the dialectical process of subordination, illustrating how they sometimes made alliances with White women because of their gender and demonstrating how the dimension of race, class, and nativity compounds the disadvantage of gender.

As individual responses to organizational control, the complex social forces operating in the intersection of race, class, and gender have produced different outcomes for various racial and ethnic groups. Joyce Ladner (1971) and other Black scholars (e.g., Davis 1981; Jones 1985; Dill 1988a) have argued that the heritage of slavery and the exigencies of ghetto life have required independence, self-reliance, and strength on the part of Black women that are not usually seen in their White counterparts. A similar argument was used by Maxine Baca Zinn (1987) to show that it is a particular class and racial experience that constructs the context, historically or today, within which Black and Hispanic women and families actively cope with structural constraints. While the seeming dependence, passivity, and submissiveness of Asian American women no doubt are characteristic to some extent, reflecting their powerless position in society, others should not equate their gentleness with passivity, their docility with timidity, and their kindness with weakness, failing to see the inner strength, firmness, and resourcefulness of these women.

While many scholars (e.g., Dill 1988b; Gilkes 1988; Terrelonge 1989) point out how Black women generally draw their strength from their community, Asian American women, though they have begun to build their diverse communities, gain strength mostly from their families. As revealed in several cases, organizational oppression and resistance seem to hamper their occupational outlook and weaken their work involvement; the family becomes an important resource to sustain them in the work world. Organizational control penetrates family life and increases, directly or indirectly, the dependence of Asian American women on the patriarchy, thus creating a paradox for women in Asian American families. An in-depth study of the interconnectedness between family and work life among Asian American women is needed to gain additional insight into this area.

In essence, women's struggles in the labor market and in the work organization are political in the sense that women have engaged in the kinds of daily activities that are enmeshed in the political and economic processes that challenge the basic power relationships in society. Only when Asian American women and others begin collectively to pressure the dominant groups in society at large to be responsible for these women's oppressed conditions will they be able to initiate structural changes at all levels where they have been denigrated historically. Alternative strategies to redesigning organizations are on the agenda for scholarly research and political action to promote a better quality of work life for all people.

## Notes

*Acknowledgments:* This article is dedicated to those Asian American women who generously shared their lives with me. The research was supported by the National Institute of Mental Health, Department of Health and Human Services, grant #1-R01 MH31218-01, and by a writing grant from the Pacific Cultural Foundation in Taiwan. The author is solely responsible for this paper's content and form of analysis. Special thanks are given to Elaine Stahl

Leo for her editorial help and to Millie DePallo and Michael Zhao for research assistance.

1. This cross-sectional survey is part of a larger multiphase study that empirically examined the effect of specific social and psychological factors on occupational outcomes for Asian American women in the San Francisco and Washington, D.C., metropolitan areas. The San Francisco data set does not include all the information used for the analysis presented in this paper. Detailed information about the study is reported more fully by Esther Chow (1982).

2. The disproportional stratified random sampling design was originally drawn from a comprehensive list of Asian American women compiled from a variety of sources. A checklist was mailed to everyone on this comprehensive list to obtain informed consent, information about the three stratified factors (ethnicity, nativity, and occupation), and other relevant information. A sample based on the results of the returned checklists was randomly selected to include approximately an equal number from each of the subgroups. The final sample included 161 employed Asian American women.

3. Many of the Asian American women seemingly appreciated having an Asian American interviewer who listened attentively to them. Empathy and sincerity were clearly evident when these women shared their life experiences and perspectives with me.

4. Ethnic diversity should be taken into consideration in analyzing the occupational characteristics and employment patterns of Asian American women. To give another example to illustrate this, while Asian-Indian Americans tend to rank highest in occupational attainment, Vietnamese Americans are at the bottom of the occupational strata, with an average income even lower that of Blacks and Hispanics in the U.S. population (Gardner et al. 1985).

5. To protect the identity of the women being interviewed and the confidentiality of the data provided, I used pseudonyms. The stories provided by the women were accurately presented, but some of the information was recomposed (a technique commonly used in field studies) to assure that distinctive characteristics of certain women could not be clearly identified.

6. While Japanese and Korean American women tended to work in predominantly White settings, Chinese and Filipino American women were more likely to report having jobs in racially mixed groups. Women of foreign birth and lower occupational status more often reported racially mixed work settings than did those of U.S. birth and higher occupational status. Due to time limitations and the lengthy interviews involved, no additional questions were asked concerning supervisors and coworkers of other racial backgrounds (i.e., Black and Hispanic). Therefore, the extent

to which Asian American women identify with other women of color at work cannot be directly examined in this study.

# References

Acker, Joan. 1987. "Hierarchies, Jobs, and Bodies: A Theory of Gendered Organizations." *Gender and Society* 4: 139–158.

Asian American Women United of California. 1989. *Making Waves: Writings About Asian American Women*. Boston: Beacon Press.

Baca Zinn, Maxine. 1987. *Minority Families in Crisis: The Public Discussion*. Research Paper no. 6. Memphis, Tenn.: Center for Research on Women, Memphis State University.

Braverman, Harry. 1974. *Labor and Monopoly Capital*. New York: Monthly Review Press.

Cabezas, Amado. 1986. "The Asian American Today as an Economic Success Model: Some Myths and Realities." Pp. 16–21 in *Break the Silence: A Conference on Anti-Asian Violence*, edited by Bill Ong Hing, Russell Lowe, Ron Wakabayashi, and Sue Wong. San Francisco: Break the Silence Coalition.

Caulfield, Mina D. 1974. "Imperialism, the Family, and Cultures of Resistance." *Socialist Revolution* 4(2): 67–85.

Chai, Alice Yun. 1987. "Adaptive Strategies of Recent Korean Immigrant Women in Hawaii." Pp. 65–99 in *Beyond the Domestic/Public Dichotomy: Contemporary Perspectives on Women's Public Lives*, edited by Janet Sharistanian. Westport, Conn.: Greenwood Press.

Cheng, Lucie, and Edna Bonacich, eds. 1984. *Labor Immigration Under Capitalism*. Berkeley: University of California Press.

Chow, Esther Ngan-Ling. 1982. *Acculturation of Asian American Professional Women*. Washington, D.C.: National Institute of Mental Health, U.S. Department of Health and Human Services.

———. 1987. "The Development of Feminist Consciousness Among Asian American Women." *Gender and Society* 1(3): 284–299.

Chow, Esther Ngan-Ling, and Catherine White Berheide. 1988. "The Interdependency of Family and Work: A Framework for Family Life Education, Policy, and Practice." *Family Relations* 37: 23–28.

Cohen, E. C. 1927. "Chinatown Has Own Spirit of Exclusiveness." *The Evening Star* (Washington, D.C.), August 14.

Davis, Angela. 1981. *Women, Race, and Class*. New York: Random House.

Dill, Bonnie Thornton. 1983. "Race, Class, and Gender: Prospects for an Inclusive Sisterhood." *Feminist Studies* 9: 131–150.

———. 1988a. " 'Making Your Job Good Yourself': Domestic Service and the Construction of Personal Dignity." Pp. 33–52 in *Women and the*

*Politics of Empowerment*, edited by Ann Bookman and Sandra Morgen. Philadelphia: Temple University Press.

———. 1988b. "Our Mothers' Grief: Racial Ethnic Women and the Maintenance of Families." *Journal of Family History* 13 (4): 415–431.

Edwards, Richard C. 1979. *Contested Terrain*. New York: Basic Books.

Ferguson, Kathy E. 1984. *The Feminist Case Against Bureaucracy*. Philadelphia: Temple University Press.

Foucault, Michel. 1972. *Power/Knowledge: Selected Interviews and Other Writings*. New York: Pantheon Books.

Gardner, Robert W., Bryant Robey, and Peter C. Smith. 1985. "Asian Americans: Growth, Change, and Diversity." *Population Bulletin* 40 (4): 1–43.

Garson, Barbara. 1975. *All the Livelong Day*. New York: Doubleday.

Gilkes, Cheryl Townsend. 1983. "Going Up for the Oppressed: The Career Mobility of Black Women Community Workers." *Journal of Social Issues* 39 (3): 115–139.

———. 1988. "Building in Many Places: Multiple Commitments and Ideologies in Black Women's Community Work." Pp. 53–76 in *Women and the Politics of Empowerment*, edited by Ann Bookman and Sandra Morgen. Philadelphia: Temple University Press.

Glenn, Evelyn Nakano. 1986. *Issei, Nisei, War Bride: Three Generations of Japanese American Women in Domestic Service*. Philadelphia: Temple University Press.

Glenn, Evelyn Nakano, and Roslyn L. Feldberg. 1989. "Clerical Work: The Female Occupation." Pp. 287–311 in *Women: A Feminist Perspective*, edited by Jo Freeman. Fourth edition. Mountain View, Calif.: Mayfield.

Harragan, Betty Lehan. 1977. *Games Mother Never Taught You: Corporate Gamesmanship for Women*. New York: Warner Books.

Hartmann, Heidi. 1981. "The Family as the Locus of Gender, Class and Political Struggle: The Example of Housework." *Signs: Journal of Women in Culture and Society* 6: 366–394.

Henning, Margaret, and Anne Jardin. 1976. *The Managerial Woman*. New York: Pocket Books.

Hochschild, Arlie Russell. 1983. *The Managed Heart*. Berkeley: University of California Press.

Jones, Jacqueline. 1985. *Labor of Love, Labor of Sorrow: Black Women, Work and the Family from Slavery to the Present*. New York: Basic Books.

Kandiyoti, Deniz. 1988. "Bargaining with Patriarchy." *Gender and Society* 2: 274–289.

Kanter, Rosabeth Moss. 1977. *Men and Women of the Corporation*. New York: Basic Books.

Kennedy, Marilyn Moats. 1980. *Office Politics: Seizing Power, Wielding Clout*. New York: Warner Books.

Ladner, Joyce. 1971. *Tomorrow's Tomorrow: The Black Woman*. Garden City, N.Y.: Doubleday.

Laws, Judith Long. 1975. "The Psychology of Tokenism: An Analysis." *Sex Roles* 1: 51–67.

Lordes, Audre. 1984. "The Transformation of Silence into Language and Action." Pp. 40–44 in *Sister Outside*, edited by Audre Lordes. Freedom, Calif.: The Crossing Press.

Martin, Patricia. 1989. "Women's Propects for Leadership in Social Welfare: A Political Economy Perspective." *Administration in Social Work* 13: 117–143.

Piore, Michael J. 1972. "Notes for a Theory of Labor Maket Stratification." Working Paper no. 95. Boston: Massachusetts Institute of Technology.

Presthus, Robert. 1962. *The Organizational Society*. New York: Alfred A. Knopf.

Rollins, Judith. 1985. *Between Women: Domestics and Their Employers*. Philadelphia: Temple University Press.

Romero, Mary. 1988. "Day Work in the Suburbs: The Work Experience of Chicano Private Housekeepers." Pp. 77–92 in *The Worth of Women's Work: A Qualitative Synthesis*, edited by Anne Statham, Eleanor M. Miller, and Hans O. Mauksch. Albany: State University of New York Press.

Scott, W. Richard. 1987. *Organizations: Rational, Natural, and Open Systems*. Second edition. Englewood Cliffs, N.J.: Prentice-Hall.

Segura, Denise. 1984. "Labor Market Stratification: The Chicano Experience." *Berkeley Journal of Sociology* 29 (Spring): 57–91.

Terrelonge, Pauline. 1989. "Feminist Consciousness and Black Women." Pp. 556–566 in *Women: A Feminist Perspective*, edited by Jo Freeman. Fourth edition. Mountain View, Calif.: Mayfield.

U.S. Bureau of the Census. 1981. *1980 Census of Population: Supplementary Reports*. Washington, D.C.: U.S. Department of Commerce, Bureau of the Census.

———. 1983. *1980 Census of Population: Detailed Population Characteristics*. Washington, D.C.: U.S. Department of Commerce, Bureau of the Census.

———. 1988. "Asian and Pacific Islander Population in the United States." In *1980 Census of Population*. Washington, D.C.: U.S. Government Printing Office.

Whyte, William H., Jr. 1957. *The Organization Man*. Garden City, N.Y.: Doubleday.

Wright, J. Patrick, and John De Lorean. 1979. *On a Clear Day You Can See General Motors*. New York: Avon Books.

Yung, Judy. 1986. *Chinese Women of America: A Pictorial History*. Seattle: University of Washington Press.

# 12

# "If It Wasn't for the Women . . .":
# African American Women,
# Community Work, and Social Change

## Cheryl Townsend Gilkes

**M**any sociologists who studied the relationships between dominant and subordinate racial-ethnic groups in the 1960s and 1970s stress the creative ways in which individuals and groups enable communities to articulate their own needs and challenge oppressive structures in the wider society (Morris 1984). Other sociologists, such as Stanford Lyman (1972), emphasize the historical experience of racial-ethnic groups in the data used for sociological interpretation. The Civil Rights Movement, the Black Power Movement, and the American Indian Movement, along with diverse movements within Asian American, Puerto Rican, and Chicano communities, challenged sociologists to explore historically rooted conflicts over power, labor, economic resources, and the appropriate strategies for achieving social change (Blauner 1972; Wilson 1973; Gilkes 1980).

Creative social conflict is inevitable and necessary if racial-ethnic, gender, and class inequities are to be eliminated and social justice achieved. When enterprising, caring members of oppressed communities become involved in public affairs, their actions often contribute to a creative cultural process that is a force for social change. This chapter is about an aspect of that creative cultural process: enterprising women in African American communities who shape social change through their community work.

Women are vital to the creative cultural process of social change. African American women and their community work highlight the importance of a group's history and culture to the process of social change. The rise of the women's liberation movement and public concern about African American women, their families, and their position in the labor force (Cade 1970; King 1987; Gilkes 1990) generated a particular interest in their roles in the process of social change. Along with Asian American, Native American, and Latina women, African American women's work outside the home was recognized as a distinctive component in their family roles. Community work is part of this work outside the home. It is labor these women perform in addition to work in the household and the labor force.[1]

This chapter describes the contemporary expression, historical foundations, and persistent activities of the community work of African American women. Community work includes a wide range of diverse tasks performed to confront and challenge racism as a total system. This work has historical foundations, and a historical perspective helps to highlight the areas of activity common to the work at different time periods. Community work consists of the women's activities to combat racism and empower their communities to survive, grow, and advance in a hostile society. The totality of their work is an emergent, dynamic, interactive model of social action in which community workers discover and explore oppressive structures, challenge many different structures and practices that keep their communities powerless and disadvantaged, and then build, maintain, and strengthen institutions within their community. These institutions become the basis for the community's political culture. The women generate an alternative organization and a set of commitments to group interests that are the basic elements of "community." They work for the community that they themselves re-create and sustain, a mutually reinforcing process.

During the late 1970s in a Northeastern city I gathered oral histories and observed the community activities of twenty-five African American women whom other African Americans had identified as those "who have worked hard for a long time for change in the Black community."[2] As these women talked about the ways in which they became involved in community work and the different kinds of organizations and activities in which they participated, I learned about the very intricate and diverse ways in which people make social change. I also learned about the many ways in which women experience racial oppression. Their family roles made them acutely conscious not only of their own deprivations but also of the suffering of their children and the men in their lives. Their insightful and enterprising responses to these many kinds of suffering led to their prominence in the community. They were responsible for maintaining a dynamic community life to create social change and an adaptive family system to foster survival in a hostile environment. Through community and

CHERYL TOWNSEND GILKES

family, these women generated a set of values and a social organization that persistently challenged and changed American society.

## Community Work

Women in American society are expected to be good managers. They organize and coordinate diverse schedules and activities within their families, and among the organizations and institutions with which family members are involved. Work outside the home is often added to this responsibility. African American women usually work, manage their families, and, if they are community workers, participate in the struggles between the communities and the dominant society.

James Blackwell's (1985) definition of the African American community helps us to understand the context of their work. Blackwell argues that the community, although diverse, is held together by both internal and external forces. It is "a highly diversified set of interrelated structures and aggregates of people who are held together by the forces of white oppression and racism. Unity within the black community is a function of the strategies developed to combat white racism and to strengthen black social, economic, and political institutions for group survival and advancement" (1985: xi).

Community work consists of all tasks contained in strategies to combat racial oppression and to strengthen African American social, economic, and political institutions in order to foster group survival, growth, and advancement. Community work is focused on internal development and external challenge, and creates ideas enabling people to think about change. It is the work that opens doors to elected and appointed positions in the political power struggle, and demands and creates jobs in local labor markets and the larger economic system. Community work also focuses on changing ideas, stereotypes, and images that keep a group perpetually stigmatized. Sometimes this is done by demanding different textbooks in the schools or publicly criticizing newspapers and other media. At the same time, community workers may insist, rightly or wrongly, that community members change their behavior to avoid being treated in terms of prevailing stereotypes. Community work is a constant struggle, and it consists of everything that people do to address oppression in their own lives, suffering in the lives of others, and their sense of solidarity or group kinship.

Women participate in every part of a community's experience of racial oppression. Racial oppression is a phenomenon that not only singles out African Americans because of their heritage and color but also places the entire community in a colonial relationship, a relationship of powerlessness and dependency, within a dominant and dominating society. Robert Blauner (1972) calls this "internal colonialism," and it involves the subordination of an entire group of people in order to take away its land, to capture its labor, or to do both. Colonized people must be excluded from the political process and, by law, have few, if any, citizenship rights. Because the primary purpose of the group is to labor unceasingly for someone else, the other dimensions of its cultural life, such as family life, health, education, and religion, become difficult, if not impossible, to pursue.

During slavery African Americans had their children and spouses sold away from them. Their family lives were repeatedly disrupted and invaded by the sexual terrorism that was part of slavery. Teaching slaves to read and write in the antebellum South was illegal. During the last decades of slavery, religious worship outside of the supervision of white people was illegal as well. The health of African Americans was constantly threatened by the violence of white slave owners, through beatings and overwork. Because they were legally nonpersons, emancipation left African Americans overwhelmingly landless and still dependent upon white landowners for a livelihood. Political powerlessness through violence and denial of the vote increased that dependence. Racist stereotypes, ideologies, and actions continued to justify the dominant group's actions and the continued subordination of another group.[3] Racial oppression is a total phenomenon that combines cultural humiliation and destruction, political subordination, and economic exploitation to maintain a hierarchy that limits the life chances of a group of people.

The economic needs and organization of the society change. Slavery was abolished in 1865; African Americans moved to northern cities in large numbers during World Wars I and II; the Civil Rights Movement did away with Jim Crow laws. However, the racist hierarchy retained a life and meaning that survived massive changes in economic, legal, political, and social institutions. Although slavery ended, the society learned to associate low-paying, dirty work with Black people and higher-paying, clean work with White people. Contemporary racial stereotypes and media images perpetuate those images rooted in slavery.

Community work confronts this totality. Everett Hughes (1971:313) suggested that an important way to conceptualize "work" is to view it as a "bundle of several tasks." Racial oppression takes up more time and creates extra work, or more "bundles of tasks," for members of a victimized group.[4] People working for and with their communities involve themselves in activities surrounding the problems associated with jobs: labor union activities, creating access to jobs, teaching strategies to fight specific problems in work settings, and seeking legislation to protect occupations where group members are concentrated. One community worker had worked for the Urban League early in her career. She described recruiting other African American women for newly created jobs during World War II by visiting churches and women's clubs. She then organized discussion groups in order to teach these women how to confront the racial harassment they would encounter in unions and factories. Another woman described in great detail the way her women's club of the 1920s and 1930s taught fellow domestic workers how to demand the full wages their White female employers had promised. That same women's club, in the 1960s and 1970s, was involved in administering job training programs for homemakers *at the same time* they were lobbying for protective legislation for household workers. Community workers involved themselves in activities that confronted ideas as well as structures within and outside the community.

Education is a case in point. Issues of self-image and self-esteem are related to educational success at the same time that employment discrimination and racist attitudes in the educational system account for the lack of African American teachers. Educational failure locks many members of the community out of the economic system at the same time that political powerlessness through gerrymandering accounts for the lack of access to low-skilled but high-paying municipal jobs. One woman who had been quite prominent in challenging the public educational system talked about the importance of self-esteem for African American students. Another woman, an elected official, displayed publications she used for raising the racial self-esteem of teenagers and described the workshops she gave for parents in order to reduce the sense of intimidation they felt when confronting White teachers. Each of these problems presents a different "bundle of tasks," yet they are all manifestations of the totality of racial oppression.

Each woman interviewed described diverse and intricate daily schedules that reflected the complexity and connectedness of the social, political, and economic problems that pervade everyday life in minority communities. One woman, for example, described getting a group of adolescent males assigned to early morning jobs, going to court as a character witness for a teenager, meeting with a board of directors in another part of the city, and coordinating a public demonstration against that same board of directors before leaving for the meeting. While levels of confrontation and activity often vary, community work persistently rejects racial oppression as a normal and natural feature of human experience. Community work, encompassing issues of challenge as well as survival, is perhaps more complicated than the racial oppression that gives rise to it.

## Historical Foundations

Community workers' expectations and obligations represent a historical role. These women, through their public participation on so many levels, claim a prominent place in the community's history. This historical prominence often provides levels of prestige and influence unmatched in the lives of White women of similar class backgrounds.[5] All of the women were connected in some way to earlier generations of organizations, activists, and confrontations. What becomes visible to outsider observers as "social movements" are the most dramatic dimensions of an intergenerational tradition of community work. Bernice Johnson Reagon (1982:82–83) emphasizes this continuity:

> If we understand that we are talking about a struggle that is hundreds of years old, then we must acknowledge a continuance: that to be Black women is to move forward the struggle for the kind of space in this society that will make sense for our people. It is different today. Things have changed. The search for high levels of humanity and space to be who we know we are is the same. And if we can make sense of our people in this society, we will go a long way in making sense for the rest of the peoples who also live and suffer here.

The historical continuity of community work depends upon an intricate fit between many kinds of organizations and people. All of the women worked within traditional and nationally recognized groups, such as churches, the National Association for the Advancement of Colored People (NAACP), the Urban League, the Student Non-Violent Coordinating Committee (SNCC), the Young Women's Christian Association (YWCA), the National Association of Colored Women's Clubs, and the National Council of Negro Women. At the same time they formed local organizations that specialized in problems of job training, drug addiction, city services, welfare rights, or public education. People in the community actively encouraged these community workers to be leaders and, once the women responded to a community need, they organized whatever was necessary to see an activity through.

Such activities were not possible without intergenerational connections. When interviewing, I asked the women to identify their heroes and heroines. These women identified specific women within the local community as well as such notables as Mary McLeod Bethune. One woman remembered very clearly being impressed when Mrs. Bethune spoke at a local church for the Women's Day service. Several women identified Mrs. Burns,[6] who was also interviewed, as their heroine and local sponsor. One said, "I walked to Mrs. Burns when I was nine months old!" This elderly community worker identified Mrs. Bethune as a coworker in the National Association of Colored Women. Older community workers, as heroines and sponsors, were the critical connection to earlier generations of community workers or "Race" women. These women who remembered Mary McLeod Bethune and Mary Church Terrell, not only as "heroines" but also as living role models in club work and church work, were the links to an unbroken tradition of community work or working for "the Race" that could be traced directly to antebellum communities, both slave and free.

Working for "the Race" began during slavery. Within the slave community, women not only played key roles in the development of family, education, and religion but also developed a women's network that was a foundation of strength, leaders, and mutual aid (White 1985; Webber 1978). Deborah Gray White (1985) names midwives, nurses, and religious leaders as critical sources of survival. One religious leader, a prophet named Sinda, preaching the imminent end of the world, precipitated a strike by an entire plantation labor force. African American women in Northern free communities built churches and developed abolitionist, literary, mutual-aid, and missionary societies that provided poor-relief and insurance benefits for their communities (Perkins 1981; Sterling 1984). Women such as Maria Stewart and Frances Ellen Watkins Harper were militant antislavery crusaders and public lecturers. Stewart was the first woman of any race in the United States to lecture publicly and leave manuscripts that are still extant (Giddings 1984; Richardson 1987), and Harper was the first female public lecturer that many women, Black or White, ever saw and heard (Sterling 1984).

After emancipation, church women and teachers organized schools and churches throughout the South. Since male ministers also worked as teachers, male and female educators (preachers and teachers) became the vital source of leaders. With the rise of Jim Crow laws, women's public activism outside the church emerged in the form of an anti-lynching movement under the leadership of Ida B. Wells Barnett.

This movement was the basis for the formation of the National Association of Colored Women, whose motto was "Lifting as We Climb." That club movement explored and confronted the way in which racism threatened or distorted every aspect of life.

In order to provide the leadership essential for their communities, African American women insisted upon their organizational autonomy while addressing their efforts to the condition of the entire community. In 1895, Josephine St. Pierre Ruffin wrote:

> Our woman's movement is a woman's movement in that it is led and directed by women for the good of women and men, for the benefit of all humanity. . . . We want, we ask the active interest of our men; . . . we are not alienating or withdrawing, we are only coming to the front, willing to join any others in the same work . . . and inviting . . . others to join us. (Davis 1933:19)

The importance of these women's clubs was evident in the interviews with the elderly community workers, who described these organizations as places where they learned to lead and administer, and where they organized to win elections in organizations seemingly dominated by men, such as the NAACP and the Urban League.[7] The oldest surviving national African American political organizations are women's organizations whose founders and members also participated in organizing the NAACP, the Urban League,[8] the Association for the Study of Afro-American Life and History, and every other national African American organization. Emerging as one of the prominent leaders during the Depression, Mary McLeod Bethune created the National Council of Negro Women as a lobby for civil rights and working women. The clubs served as training stations for both middle-class and lower-class women leaders.

Several observers in the late nineteenth and early twentieth centuries noted the prestige associated with women's public participation and work for "the Race" (Perkins 1981; Lerner 1972). In urban communities, mothers clubs were organized to deal with childbirth at home, housework, and child care. As children grew older, these clubs became scholarship clubs. Clubs for the protection, cultural "uplift," and mutual aid of household workers were formed. Carter Woodson (1930) identified the significant role of washerwomen in financing and building associations that developed into the major Black insurance companies. He argued that this was one of many examples of the way in which African American working women not only supported their families but also contributed to the possibility of economic self-sufficiency in the entire community. Through such community work,

Maggie Lena Walker became the first woman of any color to be a bank president in the United States (Brown 1989; Giddings 1983).

W. E. B. Du Bois (1975) observed that the club movement, lacking money as a resource, made its most substantial contribution through the web of affiliations it built, connecting and empowering Black people across class and status lines:

> . . . the women of America who are doing humble but on the whole the most effective work in the social uplift of the lowly, not so much by money as by personal contact, are the colored women. Little is said or known about it but in thousands of churches and social clubs, in missionary societies and fraternal organizations, in unions like the National Association of Colored Women, these workers are founding and sustaining orphanages and old folk homes; distributing personal charity and relief; visiting prisoners; helping hospitals; teaching children; and ministering to all sorts of needs. (1975:273)

The organizational history of these women is central to African American protest and survival history. They and their organizations have provided the space where contemporary community workers work as directors, managers, social workers, elected politicians, and advocates.

Because of the efforts of community workers, ideas and strategies change. People reflect on their successes and failures, and as new problems arise, these reflections contribute to new solutions or a change in ideology. Black Power activists, for instance, often accused older members of the community of complacency, accommodations, and do-nothingness. One community worker described a confrontation in which "young militants" challenged Mrs. Burns concerning what she had done for the community "lately," implying that she was an accommodationist and represented an old and useless style of leadership. Mrs. Burns reportedly replied, "I was out raising scholarship money to send you to college so you could come back here and give me sass!" When interviewed, Mrs. Burns mentioned things that she would have done differently in light of the logic of the Black Power Movement; she also named things that she was currently doing differently because of her own reflections on history. She told of one encounter with a Black federal official whom she lectured concerning his being used by his agency to steal ideas from her club rather than empowering the club to be the agency's subcontractor to teach the ideas to others. She claimed her feistiness came from her own reflections on a conflict during the 1920s when she accused another activist of "bringing Jim Crow" to her city by campaigning to build a Black hospital. Mrs. Burns conceded, in light of the late 1960s and early 1970s arguments for community control, that he had been right and she, although her view had prevailed then, had been wrong.

## Discovery, Challenge, and Development: An Emergent Model of Community Work

The totality of racial oppression and the diversity of African American communities combine to make the tasks of community work so varied as almost to defy any kind of classification. Community work comprises both responses to and catalysts for change. Successful or not, it is the effort to make things better and to eliminate the problems and structures that make life difficult. Community work is the persistent effort across time to close the gap between Black and White life chances. The work is both immediate and long term, and its effects are cumulative. There is, however, an emergent model of action that is present in all of this. It is a model of discovery, challenge, and development that represents a multifaceted model of resistance.

Discovery that there is a problem is the first critical step. Community workers observe, discover, and explore the effects of oppressive practices and structures in their own and others' lives. They are the critical connection between the abrasions of personal experience and the social and political contexts that shape experience. It can be the simple act of sending one's daughter to the mailbox that leads to critical discovery. Describing this as the impetus for her neighborhood association, one worker said, "And simply because we wanted to get together and do things for the community and get the streets cleaned up and the garbage picked up and wanted a mailbox installed on the corner, things like that . . . and then we branched out into other things."

Personal discovery does not lead immediately to community action. The discovery process is complex and involves communicating with others about the reality and nature of community problems. Another worker, a Southern migrant whose community work addressed drug problems and public education, told of her "discovery" of school problems when comparing her son's homework with that of his cousin, who attended school in another, predominantly White, neighborhood. She went on to talk about the problem of transforming personal discovery into collective action, particularly in the North:

A lot is like shadow boxing. The problem is there, but you can't quite see it. We cover them a lot. But down South everything is out in the open. . . . You knew where you stood and everybody knew where the line was drawn, and actually you could deal with it better than here. First you've got to find the problem, then you've got to pull it out from under the covers, and then if somebody says it is a problem. . . . I remember when I came to Hamptonville, I thought there was discrimination in the schools *then* . . . when my kids were in school. . . . We [she and her sister-in-law] were discussing our children's work from school one day, and I looked at my son and his cousin [who were] in the same grade, and the entire curriculum was different. And I said, "What is this!" You know, they were in the same grade, and why is this curriculum so different . . . so when I questioned these things, I was really put down; I was bringing discrimination from the South. So I really kept quiet, but I've been looking at this thing for a long time.

The activity of discovery and exploration often overlaps with challenge, since discovery itself is subversive. The actions that follow from discovery, challenge oppressive structures and practices in a variety of ways. Challenge begins when community workers raise questions among their kin and neighbors, and eventually organize some kind of action. In order to do this they must argue, obstruct, organize, teach, lecture, demonstrate, sue, write letters, and so on. They communicate in such a way that they create a critical speech community around the problem—a group of people who share a point of view on a problem, acknowledging that it exists and that it is something on which public action is necessary.

These initial acts of challenge sometimes emerge into full-blown social movements. At other times, discovery and small-scale actions in one area—welfare rights, for instance—will bring a community worker to the attention of others and involve her in a related but quite different social movement. One woman, describing her involvement on the board of directors of a large human services agency outside of her neighborhood and her own community work focus, said, "The director of the program was having some trouble. . . . She knew that I had raised Hell over in [one neighborhood], so she figured that she needed some raised over in [another neighborhood]."

At the same time they are organizing confrontations with oppressive forces outside the community, community workers address needs within their communities that enable people to resist oppression and participate meaningfully in community life. In the struggle for voting rights, for example, civil rights organizations confronted voter registrars throughout the South with demonstrations and registration campaigns at the same time workers like Septima Clark organized schools to teach African Americans how to read and take the tests (Morris 1984). This is the task of internal development, the building and maintenance of organizations and institutions indigenous to the community.

One elected official argued that the most important problem African Americans faced was internal control: " . . . the way they can't have control over their lives. Although I am not a separatist, I feel as though until we can get into the mainstream of this society . . . we are going to be third- or fourth-class citizens." Trained in elementary education, she surprised me when she told me that she had no intention of teaching children. "I felt that even though I worked with a parents' group, that because I wasn't a teacher, no one took my words very seriously, and I decided that I was going to become a teacher, not to work in the classroom but to work with parents." For some community workers, internal development was so critical, it became their full-time vocation. They either found jobs in agencies that permitted them to do such work or they organized their own agencies.

In a society in which "integration" has become the dominant theme in the politics of race, internal community development can often be very controversial, implying separatism and inter-racial hostility. Mrs. Burns experienced such a conflict and found herself, fifty years later, an advocate for the kind of community control she had earlier labeled "bringing Jim Crow." Because of the power of the dominant society, failure to build and maintain community institutions is a problem. Carter Woodson (1933) labeled it "mis-education" and suggested that it could be solved by building alternative institutions. In my own research, community workers called this activity "building Black-oriented institutions."

What has been labeled a "retreat from integration" is actually the discovery of the internal development that was sometimes accomplished in disadvantaged, segregated, Southern schools. Because education was viewed as something akin to a religious mission, African American teachers, especially after 1915, taught African American history in Southern schools at least during the month of February. Aware of the aspirations of many fathers and mothers for their daughters' college educations, and also aware of the grim realities that governed women's opportunities, these teachers often insisted that their students learn classical subjects alongside trades and business subjects. In effect they refused to compound limited social opportunities with inflexible educational policies, now called tracking. Since Southern states made it illegal for White teachers to teach Black children, those children were inadvertently provided with important

CHERYL TOWNSEND GILKES

role models. Although African American teachers in segregated schools could be very assimilationist and Anglocentric in their outlook and thinking, their commitment to the community made a real difference. The teachers believed in and supported the students, who, in turn, observed educated African American women and men in positions of leadership.

The activities of discovery, challenge, and development are interrelated and together represent a tradition of resistance. This model of social action must be seen as dynamic and interactive. The women are agents of this tradition of resistance as both volunteers and professionals. Their persistent refusal to accept the discomfort of racial oppression is the conflicted connection between the individual and the society that contributes to the emergence of a social force for change. Commenting that "revolutions happen in the funniest ways," one worker whose agency specialized in developing women for jobs and finding jobs for women said: "It just started on a physical level. It really just shocked me that I was going to be physically inconvenienced for the simple reason that I was Black. You know? It was that simple, because I was Black. There were certain things that I was not going to be able to get physically, that was going to create conditions of security and warmth and feeling good." The diversity of their work again points to the totality of the pressure on African Americans as a group. When one accounts for the full range of the women's work, it becomes apparent that every question raised about the source of community afflictions contains the seeds of rebellion and social change.

## Conclusion: If It Wasn't for the Women . . .

African American women's community work connects many "small pieces" of community life and contributes to the process of empowerment. The centrality of their work points to the need to examine the importance of women in any community resisting racial oppression. Racial oppression is a complex and interconnected phenomenon that shapes the lives of women and men. Most women of color are trapped in the worst and dirtiest sectors of the female labor market, providing the sole support of their families or supplementing the wages of their husbands, who are similarly trapped in male markets. Their families are not accorded the institutional and ideological supports that benefit White families. Additionally, African American, Asian, Latina, and Native American women also do community work. They find their historical role organized around the nurturance and defense and advancement of an oppressed public family. Women in a variety of community settings now and historically have demonstrated that it is safe to parallel the oft-repeated statement of African American church women that "If it wasn't for the women, you wouldn't have a church," to say, "If it were not for women of color, African American, Asian, Latino, and Native peoples would have far fewer alternatives and resources to maintain themselves and challenge a hostile social system."

African American women, and by extension Asian American, Native American, and Latina women, highlight the importance of women and their work for the creation of a just and more equitable society. Women bring three perspectives to community work that make them particularly rebellious. First, their consciousness is shaped by their experience in the society, especially in the labor force. Second, they see men's suffering and feel its effects in their own lives. These women observe and experience the effects of racism on the men of their community along with the effects of that racism in their own lives. The third and perhaps most important source of discontent is the effect of racial oppression in the lives of their children. Combating the damage to their children and attempting to fashion a more inclusive future for them was stated as the most important motivation for involvement. Community workers got involved "through my kids." It is in their roles as the principal caretakers of children that racial-ethnic women pose the largest political threat to the dominant society. Women and their children are the core around which group solidarity is constructed. Community workers are, in the words of Sadie Daniels, "women builders." Community work derives its character from the shared nature of the problems confronting all members of the community. The depths and complexities of racial oppression cannot be grasped without a thorough understanding of its expression in the lives of women and their children.

Although perspectives on women's roles are becoming a prominent part of the social science canon, this development has not incorporated the complex historical roles of women in powerless communities. These women must confront a politics that involves more than the politics implied by race or class or gender. When viewing the creative role of women in the simultaneous processes of social change and community survival, one must conclude that if it wasn't for the women, racially oppressed communities would not have the institutions, organizations, strategies, and ethics that enable the group not only to survive or to maintain itself as an integral whole, but also to develop in an alien, hostile, oppressive situation and to challenge it. In spite of their powerlessness, African American women and women of color generally have a dramatic impact within and beyond their communities. The translation of this historical role into real power and social justice is the ultimate goal of community work.

## Notes

1. The data for this chapter are taken from my larger study, "Living and Working in a World of Trouble: The Emergent Career of the Black Woman Community Worker." Similar studies of the Chinese American community (Yap 1983) and the Puerto Rican community (Uriarte-Gaston 1988) also identify the critical role of women community workers.

2. Earlier versions of this paper were presented to the Center for Research on Women, Memphis State University, Summer Research Institutes, 1983 and 1986.

3. Substantial insights for this discussion of racial oppression and internal colonialism are drawn from collaborative work with Bonnie Thornton Dill, Evelyn Nakano Glenn, Elizabeth Higginbotham, and Ruth Zambrana sponsored by the Interuniversity Working Group on Gender, Race, and Class.

4. The importance of the extra time and work cannot be overstated. Bettylou Valentine (1978), discussing the expanded time budgets of ghettoized African Americans, considers this to be part of the social cost of their combined poverty and racial oppression. She not only identifies "hustling" as the legal and extralegal strategies that Blackston residents used to produce and augment income, she also means the term to apply to the extra work, the extra hustle, that must be packed into each day because of poverty and racial oppression.

5. When I first began this research, people assumed I would be studying the African American equivalent of the Junior League. Although the twenty-three women who were employed full-time were in middle-class occupations, their class origins were as diverse as those of the larger community. Women with poor and working-class origins had usually experienced their upward mobility in the process of acquiring more education in order qualify for positions in human services that allowed them to do community work full-time, both as volunteers and as professionals. Calling it "going up for the oppressed," I explore this special kind of upward mobility in an earlier article (Gilkes 1983).

6. A pseudonym.

7. One Urban League consultant stated that women emerged as presidents of local Urban League and NAACP chapters as often as men, although they did not preside over the national bodies. She concluded that the role of women as local Urban League presidents combined with their

roles in Urban League Guilds (women's clubs that raised money for the Urban League) showed the importance of the unacknowledged power of women in community affairs.

8. The Urban League was formed through the merger of two organizations, one male and one female.

# References

Balbus, Isaac. 1977. *The Dialectics of Legal Repression: Black Rebels Before the American Criminal Courts.* New Brunswick, N.J.: Transaction Books.

Blackwell, James. 1985. *The Black Community: Diversity and Unity.* Second edition. New York: Harper & Row.

Blauner, Robert. 1972. *Racial Oppression in America.* New York: Harper & Row.

Brown, Elsa Barkley. 1989. "Womanist Consciousness: Maggie Lena Walker and the Independent Order of Saint Luke." *Signs: Journal of Women in Culture and Society* 14 (3): 610–633.

Cade, Toni, ed. 1970. *The Black Woman: An Anthology.* New York: Signet.

Cesaire, Aime. 1972. *Discourse on Colonialism.* New York: Monthly Review Press. (First published 1955).

Davis, Angela. 1971. "Reflections on the Black Woman's Role in the Community of Slaves." *Black Scholar* 3 (4): 2–15.

———. 1981. *Women, Race, and Class.* New York: Random House.

Davis, Elizabeth Lindsey. 1933. *Lifting as They Climb: A History of the National Association of Colored Women.* Washington, D.C.: Moorland-Spingarn Research Center.

Deloria, Vine. 1970. *We Talk, You Listen: New Tribes, New Turf.* New York: Dell.

Du Bois, W. E. B. 1975. *The Gift of Black Folk: Negroes in the Making of America* (1924). Millwood, N.Y.: Kraus-Thompson Organization.

Edelman, Marian Wright. 1987. *Families in Peril: An Agenda for Social Change.* Cambridge, Mass.: Harvard University Press.

Faris, Robert E. L. 1967. *Chicago Sociology, 1920–1932.* Chicago: University of Chicago Press.

Giddings, Paula. 1984. *When and Where I Enter: The Impact of Black Women on Race and Sex in America.* New York: William Morrow.

Gilkes, Cheryl Townsend. 1979. "Living and Working in a World of Trouble: The Emergent Career of the Black Woman Community Worker." Ph.D. dissertation, Northeastern University.

———. 1980. "The Sources of Conceptual Revolutions in the Field of Race Relations." pp. 7–31 in David Claerbaut, ed., *New Directions in Ethnic Studies: Minorities in America.* San Francisco: Century Twenty-One.

————. 1983. "Going up for the Oppressed: The Career Mobility of Black Women Community Workers." *Journal of Social Issues* 39 (3): 115–139.

————. 1990. " 'Liberated to Work Like Dogs': Labeling Black Women and Their Work." Pp. 165–188 in Hildreth Y. Grossman and Nia Lane Chester, eds., *The Experience and Meaning of Work in Women's Lives.* Hillsdale, N.J.: Lawrence Erlbaum Associates.

Hughes, Everett C. 1963. "Race Relations and the Sociological Imagination." *American Sociological Review* 28 (6): 879–890.

————. 1971. *The Sociological Eye: Selected Papers on Work, Self, and the Study of Society.* Chicago: Aldine-Atherton.

King, Mary. 1987. *Freedom Song: A Personal Story of the 1960s Civil Rights Movement.* New York: William Morrow.

Lerner, Gerda. 1972. *Black Women in White America: A Documentary History.* New York: Vintage Books.

Lyman, Stanford. 1972. *The Black American in Sociological Thought: A Failure of Perspective.* New York: G. P. Putnam.

Marable, Manning. 1983. *How Capitalism Underdeveloped Black America: Problems in Race, Political Economy, and Society.* Boston: South End Press.

Morris, Aldon. 1984. *The Origins of the Civil Rights Movement: Black Communities Organizing for Change.* New York: Free Press.

Perkins, Linda. 1981. "Black Women and Racial 'Uplift' Prior to Emancipation." pp. 317–334 in Filomina Chioma Steady, ed., *The Black Woman Cross-Culturally.* Cambridge, Mass.: Schenkman.

Reagon, Bernice Johnson. 1982. "My Black Mothers and Sisters or on Beginning a Cultural Autobiography." *Feminist Studies* 8 (1): 81–96.

————. 1986. "African Diaspora Women: The Making of Cultural Workers." *Feminist Studies* 12 (1): 77–90.

Richardson, Marilyn, ed. 1987. *Maria Stewart, America's First Black Woman Political Writer: Essays and Speeches.* Bloomington: Indiana University Press.

Sterling, Dorothy. 1984. *We Are Your Sisters: Black Women in the Nineteenth Century.* New York: W. W. Norton.

Uriarte-Gaston, Miren. 1988. "Organizing for Survival: The Emergence of a Puerto Rican Community." Ph.D. dissertation, Boston University.

Valentine, Bettylou. 1978. *Hustling and Other Hard Work: Life Styles in the Ghetto.* New York: Free Press.

Webber, Thomas L. 1978. *Deep like the Rivers: Education in the Slave Quarter Community, 1831–1865.* New York: W. W. Norton.

White, Deborah Gray. 1985. *Ar'n't I a Woman? Female Slaves in the Plantation South.* New York: W. W. Norton.

Wilson, William Julius. 1973. *Power, Racism, and Privilege: Race Relations in Theoretical and Sociohistorical Perspectives.* New York: Macmillan.

Woodson, Carter G. 1930. "The Negro Washerwoman." *Journal of Negro History* 15 (3): 269–277.

———. 1933. *The Mis-Education of the Negro*. New York: Associated Publishers.

Yap, Stacey Guat Hong. 1983. "Gather Your Strength, Sisters: The Emergence of Chinese Women Community Workers." Ph.D. dissertation, Boston University.

# 13

## Migration and Vietnamese American Women: Remaking Ethnicity

### Nazli Kibria

**E**thnicity is a gender-contested realm. It is an arena of conflict between men and women and one over which they struggle to gain control. Recent feminist scholarship has emphasized the utility of ethnic[1] bonds and institutions for immigrant women. Thus immigrant families and communities are seen as vehicles by which immigrant women resist and cope with their disadvantaged status as racial-ethnics in the dominant society, rather than as sources of gender oppression. The focus on the role of ethnicity as a mode of resistance has provided important insights into the dynamics of racial-ethnic oppression in immigrant lives. However, by making secondary the ongoing gender struggles within the immigrant community, this perspective has also given rise to an overemphasis on the consensual character of ethnic ties.

Drawing on data from my study of family life and gender relations in an urban Vietnamese American community, this chapter attempts to capture both the constraints faced by immigrant women and the resistances they offer to oppressive forces in the immigrant community as well as the dominant society.

## Women and Immigrant Ties: Oppression and Resistance

One of the most important and dominant frameworks on immigrant adaptation in the United States is the assimilationist perspective (Gordon 1964; Hirschman 1983; Park and Burgess 1969).[2] A central assumption of this perspective is that immigrant groups gradually become Americanized, that is, they shed their loyalties and connections with the traditional immigrant culture and community and become assimilated into the "melting pot" of America. In this process, women have been seen in two capacities. On the one hand, immigrant women, viewed as staunch supporters of immigrant traditions and culture, have been viewed as barriers to assimilation. Alternatively, they have been seen as important intermediaries or vehicles of integration into the dominant society (see Deutsch 1987:719–720). But regardless of the particular role into which immigrant women are cast, assimilation is viewed as synonymous with greater gender equality. Since immigrant ties are seen as a source of patriarchal oppression, as the group assimilates into American culture, immigrant women are expected to be freed from the shackles of tradition and male authority.

The assimilation model has been subject to a series of sharp and wide-ranging attacks in recent decades (Hirschman 1983; Morawska 1985). One of the fundamental criticisms has been that the characterization of the immigrant assimilation process as one of unilineal, progressive development from the "traditional" to the "modern" is far too simplistic. Instead, scholars have argued for a perspective that recognizes the uneven quality of modernization processes, and the ability of traditional values and institutions to coexist with modern ones. But perhaps the most serious criticism of the assimilation model is that it fails to take into account the distinct situation and experience of people of color within American society. The assimilation model was formulated with reference to the experiences of White European immigrants in the United States. As a result, it neglects the ways in which race shapes the adaptation of minority groups to the dominant society.

Feminist scholarship has both shared and contributed to the critique of the assimilation model. For example, the model's dichotomous characterization of migration as a movement from the "traditional" to the "modern" has been brought under question by studies which show that migration may be detrimental rather than favorable to women's status. In fact, rather than leading to greater gender equality, migration, like economic development, may result in losses for women, in terms of traditional sources of support and power in the domestic sphere as well as access to production processes and thus economic resources (Beneria and Sen 1981; Deutsch 1987). Feminist scholars have also been sensitive to the assimilation model's neglect of racial oppression and its role in shaping the experience of minority groups.

In fact, much recent scholarship on immigrant women has focused not on assimilation processes but on the disadvantaged status of immigrant women within the dominant society. Terms such as "multiple jeopardy" and "triple oppression," signifying the complex intertwining of class, racial-ethnic, and gender oppression, increasingly dominate discussions of racial-ethnic women's experience (Brettell and Simon 1986:10; King 1988). As women, as racial-ethnics, and as inhabitants of the lower rungs of the social class ladder, racial-ethnic women experience multiple disadvantages in the dominant society. This emphasis on the marginal location of racial-ethnic women within dominant society structures has been accompanied by a shift in how scholars view the relationship of racial-ethnic women to their families and communities. These "traditional" institutions are not simply sources of patriarchal oppression. Rather, family and community represent modes of resistance to dominant society constraints, or vehicles by which the minority group struggles to survive (Caulfield 1974; Glenn 1986; Dill 1988). While immigrant women may struggle against the oppression they experience as women within the immigrant family and community, the oppression they experience from the dominant society as members of a racial-ethnic group generates needs and loyalties of a more immediate and pressing nature. Thus immigrant women may remain attached to, and indeed support, traditional patriarchal family and community structures. This is due not simply to the entrenched cultural beliefs or cultural conservatism of the women, but also to the benefits that they gain from retaining these structures, given the multiple disadvantages they face in the dominant society. In short, for immigrant women, the traditional family and community are ways of surviving and maintaining cultural autonomy in the "new" society. The need to sustain family and community may take priority over the internal struggles against male dominance in the immigrant family and community.

In general, this view of ethnic affiliation—that it is a resource for coping with the dominant society—has become increasingly important in the scholarship on immigration, including studies that are not explicitly concerned with the gendered dimensions of the racial-ethnic experience. Thus many contemporary studies of ethnicity focus on the persistence and adaptive relevance of "traditional" immigrant affiliations (see, for example, Kim 1981: Morawska 1985; Portes and Bach 1985). These studies suggest that immigrant ties may actually be a vehicle for or a product of individual and collective modernization, rather than an impediment or barrier to modernity (Morawska 1985; See and Wilson 1988). Ethnic boundaries are seen as dynamic and situational, and there is an emphasis on the active part played by the immigrant group in generating and shaping group membership. To summarize, from varied and diverse currents in social science scholarship on immigrants, there has emerged a theoretical consensus of sorts about immigrant institutions, one that is critical of the assimilation model. For immigrant women and men, the immigrant family and community are sources of economic, political, and cultural resistance, vehicles for adaptation to the dominant society.

The emphasis on the notion of adaptation that has come to dominate much of the literature on the immigrant experience does, however, raise some critical questions. For one thing, the focus on the adaptive quality of the immigrant family and community has led to a neglect of the divisions and conflicts within these institutions. To see ethnic institutions only as vehicles of resistance to dominant society oppression implies a uniformity and consensuality of experience within the ethnic group. But to what extent is this true—do all participants benefit in the same way from ethnic solidarities? In recent years feminist scholarship has become increasingly critical of the concept of the family or household economy, which assumes that families act in unison and agreement in their economic strategies (Beneria and Roldan 1987). This emphasis on consensus serves to whitewash the conflictual aspects of family life (Beneria and Roldan 1987). However, this critique of familial consensus has not been fully and adequately extended to the study of ethnic ties and institutions. This is so despite the existence of many studies that document the conflicts and tensions between men and women that have been a part of the political struggles and social movements of racial-ethnic groups (Chow 1987; King 1988; Baca Zinn 1975). In general, it seems essential to acknowledge that women and men may gain vastly different kinds of benefits and rewards from ethnic resources, given the different statuses and powers of women and men in the immigrant family and community. There is evidence, for example, that the ethnic enclave economy, which has been celebrated by scholars as an example of how ethnic ties may function as a resource, confers quite different economic rewards on men and women (Zhou and Logan 1989).

Both sources of oppression—those within and those without—are important to understanding immigrant women's experience. But a perspective that acknowledges both the oppressive and the supportive dimensions of the family and community for immigrant women leaves certain questions unanswered. How do immigrant women respond to this division, the "double-edged" quality and meaning of ethnic family and community in their lives? I suggest that it is important to see immigrant family and community as contested and negotiated arenas.

NAZLI KIBRIA

Immigrants play an important part in actively shaping and constructing their ethnic institutions. But these institutions are also gender-contested, that is, arenas of conflict and struggle between men and women. The processes by which the ethnic family and community are shaped and negotiated thus ultimately reflect gender divisions, as men and women clash over the question of how to define and construct family and community. In their struggles, they attempt to gain control of and shape the resources of family and ethnicity, in ways that enhance their interests both as members of the family and community, and as men or women.

The struggle between men and women to shape immigrant institutions will vary in its strength and visibility, depending on the balance of power between women and men in the group. This balance of power is deeply shaped by the comparative access of the immigrant men and women to economic, political, and social resources in the dominant society. Particularly when migration is concurrent with a drastic shift in the resources of women and men relative to each other, the gender-based struggle to control family and community may become especially visible. While men and women jockey to control family and community, to redefine it on their terms, they are also, of course, engaged in a conflict over gender relations—the place and power of men and women within the family and community. As family and community life are reorganized by men and women, their roles and relations also undergo change. Thus the study of change in immigrant family life, gender relations, and ethnic organizations must approach these spheres as deeply intertwined rather than separate aspects of immigrant life. In my research on Vietnamese Americans, I found the impact of migration on family life and the status of women to be issues of major debate in the ethnic community. For Vietnamese Americans, the future of their family and gender relations was tied to cultural identity—what it meant "to be Vietnamese in America." In other words, the importance and fervor of the debate about family and gender stemmed in part from the implications of these debates for the core of ethnic identity and meaning itself.

## Vietnamese Americans and the Rise in Women's Power

My research on the adaptive strategies of a community of Vietnamese refugees in Philadelphia revealed some of the ways in which women and men struggled and clashed with each other in efforts to shape the social organization of family and community life. From 1983 to 1985, I gathered information on family life and gender relations through participant observation in household and community settings, as well as in-depth interviews with women and men in the ethnic community.

The Vietnamese of the study were recent immigrants who had arrived in the United States during the late 1970s and early 1980s. Most were from urban, middle-class backgrounds in southern Vietnam. At the time of the study, over 30 percent of the adult men in the households of study were unemployed. Of the men who were employed, over half worked in low-paying, unskilled jobs in the urban service sector or in factories located in the outlying areas of the city. Women tended to work periodically, occupying jobs in the informal economic sector as well as in the urban service economy. Eight of the twelve households had members who collected public assistance. Both the family economy and informal community exchange networks were important means by which the households dealt with economic scarcities. Family and community were of tremendous economic salience to the group, as they were important resources for survival in the face of a rather inhospitable economic and social environment.

As suggested by the high rate of the men's unemployment, settlement in the United States had generated some shifts in power in favor of the women in the group. Traditional Vietnamese family and gender relations were modeled on Confucian principals, which placed women in subordination to men in every aspect of life. A key aspect of the social and economic oppression of women in traditional Vietnamese life was the patrilineal extended household. Its organization dictated that women married at a young age, following which they entered the household of their husband's father. This structure ensured the concentration of economic resources in the hands of men and men's control of women through the isolation of women from their families of origin.[3]

It is important to note the deep-seated changes in traditional family and gender structures in Vietnam during this century. War and urbanization eroded the structure of the patrilineal extended household. While unemployment was high in the cities, men from middle-class backgrounds were able to take advantage of the expansion of middle-level positions in the government bureaucracy and army. Such occupational opportunities were more limited for women: the women study participants indicated that they engaged in seasonal and informal income-generating activities or worked in low-level jobs in the growing war-generated service sector in the cities. The transition from rural to urban life had generated a shift in the basis of men's control over economic and social resources. However, families relied on men's income to maintain a middle-class standard of living. Thus women remained in a position of economic subordination to men, a situation that served to sustain the ideals of the traditional family system and men's authority in the family. Restrictions on women's sexuality were important for middle-class families who sought to distinguish themselves from the lower social strata. My data suggest that families were especially conscious of the need to distance themselves from poorer "fallen" women who had become associated with the prostitution generated by the American military presence.

Within the Vietnamese American community of study, I found several conditions that were working to undermine the bases on which male authority had rested in Vietnam. Most important, for the Vietnamese men, the move to the United States had involved a profound loss of social and economic status. Whereas in pre-1975 Vietnam the men held middle-class occupations, in the United States they had access to largely unskilled, low-status, and low-paying jobs. Also, because of their difficulties with English and their racial-ethnic status, the men found themselves disadvantaged within social arenas of the dominant society. Compounding these problems was the dearth of strong formal ethnic organizations in the community that could have served as a vehicle for the men's political assertion into the dominant society.

As a result of these losses, the comparative access of men and women to the resources of the dominant society had to some extent become equalized. In contrast to the experiences of the men, migration had not significantly altered the position of the women in the economy. As in Vietnam, the women tended to work sporadically, sometimes in family businesses or, more commonly, in temporary jobs in the informal and service sector economies of the city. However, the economic contributions of women to the family budget had risen in proportion to those of the men. I have suggested that in modern, urban South Vietnam the force and legitimacy of male authority had rested heavily on the ability of men to ensure a middle-class status and standard of living for their families. In the United States, the ability of men to fulfill this expectation had been eroded. Among the men, there was widespread concern about the consequences of this situation for their status in the family, as is revealed by the words of a former lieutenant of the South Vietnamese army: "In Vietnam, the man earns and everyone depends on him. In most families, one or two men could provide for the whole family. Here the man finds he can never make enough money to take care of the family. His wife has to work, his children have to work, and so they look at him in a different way. The man isn't strong anymore, like he was in Vietnam."

Such changes had opened up the possibilities for a renegotiation of gender relations, and were the cause of considerable conflict between men and women in the family and community. The shifts in power had also enhanced the ability of women to construct and channel familial and ethnic resources in ways that they chose. Previously I suggested that the changes in the balance of power between men and women generated by migration are crucial to understanding the manner and degree to which immigrant family and community reveal themselves to be gender contested. How, then, did the fairly drastic shift in the gender balance of power among the Vietnamese Americans reflect itself in the ability of the men and women in this group to influence family and community life? In the following section, I describe some of the ways in which gender interests and conflict shaped family and community life for the Vietnamese Americans.

## Family and Ethnicity as Gender Contested

One of the most intriguing and important strategies of Vietnamese American adaptation that I observed was the rebuilding of kinship networks. Family ties had undergone tremendous disruption in the process of escape from Vietnam and resettlement in the United States. Despite this, the households of the group tended to be large and extended. The process by which this occurred was one in which the study participants actively worked to reconstruct family networks by building kin relationships. In order for this to take place, the criteria for inclusion in the family had become extremely flexible. Thus close friends were often incorporated into family groups as fictive kin. Also, relationships with relatives who were distant or vaguely known in Vietnam were elevated in importance. Perhaps most important for women, the somewhat greater significance traditionally accorded the husband's kin had receded in importance.[4] Given the scarcity of relatives in the United States, such distinctions were considered a luxury, and the demands of life made the rebuilding of family a valuable, if not a necessary, step in the process of adaptation to the dominant society.

While important for the group as a whole, the reconstruction of kinship as it took place had some special advantages for women. One consequence of the more varied and inclusive nature of the kinship network was that women were rarely surrounded exclusively by the husband's relatives and/or friends. As a result, they were often able to turn to close fictive kin and perhaps members of their families of origin for support during conflicts with men in the family. Another condition that enhanced the power of married women in the family was that few had to deal with the competing authority of their mother-in-law in the household, because elderly women have not been among those likely to leave Vietnam.

The reconstruction of kinship thus had important advantages for women, particularly as it moved the Vietnamese perhaps even further from the ideal model of the patrilineal extended household than it had been in the past. But women were not simply passive beneficiaries of the family rebuilding process. Rather, they played an active part in family reconstruction, attempting to shape family boundaries in ways that were to their advantage. I found women playing a vital part in creating fictive kin by forging close ties. And women were often important, if not central, "gatekeepers" to the family group and household. Thus the women helped to decide such matters as whether the marriage of a particular family member was a positive event and could be taken as an opportunity to expand kinship networks. At other times the women passed judgment on current or potential family members, as to whether they had demonstrated enough commitment to such important familial obligations as the sharing of economic and social resources with kin.

Although women undoubtedly played an important part in family reconstruction, their control over decisions about family membership was by no means exclusive or absolute. In fact, the question of who was legitimately included in the family group was often a source of tension within families, particularly between men and women. The frequency of disputes over this issue stemmed in part from the fluidity and subsequent uncertainty about family boundaries, as well as the great pressures often placed on individuals to subordinate their needs to those of the family collective. Beyond this, I also suggest that disputes over boundaries arose from the fundamental underlying gender divisions in the family. That is, the different interests of women and men in the family spurred efforts to shape the family in ways that were of particular advantage to them. For the reasons I have previously discussed, the Vietnamese American women had greater influence and opportunity in the shaping of family in the United States than they had in the past. The women tended to use this influence to construct family groups that extended their power in the family.

In one case that I observed, considerable tension developed between a couple named Nguyet and Phong concerning the sponsorship[5] of Nguyet's nephew and his family from a refugee camp in Southeast Asia. Nguyet and Phong had been together with their three children (two from Nguyet's previous marriage) for about seven years, since they had met in a refugee camp in Thailand. Phong remained married to a woman who was still living in Vietnam with his children, a fact that was the source of some stress for Nguyet and Phong. The issue of the nephew's sponsorship seemed to exacerbate tensions in the relationship. Phong did not want to undertake the sponsorship because of the potentially heavy financial obligations it entailed. He also confessed that he was worried that Nguyet would leave him after the nephew's arrival, a threat often made by Nguyet during their quarrels. Finally, he talked of how Nguyet's relationship with the nephew was too distant to justify the sponsorship. Nguyet had never even met the nephew, who was the son of a first cousin rather than of a sibling.

Confirming some of Phong's fears, Nguyet saw the presence of the nephew and his family as a potentially important source of support for herself. She spoke of how she had none of "my family" in the country, in comparison with Phong, whose sister lived in the city. She agreed that she did not know much about her nephew, but nonetheless felt that his presence would ease her sense of isolation and also would provide a source of aid if her relationship with Phong deteriorated. Eventually she proceeded with the sponsorship, but only after a lengthy dispute with Phong.

While the issue of sponsorship posed questions about kinship in an especially sharp manner, there were other circumstances under which women and men clashed over family boundaries. When kin connections could not be questioned (for example, in the case of a sibling), what came under dispute was the commitment of the particular person involved to familial norms and obligations. One of my woman respondents fought bitterly with her older brother about whether their male cousin should live with them. Her brother objected to the cousin's presence in the household on the grounds that he had not responded to their request for a loan of money two years ago. The woman respondent wanted to overlook this breach of conduct because of her extremely close relationship with the cousin, who had been her "best friend" in Vietnam.

Regardless of the particular circumstances, gender conflict seemed an important part of the family reconstruction process. Women and men shared an interest in creating and maintaining a family group that was large and cohesive enough to provide economic and social support. However, their responses to the family reconstruction process were framed by their differing interests, as men and women, within the family. Men and women attempted to channel family membership in ways that were to their advantage, such that their control over the resources of the family group was enhanced.

Gender divisions and conflicts also entered into the community life of the group. The social networks of the Vietnamese American women were central to the dynamics and organization of the ethnic community. They served to organize and regulate exchange between households. While "hanging out" at informal social gatherings, I observed women exchanging information, money, goods, food, and tasks such as child care and cooking. Given the precarious economic situation of the group, these exchanges played an important role in ensuring the economic survival and stability of the households. The women's centrality to these social networks gave them the power not only to regulate household exchange but also to act as agents of social control in the community in a more general sense. I found that women, through the censure of gossip and the threat of ostracism, played an important part in defining community norms. In short, the relative rise in power that had accrued to the Vietnamese American women as a result of migration expressed itself in their considerable influence over the organization and dynamics of the ethnic community. Like kinship, community life was a negotiated arena, one over which women and men struggled to gain control.

The gender-contested quality of ethnic forms was also apparent in the efforts of women to reinterpret traditional Vietnamese familial ideologies on their own terms. In general, the Vietnamese American women continued to espouse and support traditional ideologies of gender relations as important ideals. For example, when asked during interviews to describe the "best" or ideal roles of men and women in the family, most of my respondents talked of a clear division of roles in which women assumed primary responsibility for maintaining the home and taking care of the children, and men for the economic support of the family. Most felt that household decisions should be made jointly, although the opinion of the man was seen to carry more weight. About half of those interviewed felt that a wife should almost always obey her husband. Even more widespread were beliefs in the importance of restrictions on female (but not male) sexuality before marriage.

While women often professed such beliefs, their relationship to traditional ideologies was active rather than passive and inflexible. In other words, the women tended to emphasize certain aspects of the traditional familial ideology over others. In particular, they emphasized parental authority and the obligation of men to sacrifice individual needs and concerns in order to fulfill the needs of the family, traditional precepts they valued and hoped to preserve in the United States. The women's selective approach to Vietnamese "tradition" emerged most clearly in situations of conflict between men and women in the family. In such disputes, women selectively used the traditional ideologies to protect themselves and to legitimate their actions and demands (Kibria 1990). Thus, husbands who were beating their wives were attacked by other women in the community on the grounds that they (the husbands) were inadequate breadwinners. The women focused not on the husband's treatment of his wife but on his failure to fulfill his family caretaker role. Through this selective emphasis, the women managed to condemn the delinquent husband without appearing to depart from "tradition." In short, for the Vietnamese American women, migration had resulted in a greater ability to shape family and community life.

## Conclusion

For immigrant women, ethnic ties and institutions may be both a source of resistance and support, and of patriarchal oppression. Through an acknowledgment of this duality we can arrive at a fuller understanding of immigrant women's lives: one that captures the multifaceted constraints as well as the resistances that are offered by immigrant women to the oppressive forces in their lives. In patterns similar to those noted by studies of other racial-ethnic groups (Stack 1976; Baca Zinn 1975), the Vietnamese Americans presented in this chapter relied on family and community for survival and resistance. Their marginal status made the preservation of these institutions an important priority.

Like other racial-ethnic women, the ability of the Vietnamese American women to shape ethnicity was constrained by their social-structural location in the dominant society. These women saw the traditional family system as key to their cultural autonomy and economic security in American society. Migration may have equalized the economic resources of the men and women, but it had not expanded the economic opportunities of the women enough to make independence from men an attractive economic reality. The Vietnamese American women, as is true for other women of color, were especially constrained in their efforts to "negotiate" family and community in that they faced triple disadvantages (the combination of social class, racial-ethnic, and gender statuses) in their dealings with the dominant society.

Recognition of the role of ethnic institutions in facilitating immigrant adaptation and resistance is essential. However, it is equally important to not lose sight of gender divisions and conflicts, and the ways in which these influence the construction of ethnic institutions. Feminist scholars have begun to explore the diverse ways in which immigrant women manipulate family and community to enhance their own power, albeit in ways that are deeply constrained by the web of multiple oppressions that surround them (Andezian 1986; Bhachu 1986; Kibria 1990). Such work begins to suggest the complexity of immigrant women's relationship to ethnic structures, which is informed by both strength and oppression.

## Notes

1. I define "ethnicity" as a collective identity based on culture or nationality. I reserve the term "racial-ethnic" to refer to the subordinate status of the group (stemming from racial and ethnic oppression) in the dominant society. The simultaneous use of these terms is somewhat awkward but necessary in order to convey the multiple statuses occupied by many immigrant groups. For example, the Vietnamese share an ethnic identity and status as Vietnamese, based on a common nationality and culture. At the same time, they hold a racial status in the dominant society as Asian Americans.

2. My definition of the assimilationist model includes its subvariations, such as "cultural pluralism" and "Anglo conformity."

3. Some scholars stress the fact that the reality of women's lives was far different from that suggested by these Confucian ideals. Women in traditional Vietnam also had a relatively favorable economic position in comparison with Chinese women due to Vietnamese women's rights of inheritance as well as their involvement in commercial activities (see Hickey 1964; Keyes 1977). Despite these qualifications, there is little to suggest that the economic and social subordination of women was not a fundamental reality in Vietnam.

4. Hy Van Luong (1984) has noted the importance of two models of kinship in Vietnamese life, one that is patrilineal-oriented and another in which bilateral kin are of significance. Thus the flexible, encompassing conceptions of family that I found among the group were not entirely new, but had their roots in Vietnamese life; however, they had acquired greater significance in the context of the United States.

5. Refugee resettlement in the United States involves a system of sponsorship by family members or other interested parties who agree to assume part of the responsibility for taking care of those sponsored for a period of time after their arrival.

# References

Andezian, Sossie. 1986. "Women's Roles in Organizing Symbolic Life: Algerian Female Immigrants in France." Pp. 254–266 in *International Migration: The Female Experience*, edited by R. J. Simon and C. B. Brettell. Totowa, N.J.: Rowman and Allenheld.

Baca Zinn, Maxine. 1975. "Political Familism: Toward Sex Role Equality in Chicano Families." *Aztlan* 6, no. 1: 13–26.

Beneria, Lourdes, and Martha Roldan. 1987. *The Crossroads of Class and Gender*. Chicago: University of Chicago Press.

Beneria, Lourdes, and Gita Sen. 1981. "Accumulation, Reproduction and Women's Role in Economic Development: Boserup Revisited." *Signs* 7, no. 2 (Winter): 279–298.

Bhachu, Parminder K. 1986. "Work, Dowry and Marriage Among East African Sikh Women in the U.K." Pp. 241–254 in *International Migration: The Female Experience*, edited by R. J. Simon and C. B. Brettell. Totowa, N.J.: Rowman and Allenheld.

Brettell, Caroline B., and Rita J. Simon. 1986. "Immigrant Women: An Introduction." Pp. 3–21 in *International Migration: The Female Experience*, edited by Rita J. Simon and Caroline B. Brettell. Totowa, N.J.: Rowman and Allenheld.

Caulfield, Mina D. 1974. "Imperialism, the Family, and Cultures of Resistance." *Socialist Review* 4, no. 2: 67–85.

Chow, Esther Ngan-Ling. 1987. "The Development of Feminist Consciousness Among Asian American Women." *Gender and Society* 1, no. 3: 284–299.

Deutsch, Sarah. 1987. "Women and Intercultural Relations: The Case of Hispanic New Mexico and Colorado." *Signs* 12: 719–740.

Dill, Bonnie Thornton. 1988. "Our Mothers' Grief: Racial-Ethnic Women and the Maintenance of Families." *Journal of Family History* 13, no. 4: 415–431.

Glenn, Evelyn Nakano. 1986. *Issei, Nissei, War Bride*. Philadelphia: Temple University Press.

———. 1987. "Gender and the Family." Pp. 348–381 in *Analyzing Gender: A Handbook of Social Science Research*, edited by Beth B. Hess and Myra M. Ferree. Newbury Park, Calif.: Sage.

Gordon, Milton. 1964. *Assimilation in American Life*. New York: Oxford University Press.

Hickey, Gerald C. 1964. *Village in Vietnam*. New Haven: Yale University Press.

Hirschman, Charles. 1983. "America's Melting Pot Reconsidered." *Annual Review of Sociology* 9: 397–423.

Keyes, Charles F. 1977. *The Golden Peninsula*. New York: Macmillan.

Kibria, Nazli. 1990. "Power, Patriarchy and Gender Conflict in the Vietnamese Immigrant Community." *Gender and Society* 4, no. 1 (March): 9–24.

Kim, Ill Soo. 1981. *New Urban Immigrants: The Korean Community in New York*. Princeton: Princeton University Press.

King, Deborah H. 1988. "Multiple Jeopardy, Multiple Consciousness: The Context of a Black Feminist Ideology." *Signs* 14, no. 1: 42–72.

Luong, Hy Van. 1984. " 'Brother' and 'Uncle': An Analysis of Rules, Structural Contradictions and Meaning in Vietnamese Kinship." *American Anthropologist* 86, no. 2: 290–313.

Morawska, Ewa. 1985. *For Bread with Butter*. Cambridge: Cambridge University Press.

Park, Robert, and Ernest Burgess. 1969. *Introduction to the Science of Society*. Student ed. abridged by Morris Janowitz. Chicago: University of Chicago Press.

Portes, Alejandro, and Robert L. Bach. 1985 *Latin Journey: Cubans and Mexican Immigrants in the U.S.* Berkeley: University of California Press.

See, Katherine O'Sullivan, and William J. Wilson. 1988. "Race and Ethnicity." Pp. 223–243 in *Handbook of Sociology*, edited by Neil J. Smelser. Newbury Park, Calif.: Sage.

Stack, Carol. 1974. *All Our Kin*. New York: Harper & Row.

Zhou, Min, and John R. Logan. 1989. "Returns on Human Capital in Ethnic Enclaves: New York City's Chinatown." *American Sociological Review* 54 (October): 809–820.

# IV
# RETHINKING GENDER

# 14

## Images, Ideology, and Women of Color

### Leith Mullings

*So some few women are born free, and some amid insult and scarlet letters*
*achieve freedom; but our women in black had freedom thrust*
*contemptuously upon them. With that freedom they are buying an*
*untrammeled independence and dear as the price they pay for it, it will in*
*the end be worth every taunt and groan.*
—W.E.B. Du Bois, *Dark Water: Voices from Within the Veil*, p. 172.

In wondering at the way in which class and race mediate gender for African-American women, W.E.B. Du Bois, who so eloquently portrayed the double consciousness characterizing the "soul of black folks," described another conflicting duality: the freedom and constraint that mark the experience of gender for African-Americans. The fetters of racism leave them bereft of the "protection of private patriarchy" (Dill, in this volume) but also mitigate some of the constraints of gender, inadvertently creating a small measure of freedom.

But this window of freedom, narrow and equivocal as it is, poses a problem, a threat to the dominant society's rationalizations of gender hierarchy. One solution, the representation of African-American women as inappropriate women—images of them as sexually provocative, as mammies, matriarchs, castrators, as the reason for the problems of the African-American community—becomes a small part of "the price they pay."

Women of color, and particularly African-American women, are the focus of well-elaborated, strongly held, highly contested ideologies concerning race, class, and gender. The images, representations, and symbols that form ideologies often have complex meanings and associations that are not always easily or readily articulated, making them difficult to challenge. Appearing in scholarly literature as well as popular culture, they take the form of accepted truths, constructing the nature of personhood to be comprehended.

How ideologies—used here in the sense of production of meanings—are generated, maintained, and deployed is intimately related to the distribution of power.[1] Dominant ideologies often justify, support, and rationalize the interests of those in power: they tell a story about why things are the way they are, setting out a framework by which hierarchy is explained and mediating contradictions among classes, between beliefs and experiences. But dominant ideologies are also resisted and contested as people develop alternative and oppositional views of the world.

Taking African-American women as an example, this chapter will examine some of the dominant representations of African-American women, looking specifically at how they emerge in the context of class and race relations in the United States, how they function, and how they are contested. Though various writers have discussed stereotypes as they relate to sexuality and conquest, a thorough analysis must also take account of the African-American woman's relationship to work. Throughout history African-American women have been forced to work outside their homes, first by slaveholders and then by economic necessity. In a society in which the dominant ideology has held that the woman's place is in the home, the African-American woman's status as a worker becomes a point of departure for representations that function first to mobilize her labor and then to stigmatize the measure of independence gained from her relationship to work. Her historical relationship to work may be a source of discord in the African-American community, but it can also become the basis for subversion of negative ideologies. The chapter concludes with a consideration of how this analysis might apply to other women of color.

Women as mothers, virgins, and whores have been major archetypical symbols in Western thought. However, the problem of similarity and difference presents itself as we attempt to deconstruct the images, symbols, and representations of women in the United States. Although many of the images that rationalize the structuring of gender extend to all women, we need to deepen our understanding of how race and class mediate both the experience of gender and its imagery.

# Representations of Women in the Antebellum South

Some of the most enduring representations of African-American women took hold during slavery. These images, drawn from science, literature, and historical and popular accounts, as well as from the practices of the planter class, were not always consciously articulated or uniformly applied. Nevertheless, the exercise of drawing them out gives us some insight into how the planter class "made sense" of the contradictions of slavery and the post-emancipation caste system.

As the United States became a highly stratified society, the hegemonic models of womanhood accentuated the distance between races and classes. Among the planter class of the antebellum South, where women were subordinate in the gender hierarchy but reaped the benefits of race and class asymmetry, the image of the ideal woman was a highly romanticized and extreme version of what has been called the "cult of true womanhood." The model woman was portrayed as incontrovertibly identified with the home; as the ideal wife and mother; as good, passive, delicate, pure, submissive, calm, frail, small, and dependent (Atkinson and Boles 1985; Boles and Atkinson 1986).

If this model did not fit the real experiences of Euro-American working-class women, most certainly the constructions of gender were very different for enslaved women of African descent. For these women, the asymmetries of race, class, and gender gave rise to a series of images and stereotypes influenced by the universal archetypes of gender but qualitatively transformed by ideologies of race, which themselves largely grew out of the class relationships of slavery.

Historians have described two images that reflect dominant Euro-American views of African-American women during this period: (1) "Jezebel," the sexually aggressive, provocative woman governed entirely by libido; and (2) "Mammy," the religious, loyal, motherly slave devoted to the care of the slaveowner's family (see, for example, King 1973; White 1985; Simms-Wood 1988; Christian 1985; Sunquist 1987, Fox-Genovese 1988). To this I would add the underlying theme of defeminization—the African-American woman as being without a clearly ascribed gender identity: that is, as being unfeminine, in the sense of not possessing those traits, alleged to be biological, that defined, constrained, but also protected women of the time.

## "AIN'T I A WOMAN?"

While the Jezebel and Mammy stereotypes may be seen as variations of universal female archetypes, as we will discuss below, the defeminization of African-American women was more closely related to the ideologies of race that rationalized and perpetuated the brutal conditions of slavery. The belief that Africans and African-Americans constituted a distinct, possibly nonhuman, and definitely inferior species, for which slavery was the most appropriate condition, was found not only in popular thought but was elevated to "science" in the doctrine of polygenesis (see Harris 1968). Medical science, for example, marshaled evidence to demonstrate that African-Americans had smaller lungs and brains and larger genitals, supposedly constituting irrefutable proof that the enslaved were of a different species.

Sojourner Truth's haunting address to the Akron Convention for Women's Suffrage in 1851 underscored the contradiction between the model of gender in which Euro-American women were both imprisoned and protected, and the conditions of life for African-American women: "I have plowed, and planted, and gathered into barns, and no man could head me! Ain't I a woman?" The place of women was said to be in the home, but enslaved women worked outside the home at jobs traditionally defined as men's work—sawing wood, plowing, repairing roads, digging ditches, pitching hay, building post-and-rail fences, and whatever else was necessary. While the particular tasks assigned to women were influenced by the historical period and the size of the plantation, as well as the labor needs of the owner, the division of labor seems to have had more to do with the principle of division than the tasks considered appropriate for women (Fox-Genovese 1988:172–177).[2] Just as denying enslaved African-Americans human status rationalized their inhuman treatment, so the defeminization of African-American women served to mediate the contradiction between beliefs about women's abilities and limitations, on the one hand, and the intense labor exploitation of African-American women, on the other.

"I have borne thirteen children, and seen them most all sold off to slavery, and when I cried out with my mother's grief, none but Jesus heard me! And ain't I a woman?" Motherhood was a powerful and central symbol of gender definition for Euro-American women. But for African-American mothers it offered few rights—not even that of keeping their children, who could be, and often were, sold away from them. In a model of femininity based on dependence as a defining characteristic, enslaved women became "defeminized"—excluded from the protections of womanhood, motherhood, and femininity.

## JEZEBEL AND MAMMY

The Mammy and Jezebel stereotypes, evoked at different historical periods and applied to women of different ages and phenotypes, are variations of the madonna/whore dualism. But race puts a peculiar cast on how these "universal" archetypes are applied.

The "otherness" of race—the notion that African-Americans represented a distinct species—justified the attribution of excessive sexuality. Representations of the libidinous, sexually aggressive African-American woman sanctioned rape and sexual exploitation by arguing that the enslaved women were the initiators, that their sexuality elicited a "natural" response in Euro-American men. Constructing African-American women as "bad" women who were inappropriate for marriage served to allow sexual activity but to discourage marriage, thereby maintaining the caste system (see King 1973; Stoler and Cooper 1989) by drawing the boundaries along lines of race rather than of class. But as Angela Davis (1981) was the first to argue, rape of African-American women was not simply an expression of the lust of Euro-American men. Rape was primarily an instrument of control, utilized to discipline the labor force and to keep African-American men and women in line.[3]

Mammy—the servile, loyal, obedient woman who nurtures and protects the Euro-American family—a prevalent image in nineteenth-century literature (Sundquist 1987) and in other popular forms (Simms-Woods 1988), is familiar to generations of Americans through *Gone with the Wind*. But once again race puts a peculiar cast on the maternal archetype as the virtues of motherhood emerge only for the purpose of caring for elite Euro-American children. Deborah White (1985) argues that this stereotype, applied to some older women, personified the ideal slave and appeared later when Southerners were forced to defend slavery. While the Jezebel image functioned to excuse miscegenation and sexual assault, the Mammy image functioned to endorse, rationalize, and justify slavery.

The exploitation of African-American women in the spheres of production and reproduction prevailed over notions of gender differentiation. The dilemma created by the distance between the patriarchal model and the real experience of African-American women, who were denied the protections of private patriarchy, and whose men were stripped of all the attributes of male power, is in part addressed through representations of African-American women as defeminized, inappropriate, or bad. For such images serve not only to rationalize labor and sexual exploitation but also to reinforce race solidarity across gender and class lines.

## GENDER, RACE, AND CLASS

Tensions of gender seem to have been subordinated to the benefits of class position as elite Euro-American women, though dependent on men in this highly patriarchal system, clearly reaped significant material benefits from their partnership with these men. Ann Scott's curious portrayal of the planters' wives as passive, powerless, hard-working victims of the patriarchal system, humiliated by their partner's sexual access to enslaved women and burdened by the "difficult, demanding, frustrating and above all never-ending labor" (1970:36) of supervising slaves, does not give sufficient attention to why "most southern women accepted, with a few nagging questions, the racial assumptions of their time and place" (1974:61). Elizabeth Fox-Genovese (1988), on the other hand, demonstrates that the labor of the enslaved supported the leisured and advantaged life of the planters' wives. While slavery strengthened patriarchy, elite women certainly stood to gain from the labor of African-Americans (see Wertz 1984 for cross-cultural comparisons).

But what of nonelite Euro-American women? As the standards of elite women became the model for all women, class differences in gender role behavior became yet another means of strengthening social control and emphasizing the distance between classes. The model of the "lady" certainly did not fit the experience of women who projected alternative standards, such as the "farm wife," a model that placed more emphasis on the work ethic (Hagler 1980).

In a peculiarly American fashion, however, ideologies of race often obscured contradictions of class and gender. The hierarchical system is held in place not only by force but also by ideologically unifying disparate segments of the population. Euro-American women gained not only materially but also "symbolically" as the dualism inherent in Western imagery of women—good women versus bad women—was split into racial categories (Palmer 1983). These mutually defining images were the foundation for a set of beliefs about the protection of White womanhood that became a hegemonic ideology, uniting Euro-Americans across gender and class lines and justifying violence against African-Americans during slavery and in the post-emancipation period.[4]

## Shifting Realities, Changing Images

Emancipation brought freedom from slavery, but political, social, and economic discrimination prevented African-American men from earning an adequate family wage. African-Americans resisted the pressure for married women to work outside the home (Gutman 1976), often using the dominant gender role model to demand a family wage, but need propelled women into the work force. While the majority of Euro-American women did not work outside the home, African-American women worked as sharecroppers, domestics, and laundresses in order for their families to survive (Jones 1982; Mullings 1986a). By 1890, for example, 39.7 of percent of non-White women were in the labor force, compared with 16.3 percent of White women. Since the ideal was that women leave the workforce after marriage, the difference in numbers of working married women is more telling: 22.5 percent of African-American women worked outside the home, compared with only 2.5 percent of Euro-American women (Goldin 1977).

At the same time, gender role expectations dictated that African-American women carry the additional responsibility for household tasks. In short, in their struggle to maintain the family, the African-American women attempted to fulfill gender expectations, without the protections of private patriarchy, while being exploited by public patriarchy (Dill, in this volume). In the post-slavery period, the dissonance between the dominant ideology of equal opportunity and the reality of a society structured by class, race, and gender; between the dominant ideology of a woman's place and the reality of African-American women's experiences as a worker, again set the stage for the emergence of stereotypes and images.

Once again the representation of the African-American woman as sexually provocative sought, as Roland Barthes suggests, to transform "history into nature" (1991:129). Because African-American women worked outside the home, often in servant roles, they were vulnerable to sexual exploitation. These conditions nourished the stereotyping of them as "bad" women as work outside the home became symbolic of "whorish behavior" for Euro-American working-class women as well (see Palmer 1983; Rosen 1982:46). As White (1985:164) reminds us, perhaps the most graphic demonstration of the persistence of the "hot woman" image is that through two-thirds of this century no White man was convicted of raping an African-American woman. Recent rape cases suggest that this stereotype continues (Mullings 1992).

Throughout the history of African-Americans in the United States, images that concern sexuality have been particularly compelling. The dialectically intertwined images of the pure and vulnerable White woman in need of protection, the primitive, sexually aggressive African-American man, and the sexually provocative African-American woman came together to rationalize rape of African-American women and lynching of African-American men (Burton 1985:272; Hall 1983).

Although the protection of White women was the rallying cry, Hall notes that of the approximately 5,000 people murdered by lynching[5] between 1882 and 1946, less than one-fourth were actually accused, let alone found guilty, of rape. Violence, organized and rationalized through the motif of White womanhood, was primarily directed toward restricting the civil and economic rights of African-Americans. The ideology of White womanhood[6] helped preclude class unity among working class Euro-Americans and African-Americans that might have extended the gains of Radical Reconstruction, forcing redistribution of land and implementation of broad-based reforms that might have benefited both groups.

Although sexuality continues to be a major theme in the discourse about race, compliance with the dominant ideology is not always assured (Abercrombie and Turner 1978). For example, the Association of Southern Women for the Prevention of Lynching, formed in 1930— in the context of a broader interracial struggle for reform—rejected the mythology of Southern womanhood as a rationale for the epidemic of lynching. By 1943, 43,000 predominantly middle-stratum Euro-American women had repudiated lynching, stating, "Public opinion has accepted too easily the claim of lynchers and mobsters that they were attacking solely in defense of womanhood. In light of facts this claim can no longer be used as a protection to those who lynch" (cited in Laue and McCorkle 1965:83). The Association noted and rejected the split image of the pure Euro-American woman and the promiscuous African-American woman, claiming that both images served the interests of White men (Hall 1983).

## MAMMIES TO MATRIARCHS

Images of African-American women as mammies continued in media and popular and material cultural forms. Mammy as Aunt Jemima,[7] for example, has graced cereal, pancake, and syrup containers since 1889. Although she has shed her bandana for a curly Afro-like effect and lost some weight (Campbell 1989), this symbol continues to convey images of the faithful, obedient domestic servant. So attached were some Southerners to this stereotype that in 1923 they petitioned to erect a monument in Washington, D.C., to "The Black Mammy of the South" (White 1985). These representations reflected, but also helped to rationalize and reproduce, conditions where job opportunities for African-American women were largely confined to domestic work. And the image of the happy servant served, of course, to mask the economic exploitation of the domestic worker.

Despite formidable obstacles, and with exceptionally high rates of labor force participation, African-American women gradually moved out of private household work, as the expansion of the service and clerical sectors, along with the struggle against discrimination, presented new opportunities. In 1940, 60 percent of all African-American women workers were domestic servants; by 1967, the number declined to 24.5 percent (Jones 1982); and by 1980, only 7.5 percent placed themselves in this occupational category (Jones 1983). In the post–World War II revival of the cult of true womanhood and the establishment of the gender hierarchy, the "independence" created by the relationships of slavery and discrimination became particularly problematic.

In the context of these changing conditions, the imagery of African-American women shifted from that of a nurturant servant to that of the emasculating matriarch. As Barbara Christian (1985) and others have pointed out, the emergence of the matriarch is a shift of emphasis rather than a radical departure. Mammy, who gave tender care to the Massa's family, was always portrayed as uncompromisingly severe with her own. The matriarchy image is most dramatically represented by the post–World War II stereotype of Sapphire, projected on radio and television as the "bossy," "emasculating" wife of Kingfish of the "Amos and Andy Show."

In the 1960s this representation gains a new scientific stature and becomes the basis for national policy decisions. *The Negro Family: The Case for National Action*, popularly known as the Moynihan Report, goes beyond images projected by radio, television, movies, and literature. Like the rise of scientific racism at the turn of the century, this influential account gives popular stereotypes scientific status. For Daniel Patrick Moynihan (a Harvard sociologist who was elected to the U.S. Senate from New York in 1977), the African-American family is "the principal source of most of the aberrant, inadequate, or antisocial behavior that did not establish, but now serves to perpetuate the cycle of poverty and deprivation" (1965:76). The major weakness of the family is its "matriarchal structure," which is deviant from the rest of society. "Matriarchy" as used here seems to refer to the fact that a greater proportion of African-American than Euro-American women work outside the home, and presumably enjoy relatively more independence within the household. The imagery shifts, as the warm, nurturant caretaker of the children of the elite becomes a "matriarch" in her own family—a bad mother responsible for low educational attainment, crime, and delinquency (Moynihan 1965).

It is interesting that this thesis, using elements of the stereotypes fostered in slavery to place the blame for the conditions of the

African-American community on the family structure and the roles played by women, arose precisely when the civil rights movement was mounting a serious challenge to the system of racial oppression and the women's movement was challenging the structure of patriarchy. As such, it was part of a broader ideological thrust—"the culture of poverty" perspectives—that displaced concern from such issues as unemployment and discrimination to family structure and gender roles. As attention is shifted from relations between Euro-Americans and African-Americans to relations within the African-American community, the image of the warm, nurturant "Mammy" is no longer congruent with the "dysfunctional" African-American family as the cause of poverty.

## Ideology and Social Control

These images, then, are elements in ideological systems that are not unchanging but are continually re-created, modified, and defended (Williams 1977). The circumstances that force African-American women to work outside the home also give them a greater degree of freedom from dependence on men than that of Euro-American women, although at a considerable cost. However, this "independence," limited as it is, creates a dilemma that is resolved by sanctioning inappropriate independence through negative imagery.

The "matriarch" label is used to represent a deviation from a class- and race-based model of gender roles that reflects the reality neither of African-American women nor that of most Euro-American women. It brands independence as negative. Cheryl Gilkes (1983:294) points out how such labeling seeks to transform "the model of insurgency"— Afro-American women acting independently on behalf of their communities—into a "model of pathology." Stigmatizing the subordinate but more independent African-American woman, she suggests, functions to constrain women of the dominant group, keeping them in their place. Women who, by accident or design, threaten the hierarchy of the social order are labeled "bad women." Abolitionist women were branded "shameless amazons" and "unsexed females" (Scott 1970:20); similarly, the suffragists were defined as bad women and "held responsible for the increase in divorce, the decline in births, and the loss of 'home-centered life' " (Rosen 1982:45), and accused of contributing to racial suicide by concerning themselves with matters outside the home.

Sanctioning behavior deviant from that deemed appropriate by the dominant class may take a more direct form. Based on her fieldwork with incarcerated African-American women, Diane Lewis (1981) suggests that in deciding guilt or innocence and determining punishment, the police, the courts, and other criminal justice personnel sanction women as much for violating gender role expectations as for illegal behavior. African-American women and, consequently, African-American women offenders tend to be assertive, to be married less frequently, to head households, to have an independent demeanor, and to be on their own. Citing the variety of gender role constraints correctional institutions direct at "demasculinizing" deviant women, Lewis concludes that the greater number of incarcerated African-American women "may simply reflect society's view that they are in greater need of demasculinization" (1981:102). As novelists (French 1977:238), as well as social scientists (Hurtado 1989), have observed, rebellion against gender roles by Euro-American women may lead to psychiatric treatment, while for women of color who rebel, prison is the more likely consequence.

These constructions, then, seek to define the categories through which reality is to be understood, and thereby to define the limits of social action. The stereotypes are grounded in enough reality to make them credible. They are not fully articulated, which makes them difficult to confront and contest; at the same time they arouse strong affect on many levels, some not always accessible to conscious reasoning. Of particular importance is the way these symbols and images speak to a basic aspect of identity—gender attributes—move us back and forth between society and nature (cf. Barthes 1972; Turner 1967). The matriarch image, for example, transforms social relations into cultural preference, constructing matrifocality as an attribute of personality. By placing the cause in "nature" rather than "history," it obscures the role of unemployment, racism, and state policies in undermining the African-American family.

### THE STRUGGLE CONTINUES

Today, African-American women have the highest rates of labor force participation. They have made impressive gains in educational attainment and significant inroads into professions and occupations previously dominated by Euro-American women (Almquist 1989:419). Yet the same time economic policies of the 1980s produced massive unemployment among men and women, and the consequent precipitous increase in households headed by women.

African-American women now have high visibility in many fields, including media, the arts, and politics. Although there are a range of images, today some of the same themes persist in the representation of African-American women of all strata. For example, the inappropriate independence of the "matriarch" is found in the portrayal of the middle-class "superwoman,"[8] who is depicted as inappropriately independent of men because of her access to work (often seen as one of the unfortunate results of affirmative action), as well as of the "welfare mother," who is not properly dependent on men because of welfare payments by the state.

While African-American women of all strata are effected by this imagery, the cost is greatest for poor women. The themes of promiscuous sexuality and inappropriate role fulfillment converge in the discourse on women who head households. The precipitous rise in African-American women who head households is directly related to the economic policies of the last decades that have resulted in the decline of educational and employment opportunities and astounding levels of unemployment (see Wilson 1987). Yet images of the promiscuous, irresponsible welfare mother burdening society with her children serve to deflect attention from the role of the society in producing dependent African-American mothers and children. In doing so, these images reinforce racism and thus help to reproduce the conditions from which the stereotypes emerge (see Mullings 1989, forthcoming).

Most important, perhaps, these representations help to mitigate class conflict and support the status quo. As wealth becomes more and more concentrated, real wages decline and income inequality grows, economic disarray increasingly affects most Americans. In the face of massive voter discontent, politicians and the mass media stigmatize poor women who head households. They are projected as responsible not only for their own poverty but also for the ills of the entire country.

## Ideologies Contested: Accommodation, Resistance, and Transformation

These representations, projected through education, religious institutions, and the mass media, are also resisted, challenged, and altered in social struggle. Despite minimal control of the institutions that produce and reproduce these images, people develop alternative beliefs that grow out of their own experience. In varying measure they contest both the gender imagery imposed upon them and the normative gender roles of the dominant group. In their everyday lives, people accommodate, resist, and transform hegemonic models.

Models are abstractions, however, and are always mediated at particular historical moments. Further, people may hold one set of beliefs and live according to another, and may under some circumstances articulate a different ideal model. It is this process involving experiences, relationships, and beliefs expressed at a given historical moment that is difficult to capture.

As African-Americans have imagined gender roles, they have before them the dominant Euro-American model, which has historically emphasized male dominance and female dependence. This model is supported by education, law, religion, and the other major institutions of society. But they also draw on their own experience in the "new" world, informed by African traditions (Mullings 1986b) in which gender roles, domination, dependency, and work are not so strictly partitioned.

Although African-Americans have resisted negative characterizations of African-American women, they also have often accepted the hierarchical model of ideal gender relations. To the extent that the model is accepted as ideal, it must lead to the devalorization of African-American women. Because their life circumstances preclude the same sort of dependence, because they must protect themselves, their men, and their children, and be assertive on behalf of their community (see Gilkes 1983), they become "unfeminine." Uncritical acceptance of the dominant gender role model and the consequent negative characterization of African-American women by African-Americans contribute to divisions within the African-American community, diminishing the potential for united struggle.[9]

But the complexities of accommodation and resistance (cf. Anyon 1984) to class, race, and gender oppression are not easily sorted out. For example, during slavery there was masculinization of female roles but little feminization of masculine roles, that is, women did men's work but men did not do women's work. One could dispute the claim that slave households were more egalitarian and argue that sharecropping further reinforced patriarchy by reinstating traditional gender roles (cf. Mann 1989). But appropriating gender roles during slavery and sharecropping may also be seen as an attempt to resist the planters' imposition of degenderization, as an assertion of family relationships, and as a protest against the planter's tendency to ignore gender and family roles (see Jones 1982; Davis 1981; Mullings 1986a; Harley 1978). Resistance and accommodation were similarly intertwined in some of the social, nationalist, and religious movements of the late 1960s and 1970s. Women were often expected to play "traditional" roles, and noncompliant women were labelled "Sapphires" (Christian 1985) or "matriarchs" (see Giddings 1984:319–324).

But these relationships also involved a protest against the society that denied African-American men and women the means to fulfill ideal gender expectations. They constituted an attempt to extend the protections of private patriarchy to African-American women, those most exploited by public patriarchy. As such, appealing to the dominant gender role model may serve as a means of making demands—for a family wage and protection from the high personal cost of the double day, or as defense against the predatory sexual advances of Euro-American men.

What appears as accommodation may be resistance, but it does not lead to transformation. Resisting one set of oppressions may produce or reproduce another; dominant ideology may be replaced with alternative rather than oppositional forms (cf. Williams 1977). Without a critique of the hegemonic gender role model, the distance between the real and the ideal will always be a source of division in the public sphere and of tension and pain in private spheres. The foundation for this critique lies in the real experience of African-Americans. As Patricia Hill Collins (1989, 1990) and Mary Field Belenky and coauthors (1986) argue, community is essential for reconstructing ideology, as it may provide the context and validation for rejecting negative stereotypes and developing "new ways of knowing."

These "new ways of knowing" are often much more difficult to document, because they do not always appear in sources to which scholars traditionally turn. People often evolve, share, and pass along "ways of knowing" through folk tales and institutions such as the church, family (see Hill Collins 1989, 1990), and other social organizations. For example, in the slave narratives we find a very different version of Mammy—one who is "cook, housekeeper, nursemaid, seamstress, always nurturing and caring for her folk. But, unlike the white southern image of mammy, she is cunning, prone to poisoning her master, and not at all content with her lot" (Christian 1985:5). Christian reminds us that Sojourner Truth was this type of Mammy. Antebellum and postbellum writers such as Anna Julia Cooper, Ida B. Wells, Pauline Hopkins, Frederick Douglass, and others challenged the prevailing notions of gender.

Throughout their history, African-American women have been involved not only in work outside the home but also in transformative work: in individual and collective action to improve social conditions. In the course of this, they have attempted to address negative images. The National Association of Colored Women's Clubs, for example, formed in 1896, attacked the negative stereotypes of African-American women's sexuality and opened boardinghouses to protect domestic workers from living conditions that made them vulnerable to the advances of employers (Hine 1989).

Though African-American self-help organizations were characterized by some traditional gender role differentiation (Horton 1986; Neverdon-Morton 1978), they generally included both men and women and seem to have been considerably less sexist than comparable Euro-American organizations (Terborg-Penn 1978), with greater acceptance of women in activist roles (Giddings 1984:59). Emphasis on "uplifting" the race meant that education of both boys and girls was of top priority (Perkins 1983; Horton 1986:62). Thus, while gender expectations may have been comparable with those of the dominant society, objective conditions mediated the way in which people lived them, and there was some recognition that their historical experiences challenged the prevalent model.

It is perhaps in the course of attempting to effect institutional change that there is the greatest opening for transformation: the possibility of articulating new models of gender relations. Along with the struggle for civil rights, African-Americans have contested the dominant class's construction of reality. As a result of struggle in everyday life, community organizations, trade unions, the media, literature, the arts, and academia; of contestation in both the political/economic and ideological arenas, there are today a variety of images of African-American women. But as the "Black is beautiful" movement demonstrated, without control over the social relations that generate ideology, the revision of ideologies cannot be sustained.

## Women of Color:
### Identity, Gender, and National Liberation

To what extent are there similarities in the gender imagery of other women of color in the United States? Such a comparison would require a finely tuned historical analysis, examining transformations of gender imagery as these populations interact with each other as well as with Euro-Americans. In this context, I will briefly note a few possible points of comparison. While different people of color have varied histories as the dominant group has encountered and exploited them in different modes of production (Mullings 1978), they have all been subject to the exploitation of their labor and the denial of their economic, legal, and civil rights. As a result, there are many similarities in the way in which the dominant group has imaged their personhood.

For all people of color, an aspect of their exploitation centers around being defined as "the other" (see Said 1979). Representations of gender figure strongly in this process. Men are generally depicted as irresponsible and dangerous—a threat to European women (see Stoler and Cooper 1989). Women are portrayed as "wild women of other worlds" (Tiffany and Adams 1985), that is, not deserving of the social and sexual protection enjoyed by the women of the conquerors' race and class.

Thus, while men are constructed as sexually aggressive, women are depicted as sexually available. Native American women were portrayed as sexually excessive (Green 1975); Chicana women as "erotic and exotic" (Mirande 1980); Puerto Rican and Cuban women as "tropical bombshells . . . sexy, sexed and interested" (Tafolla 1985:39); Asian-American women as "cheap sexpots," prostitutes, and geisha girls (Chow 1987). Sexual domination may, as in the African-American case, serve to reinforce labor exploitation, as well as figure as a metaphor and representation of European supremacy (Said 1979).

Where there is stratification in the exploited population, the madonna/whore dichotomy may be applied differentially by class. Some of the gender constructions and protections of the women of the dominant class may be extended to the elite women of the subordinated population. For example, representations of Native Americans include the "revered" princess Pocahontas but also the "savage squaw," a sexually lax beast of burden (Green 1975; Albers 1989). Similarly, the imagery applied to Hispanic women incorporates a class distinction between the "hot-blooded working girl" and the "fervent, religious, faithful Spanish noblewoman" (Tafolla 1985:38). For African-American women, class distinctions do not seem to have been systematically applied, except perhaps by middle-class African-American women themselves.

Given the emphasis on deleterious gender role stereotypes, it is not surprising that for people of color the family becomes the focus of negative imagery. Because the family is often experienced as a source of support and refuge from oppression, as well as a powerful archetypal symbol, criticizing the family structure of people of color becomes a compelling form of victim-blaming. For example, sociological literature depicts the Mexican-American family as "totally patriarchal, pathological and unstable," with the male overly dominant, violent, and obsessed with sexual fantasies, and the women as submissive and subordinate (Ybarra 1983:92). Chicanas are portrayed as "long-suffering mothers who are subject to the brutality of insecure husbands and whose only function is to produce children—as women, who them-

LEITH MULLINGS

selves are childlike, simple, and completely dependent on fathers, brothers, and husbands" (Baca Zinn 1982:259). Note that according to these formulations, the root of family pathology, and therefore of poverty, for African-Americans is matriarchy (castrating women and emasculated men), while for Mexican-Americans, pathology stems from machismo, the exaggerated masculinity of the men, and the docility of the women. Images and symbols associated with gender roles, family, and race are particularly powerful. They evoke strong affect; they denote principles of social organization (social reproduction) on the one hand and "facts" of nature (biological reproduction) on the other (cf. Turner 1967). By transforming social categories into biological ones, they effectively perpetuate the view that these distinctions are part of a natural order, not a social order; that they are grounded in nature, not in the class structure of the society.

As women of color challenge dominant representations—generally within the context of collective action to transform economic, legal, and political constraints on both men and women—they must negotiate the difficult terrain of gender identity and national liberation (see, for example, Garcia 1989; Medicine 1983). Feminist perspectives that do not take account of national and racial oppression are unworkable. At the same time, the struggle for gender equality may be constrained by group pressure to conform to hierarchical gender roles, and women seeking to assert their rights are seen as undermining the struggle. For example, active Asian-American women have been criticized for weakening male ego and group solidarity (Chow 1987:288). Among the Lakota Sioux, Beatrice Medicine (1983) notes that, similar to the African-American experience in the 1960s, nationalist movements have often called for women to play subordinate roles and to be sexually acquiescent (1983:71–72).

In the absence of a broader vision of human liberation, both traditional movements for equality of opportunity and cultural nationalist movements may push women toward subordinate roles. In the struggle for equal rights, concepts of equality are often explicitly or implicitly circumscribed by the gender models of the dominant group. Thus the call to be "treated like a man" is based on extending to men of color the full "rights" of manhood in the United States, including those of gender privilege. Because the relations of oppression often involve "feminization" of men (cf. Said 1979), that is, stripping them of the privileges of masculinity, women of color are caught between the need to assert their equality and the desire to restore the prerogatives of masculinity denied to their men. For women, then, the struggle for racial or national equality may involve according the protections, as well as the limitations, of private patriarchy.

Women often eventually lose out where there are calls for reclamation of culture. Regaining culture is an important aspect of national liberation (see Fanon 1963; Cabral 1973), and women are often seen as culture bearers. Christian writes of the idealization of African-American women in some nationalist poetry, where they are portrayed as the keepers of moral conditions, and are "exhorted to change their ways (i.e., stop being Sapphires or loose women) in order to deserve these titles" (1985:16). Tafolla (1985:45) describes the "Guadalupe complex," in which Chicana women are seen as guardians of tradition. But again the end result may be subordination, whether the intent is to extend the "privileges" of gender roles in the dominant society or in a real or fictive traditional culture. The material base and productive, kinship, and political relations that may have given women a real independence in traditional cultures (e.g., African, Native American) no longer exist. What is reconstructed, then, is role asymmetry, which, when combined with contemporary capitalist relations, may lead to gender inequality often surpassing that of "traditional" cultures. Furthermore, as Amilcar Cabral cautions, reclaiming and developing a national culture is a process that involves criticism of negative elements of traditional culture as well as the integration of "the achievements of all of humankind" (Cabral 1973).

Women of color, for the most part, do not live with (or benefit from) partners who control, to any significant degree, societal resources and power. For this reason they tend to see the quest for women's rights, not in individual terms, but as linked to a broader struggle to transform economic, political, social, and legal constraints on both men and women. Collective actions, then, must be directed at changing the social conditions that both allow the dominant group to control the manufacture and dissemination of ideological constructions and lend strength and credibility to stereotypes.[10] By organizing to change the social relations that generate ideologies of inequality, collective action can make symbolic transformations meaningful.

## From Within the Veil

Ideologies that stigmatize women of color have been central to maintaining class, race, and gender inequality. By masking social relations, by constructing them as "natural" rather than social and historical, these representations justify the continued oppression of African Americans and support gender subordination by stigmatizing women who would challenge the patriarchal model. Further, as part of a broader ideological thrust, they help to counter challenges to the class structure, deflecting attention from structured inequality by blaming African-American women and poor people in general for poverty and economic decline.

But though "ideology may mediate contradictions . . . , it cannot resolve them" (Wolf 1982:390). African-American women, and other women of color, find themselves in a narrow historical space, caught between ideal models and real social conditions,[11] between the pressures of racial liberation and gender liberation. But such conditions also create the potential for subverting the dominant ideology. For the position of women of color may engender a unique consciousness, informed not only by the double consciousness and second sight of the veil (Du Bois 1973) but also by the triple consciousness of being at the forefront of race, class, and gender conflict. Their historical experience creates the basis for deconstructing ideologies (cf. Hill Collins 1990); for a new vision of gender roles; for building, out of "untrammeled independence" (Du Bois 1975), "standards for a new womanhood" (Davis 1981). Women of color face the major challenge of how to realize this potential in the context of a broad struggle to eliminate economic exploitation, racial oppression, and gender subordination.

## Notes

*Acknowledgments:* An earlier version of this paper was delivered as the keynote address at the 1990 workshop "Integrating Race and Gender into the College Curriculum," sponsored by the Center for Research on Women at Memphis State University, and published in their working papers series. I would like to thank Maxine Baca Zinn, Bonnie Thornton Dill, Carl Brown, Juan Flores, Sharon Harley, Aisha Khan, and Ida Susser for commenting on the manuscript.

1. See for example, Williams 1977; Wolf 1982; Abercrombie and Turner 1978.

2. The assignment of women's tasks to men and men's tasks to women seems to occur in many forms of slavery. The Nazis, too, sought out adolescent girls from among the incarcerated to move the heavy machinery in armament plants. Dorothy Wertz (1984) suggests that role reversal serves the purpose of degrading the enslaved population and demarcating the enslaved from the free.

3. Cross-cultural studies of slave systems support the view that rape functions to consolidate control of the enslaved population (Wertz 1984).

4. See Leslie 1986 for texts of antebellum apologists for slavery that employ these themes to justify violence in maintaining the social hierarchy.

5. Between 1891 and 1921, there were forty-five acknowledged lynchings of African-American women. Several were between fourteen and sixteen years old. A few were pregnant mothers, and one victim was in her eighth month of pregnancy (Katz 1965).

6. The protection of White womanhood seems to be a pervasive feature of racist ideology. In 1903, the Southern Rhodesian Immorality Act was enacted to protect White women but not Black women (Hyam 1986). In 1926, the White Woman's Protection Act imposed the death penalty in Papua New Guinea for raping a White woman (Inglis 1975). Describing similar measures in Asian colonies, Ann Stoler and Frederick Cooper (1989:641) note that "the rhetoric of sexual assault and measures used to prevent it had virtually no correlation with the incidence of rape of European women by men of color. Just the contrary." Not surprisingly, non-White women were left unprotected by these measures, though the main threat of interracial rape was generally the attack on women of color.

The invocation of the theme of protection of White woman, which surfaces all over the world as the banner to unite the White population and to justify violence against the colonized and otherwise oppressed, is a subject that requires further study. Examination of historically specific definitions of whiteness and the symbolic association of reproduction, family, race, and nation.

7. See Campbell 1989 for an interesting history of Aunt Jemima.

8. Stein and Bailey's portrait of the superwoman, who "attempts to provide her husband and children with all the benefits that they would have if she were fully devoted to traditional feminine roles . . . a physically and emotionally exhausting way of living that may have considerable psychological costs" (cited in Palm and Brewer 1979:6), does not do justice to the race and class issues.

9. That hegemony is not a meaningless concept is evident in the barrage of negative stereotypes of African-American women that have penetrated the African-American community through music, films, and popular handbooks.

10. For example, the early cohorts of Chinese women in the United States were prostitutes, but this occurred within the context of the restrictive immigration laws and subsequent gender imbalance. The Mexican-American family structure is patriarchal, but women's rights were significantly undermined by the legislation that followed conquest.

11. The distance between ideal models of femininity and actual conditions of life does exist for working-class Euro-American women and increasingly for middle-stratum women as well. However, African-Americans have historically experienced the sharpest edge of gender role

contradictions in the same way that they have experienced the brunt of labor exploitation, economic decline, and unemployment.

## References

Abercrombie, Nicholas, and Bryan S. Turner. 1978. "The Dominant Ideology Thesis." *British Journal of Sociology* 29 (2): 149–170.

Albers, Patricia. 1983. "Introduction: New Perspectives on Plains Indian Women." In Patricia Albers and Beatrice Medicine, eds., *The Hidden Half: Studies of Plains Indian Women*, pp. 1–26. Lanham, Md.: University Press of America.

——. 1989. "From Illusion to Illumination: Anthropological Studies of American Indian Women." In Sandra Morgen, ed., *Gender and Anthropology*, pp. 132–170. Washington, D.C.: American Anthropological Association.

Almquist, Elizabeth M. 1989. "The Experience of Minority Women in the United States: Intersections of Race, Gender and Class." In Jo Freeman, ed., *Women: A Feminist Perspective*, 4th ed. Mountain View, Calif.: Mayfield.

Anyon, Jean. 1984. "Intersections of Gender and Class: Accommodation and Resistance by Working-Class and Affluent Females to Contradictory Sex Role Ideologies." *Journal of Education* 166 (1): 25–48.

Atkinson, Maxine, and Jacqueline Boles. 1985. "The Shaky Pedestal: Southern Ladies Yesterday and Today." *Southern Studies* 34 (4): 398–406.

Baca Zinn, Maxine. 1982. "Mexican American Women in the Social Sciences." *Signs* 8 (2): 259–272.

Barthes, Roland. 1991. *Mythologies* (1957). New York: Hill and Wang.

Belenky, Mary Field, Blythe McVicker Clinchy, Nancy Rule Goldberger, and Jill Mattuck Tarule. 1986. *Women's Ways of Knowing: The Development of Self, Voice and Mind*. New York: Basic Books.

Boles, Jacqueline, and Maxine P. Atkinson. 1986. "Ladies: South by Northwest." *Sociological Spectrum* 6 (1): 63–81.

Burton, Orville V. 1985. *In My Father's House Are Many Mansions*. Chapel Hill: University of North Carolina Press.

Cabral, Amilcar. 1973. *Return to the Source*. New York: Africa Information Service.

Campbell, Cathy. 1989. "A Battered Woman Rises: Aunt Jemima's Corporate Makeover." *The Village Voice*, November 7, 45–46.

Chow, Esther Ngan-Ling. 1987. "The Development of Feminist Consciousness Among Asian American Women." *Gender and Society* 1 (3): 284–299.

Christian, Barbara. 1985. *Black Feminist Criticism: Perspectives on Black Women Writers*. New York: Pergamon Press.

Collins, Patricia Hill. 1989. "A Comparison of Two Works on Black Family Life." *Signs* 14 (4): 875–884.

———. 1990. *Black Feminist Thought: Knowledge, Consciousness, and the Politics of Empowerment.* Boston: Unwin Hyman.

Davis, Angela. 1981. *Women, Race, and Class.* New York: Random House.

Du Bois, William E.B. 1973. *The Souls of Black Folks* (1953). New York: Kraus-Thompson Organization Ltd.

———. 1975. *Dark Water: Voices from Within the Veil (1920).* Millwood, N.Y.: Krauss International.

Fanon, Frantz. 1963. *The Wretched of the Earth.* New York: Grove Press.

Fox-Genovese, Elizabeth. 1988. *Within the Plantation Household: Black and White Women of the Old South.* Chapel Hill: University of North Carolina Press.

French, Marilyn. 1972. *The Women's Room.* New York: Summit Books.

Garcia, Alma M. 1989. "The Development of Chicana Feminist Discourse, 1970–1980." *Gender and Society* 3 (2): 217–238.

Giddings, Paula. 1984. *When and Where I Enter: The Impact of Black Women on Race and Sex in America.* New York: William Morrow.

Gilkes, Cheryl. 1983. "From Slavery to Social Welfare: Racism and the Control of Black Women." In Amy Swerdlow and Hanna Lessinger, eds., *Class, Race, and Sex: The Dynamics of Control,* pp. 288–300. Boston: G. K. Hall.

Goldin, Claudia. 1977. "Female Labor Force Participation: The Origin of Black and White Differences." *Journal of Economic History* 37: 87–108.

Green, Rayna. 1975. The Pocahontas Perplex: The Image of Indian Women in American Culture." *Massachusetts Review* 16 (4): 698–714.

Gutman, Herbert. 1976. *The Black Family in Slavery and Freedom, 1750–1925.* New York: Pantheon Books.

Hagler, D. Harland. 1980. "The Ideal Woman in the Antebellum South: Lady or Farmwife?" *Journal of Southern History* 46 (August): 405–418.

Hall, Jacquelyn Dowd. 1983. "The Mind That Burns in Each Body: Women, Rape and Racial Violence." In Ann Snitow, Christie Stansell, and Sharon Thompson, eds, *Powers of Desire: The Politics of Sexuality,* pp. 328–349. New York: Monthly Review Press.

Harley, Sharon. 1978. "Northern Black Female Workers: 'Jackson Era'." In Sharon Harley and Rosalyn Terborg-Penn, eds. *The Afro-American Woman: Struggles and Images.* Port Washington, N.Y.: Kennikat Press.

Harris, Marvin. 1968. *The Rise of Anthropological Theory.* New York: Thomas Crowell.

Hine, Darlene Clark. 1989. "Rape and the Inner Lives of Black Women in the Middle West: Preliminary Thoughts on the Culture of Dissemblance." *Signs* 14 (4): 912–920.

Horton, James Oliver. 1986. "Freedom's Yoke: Gender Conventions Among Antebellum Free Blacks." *Feminist Studies* 12 (Spring): 51–76.

Hurtado, Aida. 1989. "Relating to Privilege: Seduction and Rejection in the Subordination of White Women and Women of Color." *Signs* 14 (4): 833–855.

Hyam, Ronald. 1986. "Empire and Sexual Opportunity." *Journal of Imperial and Commonwealth History* 14 (2): 34–90.

Inglis, Amirah. 1975. *The White Women's Protection Ordinance.* New York: St. Martin's Press.

Jones, Barbara. 1983. "The Economic Status of Black Women." In James Williams, ed., *The State of Black America 1983.* New York: National Urban League.

Jones, Jacqueline. 1982. "My Mother Was Much of a Women: Black Women, Work and the Family Under Slavery." *Feminist Studies* 8 (2): 235–269.

Katz, Maude White. 1965. "The Negro Woman and the Law." *Freedomways* 2 (3): 278–286.

King, May C. 1973. "The Politics of Sexual Stereotypes." *Black Scholar* 4 (March–April): 12–23.

Laue, James H., and Leon M. McCorkle, Jr. 1965. "The Association of Southern Women for the Prevention of Lynching: A Commentary on the Role of the 'Moderate'." *Sociological Inquiry* 35 (1): 80–93.

Leslie, Kent Anderson. 1986. "A Myth of the Southern Lady: Antebellum Proslavery Rhetoric and the Proper Place of Woman." *Sociological Spectrum* 6 (Spring): 31–49.

Lewis, Diane. 1981. "Black Women Offenders and Criminal Justice: Some Theoretical Considerations." In Marguerite Q. Warren, ed., *Comparing Female and Male Offenders,* pp. 89–105. Beverly Hills, Calif.: Sage.

Mann, Susan A. 1989. "Slavery, Sharecropping, and Sexual Inequality." *Signs* 14 (4): 774–798.

Medicine, Beatrice. 1983. "Indian Women: Tribal Identity as Status Quo." In Marian Lowe and Ruth Hubbard, eds., *Woman's Nature: Rationalizations of Inequality,* pp. 63–73. New York: Pergamon Press.

Mirande, Alfredo. 1980. "The Chicano Family: A Reanalysis of Conflicting Views." In Arlene S. Skolnick and Jerome H. Skolnick, eds., *Rethinking Marriage, Sexuality, Child Rearing, and Family Organization,* pp. 479–493. Berkeley: University of California Press.

Morton, Patricia. 1991. *Disfigured Images: The Historical Assault on Afro-American Women.* New York: Praeger.

Moynihan, Daniel Patrick. 1965. "The Negro Family: The Case for National Action." Reprinted in Lee Rainwater and W. L. Yancey, *The Moynihan Report and the Politics of Controversy,* pp. 39–124. Cambridge, Mass.: MIT Press.

Mullings, Leith. 1978. "Ethnicity and Stratification in the Urban United States." *Annals of the New York Academy of Sciences* 318: 10–22.

———. 1986a. "Uneven Development: Class, Race, and Gender in the Urban United States Before 1900." In Eleanor Leacock and Helen Safa, eds., *Women's Work: Development and the Division of Labor*, pp. 41–57. New York: Bergin and Garvey.

———. 1986b. "Anthropological Perspectives on the Afro-American Family." *American Journal of Social Psychiatry* 6 (1): 11–16.

———. 1989. "Gender and the Application of Anthropological Knowledge to Public Policy in the United States." In Sandra Morgen, ed., *Gender and Anthropology*, pp. 360–381. Washington, D.C.: American Anthropological Association.

———. 1992. *Race, Class and Gender: Representation and Reality*. Memphis, Tenn.: Center for Research on Women, Memphis State University.

———. Forthcoming. "Households Headed by Women in the United States: The Politics of Race, Class, and Gender." In Faye Ginsburg and Rayna Rapp, eds., *Conceiving the New World Order*. Los Angeles: University of California Press.

Neverdon-Morton, Cynthia. 1978. "The Black Woman's Struggle for Equality in the South, 1895–1925." In Sharon Harley and Rosalyn Terborg-Penn, eds., *The Afro-American Woman: Struggles and Images*, pp. 43–57. Port Washington, N.Y.: Kennikat Press.

Palm, Septima, and Ingrid Brewer. 1979. *The Cinderella Syndrome*. Sarasota, Fla.: Septima.

Palmer, Phyllis Marynick. 1983. "White Women/Black Women: The Dualism of Female Identity and Experience in the United States." *Feminist Studies* 9 (1): 151–170.

Perkins, Linda M. 1983. "The Impact of the 'Cult of True Womanhood' on the Education of Black Women," *Journal of Social Issues* 39 (3): 17–28.

Rosen, Ruth. 1982. *The Lost Sisterhood: Prostitution in America, 1900–1918*. Baltimore: Johns Hopkins University Press.

Said, Edward. 1979. *Orientalism*. New York: Random House.

Scott, Ann Firor. 1970. *The Southern Lady*. Chicago: University of Chicago Press.

———. 1974. "Women's Perspective on the Patriarchy in the 1850's." *Journal of American History* 61 (1): 52–64.

Simms-Wood, Janet. 1988. "The Black Female: Mammy, Jemima, Sapphire, and Other Images." In Jesse Carney Smith, ed., *Images of Blacks in American Culture: A Reference Guide to Information Sources*, pp. 235–254. Greenwich, Conn.: Greenwood Press.

Stoler, Ann, and Frederick Cooper. 1989. "Making Empire Respectable: The Politics of Race and Sexual Morality in 20th Century Colonial Cultures." *American Ethnologist* 16 (4): 634–660.

Sundquist, Asebrit. 1987. *Pocahontas & Co.: The Fictional American Indian Women in Nineteenth-Century Literature: A Study in Method.* Atlantic Highlands, N.J.: Humanities Press International.

Tafolla, Carmen. 1985. *To Split a Human: Mitos, Machos y la Mujer Chicana.* San Antonio, Tex.: Mexican American Cultural Center.

Terborg-Penn, Rosalyn. 1978. "Black Male Perspectives on the Nineteenth-Century Woman." In Sharon Harley and Rosalyn Terborg-Penn, eds., *The Afro-American Woman: Struggles and Images,* pp. 28–42. Port Washington, N.Y.: Kennikat Press.

Tiffany, Sharon, and Kathleen Adams. 1985. *The Wild Woman: An Inquiry into the Anthropology of an Idea.* Cambridge, Mass.: Schenkman.

Turner, Victor. 1967. *The Forest of Symbols.* Ithaca, N.Y.: Cornell University Press.

Wertz, Dorothy C. 1984. "Women and Slavery: A Cross-Cultural Perspective." *International Journal of Women's Studies* 7 (4): 373–384.

White, Deborah Gray. 1985. *Ar'n't I a Woman: Female Slaves in the Plantation South.* New York: W. W. Norton.

Williams, Raymond. 1977. *Marxism and Literature.* Oxford: Oxford University Press.

Wilson, William J. 1987. *The Truly Disadvantaged.* Chicago: University of Chicago Press.

Wolf, Eric. 1982. *Europe and the People Without History.* Berkeley: University of California Press.

Ybarra, Lea. 1983. "Empirical and Theoretical Developments in the Study of Chicano Families." In Armado Valdez, Albert Camarillo, and Tomás Almaguer, eds. *The State of Chicano Research on Family, Labor and Migration.* Stanford, Calif.: Stanford Center for Chicano Research.

# 15

## Different Voices, Different Visions: Gender, Culture, and Moral Reasoning

### Carol B. Stack

**A** great debate stirred my undergraduate college seminar, "Women and Justice." At midsemester, William Jones, an honors student from a rural, Southern, African-American community, stood up and addressed the class. "What," he questioned, "is gender all about?" With some reluctance, he continued. "If Carol Gilligan is right, my brothers and I were raised to be girls as much as boys, and the opposite goes for my sisters. We were raised in a large family with a morality of care as well as justice. We were raised to be responsible to kin, and to be able to face injustices at an early age. Sisters, brothers, it doesn't make a difference. Carol Gilligan should come visit my home town!"

I learn a great deal from teaching. The summer following that course I revisited families I had come to know in rural Carolina counties, bringing William's challenge to Gilligan's scholarship back home. Those observations and the debates that followed in class paralleled my own curiosity, and our collaborative hunch proved true. This chapter reports the results of my own study of the culture of gender, echoing William's question, "What is gender all about?"

Do women and men tend to see moral problems from different horizons? According to some researchers, two moral visions shape our ways of assessing these questions. Carol Gilligan argues in her book, *In a Different Voice*, that "care reasoning," which compels us to respond to those in need, and "justice reasoning," which dictates that we treat others fairly, represent separate moral orientations.[1] In her view, these are not opposites but different modes of apprehending human dilemmas. Gilligan's subsequent research suggests that these moral perspectives originate in the dynamics of early childhood relationships, solidify in adolescence, and are reproduced in the resolution of moral conflicts throughout the life course.[2]

Feminist scholars are indebted to Gilligan and her colleagues, who have brought the voice of care to moral reasoning and to our understanding of the social construction of gender. Nevertheless, as Gilligan's observations confirm, the cross-cultural construction of gender remains relatively unexplored. During the course of my study of African-American return migration to rural Southern homeplaces,[3] moral voices of both justice and care emerged from my interviews with adults and twelve- and thirteen-year-old boys and girls. However, their responses are strikingly different from the gender configurations in Gilligan's published findings.

In my research, I became interested in the vocabulary of gender and gendered discourse surrounding this return migration movement. Influenced by Gilligan's work on moral reasoning, and puzzled by the absence of reference to race and class, I chose to collect working-class adolescent and adult narratives on moral reasoning in addition to my own ethnographic research on return migration, which involved structured observation and the collection of narratives and life histories.[4] I asked these young people and adults about dilemmas similar to the difficult choices examined in Gilligan's studies. The people I interviewed were return migrants—men, women, and children who had moved back to rural Southern homeplaces. The experiences of those I interviewed differ from those of African-Americans who never left the South, and from long-term and recent dwellers in many cities in the United States. Indeed, this work does not generalize from a specific group to all African-Americans.

This study argues that moral reasoning is negotiated with respect to individual or group location within the social structure. Gender is one, but only one, of the social categories—including, among many, class, culture, racial and ethnic formation, and region—that shape the resources within which we construct morality. My goal is to contextualize gender differences in constructing moral lives within the setting of my current research on return migration, as a modest challenge to explanations that fail to situate gender differences.[5] In this chapter I report the responses of fifteen adults and eighty-seven adolescents, borrowing the orientations of "care" and "justice" in order to bring the issue of gendered strategies in moral reasoning into the race, culture, and socioeconomic context.[6]

Situating the construction of gender across race, culture, and historical conditions transforms our thinking about moral reasoning.

The creation of gender roles within specific historical and socioeconomic situations is a creative process, one better viewed as mobile than static. Gender construction is negotiated among members of specific communities, for example, as they respond to situations of institutionalized oppression and/or racial stratification. As an anthropologist concerned with the construction of gender, it has been my hypothesis that gender relationships are improvised against local and global political, economic, and familial affiliations, which are always in transition. My perspective registers serious objections to frameworks built on polarities or fixed oppositions, especially notions that create an illusory sense of "universal" or "essential" gender differences.[7]

Historically, gender as an analytic category has unfolded from early depictions of sex differences and the range of sex roles, to an examination of how gender constructs politics and how politics, class, and race construct gender.[8] Anthropological studies of gender have moved from particular, to universal, and, in this chapter, to contextual. Feminist scholars emerge from this experience with a subtle category of analysis constructed from the concrete, deeply rooted in relationships of power, class, race, and historical circumstance.

Data from my earlier research in urban Black communities in the 1970s,[9] and from my studies of the return migration of African-Americans from the Northeast to the rural South,[10] suggest new notions about the nexus of gender, race, and class relations. Class, racial formation,[11] and economic systems within rural Southern communities create a context in which African-Americans—women and men, boys and girls—experience their relationship to production, employment, class, and material and economic rewards in strikingly similar ways, rather than the divergent ways predicted by theorists of moral reasoning. It is from the vantage point of over twenty years of research on the African-American family that I situate my contributions to Carol Gilligan's discourse on moral voices.[12] I focus on gender as a social relation and suggest that it is negotiated along changing axes of difference.[13]

Although philosophers have debated Gilligan's distinction between care and justice reasoning, as well as her methods of interpreting and coding narratives or moral reasoning, in this chapter I will not challenge such concerns. This present undertaking is narrower in scope. The research does not disentangle methodological issues surrounding Gilligan and her critics,[14] or enter debates on moral reasoning or moral stages of development. It does, however, question the validity of universal gender differences.

# Moral Dilemma

On separate occasions several adults and adolescents who had returned home to rural Southern communities worked with me on this research by constructing scenarios of difficult choices they face in their own lives. The dilemmas constructed by local community members approximate Gilligan and colleagues' most current procedures, in which they ask people to talk about a situation where they were unsure what the right thing to do was, and they had to make a choice.[15] I chose to elicit culturally relevant dilemmas rather than employing the classic "Heinz dilemma" (whether Heinz should steal drugs for his dying wife) used by Gilligan. In Gilligan's current, more open-ended approach, people respond to a dilemma of their own making. What is important in this style of research is not the specific nature of the dilemma but what people say about it.

An intriguing aspect of my study of Black return migration is the cyclical migration of children. They accompany parents or extended kin, or journey alone along well-worn paths between their families' home bases in the North and in the South. Many of the parents of these children had participated in cyclical migrations and dual residences. Today, dual patterns of residence are common for young Black children whose kinship ties extend across state lines and regions of the country.[16] Their homes are in both city and countryside; their schooling is divided between public schools in Harlem, Brooklyn, or Washington, D.C., and country schools in the South. Their cyclical patterns of residence are common knowledge to school administrators, teachers, and social workers in their communities. I have been interested in how children experience their own migration, especially in light of the vivid descriptions they have given me of the tough choices they are asked to make. Straddling family ties in the North and South, and loyalties and attachments across the generations, children face real-life dilemmas over where to reside and with whom, and over what defines their responsibility to others. Their dilemmas dramatize cultural aspects of migration.

Several twelve- and thirteen-year-olds helped me construct a dilemma from the real-life situations they had described to me. One child suggested that we put the dilemma in the form of a "Dear Abby" letter, since the "Dear Abby" column is popular reading in the local community. Eighty-seven children of the North–South return migration responded to the following dilemma:

Dear Abby:

I am 12 and my brother is 10. My mother wants us to go and stay with her in New York City, and my grandparents want us to stay here in New Jericho with them. What should we do?

Love, Sally

The way children resolved the "Dear Abby" dilemma and personalized their responses reflects children's experiences as participants in this migration trend. From what children "told" "Dear Abby," and from complementary life histories, we began to understand how these boys and girls perceived their lives and constructed their roles—gender, among others—as family members caught in the web of cultural, economic, and historical forces. Their responses were infused with both a sense of responsibility to those in need and an attempt to treat others fairly.

Jimmy wrote:

I think I should stay with the one that needs my help the most. My grandmother is unable to do for herself and I should stay with her and let my mother come to see me.

Sarah wrote:

I should talk to my parents and try to get them to understand that my grandparents cannot get around like they used to. I want to make an agreement to let my brother go to New York and go to school, and I'll go to school down here. In the summer I will go and be with my parents and my brother can come down home.

Helen wrote:

I should stay with my grandparents because for one reason, there are many murderers up North, and my grandparents are old and need my help around the house.

A group of adults who had returned to Southern homeplaces, women and men between the ages of twenty-five and forty, designed the "Clyde Dilemma":

Clyde is very torn over a decision he must make. His two sisters are putting pressure on him to leave Washington, D.C., and go back home to take care of his parents. His mother is bedridden and his father recently lost a leg from sugar. One of his sisters has a family and a good job up North, and the other just moved there recently to get married. Clyde's sisters see him as more able to pick up and go back home since he is unmarried and works part-time—although he keeps trying to get a better job. What should Clyde do?

People deeply personalized their responses as they spoke of experiences within their own extended families. James Hopkins recalled, "Three of us rotated to keep my father at home," and he went on to remind me that "you must love a human being, not a dollar." Molly Henderson, who moved back in 1979, said, "Family should take care of family. It's a cycle. Someone has to do it, and it is Clyde's turn." Sam Henderson, Molly's uncle, told me, "You must take care of those who took care of you. Clyde's next in line, it's his turn." And Sam Hampton said, "He has no alternative." Others repeated, "It's not so hard if everybody helps" or "Family is the most important sacrifice we can make."

## Findings

My findings pay particular attention to class differences as well as the formation of ethnic and racial consciousness. They contrast dramatically with Gilligan's observations that while girls and women turn equally to justice and care reasoning, boys and men far less often turn to care reasoning, especially as they grow older.[17] All of the responses to the dilemmas were coded and analyzed for fifteen adults and eighty-seven adolescents (forty-two girls, forty-five boys), according to the recoded guidelines of Gilligan and colleagues. Gilligan has a separate category termed "both," which I will call "mixed" (as in a mixture that cannot be separated into constituents). In the final analysis, my results do not differ whether "mixed" is dropped or is counted as both justice and care. As shown in Table 15.1, the presence of justice as a reason (with or without care) is not different for boys versus girls. Likewise, the presence of care as a reason (with or without justice) is not different for boys versus girls (Pearson Chi-square test). Table 15.2 shows that the same conclusions are obtained for adult men versus women (Fisher exact test).

The patterns of percentages are virtually identical for boys and girls, with justice higher than care in each group. The percentage was also nearly the same for boys and girls who used both.

The adult women articulated both kinds of reasoning (care and justice) more than men did. There is no real difference between men and women in justice reasoning. Notice that only one (and that one a man) of fifteen of the adults used care reasoning alone.

The contextualization of moral reasoning in this study presents a

**Table 15.1.** Justice and Care Reasoning Among Adolescents, by Gender

| | Boys (n = 45) | Girls (n = 42) |
|---|---|---|
| Justice only | 42% (19) | 43% (18) |
| Care only | 31% (14) | 31% (13) |
| Justice and Care | 27% (12) | 26% (11) |

configuration of gender differences and similarities strikingly different from Gilligan's results. Among African-American families returning to the South, adolescents and adults are close to identical when their discourse is coded for care and justice reasoning. This suggests that situating gender difference in the context of class and race transforms our thinking about moral reasoning.

## Moral Knowledge, Social Action, and Gender

Two questions arise from these results. First, in contrast to Gilligan's findings, why the convergence between African-American male and female responses? How and why do these similarities exist? Second, what is the relationship between moral reasoning and the ways in which men and women carry out their lives and conduct social actions?

This research substantiates findings from my earlier studies of dependency relationships experienced by both African-American males and females. In many aspects of their relationship to work, to social institutions, and to political conditions, Black women and other women of color affirm the similar circumstances that encircle their lives and the lives of men. In *Talking Back*, an essay on feminist thinking, bell hooks argues the oversimplicity of viewing women as victims and men as dominators; women can be agents of domination, and men and women are both oppressed and dominated.[18] Such realities do not discount the role of sexism in public and private lives or the participation of oppressed men in the domination of others. However, data from my study of return migration suggest that the shared experience that informs the construction of self and the formation of identity among return migrants produces a convergence in the vocabulary of rights, morality, and the social good.

A collective social conscience manifests itself in several strategies across the life course. From an early age girls and boys become aware of the tyranny of racial and economic injustice. By the age of twelve or

**Table 15.2.**   Justice and Care Reasoning Among Adults, by Gender

|  | Men (n = 7) | Women (n = 8) |
|---|---|---|
| Justice only | 43% (3) | 37.5% (3) |
| Care only | 14% (1) | 0 |
| Justice and Care | 43% (3) | 62.5% (5) |

thirteen, children are aware of the workplace experiences of their parents, of sexual favors rural women must offer to keep their jobs in Southern mills and processing plants, of threats to the sanity and dignity of kin. Women and men who return to the South are imbued with a sense of both memory and history. Those who return home confront their past, and engage in a collective negotiation with social injustice. They carry back with them a mission or desire to fight for racial justice as they return to what they refer to as "my testing ground." They define themselves as "community" or as "race persons"—those who work for the good of the race.

These men and women also share a care orientation. Those who return to rural Southern communities find refuge across the generations in their Southern families. Both men and women are embedded in their extended families; they similarly experience tensions between their individual aspirations and the needs of kin. These tensions surface as a morality of responsibility; they are voiced loud and clear in the Clyde dilemma, and in life histories I collected during the course of my research.

Parallels in the experiences of men and women with reference to external forces that shape their lives, suggest that under these conditions there is a convergence between Black men and women of all ages in their construction of themselves in relationship to others. The way both men and women describe themselves indicates a sense of identity deeply connected to others—to borrow Wade Nobles's language, an "extended self." Individuals perceive their obligations within the context of a social order anchored in others rather than in an individualist focus on their personal welfare.[19] In more than 1,000 pages of self-narratives that I collected during the course of the study of return migration, people affirmed, with force and conviction, the strength of kinship ties to their rural Southern families. Over and over they emphasized, "Family is the most important sacrifice." Family ties entail intricate dependencies for Black men and women, especially for those on the edge of poverty.

Likewise, the interviews with children revealed a collective social conscience and a profound sensitivity among young people to the needs of their families. The children's voices tell a somber story of the circumstances and material conditions of their lives. Their expectations about where they will live in the coming year conform to the changing needs and demands of other family members, old and young, and family labor force participation.

The construction of gender, as Black and other feminist researchers of color have emphasized, is shaped by the experience of sex, race, class, and consciousness.[20] Future research on the construction of gender must contribute another dimension to the construction of feminist theory. It should provide a critical framework for analysis of gender consciousness, and a cautionary reminder to those theorists who argue that gender is universally shared and experienced.

My treatment of the results of coding data on care and justice reasoning among African-Americans returning to the South has startling results. Taken out of context, and compared with Gilligan's early findings, it would appear that, in contrast to the Harvard studies, gender configures fewer differences in ways of knowing among this specific group of African-Americans. But what is the relationship between ways of knowing and ways of acting?

My five-year study of African-American return migration to the rural South makes it clear that in any study we must examine multiple levels of analysis. Looking beyond the coding, the men and women who received similar scores on justice and care reasoning produced remarkably different gendered strategies for action. In their assumption of the work of kinship, the roles of wage earners and caretakers, and in their political actions, men and women in these rural Southern communities differed.

Particularly striking are gendered strategies of political action. In their battle to subvert an oppressive social order, the men who return as adults to their Southern homeplaces work principally within the local Black power structure, avoiding confrontation with the near-at-hand White power structure. When they challenge existing mores, they confront the Black male hierarchy within local landowning associations or the church. The social order women discover upon their return is a male symbolic order both within the local Black community and in relation to the local white community. Women find themselves struggling between contradictory forces of the old South and their own political missions. They face a race and gender system in which they are drawn into dependencies emerging from male structures in the local Black community. But these women, unlike the men who return, take action to circumvent this race/gender hierarchy as well as the local patronage systems. They create public programs, such as Title XX Day Care and Head Start, by creating an extensive statewide network of support in the public and private sectors. These women build community bases by carrying out their struggle in a public domain outside the jurisdiction of the local public power structure. Male preachers, politicians, and power brokers also reproduce dependency relationships between Blacks and Whites. While men participate in public spheres within their local Black communities, women bypass local black and white male structures, moving within a wider, regionally defined public domain.

There is a disjunction across race, culture, class, and gender between the study of moral voices—what people say—and observations of how people conduct themselves—what they do—as they are situated in familiar places and public spaces. We must always study, side by side, both discourse and course of action. This brings us face to face with the difference between interpretative studies of moral voices and ethnographies of gender that situate moral reasoning in everyday activity. Cross-disciplinary differences in feminist methodologies reinforce the importance within feminist scholarship of "talking back" to one another.

## Notes

1. Carol Gilligan, *In a Different Voice: Psychological Theory and Women's Development*, (Cambridge, Mass.: Harvard University Press, 1982).

2. Carol Gilligan and Grant Wiggins, "The Origins of Morality in Early Childhood Relationships," in *The Emergence of Morality*, ed. Jerome Kagan and Sharon Lamb (Chicago: University of Chicago Press, 1987).

3. Carol B. Stack, *The Proving Ground: African-Americans Reclaim the Rural South*, (New York: Pantheon, in press).

4. Between 1975 and 1980, 326,000 black individuals returned to a ten-state region of the South.

5. I am grateful to Nancy Chodorow for her view that this chapter addresses gender differentiation and gender strategies rather than gender construction.

6. Carol B. Stack, "The Culture of Gender Among Women of Color," *Signs* 12, no. 1 (Winter 1985): 321–324.

7. Laura Nader, 1989. "Orientalism, Occidentalism, and the Control of Women," *Cultural Dynamics* 2, no. 3(1989): 323.

8. Joan W. Scott, "Gender: A Useful Category of Historical Analysis," *American Historical Review* 91, no. 5 (December 1986): 1053–1075.

9. Carol B. Stack, *All Our Kin: Strategies for Survival in a Black Community* (New York: Harper & Row, 1974).

10. Stack, *The Proving Ground.*

11. Michael Omi and Howard Winant, *Racial Formation in the United States* (New York: Routledge and Kegan Paul, 1986).

12. Gilligan, *In a Different Voice.*

13. Teresa de Lauretis, "Eccentric Subjects: Feminist Theory and Historical Consciousness," unpublished MS, University of California at Santa Cruz.

14. Linda K. Kerber, Catherine G. Greeno, Eleanor E. Maccoby, Zella Luria, Carol B. Stack, and Carol Gilligan, "In a Different Voice: An Interdisciplinary Forum," *Signs* 12, no. 1 (Winter 1985): 304–333.

15. Jane Atanuchi, private communication.

16. Carol B. Stack and John Cromartie, "The Journeys of Children," unpublished MS.

17. Carol Gilligan, "Women's Place in Man's Life Cycle," *Harvard Educational Review* 49, no. 4 (1979): 413–446; and *In a Different Voice.*

18. bell hooks (Gloria Watkins), *Talking Back: Thinking Feminist, Thinking Back* (Boston: South End Press, 1989), esp. p. 20.

19. Vernon Dixon, "World Views and Research Methodology," in L. M. King, Vernon Dixon, and W. W. Nobles, eds., *African Philosophy: Assumptions and Paradigms for Research on Black Persons* (Los Angeles: Fanon Center, 1976).

20. Bonnie Thornton Dill, "The Dialectics of Black Womanhood," in *Feminism and Methodology*, ed. Sandra Harding (Bloomington: Indiana University Press, 1987).

# 16

## Feminist Rethinking from Racial-Ethnic Families

### Maxine Baca Zinn

**U**nderstanding diversity remains a pressing challenge for family scholars. Innumerable shortcomings in dominant social science studies render much thinking ill-suited to the task. The growing diversity movement in women's studies, together with new thinking on racial-ethnic groups, holds the promise of a comprehensive understanding of family life.

### The Family Transformation in Western Feminism

Two decades of feminist thinking on the family have demystified the idea of the natural and timeless nuclear family. "By taking gender as a basic category of analysis" (Thorne 1992:5), feminist theory has produced new descriptions of family experience, new conceptualizations of family dynamics, and identified new topics for investigation. The following themes show how conventional notions of the family have been transformed:

1. The family is socially constructed. This means that it is not merely a biological arrangement but is a product of specific historical, social, and material conditions. In other words, it is shaped by the social structure.

2. The family is closely connected with other structures and institutions in society. Rather than being a separate sphere, it cannot be understood in isolation from outside factors. As a result, "the family" can be experienced differently by people in different social classes and of different races, and by women and men.

3. Since structural arrangements are abstract and often invisible, family processes can be deceptive or hidden. Many structural

conditions make family life problematic. Therefore, families, like other social institutions, require changes in order to meet the needs of women, men, and children.

These themes have made great strides in challenging the myth of the monolithic family, "which has elevated the nuclear family with a breadwinner husband and a full time wife and mother as the only legitimate family form" (Thorne 1992:4). Viewing family life within wider systems of economic and political structures has uncovered great complexity in family dynamics and important variation among families within particular racial and ethnic groups. Despite these advances, women of color theorists contend that Western feminists have not gone far enough in integrating racial differences into family studies.

## Differing Feminist Perspectives on the Family

Issues that are rooted in racial (and class) differences have always produced debates within feminist scholarship. Racial differences have evoked deeply felt differences among feminists about the meaning of family life for women. Rayna Rapp's description of a typical feminist meeting about the family captured well the essence of the debate in the late 1960s and early 1970s:

> Many of us have been at an archetypical meeting in which someone stands up and asserts that the nuclear family ought to be abolished because it is degrading and constraining to women. Usually, someone else (often representing a third world position) follows on her heels, pointing out that the attack on the family represents a white middle-class position and that other women need their families for support and survival. (Rapp 1982:168)

Women of color feminists have disagreed with several feminist notions about the meaning of family life for women. As Patricia Zavella recounts the differences:

> In particular, we had problems with the separatist politics (auto-matically uncooperative with men) in some early women's organizations, and with the white middle-class focus of Americans' feminism, a focus implicitly and sometimes explicitly racist . . . both the lack of race and class consciousness in much 1970's feminist political and scholarly work came in for severe criticism. (Zavella 1991:316)

Western feminism became more contextual in the 1980s. As women of color continued to challenge the notion that gender produced a universal woman's family experience, feminism in general worked to broaden feminist studies beyond issues important to White, middle-class, heterosexual women (Ginsburg and Tsing 1990:3). Although gender remains the basic analytical category, scholars now acknowledge the relationships between families and other social divisions (Thorne 1992). The discovery that families are differentiated by race and class has had limited impact on family theorizing across groups. Feminist social scientists now routinely note the importance of race and class differences in family life. Yet we have been more successful in offering single studies of particular groups of families and women than in providing systematic comparisons of families in the same society. Although Western feminist thought takes great care to underscore race and class differences, it still marginalizes racial-ethnic families as special "cultural" cases. In other words, when it comes to thinking about family patterns, diversity is treated as if it were an intrinsic property of groups that are "different," rather than as being the product of forces that affect all families, but affect them in different ways. Feminism has taken on the challenge of diversity, yet it continues to treat race as epiphenomenal—in other words, to treat racial inequality and the social construction of race as secondary to gender (Zavella 1989:31) So far, mainstream feminism has failed to grapple with race as a power system that affects families throughout society and to apply that understanding to "the family" writ large. As Evelyn Nakano Glenn says, "Systematically incorporating hierarchies of race and class into the feminist reconstruction of the family remains a challenge, a necessary next step into the development of theories of family that are inclusive" (1987:368).

## Inclusive Feminist Perspectives on Race and Family

Families and household groups have changed over time and varied with social conditions. Distinctive political and economic contexts have created similar family histories for people of color. Composite portraits of each group show them to have family arrangements and patterns that differ from those of White Americans. Although each group is distinguishable from the others, African-Americans, Latinos, and Asians share some important commonalities (Glenn with Yap 1993). These include an extended kinship structure and informal support networks spread across multiple households. Racial-ethnic families are distinctive not only because of their ethnic heritage but also because they reside in a society where racial stratification shapes family resources and structures in important ways.

New thinking about racial stratification provides a perspective for examining family diversity as a structural aspect of society. Race is a socially constructed system that assigns different worth and unequal treatment to groups on the basis of its definition of race. While racial definitions and racial meanings are always being transformed (Omi and Winant 1986), racial hierarchies operate as fundamental axes for the social location of groups and individuals and for the unequal distribution of social opportunities. Racial and ethnic groups occupy particular social locations in which family life is constructed out of widely varying social resources. The uneven distribution of social advantages and social costs operates to strengthen some families while simultaneously weakening others.

By looking at family life in the United States across time and in different parts of the social order, we find that social and economic forces in society have produced alternative domestic arrangements. The key to understanding family diversity lies the relationship between making a living and maintaining life on a daily basis. Feminist scholars call these activities productive and reproductive labor (Brenner and Laslett 1986:117).

## PRODUCTIVE LABOR

Historically, racial differences in how people made a living had crucial implications for domestic life. In short, they produced different family and household arrangements on the part of slaves, agricultural workers, and industrial workers. European ethnics were incorporated into low-wage industrial economies of the North, while Blacks, Latinos, Chinese, and Japanese filled labor needs in the colonial labor system of the economically backward regions of the West, Southwest and South. These colonial labor systems, while different, created similar hardships for family life. They required women to work outside of the home in order to maintain even minimal levels of family subsistence. Women's placement in the larger political economy profoundly influenced their family lives.

Several women of color theorists have advanced our understanding of the shaping power of racial stratification, not only for families of color but also for family life in general. For example, Bonnie Thornton Dill (this volume) uncovers strong connections in the way racial meanings influence family life. In the antebellum United States, women of European descent received a certain level of protection within the confines of the patriarchal family. There is no doubt that they were constrained as individuals, but family life among European settlers was a highly valued aspect of societal development, and women—to the extent that they contributed to the development of families and to the economic growth of the nation—were provided institutional support for those activities. Unlike White migrants, who came voluntarily, racial-ethnics were either brought to this country or were conquered to meet the need for a cheap and exploitable labor force. Little attention was given to their family and community life. Labor, and not the existence or maintenance of families, was the critical aspect of their role in building the nation.

Women of color experienced the oppression of a patriarchal society (public patriarchy) but were denied the protections and buffering of a patriarchal family (private patriarchy). Thus, they did not have the social structural supports necessary to make their families a vital element in the social order. Family membership was not a key means of access to participation in the wider society. Families of women of color sustained cultural assaults as a direct result of the organization of the labor systems in which their groups participated. The lack of social, legal, and economic support for racial-ethnic families intensified and extended women's reproductive labor, created tensions and strains in family relationships, and set the stage for a variety of creative and adaptive forms of resistance.

Dill's study suggests a different conceptualization of the family, one that is not so bound by the notion of separate spheres of male and female labor or by the notion of the family as an emotional haven, separate and apart from the demands of the economic marketplace. People of color experienced no separation of work and family, no haven of private life, no protected sphere of domesticity. Women's work outside of the home was an extension of their family responsibilities, as family members—women men, and children—pooled their resources to put food on the table (Du Bois and Ruiz 1990:iii). What we see here are families and women who are buffeted by the demands of the labor force and provided no legal or social protection other than the maintenance of their ability to work. This research on women of color demonstrates that protecting one's family from the demands of the market is strongly related to the distribution of power and privilege in the society. The majority of White settlers had the power to shelter their members from the market (especially their women and children), and to do so with legal and social support. People of color were denied these protections, and their family members were exploited and oppressed in order to maintain the privileges of the powerful. As Leith Mullings has said, "It was the working class and enslaved men and women whose labor created the wealth that allowed the middle class and upper middle class domestic lifestyles to exist" (Mullings 1986:50).

Despite the harsh conditions imposed on family life by racial labor systems, families did not break down. Instead, they adapted as best they could. Using cultural forms where possible, and creating new adaptations where necessary, racial-ethnics adapted their families to the conditions thrust upon them. These adaptations were not exceptions to a "standard" family form. They were produced by forces of inequality in the larger society. Although the White middle-class model of the family has long been defined as the rule, it was neither the norm nor the dominant family type. It was, however, the measure against which other families were judged.

## REPRODUCTIVE LABOR

Racial divisions in making a living shape families in important ways. They also determine how people maintain life on a daily basis. Reproductive labor is strongly gendered. It includes activities such as purchasing household goods, preparing and serving food, laundering and repairing clothing, maintaining furnishings and appliances, socializing children, providing care and emotional support for adults, and maintaining kin and community ties (Glenn 1992:1). According to Evelyn Nakano Glenn, reproductive labor has divided along racial as well as gender lines. Specific characteristics of the division have varied regionally and changed over time—shifting parts of it from the household to the market:

> In the first half of the century racial-ethnic women were employed as servants to perform reproductive labor in white households, relieving white middle-class women of onerous aspects of that work; in the second half of the century, with the expansion of commodified services (services turned into commercial products or activities), racial-ethnic women are disproportionately employed as service workers in institutional settings to carry out lower-level "public" reproductive labor, while cleaner white collar supervisory and lower professional positions are filled by white women. (Glenn 1992:3)

The activities of racial-ethnic women in "public" reproductive labor suggest new interpretations of family formation. Knowing that reproductive labor has divided along racial lines offers an understanding of why the idealized family has often been a luxury of the privileged.

## Family Patterns as Relational

The distinctive place assigned to racial-ethnic women in the organization of reproductive labor has far-reaching implications for thinking about racial patterns in family diversity. Furthermore, insights about racial divisions apply to White families as well as racial-ethnic families. The new research reveals an important *relational* dimension of family formation. "Relational means that race/gender categories are positioned and that they gain meaning in relation to each other" (Glenn 1992:34). As Bonnie Thornton Dill puts it, when we examine race, class, and gender simultaneously, we have a better understanding of a social order in which the privileges of some people are dependent on the oppression and exploitation of others (Dill 1986:16). This allows us to grasp the benefits that some women derive from their race and their class while also understanding the restrictions that result from gender. In other words, such women are subordinated by patriarchal family dynamics. Yet race and class intersect to create for them privileged opportunities, choices, and lifestyles. For example, Judith Rollins uses the relationships between Black domestics and their White employers to show how one class and race of women escapes some of the consequences of patriarchy by using the labor of other women (Rollins 1985). Her study, *Between Women*, highlights the complex linkages among race, class, and gender as they create both privilege and subordination. These are simultaneous processes that enable us to look at women's diversity from a different angle.

The relational themes of privilege and subordination appear frequently in studies of domestic service (Romero 1982). Victoria Byerly (1986) found that White women who worked in the Southern textile mills hired African-Americans as domestic workers. The labor of these domestics enabled the White women to engage in formal work. Vicki Ruiz (1988) describes how Mexican-American women factory workers in Texas have eased their housework burdens by hiring Mexican domestic workers (Ward 1990:10–11). These studies highlight some of the ways in which race relations penetrate households, intersecting with gender arrangements to produce varied family experiences.

# Theorizing Across Racial Categories

Historical and contemporary racial divisions of productive and reproductive labor challenge the assumption that family diversity is the outgrowth of different cultural patterns. Racial stratification creates distinctive patterns in the way families are located and embedded in different social environments. It structures social opportunities differently, and it constructs and positions groups in systematic ways. This offers important lessons for examining current economic and social changes that are influencing families, and influencing them differently. Still, the knowledge that family life differs significantly by race does not preclude us from theorizing across racial categories.

The information and service economy continues to reshape family life by altering patterns associated with marriage, divorce, childbearing, and household composition. A growing body of family research shows that although some families are more vulnerable than others to economic marginalization, none are immune from the deep structural changes undermining "traditional" families. Adaptation takes varying forms, such as increased divorce rates, female-headed households, and extended kinship units. Although new patterns of racial formation will affect some families more than others, looking at social contexts will enable us to better understand family life in general.

The study of Black families can generate important insights for White families (Billingsly 1988). Families may respond in a like manner when impacted by larger social forces. To the extent that White families and Black families experience similar pressures, they may respond in similar ways, including the adaptation of their family structures and other behaviors. With respect to single-parent families, teenage parents, working mothers, and a host of other behaviors, Black families serve as barometers of social change and as forerunners of adaptive patterns that will be progressively experienced by the more privileged sectors of U.S. society.

On the other hand, such insights must not eclipse the ways in which racial meanings shape social perceptions of family diversity. As social and economic changes produce new family arrangements, some alternatives become more tolerable. Race plays an important role in the degree to which alternatives are deemed acceptable. When alternatives are associated with subordinate social categories, they are judged against "the traditional family" and found to be deviant. Many alternative lifestyles that appear new to middle-class Americans are actually variant family patterns that have been traditional within Black and other ethnic communities for many generations. Presented as the "new lifestyles of the young mainstream elite, they are the same lifestyles that have in the past been defined as pathological, deviant, or unacceptable when observed in Black families" (Peters and McAdoo 1983:228). As Evelyn Brooks Higginbotham observes, race often subsumes other sets of social relations, making them "good" or "bad," "correct" or "incorrect" (Higginbotham 1992:255). Yet, many of the minority family patterns deemed "incorrect" by journalists, scholars, and policymakers are logical life choices in a society of limited social opportunities.

## Growing Racial Diversity and "The Family Crisis"

Despite the proliferation of studies showing that families are shaped by their social context, conservative rhetoric is fueling a "growing social and ideological cleavage between traditional family forms and the emerging alternatives" (Gerson 1991:57). This is complicated further by the profound demographic transformation now occurring in the United States. The unprecedented growth of minority populations is placing a special spotlight on family diversity.

Racial minorities are increasing faster than the majority population. During the 1980s Asians more than doubled, from 3.5 million to 7.3 million, and Hispanics grew from 14.6 to 22.4 million. The Black increase was from 16.5 to 30.0 million. The result of these trends is that whereas Whites in 1980 were 80 percent of the population, they will only be 70 percent by 2000 (Population Reference Bureau 1989:10). Immigration now accounts for a large share of the nation's population growth. The largest ten-year wave of immigration in U.S. history occurred during the 1980s, with the arrival of almost 9 million people. More immigrants were admitted during the 1980s than any decade since 1900–1910. By 2020, immigrants will be more important to the U.S. population growth than natural increase (Waldrop 1990:23). New patterns of immigration are changing the racial composition of society. Among the expanded population of first generation immigrants, "The Asian-born now outnumber the European-born. Those from Latin America—predominantly Mexican— outnumber both" (Barringer 1992:2). This contrasts sharply with what occurred as recently as the 1950s, when two-thirds of legal immigrants were from Europe and Canada.

Changes in the racial composition of society are creating new polarizations along residential, occupational, educational, and economic lines. Crucial to these divisions is an ongoing transformation of racial meaning and racial hierarchy. Family scholars must be alert to the effects of these changes because the racial repositioning will touch families throughout the racial order.

New immigration patterns will escalate the rhetoric of family crises as immigrant lifestyles and family forms are measured against a mythical family ideal. Inevitably, some interpretations of diversity will revert to cultural explanations that deflect attention from the social opportunities associated with race. Even though pleas for "culturally sensitive" approaches to non-White families are well-meaning, they can unwittingly keep "the family" ensnared in a White middle-class ideal. We need to find a way to transcend the conflict among the emerging array of "family groups" (Gerson 1991:57). The best way to do this is to abandon all notions that uphold one family form as normal and others as "cultural variations." Immigration will undoubtedly introduce alternative family forms; they will be best understood by treating race as a fundamental structure that situates families differently and thereby produces diversity.

# References

Barringer, Felicity. 1992. "As American as Apple Pie, Dim Sum or Burritos." *New York Times* May 31, sec. 4, p. 2.

Billingsly, Andrew. 1988. "The Impact of Technology on Afro-American Families." *Family Relations* 7: 420–425.

Brenner, Johanna, and Barbara Laslett. 1986. "Social Reproduction and the Family." In *The Social Reproduction of Organization and Culture*, Ulf Himmelstrand, ed. Newbury Park, Calif.: Sage.

Byerly, Victoria. 1986. *Hard Times Cotton Mill Girls*. Ithaca, N.Y.: ILR Press.

Dill, Bonnie Thornton. 1986. *Our Mothers' Grief: Racial Ethnic Women and the Maintenance of Families*. Research Paper no. 4. Memphis, Tenn.: Center for Research on Women, Memphis State University.

DuBois, Ellen Carol, and Vicki L. Ruiz, eds. 1990. "Introduction." In *Unequal Sisters: A Multicultural Reader in U.S. Women's History*. New York: Routledge.

Gerson, Kathleen. 1991. "Coping with Commitment: Dilemmas and Conflicts of Family Life." In *America at Century's End*, Alan Wolfe, ed. Berkeley: University of California Press.

Ginsburg, Faye, and Anna Lowenhaupt Tsing. 1990. *Uncertain Terms: Negotiating Gender in American Culture.* Boston: Beacon Press.

Glenn, Evelyn Nakano. 1987. "Gender and the Family." In *Analyzing Gender*, Beth B. Hess and Myra Marx Ferree, eds. Newbury Park, Calif.: Sage.

————. 1992. "From Servitude to Service Work: Historical Continuities in the Racial Division of Paid Reproductive Labor." *Signs: Journal of Women in Culture and Society* 18 (1): 1–43.

Glenn, Evelyn Nakano, with Stacey H. Yap. 1993. "Chinese American Families." In *Minority Families in the United States: Comparative Perspectives*, Ronald L. Taylor, ed. Englewood Cliffs, N.J.: Prentice-Hall.

Higginbotham, Evelyn Brooks. 1992. "African-American Women's History and the Metalanguage of Race." *Signs: Journal of Women in Culture and Society* 17 (2): 251–274.

Mullings, Leith. 1986. "Uneven Development: Class, Race, and Gender in the United States Before 1900." In *Women's Work*, Eleanor Leacock and Helen I. Safa, eds. New York: Bergin and Garvey.

Omi, Michael, and Howard Winant. 1986. *Racial Formation in the United States.* London: Routledge and Kegan Paul.

Peters, Marie, and Harriette P. McAdoo. 1983. "The Present and Future of Alternative Lifestyles in Ethnic American Cultures." In *Contemporary Families and Alternative Lifestyles*, Eleanor D. Macklin and R. H. Rubin, eds. Beverly Hills, Calif.: Sage.

Population Reference Bureau. 1989. *America in the 21st Century: Human Resource Development.* Washington, D.C.: Population Reference Bureau.

Rapp, Rayna. 1982. "Family and Class in Contemporary America: Notes Toward an Understanding of Ideology." In *Rethinking The Family: Some Feminist Questions*, Barrie Thorne and Marilyn Yalom, eds. New York: Longman.

Rollins, Judith. 1985. *Between Women: Domestics and Their Employers.* Philadelphia: Temple University Press.

Romero, Mary. 1992. *Maid in the U.S.A.* New York: Routledge.

Ruiz, Vicki. 1988. "By the Day or the Week: Mexican Domestic Workers in El Paso." In *Women in the U.S. Mexico Border*, Vicki Ruiz and Susan Tiano, eds. Boston: Allen and Unwin.

Thorne, Barrie. 1992. "Feminism and the Family: Two Decades of Thought." In *Rethinking the Family: Some Feminist Questions*, Barrie Thorne and Marilyn Yalom, eds., 2nd ed. Boston: Northeastern University Press.

Waldrop, Judith. 1990. "You'll Know It's the 21st Century When. . . ." *American Demographics* 13 (December): 22–27.

Ward, Kathryn. 1990. *Women Workers and Global Restructuring.* Ithaca, N.Y.: Cornell University Press.

Zavella, Patricia. 1989. "The Problematic Relationship of Feminism and Chicana Studies." *Women's Studies* 17: 25–36.

———. 1991. "Mujeres in Factories: Race and Class Perspectives on Women, Work, and Family." In *Gender at the Crossroads of Knowledge,* Micaela di Leonardo, ed. Berkeley: University of California Press.

# About the Contributors

**Regina Arnold** has been an associate professor in the Social Science Division at Sarah Lawrence College since 1979. Her research has been in the areas of crime and deviance. She has conducted qualitative research and published key articles on women in prison, female criminality, and Black and Hispanic judges in New York City. Presently Dr. Arnold is engaged in educational consulting.

**Maxine Baca Zinn** is a professor of sociology at Michigan State University, where she is also a senior research associate in the Julian Samora Research Institute. She earned a Ph.D. in sociology from the University of Oregon. She specializes in race relations, gender, and the sociology of the family. In 1990, she was the Cheryl Miller Lecturer for Sociologists for Women in Society. She is the co-editor of *The Reshaping of America* and the co-author of *Diversity in Families, In Conflict and Order: Understanding Society, and Social Problems* (with D. Stanley Eitzen), as well as the author of numerous articles on racial-ethnic families.

**Esther Ngan-Ling Chow,** who received her Ph.D. from the University of California at Los Angeles, is currently a professor of sociology at the American University in Washington, D.C. She is a feminist scholar and community activist with research interests and publications in the areas of gender, women of color, work and family, race and immigration, women in development, state and local policy, feminist theories and methodologies, and organizational studies.

**Bonnie Thornton Dill** is a professor of women's studies at the University of Maryland at College Park. She was formerly a professor of sociology and founding director of the Center for Research on

Women at Memphis State University. She earned a Ph.D. in sociology from New York University and specializes in race, gender, and family. She is currently conducting a study of low-income single mothers in rural Southern communities. Her published articles have been widely reprinted in anthologies. She is the author of *Across the Boundaries of Race and Class* (forthcoming, Garland Press) and in 1993 was a co-recipient (with Elizabeth Higginbotham and Lynn Weber) of the American Sociological Association's Jessie Bernard Award and the Distinguished Contributions to Teaching Award for the work of the Memphis State Center for Research on Women.

**Cheryl Townsend Gilkes** is MacArthur Associate Professor of Sociology and Afro-American Studies at Colby College in Waterville, Maine. She received her Ph.D. from Boston University. Her articles on African American women, religion, and social change have appeared in *Signs, Gender and Society,* and the *Journal of Religious Thought.*

**Linda Grant** is an associate professor of sociology, faculty associate of the Institute for Behavioral Research, and faculty affiliate of the Women's Studies Program at the University of Georgia in Athens. She received her Ph.D. from the University of Michigan in Ann Arbor in 1981. Her current research focuses on school organizational change, experiences of diverse student subgroups, and (in collaboration with Kathryn B. Ward) the effects of mentoring on the scientific careers of women and minorities in academia.

**Elizabeth Higginbotham** is the associate director of the Center for Research on Women and an associate professor in the Department of Sociology and Social Work at Memphis State University. She has written widely in the areas of race, class, and gender, including articles on incorporating women of color into the college curriculum. She is currently completing a book manuscript on educated Black women. In 1993, she was a co-recipient (with Bonnie Thornton Dill and Lynn Weber) of the American Sociological Association's Jessie Bernard Award and the Distinguished Contributions to Teaching Award for the work of the Memphis State Center for Research on Women.

**Karen J. Hossfeld** is an associate professor of sociology at San Francisco State University. Her article in this volume draws from her forthcoming book, *Small, Foreign, and Female: Portraits of Gender, Race, and Class in Silicon Valley* (University of California Press).

**Jennie R. Joe** is an anthropologist and member of the Navajo Nation. She is an associate professor in family and community medicine and director of the Native American Research and Training Center at the University of Arizona. She holds both Ph.D. and Master's of Public Health degrees.

**Nazli Kibria** is an assistant professor of sociology at the University of Southern California. She is the author of *Family Tightrope: The Changing Lives of Vietnamese Americans* (forthcoming, Princeton University Press). Currently she is engaged in research on second-generation Asian-American ethnic identity.

**Dorothy Lonewolf Miller,** born in 1920 of Blackfoot/Irish descent, grew up in Montana and Iowa and worked for twenty years on farms and in factories. She is the mother of Dr. Ann Metcalf and Sherry Sesko and grandmother of four grown grandchildren. Educated late in life, she earned her doctorate in 1969 at the University of California, Berkeley. She is a social scientist and is founder and director of the Institute for Scientific Analysis in San Francisco, a nonprofit research firm. She is currently working with Dr. Jennie Joe of the University of Arizona on a national survey of Native American wildlands firefighters, 13 percent of whom are women. Her major research interests are in Native Americans in the workplace and Native American families in urban areas.

**Leith Mullings** is a professor of anthropology at The Graduate School, City University of New York. She is author of *Therapy, Ideology and Social Change* (University of California Press, 1987). She has written extensively on ethnicity, gender, inequality, and social policy.

**Vilma Ortiz** is an associate professor of sociology at the University of California, Los Angeles. She has published extensively on the social conditions of Latinos in the United States, with a particular focus on gender, immigration, and economic status.

**Denise A. Segura** is an associate professor of sociology at the University of California, Santa Barbara. She has published numerous articles on Chicanas and Mexican immigrant women in the labor force, Chicana feminism, and Chicana political consciousness. Currently she is working on a book manuscript on Chicana feminism co-authored with Dr. Beatriz M. Pesquera.

**Carol B. Stack,** a professor of women's studies and education at the University of California, Berkeley, is author of *All Our Kin* and co-editor of *Holding on to the Land and the Lord.* She has written extensively on rural and urban poverty and social policy and is currently completing a book manuscript on African American return migration to the rural South.

**Ruth E. Zambrana** is an associate professor of social welfare at the University of California, Los Angeles. Her research areas of interest are in racial and ethnic differences in factors that influence health status, family and children's health, and pregnancy outcome in low-income groups.

# Index

African American women (*cont.*)
30–31; family structure of, during slavery, 150–155; fertility rates among, 15, 22–23; geographic characteristics of, 15, 18; hiring biases against, in microelectronics industry, 77–82, 91n.7; images of, 265–285; income and poverty levels of, 31–32; job ceilings and, 115–118; labor force participation of, 27–29; lack of health insurance among, 136; marital status demographics of, 20–22, 27–29; median age and migration history of, 15, 17; occupational segregation of, 119–122; participation of, in professional occupations, 30–31, 113–129, 214–215; and peer relationships of primary school girls, 57–60; polarization of, 37n.1; population growth of, 15–16, 311; as preferred terminology, 12n.1; self-employment patterns among, 30–31; sexual stereotyping of, 266–267, 269–272, 280–282; and social skills ratings of primary school girls, 53–54; socioeconomic position of, 24; and teacher-student interactions of primary school girls, 51, 54–57. *See also topics related to African American women, e.g.,* Classroom roles of African American primary school girls; Images of African American women; Return migration of African Americans

Age levels: of American Indian mothers, 190–196; of Puerto Rican women in the United States, 134; racial/ethnic differences in fertility rates and, 22–23

Aggressive behavior, of African American primary school girls, 59. *See also* Assertive coping strategies

Agricultural work, Chicano prevalence in, 84, 161

AIDS transmission, among Puerto Rican women, 139

Alcohol abuse: American Indian social problems and, 195–196, 198; among Puerto Rican women, 139. *See also* Drug abuse

Alers, Jose, 134

American Indian women: acculturation of, in Tucson, 188–190; cultural survival of, amid urbanization, 185–199; defined, 37n.5; demographic characteristics of, 16–18, 20, 190–196; educational attainment of, 26–27; encapsulation strategy of, 196–198; female-headed households among, 33–34; fertility rates among, 23; income and poverty levels of, 31–34; and labor force participation, 27–28; off-reservation populations of, 187–188; participation of, in professional occupations, 30–31; self-employment patterns among, 30–31; sexual stereotyping of, 280; socioeconomic position of, 24

Andersen, Margaret L., 11

Anger desensitization technique, African American women's use of, 214–215

Anti-Semitism, in workplace, 219

Arnold, Regina, 8, 315

Asian American women: census data on, 36; coping strategies of, 216–222; country of origin of, 13–14; demographic characteristics of, 13–14, 18–22; earning potentials of, 30–31; educational attainment of, 25–26; ethnic diversity among,

224n.4; and female-headed households, 24; fertility rates among, 22–23; hiring bias in favor of, for microelectronics assembly, 79–82; labor force participation of, 27–28; marital status of, 21–22; as "model minority," 69–71, 82–85, 210–212; participation of, in professional occupations, 29–31; population growth of, 311; productivity myths surrounding, 82–85; self-employment patterns among, 30–31; socioeconomic position of, 24; stereotyping of, 8–9, 210–212; working conditions for, 203–223. *See also* Asian Indian women; Chinese American women; Filipino American women; Japanese Americans; Korean American women; Vietnamese American women

Asian Indian women: demographic characteristics of, 16–19; educational attainment of, 25–27, 224n.4; fertility rates among, 23; income and poverty levels of, 32; labor force participation of, 27–28; marital status demographics of, 21–22; participation of, in professional occupations, 29–31; racial stereotyping of, 68–69; sexual stereotyping of, 280–281; socioeconomic position of, 24

Assembly work, concentration of immigrant women in, 73; racial stereotyping in hiring patterns for, 74, 82–85

Assertive coping strategies: negative images of, for African American women, 274–275; use of, by Asian American women, 218–221

Assimilation: American Indian women's resistance to, 188–190,

196–199; as model for immigration policies, 247–248, 259n.2. *See also* Adaptation, immigrant experience and

Association for the Study of Afro-American Life and History, 236

Association of Southern Women for the Prevention of Lynching, 272

Automation, labor force participation of Puerto Rican women and, 135

Baca Zinn, Maxine, 166–167, 222–223, 315

*Backlash*, 11

Backlash: against Japanese, 70–71; against Vietnamese, 83–84

Baptism rites, Chicano kinship networks and, 164

Barnett, Ida B. Wells, 235–236

Barthes, Roland, 271

Becerra, Rosina, 138

Belenky, Mary Field, 278

Bethune, Mary McLeod, 235–236

*Between Women*, 309

Bilingualism, among American Indians, 193–194

Black American women. *See* African American women

*Black Feminist Thought*, 9

*Black Metropolis*, 116

Black Power activists, and confrontation with community groups, 237

Blackwell, James, 231

Blassingame, John, 153

Blauner, Robert, 232

*Bodegas*, 141

*Botanicas*, 141

Burciago-Valdez, Robert, 136

Bureaucracy: organization of inequality in, 208–212; working con-

Bureaucracy (*cont.*)
ditions for Asian American
women and, 203–204, 208–212
Burns, Mrs. (pseudonym), 235,
237–238, 240
Business ownership, racial/ethnic
patterns in, 90n.4
Byerly, Victoria, 309

Cabral, Amilcar, 282
Caetano, Raul, 139
Camarillo, Albert, 160–161, 164
Capitalism, necessity of bureau-
cracy within, 208–209
Capital logic, strategies for hiring
immigrant labor and, 68–71
"Care reasoning," 291–298
Caretaker role, of African American
primary school girls, 45–47
Case studies, of Chicana and Mexi-
cana occupational segregation,
95, 101–107
Cayton, Horace, 116
Census data: on Latino population
groups, 143n.1; on Puerto Ricans,
143n.1; research methodology
and, 36, 37n.8. *See also* Demographic characteristics
Cervical cancer, rates of, among
Puerto Rican women, 137
CETA (Comprehensive Employment Training Act), 98–99
Chapman, Jane, 179
Chesney-Lind, Meda, 176, 180
Chiang Kai, 204
Chicana women: defined, 108n.1;
demographic characteristics of,
15–16; "Guadalupe complex" of,
282; lack of health insurance
among, 136; occupational segregation of, 96–98; overrepresentation of, in female-dominated
occupations, 108n.2; sexual stereo-

typing of, 280–281; survival of
family structure and, 158–164;
working conditions of, 95–109
Chicanos: class and racial stereotyping of, 83–85; family structure
among, 158–164; mortality rates
among, gender-based comparisons of, 160
Chinese Americans: community
work by, 243n.1; and immigration to eastern United States,
204–205; as "model minority,"
70; "paper sons" of, 156–158;
and sojourner population, 155–
158
Chinese American women: demographic characteristics of, 16–19;
educational attainment of, 25–27;
and female-headed household
demographics, 24; fertility rates
among, 22–23; labor force participation of, 27–28; and marital
status, 21–22; occupational segregation of, 224n.6; and prostitution among early immigrant
women, 157–158; socioeconomic
position of, 24
Chinese Exclusion Act, 18, 205
Chow, Esther Ngan-Ling, 8, 315
Churches: as community resource,
234–238; return migration patterns and, 299–300
Civil Rights Act of 1964, 14
Clark, Septima, 240
Classroom roles of African American primary school girls: academic skills ratings linked with,
51–53; categories of, 45–51; commonalities among, 51; emergence
and maintenance of, 51–61; peer
relationships and, 57–60; policy
implications of, 60–61; social
skills ratings linked with, 53–54;

teacher-student interactions and, 51, 54–57

Class structure: accommodation and resistance to, 276–279; in antebellum South, 267–270; Asian American women's immigration patterns and, 206; changes in, for Vietnamese American community, 251–254; Chicana/Mexicana occupational mobility and, 99, 104–105; criminalization of African American women and, 171–182; diversity of, in community work, 243n.5; division of labor and, 72–73; emergence of African American middle class, 114–115; family structure and, 165–167; feminist theory and, 304–305; gender images and, 270; impact of, on gender and race, 4–6; job ceilings and employment sectors for African American professional women and, 113–129; moral reasoning and, 9–10, 296–297; peer interactions of African American school girls and, 58; versus racism, in labor force participation, 69–71; sexual stereotyping of minorities and, 280–282; stereotyping of Asian workers and, 83–85. *See also* Middle class

*Club sociales*, 141–142

"Clyde Dilemma," 295–296

Collective shame control, use of, by Asian American women, 215

Collins, Patricia Hill, 9, 278

Collins, Sharon, 119

Colonialism: impact of, on African American family structure, 149–150; impact of, on Tohono O'odham American Indians, 189–190; incorporation of Mexicans under, 158–160; "internal coloni-

alism" in communities, 232; labor system under, 306–307

Community: African American community defined, 231–234; African American women and, 8, 222, 229–244; characteristics of, 230; Chicano family structure and, 159–164; historical foundations of, 234–238; ideology and, 278–279; internal development of, 240–241; model for, 238–241; as part of Puerto Rican natural support system, 141–142; reproductive labor of women and, 165–166; return migration patterns and, 299–300; social change through, 229–244; of Vietnamese Americans, 249–251, 257–258

*Como familia* concept, 140–142

*Compadrazgo*: Chicano family structure and, 159–164; Puerto Rican women's reliance on, 140–142. *See also* Fictive kinship; Kinship networks

"Conduits for oppression," social institutions as, 6

Confrontational opposition to discrimination, Asian American women's use of, 217–218

Confucianism, Vietnamese American culture and, 252, 259n.3

Cooper, Anna Julia, 278

Coping strategies of minorities: affiliation coping strategy, 219, 221; of Asian American women in workplace, 216–222; assertive coping strategy, 218–222; criminal behavior as, 171; ethnic boundaries as, 248–251; racial/ethnic differences in, 222–223; reciprocity as, 218–219, 222; resistance as, 8, 172–178, 213–221, 241; silence as, 220–222

Diversity: diminishment of racial-ethnic differences with, 58; versus dominance, 3–12; in family structure, 309–312; gender and, 10; intellectual unity and, xiv-xv

Division of labor: among Asian immigrants, in microelectronics, 71–72, 89–90; gender-based, in African American slave community, 153–155; racial/ethnic/gender factors in, 68–73. See also Female-dominated occupations; Male-dominated occupations; Occupational segregation

Domestic service, racial/class relations in, 309

Domination: of cultural values, by white European groups, xiii-xiv; versus diversity, 3–12; of management profession, by white males, 72–73. See also Oppression, resistance to

"Double day," of African American slave women, 153–154, 165

Douglass, Frederick, 278

Drake, St. Clair, 116

Drug abuse: American Indian social problems and, 195–196, 198; among Puerto Rican women, 139; as response to race/gender criminalization of African American adolescents, 8, 175–181

Dual residency patterns of African American children, 294–296

Du Bois, W. E. B., 237, 265

Earnings. See Income levels; Wages

Educational attainment: of African American women, 177–178, 275–276; of American Indian women, 190–196; Chicana/Mexicana occupational mobility and, 99; community and, 233; criminalization of African American adolescent girls and, 177–178; of Puerto Rican women, 135, 142–143; racial/ethnic differences in, 24–27, 38n.12; survival of American Indian cultural values and, 185–199. See also Academic performance; School dropout rate

Educational institutions: African American teachers in, 44–46, 240–241; American Indian boarding schools and public schools, 193–194; Classroom roles of African American students in, 6, 43–61; job ceilings for African Americans and access to, 116–118, 126–129; organization of, by African American women, 235–236

Edwards, Richard, 203

Emancipation, impact of, on African American family structure, 155

Employer discrimination, Chicana/Mexicana occupational mobility and, 98

Employment. See Labor force participation

Employment sectors: gains in percentage of professional occupations for African American women and, 123–126; job ceilings for African American women and, 119–122. See also Occupational segregation; Public sector jobs

Enforcer role, of African American primary school girls, 47–48, 56–57

Entry-level manufacturing jobs: declining number of, 35; denial of access to, for white and African American workers, 77–78

Equal Employment Opportunity Commission (EEOC), 81–82

Fictive kinship: in African American slave community, 150–155; in Vietnamese American community, 254–258. *See also* Kinship networks; "Paper sons" of Chinese immigrants

Filipino American women: demographic characteristics of, 16–19; educational attainment of, 25–26, 38n.12; fertility rates among, 23; full-time employment patterns of, 29–30; income and poverty levels of, 32; labor force participation of, 27–28; marital status of, 21–22; occupational segregation of, 224n.6; participation of, in professional occupations, 29–31; percentage of female-headed households among, 24; socioeconomic position of, 24

Fisher exact test, analysis of justice and care reasoning, 296, 298

Folk healers, Puerto Rican reliance on, 140–142. *See also* Herbalists; Medicine people (American Indian)

Foraker Act, 144n.2

Fox-Genovese, Elizabeth, 270

Full-time employment patterns, income levels and racial/ethnic/gender differences in, 29–31

Gamio, Manuel, 163

Garcia, Mario, 160–162

Gender logic, in hiring patterns for immigrant labor, 74

Gender roles: accommodation and resistance to, 276–279; of African American women, 116–118, 275–279; for Asian American women, 205–206; of Chicanas and Mexicanas, 95–109; class structure and, 4–6, 9–11, 303–312; concepts of,

xv; criminalization of African American women and, 171–182; cultural values and moral reasoning and, 291–300; as factor in immigrant labor hiring discrimination, 85–89; family structure and, 159–164, 167n.4; health status of Puerto Rican women and, 136–142; hierarchy of, 265–266; identity and national liberation and, 279–282; moral reasoning impacted by, 9–10; occupational segregation and, 95–109, 116–118, 205–206; race and class as factors in images of, 270; racial-ethnic issues in, 303–312; Vietnamese Americans and, 249–258

Geographic demographics: African American women's access to employment sectors and, 125–126; racial patterns in, 18

Giachello, Aida, 138

Gilkes, Cheryl Townsend, 8, 274, 316

Gilligan, Carol, 291–300

Glenn, Evelyn Nakano, 10, 156–157, 304, 308

Go-between role, of African American primary school girls, 48–50, 56–57

Goffman, Erving, 50, 60–61

*Gone with the Wind*, 269

Graduation rates, racial/ethnic differences in, 25–26. *See also* Educational attainment

Granovetter, Mark, 56

Grant, Linda, 6, 316

Greenblatt, Milton, 138

"Guadalupe complex," 282

Guadalupe Hidalgo, treaty of, 158–159

Gutierres, Sara E., 174

Gutman, Herbert, 151–152, 154–155

Hare, Bruce, 56
Harper, Frances Ellen Watkins, 235
Harragan, Betty, 214
Health insurance, lack of, among Latino groups, 136, 138
Health Opinion Survey (HOS) mental health scale, 195–196
Health services: American Indian women's operation of, 194–196; Puerto Rican women's underutilization of, 138–139
Health status: of American Indians, 194–196; of Puerto Rican women, 134
"Heinz" dilemma, 294
Helper role, of African American primary school girls, 45–47, 56–59
Herbalists: Chicano use of, 163; as part of Puerto Rican natural support system, 141
Hierarchical structure: Asian American coping strategies regarding, 213–216; strategies for hiring immigrant labor and, 68–71. *See also* Bureaucracy; Patriarchal system
Higginbotham, Elizabeth, 6, 316
Higginbotham, Evelyn Brooks, 311
Hirata, Lucia Cheng, 157
Hiring patterns: bias against whites and African Americans for entry-level jobs and, 77–78; division of labor and, 71–72; gender logic in, 74; "immigrant logic" in, 74–78; of immigrant women workers, 85–89; race as factor in, 69–71; racial/ethnic/gender variations in, 72–73; racial logic in, 78–82; of Silicon Valley immigrant labor force, 65–91; stereotyping of Asian women and, 82–85
Hispanic, defined, 108n.1. *See also* Latinos

HIV infection, among Puerto Rican women, 139
Hmong population, demographics of, 20
Hochschild, Arlie, 214–215
Homeless women, 172, 181
Homosexuality, matrix of domination and, 10
Hooks, bell, 297
Hopkins, Pauline, 278
Hossfeld, Karen J., 6, 316
Housing segregation: American Indians' encapsulation strategy and, 196–198; for Puerto Ricans, 136
Housing styles, African American slave culture and, 152–153
Hughes, Everett, 232–233
Human capital theory, employment and mobility under, 96–101
Humm-Delgado, Denise, 140
Hurst, Marsha, 138
"Hustling" as coping strategy, 243n.4

Ichi, 215
Ideology: accommodation, resistance, and transformation in, 276–279; of bureaucracies, 209–212; empowerment of Vietnamese American women and, 256–258; gender-based, 90n.5, 282–283; images of women of color and, 265–285; of race, 270; social control and, 274–275; stereotyping of immigrant labor and, 68–71, 86–89
Images of African American women: in antebellum South, 267–270; impact of ideology on, 265–285; national liberation and, 279–282; post-emancipation era and, 270–276

versity in family structure and, 311–312; among Puerto Rican women, 139

Literacy rates, Chicano kinship networks and, 164. *See also* Educational attainment

*Longtime Californ'*, 156

Lopez, Iris, 137

Lopez de la Cruz, Jesse, 161–162

Low birth weight (LBW) infants, rates of, among Puerto Rican women, 136–137

Luong, Hy Van, 259n.4

Lyman, Stanford, 229

Lynching: of African American women, 284n.6; ideology as force behind, 271–272

McEntee, Jim, 83–84

Machismo, gender role stereotypes and, 281

Male-dominated occupations: Chicana/Mexicana occupational mobility and segregation and, 100–101; microelectronics industry positions as, 71–72

"Mammy" image of African American women, 267–270, 273–274; in slave narratives, 278

Management occupations: African American women's job ceilings and employment patterns and, 113–129; Chicana/Mexicana participation in, 96–97, 109n.3; minority representation in, 72; white male dominance of, 72–73

Marable, Manning, 69

"Marielitos," 17

Marriage patterns: African American middle-class women and, 129n.1; Chicana/Mexicana occupational mobility and, 99; of early Chinese women immigrants,

157–158; intertribal and interracial, among American Indians, 187–188, 194–195; labor force participation and, 27–29; racial/ethnic differences in, 20–22

Master-slave relationships, impact of, on African American family structure, 150–155

Matriarchal stereotype of African American women, 273–274, 277, 281

"Matrix of domination," 9–10

Medicine, Beatrice, 281

Medicine people (American Indian), 192–196

Merchants, as part of Puerto Rican natural support system, 140–142

Mexican American women. *See* Chicana women

Mexicana women (immigrant women from Mexico): class and racial stereotyping of, 83–85; educational attainment of, 25–26; female-headed households among, demographics on, 23–24; fertility rates among, 22–23; gender role stereotypes and, 281; hiring of Mexican domestic workers by, 309; immigration patterns among, 34–35; labor force participation of, 27–28; overrepresentation of, in female-dominated occupations, 108n.2; working conditions of, 95–109

Mexican men and women, occupational distribution of, versus non-Hispanic workers, 96–98

Mexican Revolution, impact of, on American Indians, 190

Microelectronics industry, immigrant labor force participation in, 69–71

Middle class: African American women, job ceilings, and employ-

Middle class (*cont.*)
ment sectors in professional occupations, 37n.1, 113–129; polarization of, in African American community, 37n.1; racial segmentation of, 128–129. *See also* Class structure.
Migrant workers, working conditions for, 161
Miller, Dorothy Lonewolf, 7, 317
Missionization of American Indians, 185
"Model minority:" Asian American women as, 210–212; productivity myths surrounding Asian workers and, 82–85; race-employment dynamics and, 69–71
Moore, Joan, 134–135
Moral reasoning: class structure and, 296–297; family structure and, 294–296; gender, race, class, and culture and, 9–10, 291–300; social action, gender-based trends in, 297–300
Motherhood as gender definition, 268–270
Mothers clubs, organized by African American women, 236
Moyer, Eugene, 136
Mullings, Leith, 9, 308, 317
Multiculturalism, backlash against, 3–4. *See also* Cultural values
Multiracial feminism, 11
Mutual-aid associations, 141–142

Naming patterns, in African American slave culture, 151–152
National Association for the Advancement of Colored People (NAACP), 234, 236, 243n.7
National Association of Colored Women's Clubs, 234–236, 278–279

National Council of Negro Women, 234, 236
Nationalist movements, subordination of women in, 281
National Juvenile Justice Assessment Center, 174–175
National origin quotas, 18
Native Americans. *See* American Indian women
Naylor, Gloria, 5
Nazis, use of gender role reversal, 283n.2
Nee, Brett de Bary, 156
Nee, Victor, 156
Networking: by African American primary school girls, 57–60; Chicana/Mexicana occupational mobility and, 98; Puerto Rican women's reliance on, 140–142
Nobles, Wade, 298
Nursing profession, job ceilings for African Americans in, 118

Occupational health, in semiconductor industry, 78
Occupational mobility: for Asian American women, 205–208; for Chicana and Mexicana women, 96–98; immigrant workers' illusions regarding, 74–78, 84–89; job ceilings for African Americans and, 116–118; myth of hard work as key to, 216
Occupational segregation: of Asian American women, 65–91, 205–208; of Chicanas, 95–109; criminalization of African American women and, 180–181; encouragement of African American elementary students toward, 44; family structure and, 306–308; gender/racial/ethnic factors in,

95–109; job attachment and mobility and, 107. *See also* Female-dominated occupations

Omi, Michael, 69

Operative jobs, dominance of minorities in, 71–72

Oppression, resistance to: community work as, 241; consequences of, 8; coping strategy for Asian American women workers, 213–221; criminalization of African American adolescent girls as, 172–178; negative images of, for African American women, 277–279; organizational dimensions of, 221–222; quitting a job as, 217–218, 220–221

Ortiz, Vilma, 137, 317

Outsider within, illusions of unity and, xiii-xv

Pachon, Harry, 134–135

Pakistanis, racial stereotyping of, 68–69

Papago. *See* Tohono O'odham tribe

"Paper sons" of Chinese immigrants, 156–158

"Passing" strategy, 8

Patriarchal system: adaptation of, in Vietnamese American families, 251–254; Asian American women's power struggles with, 206–208, 214–215; Chicano family structure and, 158–159; Chinese family structure and, 157–158; family structure and, 149–150, 157–159, 306–308; private patriarchy missing in slavery, 265–266, 271–272, 278–279, 306–307; slavery as support of, 150–155, 270

Patrilineal family model, adaptation of, in Vietnamese American community, 251–258, 259n.4

Pearson Chi-square test, 296–297

Peer relationships, African American classroom roles and, 46–48, 57–60

People of color, as preferred terminology, 12n.1

Physical abuse, criminalization of African American girls and, 172–181

Pines, Ayola, 176

Political unity, illusion of, xiii-xiv

Population growth, racial patterns in, 15–16, 20, 311–312

Poverty levels: American Indian cultural values assaulted by, 185–199; criminalization of African American girls as result of, 172–178; female-headed households and, 33–34; health status of Puerto Rican women and, 136–142; measurements of, 38n.11; of Puerto Rican women, 134–142; racial/ethnic/gender differences in, 31–32

Power, distribution of: ideology and, 266; increase in, for Vietnamese American women, 251–259; return migration patterns and, 299–300

Prenatal care, lack of, among Puerto Rican women, 136–138

Presthus, Robert, 216

Prisons: demographics of African American women in, 171–182; recidivism among African American women criminals in, 178–181; social control through, 275

Private sector occupations, African American professional women's access to, 119–126

Productivity: family structure and, 306–308; stereotyping of Asian American women concerning, 82–85

Professional occupations: African American visibility in, 275–276; Asian American women in, 214–215; Chicana/Mexicana participation in, 96–97, 109n.3; job ceilings and employment sectors, 113–129; minority representation in, 72; racial/ethnic differences in access to, 24–33; white male dominance of, 72–73

Property ownership, equality of, among Chicanos, 162

Prostitution: criminalization of African American adolescents and, 175–182; among early Chinese women immigrants, 157–158, 284n.10; stereotyping of African American women with, 271–272

Public health occupations, job ceilings for African Americans and, 118, 127

Public sector jobs: African American professional women's access to, 119–128; job ceilings for African Americans and, 118

Puerto Rican women: citizenship rights of, 144n.2; community work by, 243n.1; demographic characteristics of, 16–18, 133–136; demographics on female-headed households among, 23–24, 33–34; educational attainment of, 25–26, 135; family structure of, 133–143; fertility rates among, 22–23; immigration patterns among, 35, 37n.4; income levels of, 30–32, 34–35; labor force participation of, 27–29, 135; marital status demographics of, 20–22, 27–29; natural support systems for, 140–142; and participation in professional occupations, 30–31; as percentage of U.S. population, 143n.1; poverty levels among, 33–34, 136–142; racial diversity of, 140; reproductive health status of, 136–138; research and policy issues concerning, 142–143; sexual stereotyping of, 280; urban concentration of, 17–18, 136

Quitting a job, as resistance technique, 217–218, 220–221

Racial-ethnic, defined, 12n.1, 259n.1

Racial logic, in hiring patterns for immigrant labor, 78–82

Racism: African American primary school girls and, 59–60; African American women and, 122, 241–244; American Indian tribal identification and, 192–196; Asian American women and, 83–85, 207–208, 216–221; community work as weapon against, 231–234; criminalization of African American adolescents and, 176–178; family structure and, 149–150, 165–167, 305–306; feminist theory and, 304–305; gender images and, 265, 270; immigrant labor and, 69–71, 87–89, 248–249; job ceilings for African Americans and, 117–118; Mexicana/Chicana perceptions of, in labor market, 103–107; middle-class minorities and, 115, 128–129; Puerto Rican racial diversity and, 140; stereotyping of Asian workers and, 83–85

Rape: of African American slave women, 150–151, 269–276; as in-

School dropout rate (*cont.*)
American adolescents and, 172–178

Scott, Ann, 270

"Secondary labor market," Chicana/Mexicana occupational mobility and, 98

Segregated schools, Puerto Rican attendance in, 135

Segura, Denise A., 5, 317

Self-employment patterns, racial/ethnic/gender differences in, 30–31

Self-esteem: of African American elementary students, 44; community-based efforts to raise, 233–234

Self-help organizations of African Americans, 234–236, 279

Semiconductor industry: division of labor within, 71–72; immigrant labor force in, 65–91; production job categories in, 90n.3

Service sector: African American elementary students encouraged toward, 44; Asian American women's concentration in, 205; Puerto Rican access to jobs in, 135

Sexism: African American primary school girls as victims of, 59–60; impact of, on Asian American women, 207–208, 216–221

Sexual abuse: criminalization of adolescent African American girls as result of, 172–181; prostitution linked with, 175–178. *See also* Rape

Sexual equality: African American slave culture and, 152–153; emergence of, in Vietnamese American community, 251–254

Sexuality: cross-minority comparisons of, 280–282; stereotyping of,

in African American women, 266–267, 269–272, 280–282

Sherover-Marcuse, Erica, 88

Silbert, Mimi, 176

Silence, as coping and resistance strategy for Asian American women, 220–221

Silicon Valley, hiring of immigrant women in, 65–91

Slave narratives, 153

Slavery: assertive coping strategies as heritage from, 222–223; community work within confines of, 235; cross-cultural studies of, 283n.3; family structure disrupted by, 232; gender role reversal in, 277–279, 281–282, 283n.2; impact of, on African American family structure, 150–155

Social action: African American women's community work for, 229–244; discovery, challenge, and development as agents for, 238–241; gender-based strategies for, 299–300; moral reasoning and, 297–300

Social agency: American Indian women's struggle for cultural survival and, 185–199; Asian American women's confrontational strategies and, 203–223; community work of African American women, 229–244; family structure impacted by, 159–164; and matrix of domination, 6–9; prisons as agents of control, 171–182, 274–275; Vietnamese American women's ethnicity and, 247–259

Social clubs: as avenues for community work, 233–238; as part of Puerto Rican natural support system, 140–142

Social control, ideology and, 274–275

Social isolation in work environment: bureaucratization of workplace and, 209–212; Chicana/Mexicana occupational mobility and, 102–107

Socialization: of African American primary school girls, 56–60; Asian American women's coping strategies for, in workplace, 216–221; Chicana/Mexicana occupational mobility and, 98; emphasis on skills, in evaluation of African American school girls, 52–57, 61; opportunities for, in female-dominated occupations, 105–108; Puerto Rican women's reliance on, 140–142

Social mobility, barriers to, for women of color, 5–6

Social stratification: Chicana/Mexicana occupational mobility and, 96–108; classroom roles of African American primary school girls, 43, 51–61; constraints of, for women of color, 4–6; demographic characteristics and, 14–38; domination of women and, 3–12; job ceilings for African American professional women and, 113–129; Puerto Rican family structure and, 133–143; racial/ethnic differences in, 24–33; Silicon Valley hiring patterns based on, 65–91

Socioeconomic conditions: adaptation of family structure and, 310–311; Chicano kinship networks and, 164; criminalization of African American adolescent girls and, 176–178; family structure and, 305–309; Puerto Rican family structure and, 133–143. *See also* Class structure

Sojourning, by Chinese immigrants, 155–158

Southern Rhodesian Immorality Act, 284n.6

Spanish language, perpetuation of, by Chicanos, 163

Spicer, Edward H., 197

Spiritism, as part of Puerto Rican natural support system, 141–142

"Split household" family structure among Chinese, 157–158

Sponsorship, conflicts in Vietnamese American families over, 255–257, 260n.5

Stack, Carol B., 9–10, 318

Standard of living, disregard of, among immigrant workers, 86–87

Stealing, as survival technique, criminalization of African American adolescents and, 172–178

Stereotyping of minorities: and Asian American workers, 210–212; community work as weapon against, 232–233; gender role expectations and, 271–272; as rationale for hiring immigrant labor, 68–71, 74, 78–82; sexual stereotyping of African American women, 265–267, 269–272; sexual stereotyping, cross-minority comparisons, 280–282

Sterilization, rates of, among Puerto Rican women, 137

Stewart, Maria, 235

Stoler, Ann, 284n.6

Stroup-Benham, Christine, 136

Structural dislocation: criminalization of adolescent African American girls and, 172–178; transformation of family in Western feminism and, 303–304